# NEW REVISED CAMBRIDGE GED PROGRAM

# Interpreting Literature and the Arts

## Stella Sands
## Virginia Lowe

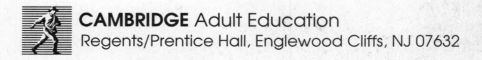

**CAMBRIDGE** Adult Education
Regents/Prentice Hall, Englewood Cliffs, NJ 07632

Pre-press Production: **TopDesk**
Acquisitions Editor: **Mark Moscowitz**
Production Editor: **Shirley Hinkamp**
Interior Design: **LCI Designs**
Cover Photo: **The Stock Market/Craig Tuttle**
Prepress Buyer: **Ray Keating**
Manufacturing Buyer: **Lori Bulwin**

ISBN   0-13-116443-0

The editors have made every effort to trace the ownership of all copyrighted material and express regret in advance for any error or omission. After notification of an oversight, they will include proper notification in future printings.

Prentice-Hall International (UK) Limited, *London*
Prentice-Hall of Australia Pty. Limited, *Sydney*
Prentice-Hall Canada, Inc., *Toronto*
Prentice-Hall Hispanoamericana, S.A., *Mexico*
Prentice-Hall of India Private Limited, *New Delhi*
Prentice-Hall of Japan, Inc., *Tokyo*
Simon & Schuster Asia Pte. Ltd., *Singapore*
Editora Prentice-Hall do Brasil, Ltda., *Rio de Janeiro*

## New Revised Cambridge GED Program

### Executive Editor

James W. Brown

### Project Director/Senior Editor

Robert McIlwaine

### Writers

Beverly Ann Chin
Gloria Levine
Karen Wunderman
Stella Sands
Michael Ross
Alan Hines
Donald Gerstein

### Consultants/Reviewers

Marjorie Jacobs
Cecily Bodnar
Diane Hardison
Dr. Margaret Tinzmann
Nora Chomitz
Bert C. Honigman
Sylvester Pues

### Photo Researchers

Page Poore
Ellen Diamond

### Electronic Design

Molly Pike Riccardi
Freddy Flake

# Contents

# TO THE STUDENT

The following pages will introduce you to the Interpreting Literature and the Arts Test and to the organization of this book. You will read about ways that you can use this book to your best advantage.

## What is the Interpreting Literature and the Arts Test?

The Interpreting Literature and the Arts Test of the GED exam examines your ability to understand and analyze popular and classical literature, as well as commentary about literature and the arts, such as book and film reviews.

## What Kind of Questions Are on the Test?

When you take the test, you will read passages and answer questions that test your comprehension—your understanding of what the author says directly—as well as your ability to apply and analyze what you understand. In analysis questions, you may be asked to show how the passages achieve certain literary effects. For example, you might be asked to identify the words in a poem that help create a certain mood. In application questions, you may be asked questions about the characters in a passage. For example, you might be asked to decide what a character would do in a situation other than the one described in the passage.

The questions will not test your prior knowledge of literature and the arts. You will not be asked to name any authors or dates. You will be asked only to demonstrate that you understand and can analyze various types of writing.

As with most of the other GED tests, all of the questions on the Interpreting Literature and the Arts Test are in multiple choice format.

## What Are the Reading Passages Like?

The passages you will read are all taken from actual published works. About half of the questions will be based on *popular literature*—nonfiction, fiction, drama, and poetry (including song lyrics) recently written and widely enjoyed by today's readers. About one-fourth of the questions will be based on passages from *classical literature*—works that are considered to have earned a place in literary history. Finally, one-fourth of the questions will be based on *commentary*—writing about literature, theater, music, dance, film, and art. Questions based on commentary might ask you to decide what a critic liked or disliked about a play, or to imagine what the same critic might think of a different play.

## What You Will Find in This Book

This book gives you a four-step preparation for taking the Interpreting Literature and the Arts Test. The four steps are as follows:

## Step One: Prediction

In this first step, you will find the Predictor Test. This test is very much like the actual Interpreting Literature and the Arts Test, but is only half as long. Taking the Predictor Test will give you an idea of what the real GED will be like. By evaluating your performance on the Predictor Test, you will get a sense of your strengths and weaknesses. This information will help you to plan your studies accordingly.

## Step Two: Instruction

Interpreting Literature and the Arts focuses on literature itself. Here you will practice reading various types of literature and commentary, similar to those on the real test. This section will also teach you how to be a critical reader by pointing out features of literature that you should be aware of.

This section is divided into chapters. There is a chapter for each type of literature covered on the test: Nonfiction, Fiction, Drama, Poetry, and Commentary. Each chapter is divided into lessons. A lesson consists of instruction based on example passages and GED-style questions to help you learn the skills covered in the lesson.

## Step Three: Practice

This section gives you valuable practice in answering the type of questions you will find on the actual Interpreting Literature and the Arts Test. There are two separate types of practice activity in Step Three.

- *Practice Items:* The Practice Items are GED-style questions grouped according to the types of literature taught in the text. For example, you will find items based on nonfiction grouped together, items based on fiction grouped together, and so on. The Practice Items allow you to test your understanding of one type of literature at a time.
- *Practice Test:* The second type of practice, the Practice Test, is structured like the actual Interpreting Literature and the Arts Test. In the Practice Test, the types of literature vary from passage to passage, just as they do on the real test. This section gives you an opportunity to practice taking a test similar to the GED.

Both types of practice activities have 45 items, the same number of questions as are on the actual Interpreting Literature and the Arts Test. You can use your results to track your progress and give yourself an idea of how prepared you are to take the real test.

## Step Four: Simulation

Finally, this book offers a simulated version of the Interpreting Literature and the Arts Test. It is similar to the real test in every way. The number of questions, their level of difficulty, and the way they are organized are the same as you will find on the actual test. You will have the same amount of time to answer the questions as you will have on the actual test. Taking the Simulated Test will be useful preparation for taking the GED. It will help you find out how ready you are to take the real exam.

## The Answer Keys

At the back of this book, you will find answers and explanations. The answer key contains the answers to all the questions in the Predictor Test, the Lesson Exercises, the Practice Items, the Practice Test, and the Simulated Test. The answer keys are a valuable study tool: They not only tell you the right answer, but explain why that answer is right and point out the reading skill you need to answer the questions successfully. You can benefit a great deal by carefully consulting the answer keys after completing an activity.

There are many ways to use this book. Whether you are working with an instructor or alone, you can use this book to prepare for the Interpreting Literature and the Arts Test in the way that works best for you.

# What is the GED?

You are preparing for the GED Tests. The initials GED stand for General Educational Development. You may also have heard the tests referred to as the High School Equivalency Tests.

The GED Test is a way for millions of adults in the United States and Canada to get diplomas or certificates without returning to high school. Each year about half a million people take advantage of the opportunity to take the GED tests.

## Who Recognizes the GED?

The GED is recognized by employers, unions, and state and federal civil services. Many vocational institutes, colleges, and universities accept students who have obtained GED. All fifty states and parts of Canada use the GED Test results to issue high school equivalency credentials. However, each state has its own standards for what constitutes a passing grade. For information on the requirements in your state, contact the High School Equivalency Program of the State Department of Education in your state's capital.

## What is Tested on the GED?

The material on the GED is based on high school curricula. Thus you will be tested on materials present-day high school students study. However, the focus of the GED is not on content, but on skills. You will not have to memorize specific dates, names, and places. For example, whether you recall the date of a battle or the title of a novel is less important than whether you can understand and use information from a passage on history or literature.

You already use many of the thinking skills that will be tested on the GED. You do some writing in your life: the GED includes a test of writing skills. You read in your job or for pleasure: the GED tests reading skills. You use basic mathematics for such things as figuring out a budget or doubling a recipe: the GED includes a test of basic math skills.

Instead of testing your memory, the GED will test your ability to absorb information and to apply your thinking to that information.

## How is the GED Structured?

The GED is actually five separate tests. With one exception, the tests are composed entirely of multiple choice questions. The one exception is the 200-word essay that you will write as part of the Writing Skill Test.

## The Five GED Tests

There are five content areas tested by the GED: writing skills, social studies, science, literature and the arts, and mathematics. The specifics of each test are listed below.

- *Writing Skills, Part I:* You will have 75 minutes to answer 55 questions (Sentence Structure 35%; Usage 35% Mechanics 30%). Most questions involve detecting and correcting errors.
- *Writing Skills, Part II:* You will have 45 minutes to write a 200-word composition on a given topic, The.topic will be familiar to most people.
- *Social Studies:* You will have 85 minutes to answer 64 questions (History 25%; Geography 15%; Economics 20%; Political Science 20%; Behavioral Science 20%. Note: In Canada, Geography is 20% and Behavioral Science is 15%). Most questions are based on reading passages. About 1/3 are based on graphic material.
- *Science:* You will have 95 minutes to answer 66 questions (Biology 50%; Physical Sciences 50%). Most questions are based on reading passages. Others are based on graphic material.
- *Literature and the Arts:* You will have 65 Minutes to answer 45 questions (Popular Literature 50%; Classical literature 25%; Commentary 25%). Questions are based on reading passages.
- *Mathematics:* You will have 90 minutes to answer 56 questions (Arithmetic 50%; Algebra 30%, Geometry 20%). Most questions are word problems.

Actual passing scores differ from area to area, but regardless of where you are, there are two scores you will need to pay attention to. One is the *minimum score* you must get on each test. If your area sets a minimum score of 35, that means you have to score at least 35 points on *each* of the five tests. The second score is a *minimum average score* on all five tests. If your area requires a minimum average score of 45, that means you have to get a total of 225 points to pass (45 x 5 = 225). To pass on the GED, you must meet *both* requirements: (1) the minimum score on each of the five tests and (2) the minimum average score for all five tests. Failure to meet one or the other score will result in failure to pass the GED.

All is not lost if you don't pass the test the first time around. You can take one or all five tests again if you don't pass. You will receive a different form of the test each time you take it, but the experience of having taken the test before should improve your score the next time around. Of course, you will want to study again to be fully prepared for the test.

You can contact: the office of the superintendent of schools in your area; a vocational education center; local community colleges; and adult education courses; or write to:

> General Education Development
> GED Testing Service of the American Council on Education
> One Dupont Circle
> Washington, DC 20036

## How To Be a Better Test Taker

Often you will hear people say that they are not good test-takers. These people may be quite intelligent and get good grades in school, but they simply do not do well on standardized tests. You may think of yourself as one of these people. However there are things people can do to improve their chances of doing well on a test. Listed below are some helpful hints to make you a better test taker.

- *Study the Content Areas of the GED*
- *Practice Taking Tests*
- *Be Well Rested for the Actual Test*
- *Allow Yourself Enough Time to Get to the Test Center*
- *Follow Directions Carefully*
- *Pay Attention to the Time*
- *Use Your Test-Taking Skills*
- *Answer All Questions on the Test*
- *Mark Your Answers Carefully*
- *Above All, Relax.*

# Using This Book

## Take a Glance at the Table of Contents

Before doing anything else, look over the Table of Contents and get a feel for this book. You can compare the headings in the Table of Contents with the descriptions found in the preceding pages. You might also want to leaf through the book to see what each section looks like.

## Take the Predictor Test

Next, you will probably want to take the Predictor Test. As the introduction before the test explains, there is more than one way to take this test. Decide which is best for you.

The Performance Analysis Chart for the Predictor Test will be very useful to you as you work with the rest of this book. It will point out your particular strengths and weaknesses, which can help you plan your course of study.

## Beginning Your Instruction

After you have analyzed your strengths and weaknesses, you are ready to begin instruction. You will probably want to go through the lessons in normal order starting with Chapter 1 because in many cases the reading strategy taught in one lesson builds on the ones taught in the lessons before.

## Using the Practice Section

When you complete a chapter, you have a choice. You may proceed to the next chapter or you can get some practice on the type of literature you just studied. The Practice Items (pages 269-282) are grouped according to the types of literature covered by each chapter. Thus you can test yourself immediately after each chapter. If you wish, you can wait until you've finished all the chapters and then do the Practice Items. You should take the Practice Test, however, only after you have finished the entire book.

## Taking the Simulated Test

Finally, once you have completed the Instruction and Practice sections, you can take the Simulated Interpreting Literature and the Arts Test. This will give you the most accurate assessment of how ready you are to take the actual test.

## Try Your Best!

As you study the lessons and complete the activities and tests in this book, you should give it your best effort. To attain a passing score on the GED, you will probably need to get half or more of the items correct. To give yourself a margin for passing, try to maintain a score of at least 80% correct as you work through this book. If you maintain 80% scores, you are probably working at a level that will allow you to do well on the GED test.

# Introduction

How would you score on the GED test if you took it today? What questions would you find the easiest to answer? Which ones might give you the most difficulty? Take the Predictor Test that follows to help you answer these questions. It is called a Predictor Test because it can help you predict your strengths and weaknesses before you take the actual Interpreting Literature and the Arts Test of the GED.

The Predictor Test is similar to the actual GED in two main ways. First, it contains the same types of questions you will find on the GED. Second, it follows the same format as the GED. This way, the Predictor Test allows you to check your skills against the types of questions you will encounter on the GED.

## How to Take the Predictor Test

You will get the most accurate results if you take the Predictor Test as you would take the real GED. If you can, finish the Predictor Test in one sitting, in a quiet place. Write your answers on a sheet of paper, or use an answer sheet provided by your teacher.

Don't be discouraged if you find many of the questions are hard to answer. Remember that the purpose of this test is to find out what areas you need to learn more about for the GED. Since there will be plenty of time to correct any weaknesses later on, try to relax when you take the Predictor Test.

Time yourself as you work through the Predictor Test so that you can see how long it takes you to answer GED-type questions. Use a timer or write down the time when you start the test. You will be given 65 minutes for the actual Interpreting Literature and the Arts Test. The Predictor Test is about half the length of the actual GED test, so if you finish in about 37-1/2 minutes, you're right on target. Don't worry if it takes you longer, though. Remember that you're predicting how you will react to the actual GED test.

When you complete the Predictor Test, check your answers by using the answer key that begins on page 9. To score your results, put a check next to each item you answered correctly.

## How to Use Your Score

At the end of the test is a Performance Analysis Chart. Complete the chart, because it will help you find out which parts of the test you know well, and which ones you will have to study more intensively.

As you begin each chapter of the book, you can refer back to the Performance Analysis Chart to see how you scored on that portion of the Predictor Test.

# PREDICTOR TEST

**TIME:** 37-1/2 minutes

**Directions:** Choose the one best answer for each question.

Items 1 to 4 refer to the following passage.

## HOW DOES JEROME FEEL ABOUT HIS FATHER?

"I've had a telephone call, Jerome. From your aunt. I'm afraid I have bad news for you."

"Yes, sir?"

(5) "Your father has had an accident."

"Oh."

Mr. Wordsworth looked at him with some surprise. "A serious accident."

"Yes, sir?"

(10) Jerome worshipped his father: the verb is exact. As man re-creates God, so Jerome re-created his father—from a restless widowed author into a mysterious adventurer who travelled in far places—
(15) Nice, Beirut, Majorca, even the Canaries. The time had arrived about his eighth birthday when Jerome believed that his father either "ran guns" or was a member of the British Secret Service. Now it
(20) occurred to him that his father might have been wounded in "a hail of machine-gun bullets."

Mr. Wordsworth played with the ruler on his desk. He seemed at a loss how to
(25) continue. He said, "You know your father was in Naples?"

"Yes, sir."

"Your aunt heard from the hospital today."

(30) "Oh."

Mr. Wordsworth said with desperation. "It was a street accident."

"Yes sir?" It seemed quite likely to Jerome that they would call it a street
(35) accident. The police of course had fired first; his father would not take human life except as a last resort.

"I'm afraid your father was very seriously hurt indeed."

(40) "Oh."

"In fact, Jerome, he died yesterday. Quite without pain."

"Did they shoot him through the heart?"

(45) "I beg your pardon. What did you say, Jerome?"

"Did they shoot him through the heart?"

"Nobody shot him, Jerome. A pig fell
(50) on him." An inexplicable convulsion took place in the nerves of Mr. Wordsworth's face; it really looked for a moment as though he were going to laugh. He closed his eyes, composed his features and said
(55) rapidly as though it were necessary to expel the story as quickly as possible, "Your father was walking along a street in Naples when a pig fell on him. A shocking accident."

Graham Greene, "A Shocking Accident." From *Graham Greene: Collected Stories* (New York: The Viking Press, 1935).

1. How did Jerome "re-create" his father (lines 11-15)?

   **(1)** He told lies about his father.

   **(2)** He believed that his father would never die.

   **(3)** He imagined that his father was God.

   **(4)** He invented new occupations for his father.

   **(5)** He pretended that Mr. Wordsworth was his father.

**2.** How does Jerome react to the news of his father's death?

   **(1)** Crushed, he asks to be left alone.
   **(2)** Hysterical, he demands that Mr. Wordsworth tell him every detail of the accident.
   **(3)** Detached, he dreams that his father died, as he had lived, a hero.
   **(4)** Shocked, he turns in his anger against Mr. Wordsworth.
   **(5)** Relieved, he rejoices that his cruel father is gone.

**3.** How might Jerome react to news that his father had been arrested?

   **(1)** He would plan a way for his father to escape.
   **(2)** He would be ashamed of his father's crime.
   **(3)** He would imagine that his father was a captured spy.
   **(4)** He would think that the report was a lie.
   **(5)** He would plead with Mr. Wordsworth to be allowed to go to his father.

**4.** Which of the following words best describes the tone that the author uses in describing this situation?

   **(1)** humorous
   **(2)** grief-stricken
   **(3)** menacing
   **(4)** sad
   **(5)** condemning

Items 5 to 8 refer to the following passage.

**HOW DOES RED SUN SURPRISE EVERYONE AT THE HOME?**

Among the funny incidents that happened at the Home I will never forget the stunt Red Sun pulled off. He had been sent to the Home for stealing. It was a (5) mania with him; he would steal anything which was not nailed down. Before I ever saw the Home he had served two or three terms there. He would be released, and two or three months later he would be (10) back again to serve another term for stealing.

After serving six months while I was at the Home he was paroled by the judge. Three months passed, and he was still on (15) the streets. We took it for granted that Red Sun had gone straight at last and we practically forgot all about him.

One day while Mr. Jones was drilling us in front of the Home we saw somebody (20) coming down the road riding on a real beautiful horse. We all wondered who it could be.... To our amazement it was Red Sun. Above all he was riding bareback. We crowded around him to tell how glad (25) we were to see him looking so good and to admire his horse....

"I have been working," he said. "I had such a good job that I was able to buy the horse. What do you think of him?"

(30) Mr. Jones thought he was pretty and so did the rest of us. Red poked his chest way out.

He spent the whole day with us, letting us all take turns riding his horse. Oh, we (35) had a ball! Red stayed for supper, the same as I did in later years, and when I blew the bugle for taps he mounted his fine horse and bade us all good-bye.

"Ah'll see you-all soon," he said and he (40) rode away as good as the Lone Ranger. After he had left, Red was the topic of conversation until the lights went out. We all went to sleep saying how great ol' Red Sun had become.

(45) After dinner the next evening while we were looking out the windows we saw Mr. Alexander—he generally went to the Juvenile Court for delinquents—bring a new recruit into Mr. Jones' office. We (50) wondered who it could be: it was Red Sun—bless my lamb—who had been arrested for stealing a horse.

**5.** According to the author, the Home is similar to

**(1)** a prison
**(2)** a hospital
**(3)** a military base
**(4)** a rescue mission
**(5)** a factory

**6.** Why does Red Sun continue to steal?

**(1)** He is sure he won't be caught.
**(2)** He enjoys the danger involved.
**(3)** He must steal to stay alive.
**(4)** He is addicted to stealing.
**(5)** He steals to help needy people.

**7.** The praise that Mr. Jones and the residents gave to Red Sun made him

**(1)** feel angry
**(2)** feel proud
**(3)** decide to go straight
**(4)** become a horse thief
**(5)** want to come back to the Home

**8.** The author quotes Red Sun as saying "Ah'll see you-all soon" (line 39) to

**(1)** emphasize the humor of Red coming back the next day as a new prisoner
**(2)** make a serious comment on human foolishness
**(3)** show how little faith Red had in himself
**(4)** reveal how uneducated Red was
**(5)** suggest that Red is a friendly person

Items 9 to 12 refer to the following passage.

### WHAT ARE THESE CHARACTERS ARGUING ABOUT?

LOPAHIN: That rich man, Deriganov, wants to buy your estate. They say he's coming to the auction himself.

(5) MME. RANEVSKAYA: Where did you hear that?

LOPAHIN: That's what they are saying in town.

GAYEV: Our aunt in Yaroslavl has (10) promised to help; but when she will send the money, and how much, no one knows.

LOPAHIN: How much will she send? A hundred thousand? Two hundred?

(15) MME. RANEVSKAYA: Oh, well, ten or fifteen thousand; and we'll have to be grateful for that.

LOPAHIN: Forgive me, but such frivolous people as you are, so queer and (20) unbusinesslike—I never met in my life. One tells you in plain language that your estate is up for sale, and you don't seem to take it in.

MME. RANEVSKAYA: What are we to do? Tell us what to do.

(25) LOPAHIN: I do tell you, every day; every day I say the same thing! You must lease the cherry orchard and the land for summer cottages, you must do it and as soon as possible—right (30) away. The auction is close at hand. Please understand! Once you've decided to have the cottages, you can raise as much money as you like, and you're saved.

(35) MME. RANEVSKAYA: Cottages—summer people—forgive me, but it's all so vulgar.

GAYEV: I agree with you absolutely.

LOPAHIN: I shall either burst into tears (40) or scream or faint! I can't stand it! You've worn me out! (*To Gayev.*) You're an old woman!

GAYEV: Who?

LOPAHIN: An old woman! (*Gets up to go.*)

(45) MME. RANEVSKAYA (*alarmed*): No, don't go! Please stay, I beg you, my dear. Perhaps we shall think of something.

LOPAHIN: What is there to think of?

Anton Chekhov, *The Cherry Orchard*, translated by Avraham Yarmolinsky (New York: The Viking Press, 1947).

9. The comments of Gayev and Mme. Ranevskaya indicate that they

   (1) understand their situation better than Lopahin does
   (2) enjoy the simple pleasure of life
   (3) view the world quite unrealistically
   (4) have allowed their greed to blind them to the truth
   (5) are insane

10. Lopahin's outburst (lines 39-41) indicates that, prior to this exchange,

   (1) Gayev and Mme. Ranevskaya had misled him about their wealth
   (2) he had other arguments with the pair about this subject
   (3) he had received an offer to buy the cherry orchard
   (4) he had been in contact with the aunt in Yaroslavl
   (5) Gayev's once-prosperous business had failed

11. What would be Mme. Ranevskaya's most likely response if asked about democratic government?

   (1) "I am a socialist, not a democrat."
   (2) "Ask Gayev; he's the politician in the family."
   (3) "It seems to be a fashionable idea, so let's follow fashion."
   (4) "A vote for every person? What a crude idea!"
   (5) "Democracy is the only form of government that makes sense in this day and age."

12. To show that Lopahin is a sensible man, the author

   (1) has Lopahin talk about large sums of money
   (2) says Lopahin is sensible in the stage directions
   (3) describes Lopahin's sensible way of speaking
   (4) has Lopahin use facts and logic in his speeches
   (5) has other characters agree with Lopahin

Items 13 to 16 refer to the following passage.

## WHY WILL SHAKER DESIGNS STAND THE TEST OF TIME?

Consider a Shaker chair: four posts, three slats, a handful of stretchers, a few yards of woolen tape for the seat. It could scarcely be more simply made, but look
(5) more closely at this product of an unhurried hand. The proportions were chosen with care. The posts are slender, no thicker than needed for strength. You can lift this chair with a finger. The slats increase
(10) slightly in height as they rise, as does the space between them, so that the back seems to float above the seat and legs. The chair slants at a backward angle agreeable for sitting. Time has not faded
(15) the clear red and blue of the seat, nor bowed the back, in some hundred and thirty years since it was new.

It was not design, however, for which the Shakers were known in their own
(20) day.... They turned away from the rest of society, which they simply called the World. They lived in large Families that were both celibate and communal, devoted their lives to work, and celebrated their
(25) love of God in the rousing dance worship that gave them their name. Simplicity was their hallmark. They cared little for possessions. "Set not your hearts upon worldly objects," they said, "but let this be
(30) your labor, to keep a spiritual sense." Their purpose was to bring heaven to earth, not make beautiful things.

But as they created a new, more perfect society, the Shakers also produced a visu-
(35) al environment of such quiet power that it continues to impress the observer even as they themselves are passing from the American scene. Today, fewer than a dozen Shakers remain in two communi-
(40) ties—Canterbury, New Hampshire, and Sabbathday Lake, Maine—yet Shaker work endures. It is unadorned, functional, and well-made. But these qualities themselves do not account for the excel-
(45) lence of design. Examine a basket. Mere utility did not shape the curve of the handle above. Look at a three-legged stand. Simplicity alone did not cause the legs to soar. What really distinguishes Shaker
(50) design is something that transcends utility, simplicity, and perfection—a subtle beauty that relies almost wholly on proportion. There is harmony in the parts of a Shaker object.

June Sprigg, "Introduction", *Shaker Design* (New York: Whitney Museum of American Art and W.W. Norton & Company, Inc., 1986).

13. Which of the following pairs of words best describes Shaker design?

   (1) light and well-designed
   (2) decorative but fragile
   (3) long-lasting and fancy
   (4) sturdy and heavy
   (5) functional but unattractive

14. According to the author, what was the chief goal of the Shakers?

   (1) to make excellent, unique furniture
   (2) to spread their ideas across the world
   (3) to pool their talents to produce great works of art
   (4) to create communities of large families
   (5) to establish a society that was in harmony with God

15. Which of the following examples would the author be most likely to say is similar to objects of Shaker design?

   (1) a symbolic film in which the viewers are expected to determine the meaning for themselves
   (2) a new building whose architecture reflects the latest style
   (3) a china vase with a simple but elegant form
   (4) a diamond ring with an elaborate, eye-catching setting
   (5) a mystery novel in which the readers are encouraged to look for references to the author's own life

**16.** The style of writing found in this passage is most similar to the style that would be found in a

    **(1)** historical novel
    **(2)** biography
    **(3)** political speech
    **(4)** review of a painting
    **(5)** business report

Items 17-20 refer to the following passage.

## WHEN WILL THE VOICES COME AGAIN?

The traveler reached the star system of the nondescript blue planet. The voices it sought remained silent. It passed the system's outer worlds, frozen rocky spheres
(5) and great gas giants, and it sang its grief to space and all worlds' skies. It sensors traced the planet's surface, cutting through the electromagnetic radiation that often surrounded such worlds. It
(10) found several small spaceborne nodes of power and drained them.

This was a marginally acceptable world. The traveler could give it new voices. First its surface must be sterilized. The traveler
(15) would lower the temperature until glaciers covered the land and the seas froze solid. Whatever had destroyed the intelligence that once existed here would itself be destroyed. After a few eons, the traveler
(20) would permit the temperature to rise again, leaving a tropical world devoid of life. Then the traveler could reseed.

The traveler centered its attention on a wide expanse of ocean and began feeding
(25) power to the focus.

An enormous sea wave burst upward and exploded into steam. The traveler observed and approved the results. It intensified its power discharge, which
(30) plunged into the ocean and vaporized tremendous volumes of water. The vapor rose into the atmosphere and collected into a cloud cover that rapidly thickened and spread, obscuring the surface of the
(35) world.

On the surface of earth, it began to rain.

Vonda N. McIntyre, *Star Trek IV The Voyage Home* (New York: Pocket Books, a division of Simon & Schuster, Inc., 1986).

**17.** What best describes the traveler's mission?

    **(1)** Search and Explore
    **(2)** Search and Destroy
    **(3)** Search and Instruct
    **(4)** Search, Explore, and Instruct
    **(5)** Search, Destroy, and Restore

**18.** Which of the following is the traveler's most likely origin?

    **(1)** the blue planet
    **(2)** a great gas giant
    **(3)** somewhere in outer space
    **(4)** the ocean
    **(5)** a frozen world

**19.** What caused the rain to fall on the earth's surface (line 29)?

    **(1)** a tropical storm
    **(2)** an action by the traveler
    **(3)** an accident
    **(4)** a melting glacier
    **(5)** a hole in the ozone layer

**20.** The author's description of the traveler suggests that

    **(1)** scientists are inside a space ship called "the traveler"
    **(2)** scientists are watching the traveler
    **(3)** the traveler is a rational but non-human power
    **(4)** the traveler is not in control of its power
    **(5)** the traveler is controlled by another power

Items 21-23 refer to the following poem.

## HOW DOES THIS WOMAN FEEL ABOUT HER BELOVED GOING OFF TO WAR?

### The Sonnet-Ballad

Oh mother, mother, where is happiness?
They took my lover's tallness off to war,
Left me lamenting. Now I cannot guess
What I can use an empty heart-cup for.
(5) He won't be coming back here any more.
Some day the war will end, but, oh, I knew
When he went walking grandly out that door
That my sweet love would have to be untrue.
Would have to be untrue. Would have to court
(10) Coquettish death, whose impudent and strange
Possessive arms and beauty (of a sort)
Can make a hard man hesitate—and change.
And will he be the one to stammer, "Yes."
Oh mother, mother, where is happiness?

Gwendolyn Brooks, "The Sonnet-Ballad," from *The World of Gwendolyn Brooks* (New York: Harper and Row, ©1971 Gwendolyn Brooks, the David Company.)

**21.** "My lover's tallness" (line 2) refers to his

    **(1)** stubbornness
    **(2)** unfaithfulness with another woman
    **(3)** youth, good looks, and health
    **(4)** desire to fight in the war
    **(5)** appearance in his coffin

**22.** Death is described in this poem as

    **(1)** a beautiful, flirtatious woman
    **(2)** a cruel victor
    **(3)** an empty heart-cup
    **(4)** a sweet love
    **(5)** one who hesitates, stammers, and changes

**23.** The *tone* of this poem is best described as

    **(1)** hopeful and uplifting
    **(2)** confused
    **(3)** furious
    **(4)** sad but relieved
    **(5)** sad and bitter

Answers are on pages 9-11.

# ANSWERS AND EXPLANATIONS FOR THE PREDICTOR TEST

1. **(4)** *Literal Comprehension/Fiction.* The author states that Jerome "changed" his father "from a restless widowed author into a mysterious adventurer" (lines 12-14). Jerome did not imagine him to be God (3) or immortal (2)—just a hero. There is no evidence that he told any lies about his father or that he tried to make Mr. Wordsworth his father, so (1) and (5) are wrong.

2. **(3)** *Inferential Comprehension/Fiction.* Jerome's short responses and matter-of-fact questions reveal that he is quite detached from the reality of death; he continues to live in a dream world. He seems neither upset, (1) and (2), nor shocked and angry (4); instead, he hopes for information that will reinforce his fantasies about his father. He is not all relieved at his father's death, and there is no evidence that his father was cruel. Therefore, (5) cannot be correct.

3. **(3)** *Application/Fiction.* Again, Jerome probably would use his imagination to color reality. Just as he did not pretend that his father was alive, he would not pretend that the news of his imprisonment is false (4). He would not try to plan his father's escape (1), since he failed to ask any realistic questions when he was told that his father had an accident. There is no evidence that he would be ashamed (2). Because he did not want to be taken to see his father's body, we cannot assume that he would want to see his father in prison (5). He would accept the situation by fantasizing about it (3).

4. **(1)** *Analysis/Fiction.* The author deals with the humor in this ridiculous situation. In particular, he draws attention to the absurdity in the pig being the instrument of the father's death—how many people are killed by falling pigs? The tone of the passage is not grief-stricken (2), menacing (3), or sad (4), nor does it condemn any of the characters involved (5).

5. **(1)** *Literal Comprehension/Nonfiction.* Like a prison, the Home is a place where people serve terms for committing crimes (lines 3-8). It is a place from which one can be paroled by a judge (line 13) and to which "recruits" can be brought from Juvenile Court (lines 47-49). Since no one is ill or recovering from an illness, it cannot be a hospital (2). None of the people in the Home are making any products, so it cannot be a factory (5). Similarly, there is no indication that it is a military base (3) or a rescue mission (4).

6. **(4)** *Literal Comprehension/Nonfiction.* The author calls Red Sun's stealing a "mania" and declares that "he would steal anything that was not nailed down" (lines 4-6). Red Sun is not even concerned with being caught (1), nor does the passage show that he enjoys the danger involved (2). Likewise, the passage does not state that he must steal to survive (3) or to help others (5).

7. **(2)** *Inferential Comprehension/Nonfiction.* Red Sun "poked his chest way out" (line 31-32) after being praised. Since this is a way of showing pride, you can infer that Red felt proud about being praised. (4) cannot be correct because Red Sun already was a horse thief. The praise clearly did not make him decide to go straight (3), since he is arrested for stealing the horse that gains him the praise. Nothing suggests that the praise makes him feel angry (1) or makes him want to return to the Home (5).

8. **(1)** *Analysis/Nonfiction.* In line 1, the author states that this is a "funny incident." The humor comes partly from the reversal of the other residents' assumptions that Red Sun had "gone straight" (lines 15-16). Red Sun's words are particularly comic. "See you-all soon" is a standard way of saying goodbye, yet Red doesn't think that he really will be back soon as a resident. Because of the humorous tone, the author cannot be making a serious comment on human foolishness (2). He is not concerned with Red's feelings (3) or his education (4), as shown by his opening comment about the "funny incident." Aside from this one comment, we have no other indication that Red is friendly (5), so reject this choice.

9. **(3)** *Inferential Comprehension/Drama.* Gayev and Mme. Ranevskaya's apparent wealth seems to have allowed them to live sheltered lives. They think that the small contribution from an aunt will make a difference in the situation (lines 8-11). They discredit Lopahin's plan to lease their land—the only way they can keep it—as "all so vulgar" (lines 38-39). Lopahin calls them "frivolous" and "unbusinesslike" (lines 17-19) and is completely frustrated in his attempts to make them understand the severity of their situation, so (1) cannot be correct. They live well, not simply, (2), and are completely sane (5). If they were greedy, they would seize on Lopahin's plan, so reject (4).

10. **(2)** *Inferential Comprehension/Drama.* Lopahin exclaims, "I shall either burst into tears or scream or faint! I can't stand it! You've worn me out!" (lines 39-41). He is frustrated because they will not listen to his plan; rather, they seem to expect some miraculous solution. We know his outburst is caused by many previous arguments with them because in lines 25-26 Lopahin says, "I do tell you [what to do] every day; every day I say the same thing!" There is no evidence that Gayev and Mme. Ranevskaya lie about their assets (1) or that Lopahin had received an offer to buy the orchard (3)—only that Lopahin wants them to leave the land. (4) is wrong because Gayev and Mme. Ranevskaya have been in contact with the aunt, not Lopahin. There is no evidence that Gayev had a business at all (5).

11. **(4)** *Application/Drama.* Aristocratic Mme. Ranevskaya's views about "common people" (the kind who might rent summer cottages on her land) are summed up in the word "vulgar" (line 37). The passage indicates that she has had little to do with such people in the past and that she wants little to do with them in the future. She does not see why they would be put in the position of exercising some control over her financial well-being. Mme. Ranevskaya would probably look at democracy—a system that would give such people some control over her political rights and freedoms—in a similar light. Thus, she would not endorse the statement in (5). Since she considers the middle class or working class "vulgar," she would never want to be a socialist (1) and share power with these people. There is no indication that she is concerned with fashion above all else (3). She does not delegate authority to Gayev, so (2) cannot be correct.

12. **(4)** *Analysis/Drama.* Most of Lopahin's speeches contain facts and logic, the signs of a sensible person. He does talk about large sums of money, but so do the other two characters. It is his use of facts and logic in his discussion—and the others' lack of logic—which makes his talk about money sensible compared to theirs. Therefore, (1) is wrong. The stage directions do not say that Lopahin is sensible, so reject (2). Likewise, the author does not describe Lopahin in any way, so (3) is false. Reject (5), because the other characters do not agree with Lopahin at all.

13. **(1)** *Literal Comprehension/Commentary.* Shaker designs may be decorative, long-lasting, sturdy, and functional, but they are not fragile (2), fancy (3), heavy (4), or unattractive (5). Only (1) offers two correct descriptions.

14. **(5)** *Literal Comprehension/Commentary.* The Shakers' "purpose was to bring heaven to earth, not make beautiful things" (line 31-33). To do so, they tried to make every aspect of their community reflect "a spiritual sense" (line 30-31). The large families in their communities were "both communal and celibate"—that is, they were not families created by sexual reproduction. Instead, they were unrelated groups of people who lived and worked together out of a common sense of purpose. Such "families" were not the Shakers' main purpose but only a way of living apart from the world. Therefore, (4) is wrong. Since the Shakers turned away from society, (2) cannot be correct. Clearly their act of furniture-making and other crafts was only an expression of their desire to live a completely spiritual life, so (1) and (3) are incorrect.

15. **(3)** *Application/Commentary.* The main idea of the passage is that Shaker designs have power and beauty because of their simplicity (line 27) and their sense of proportion (lines 52-54). Because of their desire to live apart from the "the World," the Shakers would not like or make art that was "showy" or called attention to the artist instead of God. Therefore, reject (4) and (5), which would call attention to themselves or to their creators. The film (1) cannot be correct because it would allow a variety of interpretations, whereas the Shakers intended only one interpretation of their work—the glory of God. (2) would reflect the fashion trends of "the World"; the Shakers had little interest in what "the World" thought of anything (lines 21-22). Of the choices given, the vase (3) come the closest to reflecting the Shakers' own love

of simplicity and a sense of proportion, or elegance.

16. **(4)** *Analysis/Commentary.* The author's style reflects the purpose of the passage—namely, to discuss the reasons why the author finds objects made by the Shakers so attractive. The author concentrates on "harmony," "proportion," and "excellence of design." Such terms could also be applied to a review of a painting, but not to any of the other choices.

17. **(5)** *Literal Comprehension/Fiction.* Throughout the passage, the traveler—referred to as "it" rather than as "he" or "she"—is described as seeking the voices. Since the voices are not heard, the traveler will create conditions under which the voices could return. Lines 17-19 reveal that the traveler will first destroy "whatever had destroyed the intelligence that once existed here." Line 22 tells us that later the traveler will "reseed." The traveler also sends power into the planet's ocean, turning it into a huge cloud of water vapor which then becomes rain that will help restore the planet's life (lines 29-31). Only (5) has all three of the traveler's main activities. The traveler's mission is not to simply find out what is there (1), merely destroy (2), or only instruct (3).

18. **(3)** *Inferential Comprehension/Fiction.* From the description of the traveler reaching the "star system" (line 1), the "nondescript blue planet" (line 2), and the "system's outer worlds" and "great gas giants" (line 5), you can infer that the traveler is most likely from somewhere in outer space. (1) is wrong because the blue planet is the traveler's *destination*, not its place of origin. Eliminate (2) because the traveler *passes through* the great gas giant on its way to Earth. (4) is incorrect for the same reason: the ocean is located on the blue planet. It is unlikely that the traveler came from a frozen world (5), since it knows how to freeze, thaw, water, and reseed the Earth to make it acceptable.

19. **(2)** *Inferential Comprehension/Fiction.* The traveler's actions create the vapor which condenses into rain clouds. You can infer this from the second and third paragraphs, where the traveler "centered its attentions on a wide expanse of ocean and began feeding power to the focus" (line 23-25). These actions are intentional, not accidental, so (3) is wrong. There is no mention of a tropical storm, melting glacier, or hole in the ozone layer, so (1), (4), and (5) are incorrect.

20. **(3)** *Analysis/Fiction.* By analyzing the traveler's actions, you can see that they are rational—each action makes logical sense. The traveler knows to freeze, thaw, water, and reseed the Earth to make it acceptable to life. The traveler does not have any human traits, either physical—such as eyes or hands—or emotional—such as fears or hopes. Further, the author refers to the traveler as "it." It might be a kind of computer creature, for example. Nothing in the passage supports any of the other choices. There is no mention of a space ship (1), scientists (2), or outside forces (5). (4) is directly contradicted by the passage, for the traveler is fully in control of the powers it unleashes.

21. **(3)** *Inference/Poetry.* "They took my lover's tallness off to war" (line 2). Therefore, you an infer that the phrase refers to everything that the war has robbed from the couple—his youth, good looks, health. There is no indication that he is stubborn, so reject (1). The "other woman" with whom he has been unfaithful is death, so eliminate (2). We do not know that he wanted to fight in the war, only that he is willing to be courted by death, so (4) is wrong. There is no description of his appearance in his coffin, so (5) cannot be correct.

22. **(1)** *Inference/Poetry.* From lines 10-12, you can infer that the speaker is describing death as a flirtatious woman. Line 10 tells you that she is "coquettish" (flirtatious); line 11 describes her "possessive arms and beauty (of a sort)." "Sweet love" (line 8) and "one who hesitates, stammers, and changes" (line 12-13) both describe the soldier, not death, so reject (4) and (5). There is nothing to suggest that death is a "cruel victory" ; rather, death is described as a woman. Therefore (2) is not correct. The "empty heart-cup" describes how the speaker feels, not death.

23. **(5)** *Analysis/Poetry.* The word "lamenting" (line 3) and the description of the soldier's death (line 5) establish the sad tone. By showing death as a successful rival, the speaker conveys her bitterness at losing her beloved. "Furious" is too strong a word for her feelings, so reject (3). She is certain that her beloved is dead, so she cannot be confused. Thus, eliminate (2). She is sad, but far from relieved, so reject (4). (1) is wrong because it directly contradicts the speaker's feelings at losing her beloved to a war.

# *Predictor Test*

# Performance Analysis Chart 1

Directions: Circle the number of each item that you got correct on the Predictor Test. Count how many items you got correct in each row; count how many items you got correct in each column. Write the amount correct per row and column as the numerator in the fraction in the appropriate "Total Correct" box. (The denominators represent the total number of items in the row or column.) Write the grand total correct over the denominator, **23**, at the lower right corner of the chart. (For example, if you got 19 items correct, write 19 so that the fraction reads 19/**23**.)

| Item Type | Nonfiction (page 14) | Fiction (page 90) | Drama (page 168) | Poetry (page 210) | Commentary (page 246) | TOTAL CORRECT |
|---|---|---|---|---|---|---|
| Literal Comprehension | 5, 6 | 1. 17 | | 21, 22 | 13,14 | /8 |
| Inferential Comprehension | 7 | 2, 18, 19 | 9, 10 | | | /6 |
| Application | | 3 | 11 | | 15 | /3 |
| Analysis | 8 | 4, 20 | 12 | 23 | 16 | /6 |
| TOTAL CORRECT | /4 | /8 | /4 | /3 | /4 | /23 |

The page numbers in parentheses indicate where in this book you can find the beginning of specific instruction about the various types of literature and commentary and about the types of questions you encountered in the Predictor Test.

# CHAPTER 1

Some writers of literature make up the stories they write. They invent imaginary people, places, and events. Other writers, however, write about people, places, and events in the real world. This type of literature, called nonfiction, begins with facts. The facts are put together in new and unique ways so that readers can look at the real world in a new and challenging way.

Mark Twain
Credit: Bancroft Library, University of California at Berkley

## Prereading Prompt

Nonfiction literature is about real people and events. Think of a recent book, magazine article, or movie that was nonfiction. What kind of lives did the people live? What did they do that made their story or situations worth telling? Is there some part of your life that you think would make an interesting book or movie?

# NONFICTION

## What is Nonfiction?

Nonfiction writing is about real people, places, and events. Most of the writing we read in magazines, newspapers, and textbooks is nonfiction. Nonfiction writers are careful observers. They research their topic fully. They gather the *facts*, information that can be proven. They organize the facts into writings that allow a reader to see the world in a new way. Some nonfiction writers include their own opinions about their subjects.

Nonfiction writing that has universal interest and that says something of lasting value is considered literature.

## Key Words

**autobiography**—an account of a person's life written by that person

**biography**—an account of a person's life written by another person

**article or essay**—a formally or informally written expression of a writer's thoughts and feelings about a subject

# Understanding Words By Using Context Clues

## Prereading Prompt

Most people like to read and talk about topics that interest them. If you are a sports fan, you probably read the sports section of the paper and discuss yesterday's games with friends. You may even subscribe to a sports magazine or buy issues of interest at the newsstand. If you are considering a career in computers, you probably read the want ads and articles about computers and talk with friends and experts about the subject.

Every once in a while in your reading and talking, you come across an unfamiliar word. When this happens, you can often figure out its meaning by paying close attention to the words nearby for clues. Knowing how to find word meanings in this way is very important for answering GED questions. You will learn how in this lesson.

## Key Words

**definition**—the direct statement of the meaning of a word

**paraphrase**—The reinstatement of the meaning of a word or phrase in different words

**example**—something used to show what a certain type of things is like

**parallelism**—similarity in meaning between two statements

**contrast**—explanation of the meaning by stating what it does *not* mean

## Understanding Words by Using Context Clues

While giving the news, the TV announcer says, "After a long police search, the dangerous *sociopath* was apprehended." Even if you have never heard the word *sociopath* before, you can figure out that it means "a person whose behavior is antisocial." You use clues from your own experience. You have heard words using the root "socio" such as **society, social**, and **sociology**. All these words describe communities of people. You may also have heard words using "patho" such as **pathology**. You know that this root means **disease**, so it makes sense that a sociopath would be a person who is, like a disease, dangerous to life—here, the lives of people in society. When you come across an unfamiliar word or phrase in your reading, you can often figure out the meaning by looking at the surrounding words for clues.

There are five basic types of context clues:

**(1) Definition:** "An *autobiography* is *the story of a person's life as written by that person*." This is probably the easiest type of clue to use, since the word's meaning is given directly to you.

**(2) Paraphrase:** "The store on the corner sells *organic* food, food *grown without chemicals*." A paraphrase gives the meaning of a word or phrase by restating its meaning in other words. The paraphrase occurs in the same sentence or the next sentence. *Organic* means *grown without chemicals*.

**(3) Example:** "The conductor was known for such *dramatics* as *leaping into the air, gesturing wildly, and looking heavenward for inspiration*." By thinking about how all the examples of what the conductor does are the same, you can figure out the meaning of *dramatics*. Leaping up, gesturing wildly, and looking heavenward are all examples of "hamming it up," so *dramatics* must mean overemotional behavior.

**(4) Parallelism:** "Her stories portray *the separation of blacks and whites in South Africa*. Each is a powerful argument against *apartheid*." When two statements talk about the same thing in slightly different ways, they are said to be *parallel*: like two train tracks, they are separate but go in the same direction. By parallelism, you can figure out that *apartheid* must be the separation of blacks and whites in South Africa.

**(5) Contrast:** "All is *flux*; nothing stays still." In a contrast, an explanation of what something does *not* mean is given. *All* and *nothing* are opposites, so *flux* must mean the opposite of *staying still*. Something that is "in flux" must mean *moving, changing*.

## Model Question and Strategy

In the Interpreting Literature and the Arts section of the GED test, you will sometimes be asked to find the meaning of a word from a passage. Here is a sample question:

> As used in the article on line 00, what does the term_____ mean?

Here is a strategy you can use to find the answer:

Step 1: Locate the word in the passage.

Step 2: Look at nearby words and sentences for clues to the word's meaning.

Step 3: Make a prediction about the answer before looking at the choices.

Step 4: Examine each choice. Eliminate any choices that seem far-fetched.

Step 5: Choose the best answer.

## Model Passage and Question

The question below refers to the following passage. Use the strategy and see if you can select the correct meaning of **deserted**.

### WHAT IS A SUBWAY PLATFORM LIKE ON THE EVE OF MEMORIAL DAY?

As the train was entering the Atlantic City station, some white man stood up from his seat and helped her out of the car, placing the children on the long, deserted platform. There were only two adult persons on the long platform sometime
(5) after midnight on the eve of Memorial Day.

From *A Puerto Rican in New York* by Jesus Colon. Reprinted by permission of International Publishers, Inc.

The word *deserted* in line 3 means

**(1)** nearly dark
**(2)** bitterly cold
**(3)** almost empty
**(4)** very crowded
**(5)** well-lighted

Step 1: Locate the word in the passage. Run your finger down to line 3 and find *deserted*.

Step 2: Look at nearby words and sentences for clues to the word's meaning. The platform is almost empty when the train pulls into the station. You know this because the sentence after the one containing *deserted* tells you, "There were only two adults on the long platform sometime after midnight . . ."

Step 3: Make a prediction about the answer before looking at the choices. *Deserted* probably means "fairly empty."

Step 4: Examine each choice. Eliminate any choices that seem not to fit. Choices (1) and (5) are incorrect because no details in the passage tell you about the lighting on the platform. Choice (2) is incorrect because there are no details in the passage to support the idea that it was cold on the platform. Choice (4) is incorrect because there were "only two adult persons on the long platform." A subway platform with only two people on it is not a very crowded one.

Step 5: Look at the passage again and choose the best answer. The correct choice is (3). "Almost empty" is the best match for your prediction—"fairly empty."

Items 1 to 3 refer to the following passage. Choose the one best answer to each item.

### HOW ARE "HUMOROUS" AND "COMIC" STORYTELLERS DIFFERENT?

I do not claim that I can tell a story as it ought to be told. I only claim to know how a story ought to be told, for I have been almost daily in the company of the most expert storytellers for many years.

(5) There are many kinds of stories, but only one difficult kind—the humorous. I will talk mainly about that one . . .

The humorous story may be spun out to great length, and may wander around as much as it pleases, and arrive nowhere in particular; but the comic and witty stories must be brief and end with a point. The humorous story bubbles

(10) gently along; the others burst.

The humorous story is strictly a work of art—high and delicate art—and only an artist can tell it. But no art is necessary in telling the comic and the witty story; anybody can do it. The art of telling a humorous story—understand, I mean by word of mouth, not print—was created in America, and has remained at home.

(15) The humorous story is told gravely. The teller does his best to conceal the fact that he even dimly suspects that there is anything funny about it. But the teller of the comic story tells you beforehand that it is one of the funniest things he has ever heard, then tells it with eager delight, and is the first

(20) person to laugh when he gets through. Sometimes, if he has had good success, he is so glad and happy that he will repeat the "nub" of it and glance around from face to face, collecting applause, and then repeat it again. It is a pathetic thing to see.

(25) Very often, of course, the rambling humorous story also finishes with a nub, point, snapper, or whatever you like to call it. Then the listener must be alert, for in many cases, the teller will divert attention from that nub by dropping it in a carefully casual and indifferent way, as though he does not

(30) even know it is a nub.

But the teller of the comic story does not slur the nub; he shouts it at you—every time. And when he prints it, in England, France, Germany, and Italy, he *italicizes* it, puts some whooping exclamation points after it, and sometimes

(35) explains it in a parenthesis. All of which is very depressing, and makes one want to renounce joking and lead a better life.

From "How to Tell A Story" by Mark Twain. Published by Harper Collins Publishers, Inc.

1. The word *gravely* in line 18 means

    (1) in a humorous manner
    (2) in a serious and solemn manner
    (3) in a slow, quiet manner
    (4) in a loud manner
    (5) in a rapid, excited manner

2. The word *divert* in line 31 means

    (1) distract
    (2) call
    (3) italicize
    (4) depress
    (5) snap

3. The word *slur* in line 34 means

    (1) consider
    (2) scream
    (3) remember
    (4) wisecrack
    (5) mumble

Answers are on page 311.

# Finding Details and Restating Information

## Prereading Prompt

When you read, you often look for specific details. In a magazine article about an oil spill, you might look to see how many gallons were spilled, where the spill occurred, and the kind of damage that was done. Knowing how to find specific details—and recognize restatements of them— is important for answering GED questions. You will learn how in this lesson.

## Key Words

**specific details**—details that give precise information

**literal comprehension**—understanding something that is expressed directly

## Finding Details

On the *Interpreting Literature and the Arts* section on the GED test, you will sometimes be asked to find specific details from a passage and show that you understand their meaning. These specific details can be found directly in the passage.

## Model Questions and Strategy

Here are two sample questions that ask for literal comprehension of specific details that you could find on the GED test. The questions are followed by a strategy you can use to find the answer.

- The event described in lines 00-00 is _____.

- According to line 00, why did ____ happen?

**Strategy:**

<u>Step 1</u>: Look at the cited line or find the detail in the passage.

<u>Step 2</u>: Look nearby to find additional information about the detail.

<u>Step 3</u>: Make a prediction about the answer before looking at the choices.

<u>Step 4</u>: Examine each choice. Eliminate any choices that do not fit.

<u>Step 5</u>: Read the passage again and choose the best answer.

## Model Passage and Question

The question below refers to the following passage. Use the strategy to help you find the specific detail.

### WHAT DO THESE PERFORMERS HAVE IN COMMON?

In the 1940's, the image of black performers began to change. With the rise of modern dance, they found an artistic means for free expression without betraying their ethnic past. The earliest contributions came from Katherine Dunham and
(5) Pearl Primus. A host of dancer-choreographers followed whose intensity is of astonishing power. From Donald McKayle to Alvin Ailey, they have added a flavor to the American dance theatre without which it would be the poorer. The Dance Theatre of Harlem, the first all-black ballet compa-
(10) ny, is one of our nation's most accomplished groups. Blacks may not yet have achieved all their desired goals on a social level, but they have certainly secured an adequate place on the dance stage.

From *Dance in Its Time: The Emergence of an Art Form* by Walter Sorel Copyright ©1981 by Walter Sorel. Used by permission of Doubleday, an imprint of Bantam Doubleday Dell Publishing Group, Inc.

What do Donald McKayle and Alvin Ailey have in common?

**(1)** They are African-American male performers from the 1920's.

**(2)** They tried to be artists, but failed.

**(3)** They are painters.

**(4)** They are African-American dancer-choreographers.

**(5)** They betrayed their ethnic past.

<u>Step 1: Look at the cited line or find the detail in the passage.</u> Donald McKayle and Alvin Ailey are mentioned on line 7.

<u>Step 2: Look nearby to find additional information about the detail.</u> From the sentence before McKayle and Ailey are mentioned, we know that these men are two of a "host of dancer-choreographers . . . whose intensity is of astonishing power." McKayle and Alvin Ailey, then, are dancer-choreographers.

<u>Step 3: Make a prediction about the answer before looking at the choices.</u> There should be a choice that mentions that both men are African-American and/or that both are dancer-choreographers.

<u>Step 4: Examine each choice. Eliminate any choices that do not fit.</u> Choice (1) cannot be correct because the first sentence of the passage tells you that the article is about African-American performers from the 1940's and after. Choice (2) is incorrect because the passage never mentions that any of these performers failed. On the contrary, the article tells us that these performers have "astonishing power" and "have added a flavor to the American dance theater without which it would be the poorer." Choice (3) cannot be correct because painting is never mentioned in the passage. Choice (5) is incorrect because it is contradicted by the passage. The passage directly states that the African-American performers found "an artistic means for free expression without betraying their ethnic past."

<u>Step 5: Look at the passage again and choose the best answer.</u> The correct answer is (4). You know this because it is directly stated in lines 5-7 that McKayle and Ailey are dancer-choreographers.

## Restating Information

On the *Interpreting Literature and the Arts* section of the GED test, you will sometimes be asked to restate information. When you restate ideas, you put them in your own words. Be careful not to alter the meaning of the original information. Suppose you read this sentence:

> "Justice in a society must include both an impartial trial for the accused and the selection of an appropriate punishment for the guilty."

You might restate this sentence as: "Justice means that people charged with a crime must be given a fair trial, and those who are found guilty must be given a suitable punishment."

# Model Question and Strategy

Below is a sample question that asks for a restatement of information that you could find on the GED test. The question is followed by a strategy you can use to find the answer.

- According to the passage, which of the following is true?

## Strategy:

Step 1: Preview the test question.

Step 2: Read the passage and the choices. Put each choice in your own words.

Step 3: Check each choice carefully against information in the passage to make sure that it is accurate.

Step 4: Eliminate choices that are not accurate. Recheck the remaining choice against the information in the passage to make sure that it is accurate.

The question below refers to the following passage. Use the strategy to help you find the correct answer.

### WHAT DID THIS MAN GAIN BY HIS APPRENTICESHIP?

During the two and a half years of my apprenticeship I served under many pilots and had experience of many kinds of steamboatmen and many varieties of steamboats. I am to this day profiting somewhat by that experience; for in that
(5) brief, sharp schooling, I got personally and familiarly acquainted with about all the different types of human nature that are to be found in fiction, biography, or history.

Excerpted from "Cub Pilot on the Mississippi" by Mark Twain from *Life on the Mississippi*. Published by HarperCollins Publishers.

According to the passage, the major benefit of an apprenticeship is that it gives an opportunity

**(1)** to have a two-and-a-half year vacation

**(2)** to earn a profit at an early age

**(3)** to avoid brief, sharp schooling

**(4)** to serve others at an early age

**(5)** to get to know many kinds of people

<u>Step 1: Preview the test question</u>. Notice that with this type of test question you cannot predict the answer.

<u>Step 2: Read the passage and the choices. Put each choice in your own words.</u>

<u>Step 3: Check each choice carefully against the information in the passage to make sure that it is accurate</u>. Each of the first four choices mixes up words and meanings in the passage to make false statements. The first sentence in the passage says that the speaker had "two and a half years of... apprenticeship"—not a vacation (1). Line 5 refers to that period of "brief, sharp schooling." The apprenticeship was a time of learning job skills—not taking time off from work. (2) is incorrect because the author says he profited from his experience as an apprentice, not that he earned a profit. (3) is incorrect because the author says that his apprenticeship served as a "brief, sharp schooling"; the author did not avoid schooling. (4) While it is true that the speaker "served under many pilots", this was a requirement of apprenticeship, not an act of unselfish service to people in general, as (4) suggests.

<u>Step 4: Eliminate choices that are not accurate. Recheck the remaining choice against information in the passage to make sure that it is accurate.</u> (5) is the answer because it restates information found in the last line of the passage about apprenticeship. "To get to know many kinds of people" is another way of saying to get "personally and familiarly acquainted with about all the different types of human nature that are to be found...."

Items 1 to 3 refer to the following passage. Choose the one best answer to each item.

### HOW DO THINGS TURN?

When something turns, it can turn in just one of two ways, clockwise or counterclockwise, and we all know which is which. Clockwise is the normal turning direction of the hands of a clock and counterclockwise is the opposite of that. Since
(5) we all stare at clocks (dial clocks, that is), we have no trouble following directions or descriptions that include those words. But if dial clocks disappear, so will the meaning of those words for anyone who has never stared at anything but digitals. There are no *good* substitutes for clockwise and counter-
(10) clockwise. . . .

Nor is this a minor matter. Astronomers define the north pole and south pole of any rotating body [in outer space] in such terms. If you are hovering [in a space ship] above a pole of rotation and the body is rotating counterclockwise, it is the
(15) north pole; if the body is rotating clockwise, it is the south pole. Astronomers also speak of "direct motion" and "retrograde motion," by which they mean counterclockwise and clockwise, respectively.

From "Dial Versus Digital," by Isaac Asimov. Reprinted by permission of *American Way,* inflight magazine of American Airlines. Copyright ©1985 by American Airlines.

1. According to the author, if dial clocks disappear, what will disappear along with them?

   (1) the ability to understand digital clocks
   (2) the ability to hover about a pole of rotation
   (3) the ability to understand the words *clockwise* and *counterclockwise*
   (4) the ability to understand the concepts *retrograde motion* and *direct motion*
   (5) the ability to study motion around the North and South poles

2. Losing the terms *clockwise* and *counterclockwise* is "no minor matter" because

   (1) astronomers describe rotating bodies using these terms
   (2) people cannot tell time without them
   (3) the hands of a clock usually turn clockwise
   (4) they show the different between the south pole and direct motion
   (5) digital clocks will become meaningless

3. Of the following pairs of terms, the two with the opposite meanings are

   (1) clockwise and normal turning direction
   (2) counterclockwise and north pole rotation
   (3) clockwise and retrograde motion
   (4) counterclockwise and direct motion
   (5) direct motion and retrograde motion

Answers are on page 311.

# Finding the Main Idea of a Paragraph

## Prereading Prompt

You probably spend some time each day talking with friends about a variety of topics, Sometimes you or your friends have a specific point to make. For example, you might think one singer or team is the best.

In a piece of writing, the main point made about a topic is the writer's main idea.

On the GED, you will be asked to find the main idea of a paragraph. You will learn how in this lesson.

## Key Words

**main idea**—the point the writer is making about a topic

**topic**—what a piece of writing is about

**topic sentence**—one sentence that states the main idea

## Finding the Main Idea of a Paragraph

On the *Interpreting Literature and the Arts* section of the GED test, you will sometimes be asked to find the main idea of a paragraph. The **main idea** is the point the writer is making about a subject. To find the main idea, read the work carefully to find the **topic sentence**, a sentence that answers the question, "What point is the author trying to make about the topic?" The topic sentence may be the first sentence of a paragraph, the last sentence, or one of the sentences in the middle. Regardless of where the topic sentence is placed, all the other sentences in the paragraph should give details that support the main idea it expresses.

## Model Questions and Strategy

Below are three sample questions about the main idea of a paragraph that you could find on the GED test. The questions are followed by a strategy you can use to find the answer.

- The event described took place as it did because _____.
- Which of the following sentences states the author's general attitude toward_____ [the topic]?
- According to the paragraph, how is _____ [the topic] explained?

**Strategy:**

<u>Step 1:</u> Identify the topic. Ask yourself what the paragraph is about. Look for repeated words, statements about the same thing.

<u>Step 2:</u> Summarize the author's main point about the topic.

<u>Step 3:</u> Read through the paragraph for the sentence that states the main idea of the paragraph.

<u>Step 4:</u> Look at the answer choices and eliminate those that do not seem to fit your summary of the paragraph's point. Eliminate the details—that is, statements not general enough to be the main idea of the paragraph.

<u>Step 5:</u> Choose the best answer.

## Model Passage and Questions

The two questions below refer to the following passage. Use the strategy to help you find the topic and main idea of the paragraph.

### WHAT DO ACORNS TASTE LIKE?

I was a member of a party of six in the mountains of central Pennsylvania one autumn when the chestnut oaks, Quercus Muhlenberglii, had borne an extra heavy crop of acorns. We easily gathered a bushel in an hour. All of us tried
(5) them raw, and three members of the party liked them well enough to eat several. I thought them considerably improved when we roasted some in the oven of the wood stove that heated the cabin in which we were staying. This experience convinced me that... unleached acorns of some species are
(10) worth the attention of anyone who is really hungry.

From *Stalking the Wild Asparagus*, by Euell Gibbons. Copyright ©1962 by Euell Gibbons. Used by permission of Alan C. Hood & Co., Brattleboro, VT.

The topic of the paragraph is

**(1)** roasting acorns
**(2)** mountain climbing
**(3)** eating raw acorns
**(4)** finding a heavy acorn crop
**(5)** gathering and eating acorns

<u>Step 1: Identify the topic.</u> Remember, the topic is one or two words stating what the entire paragraph is about. Ask yourself, "What are all the details in the paragraph about?" Repeated words are often clues to the topic. You can tell that the topic is gathering and eating acorns (5) because *all* of the sentences tell you about this. The entire paragraph—not simply one or two sentences—is about acorns. Choice (1), roasting acorns, is one of the details mentioned, but the whole paragraph is not about roasting acorns. Likewise, there are details about being in the mountains (2), eating raw acorns (3), and a heavy crop of acorns (4), but the *whole* paragraph is not about any of these.

The main idea of the paragraph is

**(1)** it may be easy to gather a bushel of acorns in an hour
**(2)** anyone who is really hungry can eat unleached acorns
**(3)** roasted acorns are better-tasting than raw acorns
**(4)** everyone should have the experience of gathering acorns
**(5)** chestnut oaks can bear a very heavy crop of acorns

<u>Step 2: Summarize the author's main point about the topic.</u> Ask yourself, "Why is the writer telling me all these details? What point is the writer trying to make about the topic?" Your summary might be something like this: I learned that you can eat acorns either raw or roasted.

<u>Step 3: Read through the paragraph for the sentence that states the main idea of the paragraph.</u> The main idea of the paragraph is stated in the last sentence: "This experience convinced me that even unleached acorns of some species are worth the attention of anyone who is really hungry." This is very close in meaning to the summary you drew up for yourself. All of the other sentences in the paragraph are details that support this main idea.

<u>Step 4: Look at the answer choices and eliminate those that do not fit your summary of the main idea or the topic sentence. Eliminate the choices that are not general statements.</u> (1), (3), and (5) are all details about various aspects of acorn gathering and eating, so eliminate them. (1) and (5) are details about gathering acorns; both are true, but they don't state the main idea. (3) is a detail about the author's viewpoint on whether acorns taste better raw or cooked. (4) is general but inaccurate because the author does not suggest that people should "experience gathering acorns"; he only says that he has done so.

<u>Step 5: Choose the best answer.</u> (2) is the best answer—the one that best matches your own prediction. The main idea is that both raw and roasted acorns can be eaten by people who are truly hungry. All of the other sentences in the paragraph support that idea.

Items 1-2 refer to the following paragraph. Choose the one best answer to each item.

### WHAT WAS IT LIKE TO ATTEND LINCOLN?

At Lincoln, making us into Americans did not mean scrubbing away what made us originally foreign. The teachers called us as our parents did, or as close as they could pronounce our names in Spanish or Japanese. No one was ever
(5) scolded or punished for speaking in his native tongue on the playground. Matti told the class about his mother's quilt, which she had made in Italy with the fine feathers of a thousand geese. Encarnacion acted out how boys learned to fish in the Philippines. I astounded the third grade with the story
(10) of my travels on a stagecoach, which nobody else in the class had seen except in the museum at Sutter's Fort. After a visit to the Crocker Art Gallery and its collection of heroic paintings of the golden age of California, someone showed a silk scroll with a Chinese painting. Miss Hopley herself had a way
(15) of expressing wonder over these matters before a class, her eye wide until they popped slightly. It was easy for me to feel that becoming a proud American, as she said we should, did not mean feeling ashamed of being a Mexican.

From *Barrio Boy* by Ernesto Galaza. Copyright ©1971 by University of Notre Dame Press. Reprinted by permission.

1. The outstanding characteristic of Lincoln High was that

   (1) Mexican-American students felt the most pride in their heritage
   (2) students were often transformed from foreigners into 100% Americans
   (3) students were happy because they were not reminded of their backgrounds
   (4) Asian and American students shared experiences
   (5) foreign-born students were made to feel proud of their backgrounds and becoming Americans

2. What were "these matters" (line 15) over which Miss Hopley expressed wonder?

   (1) field trips taken by the third-grade class
   (2) the collection of heroic paintings at the Crocker Art Gallery
   (3) stories and objects from the children's native lands
   (4) the ways in which the children communicated on the playground
   (5) museum pieces from the golden age of California

Item 3 is based on the following passage.

## WHAT'S WRONG WITH WATCHING TELEVISION?

The trouble with television is that it discourages concentration. Almost anything interesting and rewarding in life requires some constructive, consistently applied effort. The dullest, the least gifted of us can achieve things that seem
(5) miraculous to those who never concentrate on anything. But television encourages us to apply no effort. It sells us instant gratification.

From "The Trouble with Television," by Robert MacNeil. Reprinted with permission of the author and *Reader's Digest*. From the March 1985 Reader's Digest.

3. The author's main point about television is that it

(1) makes life seem too interesting and rewarding
(2) enables even the dullest and least gifted people to do miraculous things
(3) does not encourage concentration
(4) tries to sell us products that most of us really don't need
(5) allows us to do something constructive with little or no effort

Answers are on page 312.

# Finding the Main Idea of a Passage

## Prereading Prompt

When you read an article that really grabs your interest—about a scandal in Hollywood or about a hot political issue close to home—you ask yourself: What is this writer's main point? In reading, as in real life, you are often required to sift through all the details and come up with the main point. On the GED you may be asked to answer questions about the main idea of a passage—a series of paragraphs on the same topic. You will learn how in this lesson.

## Key Words

**supporting details**—details that support the main idea

**passage**—a series of paragraphs on the same topic

## Model Questions and Strategy

Below are three sample questions about the main idea of a passage that you could find on the GED test. The questions are followed by a strategy you can use to find the answer.

- What is the main idea of the passage?
- What sentence states the author's overall attitude toward _____ [the topic]?
- According to the passage, how is _____ [the topic] explained?

Here is a strategy you can use to find the answer:

Step1: Read the purpose question carefully. It will give you an important clue to the main idea.

Step 2: Keeping the purpose question in mind, read the passage.

Step 3: Look for the topic sentence in each paragraph. The main ideas the topic sentence state will help you find the topic of the passage.

Step 4: Now ask yourself: What is the most important thing this passage says about the topic? Look for a sentence that states this most important idea. This sentence will give you the main idea of the passage.

Step 5: Test the main idea of the passage by making sure that the main idea of each paragraph supports it.

Step 6: Choose the answer that best restates the main idea of the passage. Check your answer by eliminating choices that do not restate the main idea accurately, or which inaccurately restate details.

It will help you get the main idea of a passage more quickly in a GED question if, before you read it, you look for key words—underlined and capitalized words, titles and names—and try to guess its topic. If you have heard of the key things and people mentioned, remind yourself of anything you might know about them. For instance, in the passage below, ask yourself: What do I know about John Lennon or any of the people mentioned?

## Model Passage and Question

Read Item 1 and the passage that follows. Then use the strategy above to help you find the main idea of the passage.

### WHAT IS GOOD ABOUT THE MUSIC OF RICHARD RODGERS?

[Richard Rodgers] came into our house with the first Victrola... and stayed. By the time I was ten I knew every song on our boxed and scratched "78" records: songs from *Oklahoma!* and *Carousel* and *South Pacific.* They were, very
(5)  simply, the earliest tunes in a house that was more alive with the sound of politics than the sound of music.

As I grew older, I knew he was no Beethoven or Verdi, or John Lennon for that matter. By then his songs had been orchestrally overkilled into the sort of Muzak that kept you
(10)  company in elevators or "on hold" at the insurance company lines.

But the fact is that from the time I was a child,... there has always been a Richard Rodgers song in the background.

From "The Sounds of Richard Rodgers," from *At Large* by Ellen Goodman. Copyright ©1981 by the Washington Post Co. Reprinted by permission of Simon & Schuster, Inc.

1. What is the author's main point in the passage?

   **(1)** The music of Richard Rodgers has been important to the author most of her life.
   **(2)** Richard Rodgers is nearly worthless compared to Beethoven, Verdi, or John Lennon.
   **(3)** The earliest songs the author heard are the best songs.
   **(4)** Richard Rodgers songs have been killed by Muzak.
   **(5)** Politics and Rodgers' music were combined in the author's family.

Step 1: Read the purpose question carefully. It will give you an important clue to the main idea. The purpose question is: WHAT IS GOOD ABOUT THE MUSIC OF RICHARD RODGERS?

Step 2: Read the passage, keeping the purpose question in mind.

Step 3: Look for the topic sentence of each paragraph. The main idea each topic sentence states will help you find the topic of the passage. All of the paragraphs are about the same topic: the songs of Richard Rodgers. The topic sentence of the first paragraph is the first sentence. All the other sentences in that paragraph describe how "[Richard Rodgers] came into our house with the first Victrola . . . and stayed." The topic sentence of the second paragraph is the first sentence as well: "As I grew older, I knew he was no Beethoven or Verdi . . ." The other sentences explain why this is so.

Step 4: Now ask yourself: What is the most important thing this passage says about the topic? Look for a sentence that states the most important idea. This sentence will give you the main idea of the passage. Your summary might look something like this: The music of Richard Rodgers has always been a part of the author's life. The final line in the passage matches the summary most closely: ". . . from the time I was a child . . . there has always been a Richard Rodgers' song in the background."

Step 5: Test the main idea of the passage by making sure that the main idea of each paragraph supports it. The main idea of the first paragraph (Richard Rodgers's music was always around during the author's childhood) and the main idea of the second paragraph (the music was still around as she grew older) both support the main idea in the final sentence (". . . there has always been a Richard Rodgers' song in the background.")

Step 6: Choose the answer that best restates the main idea of the passage. Check your answer by eliminating choices that do not restate the main idea accurately, or which inaccurately restate details. (2) is wrong because even though the author states that Rodgers is "no Beethoven or Verdi, or even a John Lennon," nevertheless she has been enjoying his songs "in the background" since she was a child. (3) is incorrect because the author does not say that Rodgers's songs, the earliest songs she heard, are the best. Rather, she says they are not as good as Lennon's songs. (4) is also incorrect. The author says that Rodgers's songs have been "orchestrally overkilled into a sort of Muzak," meaning that performers have often ruined them. However, she also says that she and her child still enjoy Rodgers's songs. (5) is also incorrect because the author says that her home "was more alive with the sound of politics than the sound of music," not that the two things were enjoyed together.

Items 1 to 3 refer to the following passage. Choose the one best answer to each item using the strategies you have learned.

## WHY IS BERTHA FLOWERS SPECIAL TO MAYA ANGELOU?

For nearly a year, I sopped around the house, the Store, the school and the church, like an old biscuit, dirty and inedible. Then I met, or rather got to know, the lady who threw me my first lifeline.

(5) Mrs. Bertha Flowers was the aristocrat of [the town of] Black Stamps. She had the grace of control to appear warm in the coldest weather, and on the Arkansas summer days it seemed she had a private breeze which swirled around, cooling her. She was thin without the taut look of wiry people,

(10) and her printed voile dresses and flowered hats were as right for her as denim overalls for a farmer. She was our side's answer to the richest white woman in town.

Her skin was a rich black that would have peeled like a plum if snagged, but then no one would have thought of get-

(15) ting close enough to Mrs. Flowers to ruffle her dress, let alone snag her skin. She didn't encourage familiarity. She wore gloves too.

I don't think I ever saw Mrs. Flowers laugh, but she smiled often. A slow widening of her thin black lips to show even,

(20) small white teeth, then the slow effortless closing. When she chose to smile on me, I always wanted to thank her. The action was so graceful and inclusively benign.

She was one of the few gentlewomen I have ever known, and has remained throughout my life the measure of what a

(25) human being can be.

From *I Know Why the Caged Bird Sings*, by Maya Angelou. Copyright ©1969 by Maya Angelou. Reprinted by permission of Random House, Inc.

1. Which sentence best expresses the main idea of the passage?

   (1) Mrs. Flowers was the first person to give the author support and a hope for a better life.
   (2) Mrs. Flowers has always been for the author an ideal of femininity and human potential.
   (3) The author was especially impressed by Mrs. Flowers because the author was depressed when she first met her.
   (4) Mrs. Flowers was dignified and kind but not high-spirited or easy to know.
   (5) When the author was young, she always felt grateful to Mrs. Flowers whenever she was friendly to her.

2. All of statements below are true of Mrs. Bertha Flowers EXCEPT

   (1) she rarely laughed
   (2) she acted as though she was from a high social class
   (3) she was able to appear warm in cold weather
   (4) she had breezes swirling around her on summer days
   (5) she often smiled

3. The main point of the description of Mrs. Bertha Flowers in the second paragraph is that she was

   (1) the most dignified person of Black Stamps
   (2) a private person who controlled those around her
   (3) a thin, wiry person who was not nervous
   (4) the best-dressed woman in town
   (5) the richest woman in town

Answers are on page 312.

# Inferring a Detail

## Prereading Prompt

In daily life, you can often figure out what is happening from things you observe: if your fellow worker's car is parked outside and his coat is on his chair, you will probably decide that he is in the office somewhere. In a similar way, you may use a writer's direct statements as clues to figure out an unstated, or implied, meaning. Figuring out meaning in this way is called *inferring*, or *making an inference*. This lesson will teach you this reading skill, which you will need for the GED test.

### Key Words

**inference**—an unstated meaning understood by using direct statements as clues

**infer**—to use direct statements to figure out an unstated meaning

In the past few lessons you have been working on finding details and main ideas. This requires your understanding of what is stated in a passage. This ability to read what the lines say is called literal comprehension.

Often, however, the author expresses an idea without coming right out and saying it. In these instances, you must "read between the lines" to figure out the unstated meaning. This ability to read what is implied in a passage is called *inferential* comprehension. In Lesson 1, when you used a word's context to help you figure out its meaning, you were putting context clues together to make inferences.

Here is a five-step strategy you can use to find out if you can answer a question by reading between the lines.

Step 1: Look at the test question.

Step 2: Scan the paragraph to see if the answer to this question is stated directly. When the details in the passage do not answer a question, go to Step 3.

Step 3: Scan the paragraph to see if there are any clues that can help you answer the question. When you put clues together to answer a question, you are reading between the lines.

Step 4: Make a prediction about the answer before looking at the choices.

Step 5: Examine each choice. Eliminate choices that leap to illogical or unsupported conclusions.

Step 6: Chose the best answer.


## Model Passage and Question

Read this passage and the question that follows. Use the strategies above to help you infer the unstated details.

### HOW DO ARBITRAGERS TAKE OVER COMPANIES?

Arbitragers make money in three ways: hostile takeovers, friendly takeovers, and greenmail takeovers. In a hostile takeover, these investors take over the control of a company that does not want to be taken over by buying a controlling
(5) interest in it. However, sometimes the people who control a company or who own a lot of stock in it are not hostile to the arbitrager's takeover. They want him to take over the company so that it can be reorganized and the people running it replaced. At times, the arbitrager does not want control of the
(10) company. Instead, he forces the company to buy the stock he owns in their company in order to prevent him from taking it over. In other words, he uses a kind of financial blackmail.

In a friendly takeover, the people controlling the company seem to believe the arbitrager will

**(1)** pay them to let him take over the company
**(2)** make himself president of the company
**(3)** reduce their control of the company
**(4)** enlarge the company's operations
**(5)** make the company more efficient

Step 1: Preview the test question. Your preview shows that the test question will ask about a friendly takeover.

Step 2: Scan the paragraph to see if the answer to this question is stated directly. The "friendly takeover" is mentioned once in the first sentence of the paragraph, but nowhere does the author directly state what the people expect of the arbitrager in a friendly takeover.

When the details in the passage do not answer a question, go to Step 3.

Step 3: Scan the paragraph to see if there are any clues that can help you answer the question. In the first sentence of the paragraph, friendly takeovers are second in a list of three ways that arbitragers make money: hostile takeovers, friendly takeovers, and greenmail takeovers. The rest of the paragraph goes on to explain these three ways, beginning with "In a hostile takeover . . ." It is logical to assume that friendly takeovers will be explained after hostile takeovers and before greenmail.

Step 4: Make a prediction about the answer before looking at the choices. In the sentence after the explanation of hostile takeovers, the word "However . . ." signals that a contrasting situation will be presented. The author then states that the people controlling the company sometimes are not hostile to the takeover because they think the arbitrager will reorganize the company and replace the people operating it. Putting this information together, then, you might predict that in a friendly takeover, the people controlling the company believe the arbitrager will benefit the company.

Step 5: Examine each choice. Eliminate choices that leap to illogical or unsupported conclusions. (1) is wrong because nothing is said to suggest that the arbitrager is going to pay people controlling the company—only that he is investing in the company. (2) is incorrect because there is no evidence to suggest that the people want the arbitrager to make himself president of their company. Such a meaning would be suggested only if the passage said, for example, that the people welcomed the takeover so that their company could get new leadership from outside the company. Eliminate (3); it would not make sense for the people controlling the company to want their control reduced. (4) is also incorrect. The passage only states that the people who control the company want it reorganized; you shouldn't leap to the conclusion that they want it enlarged. In fact, the result of reorganization might be a smaller company or several smaller companies. (5) is the correct answer and the one that fits your prediction. In the passage, the author states that the people controlling the company are not hostile to the takeover because they think the arbitrager will reorganize the company and replace the people operating it. It would be logical for them to think the takeover would benefit their company by making it more efficient.

Use the strategies to help you infer the answer to this question on the passage about arbitragers on page 39.

In greenmail, people who control a company

**(1)** lose control against their will

**(2)** pay investors to buy a controlling interest

**(3)** pay off an arbitrager to keep control

**(4)** sell the company because they do not really want control

**(5)** force the arbitrager to buy stock he does not really want

(3) is the correct answer. The final two sentences describe a "kind of financial blackmail." Think about what you may already know about blackmail plus what you have learned from the paragraph about the meanings of "hostile takeovers" and "friendly takeovers." It is logical to assume that his "blackmail" situation, in which the arbitrager forces the company owners to pay him not to take over, is the "greenmail" mentioned in the first sentence of the paragraph. (1) is incorrect because the paragraph states that with greenmail the company *keeps from* losing control by paying off the arbitrager. In greenmail, people who control the company pay off, or bribe, the arbitrager so that he will *not* buy control of the company, which is the opposite of what is described in (2). None of the types of takeovers dealt with in the paragraph involve the activities described in (4) and (5).

Items 1-3 are based on the following passage. Read the passage and answer the question, using the strategy you have just learned.

### WAS ALBERT EINSTEIN ALWAYS CONSIDERED A GENIUS?

Einstein was born in 1879 in the German city of Ulm. He had been no infant prodigy; indeed, he was so late in learning to speak that his parents feared he was a dullard. In school, though his teachers saw no special talent in him, the signs
(5) were already there. He taught himself calculus, for example, and his teachers seemed a little afraid of him because he asked questions they could not answer. At the age of 16, he asked himself whether a light wave would seem stationary if one ran abreast of it. From that innocent question would
(10) arise, ten years later, his theory of relativity.

Einstein failed his entrance examination at the Swiss Federal Polytechnic School, in Zurich, but was admitted a year later. There he went beyond his regular work to study the masterworks of physics on his own. Rejected when he
(15) applied for academic positions, he ultimately found work in 1902 as a patent examiner in Berne, and there in 1905 his genius burst into fabulous flower.

Among the extraordinary things he produced in that memorable year were his theory of relativity, with its famous off-
(20) shoot, $E=MC^2$ (energy equals mass times the speed of light squared), and his quantum theory of light. These two theories were not only revolutionary, but seemingly contradictory: the former was intimately linked to the theory that light consists of waves, while the latter said it consists somehow of parti-
(25) cles. Yet this unknown young man boldly proposed both at once—and he was right in both cases, though how he could have been is far too complex a story to tell here.

From "Unforgettable Albert Einstein," by Banesh Hoffmann.in *Reader's Digest*, January 1968. Copyright ©1967 by The Reader's Digest Association, Inc.

1.  In line 2, the word *prodigy* means

    (1) an exceptionally talented child
    (2) a dull child
    (3) a late learner
    (4) someone who cannot speak
    (5) a crybaby

2.  Einstein in his early years

    (1) neglected assigned work to study physics
    (2) disliked his academic positions intensely
    (3) could not find his real interests until late in life
    (4) took time to explore his interests in math and science
    (5) produced brilliant ideas when stimulated by his patent job

3.  Einstein's theories were extraordinary because

    (1) they did not seem to fit together
    (2) no one expected him to come up with anything like them
    (3) they brought together what looked like opposite ideas
    (4) no one had thought of them before
    (5) he made a great deal of money from them

Answers are on page 313.

# Inferring the Main Idea

## Inferring the Main Idea of a Paragraph

In Lesson 4, you practiced finding the main idea when it was stated. This lesson shows you how to find the main idea when it is not directly stated in a paragraph or passage. Here is a strategy you can use when you need to infer the main idea.

**Strategy:**

<u>Step 1</u>: Identify the topic of the paragraph. What is the entire paragraph saying? Look carefully at all the details.

<u>Step 2</u>: Infer the main idea by putting the details in the sentences together and figuring out what important statement they are making about the topic. Try to restate the main idea in your own words.

<u>Step 3</u>: Test the main idea by making sure that most of the sentences support or tell about it. If they don't, start again by creating a new sentence that states the main idea.

## Model Question and Passage

Read this paragraph and see if you can infer the main idea. Use the strategy above to help you figure it out.

### WHAT CAN COMPUTER SCREENS DO TO YOUR EYES?

A video display terminal (VDT) is a computer screen. Many people who work on VDTs get headaches from straining their eyes. They also suffer from eye irritation. Often, their vision blurs or doubles, or the way they see color changes.
(5) Sometimes people who use VDTs can't see clearly when they look up from the screen. These problems are caused by blurred characters on the screen and poor lighting. They are also caused by operators constantly moving their eyes around from the VDT to the keyboard, and to what is being typed on
(10) the screen.

Step 1: Identify the topic of the paragraph. Looking back over the paragraph, you'll see that *VDT*, the abbreviation for video display terminal, is repeated several times. Further, all the details in the paragraph seem to refer to *VDTs*. From this, you can infer that the topic of the paragraph is *VDTs*.

Step 2: Infer the main idea by putting the details in the sentences together and figuring out what important statement they are making about the topic. Think about all the details you read. Then restate them in your own words. You may come up with a statement something like this: *Working on a VDT may cause eye problems.*

Step 3: Test the main idea by making sure that most of the sentences support or tell about it. Your possible main idea is: *Working on a VDT may cause eye problems.* Do the details support it? Sentence 1 defines a VDT. Sentences 2, 3, 4, and 5 describe eye problems caused by working on VDTs. Sentences 6 and 7 explain why VDTs cause eye problems. Therefore, all the sentences in the paragraph do support the main idea. While none of the sentences directly state the main idea, all of them together imply it because each gives information about the eye problems caused by VDTs.

What should you do if most of the sentences do not support the main idea? Read back over the paragraph and write a new sentence that you think states the main idea. Then test this statement by making sure that most of the sentences support or tell about it.

## Inferring the Main Idea of a Passage

On the GED, you may be asked questions that require you to infer the main idea of a series of paragraphs on a single topic, that is, to infer the main idea of a whole passage.

Here are some typical GED questions that may require you to infer the main idea of a paragraph, of several paragraphs, or of the whole passage.

- According to the article, what is the major reason for _____?
- The essay suggests that this kind of event/action will occur when_____.
- According to the review, these people have the common characteristic of _____.

Here is a strategy you can use to find the answer to these questions when you need to infer the main idea of the whole passage:

1.  As you read, try to identify the topic. Use the purpose question to help you.
2.  Identify the main idea of each paragraph (the topic sentence of each paragraph).
3.  Infer the main idea by putting the main ideas of all the paragraphs together and figuring out what important statement they are making about the topic.

Here is how this three-step strategy is applied to the following passage.

### WHAT SHOULD YOU KNOW WHEN BUYING A HOUSE?

When buying a house, it is important to know exactly how much money you can spend. The mortgage department of a local bank.can help you figure out what you can afford to spend on a house. This is based on your monthly income and
(5) expenses. When you buy a house, you must pay part of the total cost right away. This is known as the down payment. Down payments are at least 10 percent of the price of the house. A bank (or other lender) lends you the rest of the money by making a payment directly to the seller. You must
(10) repay the loan plus interest over a set period of time. The more money you put down, the smaller your loan or mortgage payments will be.

Once you know exactly how much money you can spend, its time to choose a location. Some locations are more expen-
(15) sive than others; therefore, it is important to choose a neighborhood that is within your budget. If you rely on public transportation, a train or bus should be within walking distance. If you have children, you may want to be near their school or school bus route. In addition, you may want to be
(20) within walking distance of a grocery store, bank, church, park, playground, or library.

Finally it is important to decide how much space you need ...or how little you'll settle for. Generally, the larger the house, the more it will cost. Your family's needs will determine the
(25) size of the house, how many bedrooms you will need, and whether or not you will need a big yard.

<u>Step 1: Identify the topic of the passage.</u> The first sentence, the third sentence, and in fact all the details of the passage let you know that the topic of the passage is *buying a house.*

<u>Step 2: Identify the main idea of each paragraph.</u> The main ideas of the the paragraphs, which are the supporting ideas of the passage, are as follows:

1. When buying a house, it's important to know exactly how much money you can spend.
2. Once you know exactly how much money you can spend, it's time to choose a location.
3. Finally, it's important to decide how much space you need... or how little you'll settle for.

<u>Step 3. Infer the main idea of the passage.</u> You might summarize the meaning of the three paragraphs' main ideas as follows: When buying a house, you should decide on how much you can spend, the location, and how much space you need. You might shorten this to: *When buying a house, decide first how much you can spend, then chose location and size.*

Read this passage and the question that follows. Use the strategy above to help figure out the unstated main idea.

### WHY IS FOOTBALL "A FINE SPORT"?

(5)

(10)

(15)

Some boys taught me to play football. This was fine sport. You thought up a new strategy for every play and whispered it to the others. You went out for a pass, fooling everyone. Best, you got to throw yourself mightily at someone's running legs. Either you brought him down or you hit the ground flat out on your chin, with your arms empty before you. It was all or nothing. If you hesitated in fear, you would miss and get hurt: You would take a hard fall while the kid got away, or you would get kicked in the face while the kid got away. But if you flung yourself wholeheartedly at the back of his knees—if you gathered and joined body and soul and pointed them, diving fearlessly—then you likely wouldn't get hurt, and you'd stop the ball. Your fate, and your team's score, depended on your concentration and courage. Nothing girls did could compare with it.

From *An American Childhood,* by Annie Dillard. Copyright ©1987 by Annie Dillard.. Reprinted by permission of HarperCollins Publishers.

The author's main point about football is that it

**(1)** is an exciting but dangerous "all or nothing" game
**(2)** is not a sport for girls
**(3)** will injure only girls if they hesitate in tackling
**(4)** is more exciting than any activity for girls
**(5)** helps girls and boys develop courage and concentration

The correct answer is (4). From the details "This was fine sport" and "Nothing girls did could compare with it" you can infer the main idea. (1) is incorrect because it is only one detail about the sport, not the main idea. (2) is incorrect because the author never says that football is *not* a game for girls. She states that "nothing girls did could compare with it," not that girls shouldn't play. (3) is incorrect because the author doesn't suggest that only girls will get hurt if they hesitate in tackling; she states that all players who hesitate in fear will miss and get hurt. (5) is incorrect because it is one detail mentioned by the author, not the main idea of the paragraph.

# Lesson 6 Exercise

Items 1 and 2 refer to the following passage. Choose the one best answer to each item.

## WHY DOES THE SPEAKER LIKE WALKING?

I have met with only one or two persons in the course of my life who understand the art of walking, that is, of taking walks.... I think that I cannot preserve my health and spirits unless I spend four hours a day at least...sauntering through
(5) the woods.... When sometimes I am reminded that the mechanics and shopkeepers stay in their shops not only all morning, but all the afternoon too, sitting with crossed legs, so many of them—as if the legs were meant to sit upon, and not to stand and walk upon—I think that they deserve some
(10) credit for not having all committed suicide long ago. I...cannot stay in my room for a single day without acquiring some rust. I confess that I am astonished at the power of endurance of my neighbors who confine themselves to shops and offices the whole day for weeks and months and
(15) years almost together.

But the walking of which I speak has nothing in it akin to taking exercise, as it is called, as the sick take medicine at stated hours—as the swinging of the dumbbells or chairs; but is itself the enterprise and adventure of the day.

From "Walking" by Henry David Thoreau. Reprinted in *The Oxford Book of American Essays.*

1. The author's main point about walking is that he, unlike many others,

   **(1)** chooses not to give it up for a job in a shop
   **(2)** finds it a better form of exercise than lifting weights
   **(3)** considers it a necessary and enjoyable part of his routine
   **(4)** takes it as regularly as the sick take medicine
   **(5)** spends four hours a day taking walks through the woods

2. You can infer from the passage that the author

   **(1)** works in an office less than four hours a day
   **(2)** could not tolerate a full-time indoor job
   **(3)** would be an excellent instructor
   **(4)** admires people who can endure regular office work
   **(5)** swings dumbbells or chairs as well as walks

Item 3 refers to the following passage.

## HOW CAN SUNBATHING HURT YOU?

Getting too much sun causes sunburn, which makes the skin burn, itch, and blister. It can also cause a fever. Besides the immediate results of sunburn, a long term effect of too much sun is premature aging of the skin. The skin loses its
(5) ability to stretch, causing sags and wrinkles. The most serious long term effect of the sun is skin cancer. People who enjoy being outdoors in the summer need to be aware of the harmful effects of too much sun.

One way to avoid the harmful effects of the sun is to use a
(10) sunscreen. Sunscreens protect the skin from ultraviolet (UV) rays. Sunscreens protect the skin by soaking in or reflecting the ultraviolet rays. The substance in many sun screens that blocks the harmful burning rays is PABA, a B vitamin. Sunscreens have Sun Protection Factor (SPF) numbers from
(15) 1 to 30 that show how much protection they give. The higher the number, the more protection they give,

Another way to avoid the harmful effects is to sunbathe wisely. Try to stay out of the sun between 11: 00 A.M. and 2:00 P.M. At that time of day, people tend to burn faster
(20) because the sun is directly overhead.Also start sunbathing slowly. On your first day, spend only about fifteen minutes in the sun. Then gradually spend more time in the sun each day. Don't count on clouds to protect you; the ultraviolet rays can get through clouds.

3.  According to the article, the major reason that sunbathers are harmed by the sun rays is which of the following?

    **(1)** lack of knowledge and sensible protection
    **(2)** failure to use sunscreens with a high SPF
    **(3)** inability to prevent skin cancer
    **(4)** premature aging of the skin
    **(5)** gradual increase of ultraviolet rays

Answers are on page 313.

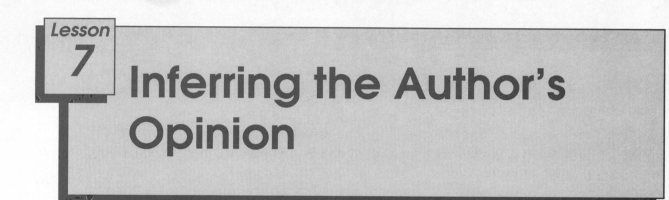

# Inferring the Author's Opinion

## Prereading Prompt

If you read that the principal of the local high school had just put into effect a strict dress code, you can probably make a good guess why: She most likely feels that looking neat and clean helps create a positive learning atmosphere. In this example, you have inferred an opinion based on details. On the GED you may be asked to infer an author's opinion. This lesson will show you how.

## Key Words

**opinion**—a personal view that cannot be proved

**fact**—something that can be proved by measurement or observation

## Inferring the Author's Opinion

An *opinion* is a belief that a person holds that is not based on facts but is based on what the person thinks. You may agree or disagree with a person's opinion. Authors support their opinions with *facts*, statements that can be proven, to try to convince readers to share their beliefs. On the *Interpreting Literature and the Arts* section of the GED test, you may be asked to infer the author's opinion. To do so, you must look at details and facts to figure out what they suggest about the author's beliefs. These details and facts are like clues to help you solve a mystery.

Below are three simple questions about inferring the author's opinion that you could find on the GED test. The questions are followed by a strategy you can use to find the answer.

- How does the author feel about _____ [the topic]?
- Which of the following words best describes the author's attitude toward _____ [the topic]?
- With which of the following statements would the author agree?

Here is a strategy you can use to find the answer:

Step 1: Read the purpose question, the passage, and the items that follow.

Step 2: Summarize the main idea in your own words. Ask yourself: What is the author's purpose in making this point? What is the author trying to convince me to do or think?

Step 3: Think about the details that support the main idea and what these details suggest about the author's attitude.

Step 4: Make a prediction about the answer before looking at the choices.

Step 5: Examine each choice.

Step 6: Look at the passage again and choose the best answer.

Read the passage below and the question that follows it. Use the six-step strategy you have just learned to find the answer.

### WHAT SHOULD YOU DO
### WHEN PREDATORS ARE NEAR?

I once presented a paper at a meeting of anthropologists on the subject of "primates as prey." I ended by noting that when a sloth bear, which lives in the same habitat as leopards and tigers in India, is in a defensive mode, it stands up. So do

(5) grizzly bears when they encounter big cats. I made some half-joking remarks about why early hominids took to standing up—perhaps this worked to scare off predators. On the other hand, a person sitting, squatting or bending over looks a lot like a four-legged prey animal.

(10) Tigers sometimes kill Asian rubber tappers who go out to work in the darkness of early morning and bend down to cut into trees to start the latex flowing. They also kill grass cutters who are bending over, and people who go out at night and squat to relieve themselves. Some of the people killed

(15) every year by tigers in the Sundarbans, a great mangrove for-

est at the mouth of the Ganges in India and Bangladesh, are honey collectors. They travel through the forest at low tide, frequently alone or well away from other collectors, and must bend down in order to get under the branches of the man-
(20) groves.

From "Mountain Lions Don't Stalk People. True or False?" by John Seidensticker with Susan Lumpkin, *Smithsonian*, Feb 1992.

Which of the following words best describes the author's attitude toward primate-killers?

**(1)** supreme disgust

**(2)** scientific interest

**(3)** bold humor

**(4)** paralyzing fear

**(5)** pretended indifference

Step 1: Read the purpose question, the passage, and the items that follow.

Step 2: Summarize the main idea in your own words. Ask yourself: What is the author's purpose in making this point? What is the author trying to convince me to do or think? You might come up with a statement like this: The author's purpose is to share his observation that some predators tend to strike when their prey is bending over.

Step 3: Think about the details that support the main idea and what these details suggest about the author's attitude. Details that support the main idea include examples about tigers who kill rubber tappers, grass cutters, and honey collectors who all bend down to complete their tasks. The author seems objective about these examples. He does not blame the predators; rather, he seems to find their behavior interesting. There is a trace of humor in his comment about making "half-joking remarks" about early hominids.

Step 4: Make a prediction about the answer before looking at the choices. Since the author does not seem to condemn the primate-killers, the answer choice should not blame these creatures for their habits. The answer should have something about how interesting their habits are to him.

Step 5: Examine each choice. Although there is one humorous comment in the passage, the overall tone is neutral. Therefore, (3) does not fit. In addition, there is nothing in the passage to suggest disgust (1) or fear (4), so these answers are not valid either. The very fact that the author found his topic worthy of sharing with us contradicts the idea of his being indifferent, (5).

Step 6: Look at the passage again and chose the best answer. (2) fits our prediction and the passage the best.

The question below refer to the following passage. Use the strategy and see if you can infer the author's purpose.

### HOW ARE SITCOMS UNREAL?

To watch American sitcoms, then and now, is to enter an "America" in which adults spend virtually all their time in their well-appointed, commodity-filled kitchens and dens talking to and about their children, worrying over and solving
(5) their children's problems, successfully teaching their loving, respectful offspring moral lessons about honesty, tolerance, charity, and compassion. It is a world in which violence, drugs, racism, and sexism barely exist; in which social issues of any kind, when they are raised at all, are seen to be
(10) quickly and easily solved in twenty-two minutes in the privacy of the family living room by fathers and mothers who still know best, with no help at all from government, schools, or social-service agencies.

Excerpt from "A Family Affair", by Elayne Rapping, *The Progressive*, April 1992. Reprinted by permission from *The Progressive*, Madison, WI.

Which of the following best describes the author's opinion of sitcoms?

**(1)** They portray too much subtle racism and sexism.

**(2)** They are dishonest denials of the hardships children face.

**(3)** They offer a welcome escape from the harsh realities of life.

**(4)** They provide a vital reminder of the importance of family.

**(5)** They teach important moral lessons about honesty and charity.

The correct answer is (2). Think about the author's attitude as you read. The first sentence is especially ironic, as the author comments on "well-appointed commodity-filled kitchens," and world in which violence, drugs, and racism barely exist. This sarcastic tone clues you in to the fact that the author believes that these problems *should* be addressed. For this reason, eliminate (3), for the tone of the passage indicates that the author feels that "escape from the harsh realities of life" is undesirable. (1) is wrong because it is contradicted by the passage. In lines 7-8 the author says, "It is a world in which violence, drugs, racism, and sexism barely exist...." Watch out for (4) and (5); both echo details in the paragraph but do not describe the author's opinion. The author's purpose in including both is to show how TV *fails* by portraying a world where the families and moral lessons are unreal.

Read the following passage and answer the questions using the strategy you have learned.

### WHAT IS RAINY MOUNTAIN?

A single knoll rises out of the plain in Oklahoma, north and west of the Wichita Range. For my people, the Kiowas, it is an old landmark, and they gave it the name Rainy Mountain.
(5) The hardest weather in the world is there. Winter brings blizzards, hot tornadic winds arise in the spring, and in summer the prairie is an anvil's edge. The grass turns brittle and brown, and it cracks beneath your feet. There are green belts along the rivers and creeks, linear groves of hickory and
(10) pecan, willow and witch hazel. At a distance in July or August the steaming foliage seems almost to writhe in fire. Great green and yellow grasshoppers are everywhere in the tall grass, popping up like corn to sting the flesh, and tortoises crawl about on the red earth, going nowhere in the
(15) plenty of time. Loneliness is an aspect of the land. All things in the plain are isolate; there is no confusion of objects in the eyes, but *one* hill or *one* tree or *one* man. To look upon that landscape in the early morning, with the sun at your back, is to lose the sense of proportion. Your imagination comes to life, and this, you think, is where Creation was begun.

From *The Way to Rainy Mountain*, by N. Scott Momaday. Copyright ©1969 University of New Mexico Press. First published in *The Reporter*, 26 January 1967.

1. Which of the following best describes the author's attitude toward Rainy Mountain?

   (1) It is a terrible place with no meaning for human beings.

   (2) It is an inspirational place that makes one think of the beginning of time.

   (3) It is a cluttered, busy place where animals must compete for every bite of food.

   (4) It is a dead place, which makes you feel uninspired and bored.

   (5) It is a worthless place that develops for the use of people in surrounding areas.

2. What is the meaning of *grove* (line 8)?

   (1) group of meadows
   (2) group of trees
   (3) group of nuts
   (4) group of streams
   (5) group of ditches

3. In lines 14-19 (the last six lines of the passage) the author suggests that the loneliness of the land will make a person feel

   (1) confused
   (2) exhausted
   (3) thoughtful
   (4) hopeful
   (5) frightened

Answers are on page 314.

# Applying the Author's Opinion

## Prereading Prompt

Suppose you read that a mayor is sponsoring a bill to ban smoking in public places. Based on that information, which of the following bills do you think he would most likely support? A bill that gives fines to people and businesses for polluting the environment, or a bill that lessens environmental controls on businesses?

You would probably guess that he would have polluters fined for their actions. You concluded that because he wants smoking banned in public places, he must be concerned about a clean environment. On the GED you may be asked to take information from a passage and use it in a new situation. You will learn how in this lesson.

## Key Words

**apply**—to make use of something in a new situation; to put a general idea to a specific use

## Applying the Author's Opinion

To apply something means to *use* it. In application, you use your understanding of some information to solve a problem in a new situation. But before you apply an opinion, you must first understand it. In Lesson 7, you learned how to infer the author's opinion. If you understand an author's opinion about a subject, you can sometimes predict how the author will feel about a different subject.

In the *Interpreting Literature and the Arts* section of the GED, you may be asked to take information from a passage and use it to predict the author's attitude in a new situation. Any time you say to yourself, "I wonder what the author would say about . . .?" you are asking an application question, or applying what you read to a new situation. You have to build a bridge of ideas about what you have read and what might happen in the new situation. In this lesson, you will learn about applying the author's opinion to a new situation.

## Model Questions and Strategy

Below are three sample questions about applying the author's opinion that you could find on the GED test. The questions are followed by a strategy you can use to find the answer.

- What would the author probably think about _____ [the topic]?
- Would the author of the passage most likely enjoy _____ ?
- With which of the following ideas would the author most likely agree?

Here is a strategy you can use to find the answer:

Step 1: Preview the passage and questions.

Step 2: Read the passage and summarize the main idea of the passage.

Step 3: Examine each choice, and build a bridge connecting the ideas in the passage with the situation in one of the choices. Ask yourself: Which choice is closest to the attitude the author expresses in the passage?

Step 4: Choose the best answer.

## Model Passage and Question

Read the passage below and the question that follows it. Use the four-step strategy you have just learned to find the answer to the question.

### HOW ARE WE FAILING OUR CHILDREN?

The message is clear. And we don't actually need TV drama to tell it to us. The schools are collapsing and are not being repaired. Child care is nonexistent, yet most parents must work, and more and more of us are single parents. Drugs and
(5) guns are easily available, and no one in government is seriously interested in stopping them at their sources. Sexually transmitted diseases and illegitimate and addicted babies are rampant, but our courts are working hard to keep us from getting treatment, birth control, and legal abortions. And,
(10) most chillingly, we are raising a generation of kids who do not even consider the possibility of following the rules, obeying the laws, even respecting the sanctity of life itself, their own or others.

We are indeed a nation of hypocrites, mouthing platitudes
about childhood innocence, putting cherubic faces on posters
(15) and milk cartons, crying crocodile tears over specially selected infants who fall into wells or receive organ transplants.
But our infant-mortality rate is outrageous and one in five of
our children gets no medical attention at all.

From "A Family Affair" by Elayne Rapping, *The Progressive*, April 1992. Reprinted by permission from *The Progressive*, Madison WI.

If the local school board had to make budget cuts, with which one of the following would the author be most likely to agree?

**(1)** Cut the all-day kindergarten.

**(2)** Cut free breakfasts.

**(3)** Cut extramural sports.

**(4)** Cut sex ed programs.

**(5)** Cut the school nurse's hours

Step 1: Preview the passage and questions. Notice that this is the sort of question that requires you to read each choice carefully before selecting an answer.
You cannot predict the answer ahead of time. A quick glance at the question
choices tells you that each describes a possible school budget cut. You know
that you need to read the passage for information that will help you pick out
the budget cut the author would find most acceptable.

Step 2: Read the passage and summarize the main idea of the passage. Your
summary might be something like this: *We aren't giving most of our children the
safe, healthy environment they need.*

Step 3: Examine each choice, and build a bridge connecting the ideas in the
passage with the situation in one of the choices. You are trying to connect the
author's concerned, angry statements about basic unmet needs of children
with the new school board situation. Eliminate (1) because all-day kindergarten
provides working parents with child-care, one of the author's stated concerns.
Eliminate (2) and (5) because proper nutrition and attention by medical person-
nel are important to children's health. You can infer from the author's last line
("one in five of our children gets no medical attention ...") and from her overall
concern with children's welfare that health care is important to her. Choice (4)
is wrong because the author's statements about sexually transmitted diseases
and illegitimate babies indicates that she probably considers sex education a
must.

Step 4: Choose the best answer. (3) is the best answer. This question shows
how important it is to read the question carefully. You are trying to connect the
ideas the author lists in the passage with the program she would probably
agree to cut. Such a program would be the one that fits *least* well with those
she mentions in the passage. You probably know that extramural sports take
place after school, and are optional activities. Therefore, you can put together
what you have learned from the passage—about the author's cry for meeting
the basic needs of children—with what (3) describes—an activity that is fun for
some, but not crucial to a large number of kids. All-day kindergarten, free-
breakfasts, sex ed programs, and access to the school nurse are more crucial to
health and safety, and the author would not be likely to approve of losing any
of these programs.

Read the following excerpt and choose the best answer to the question. Use the strategy you have just learned to answer the question

## WHAT MAKES A PERSON FEEL PROUD?

You can't take pride anymore. You remember when a guy could point to a house he built, how many logs he stacked. He built it and he was proud of it. I don't really think I could be proud if a contractor built a home for me. I would want to (5) get in there and take the saw away from him. 'Cause I would have to be part of it, you know.

It's hard to take pride in a bridge you're never gonna cross, in a door you're never gonna open. You're mass-producing things and you never see the end result of it. (*Muses.*) I (10) worked for a trucker one time. And I got this tiny satisfaction when I loaded a truck. At least I could see the truck depart loaded. In a steel mill, forget it. You don't see where nothing goes.

From "Steelworker: Mike Lefevre" in *Working: People Talk About What They Do All Day and How They Feel About What They Do*, by Studs Terkel. Copyright © Published by Random House.

The steelworker who was interviewed would feel the most pride when

**(1)** hiring people to landscape his garden

**(2)** working as a factory foreman

**(3)** building and flying a model airplane

**(4)** watching people construct a bridge

**(5)** working on an assembly line

The correct answer is (3). The steelworker would most likely take pride in building and flying a model plane because he enjoys doing things himself: "I don't really think I could be proud if a contractor built a home for me" as he remarks in line 3. He is a man who gets satisfaction in seeing how his work turns out. Building and flying a model airplane would make him feel both proud and satisfied.

(1), (2), and (4) are incorrect because hiring people to do work or watching them work does not make him feel proud. On the contrary, doing the work and seeing the end product gives him a feeling of pride. (5) is incorrect because the steelworker says that when "you're mass producing things... you never see the end result of it," which shows that he gets satisfaction from seeing the end result of his work, which he would not get on an assembly line.

Items 1-3 refer to the following passage. Choose the best answer to each item.

## HOW ARE SOME PEOPLE MAKING MONEY FROM AIDS?

...*The New York Times* recently revealed a scheme by which American entrepreneurs are cashing in on AIDS. The deal consists of buying up at a discount the life insurance policies of victims of this fatal illness while they are still alive. The

(5) buyers obtain the policies cheaply (at discounts between 10 percent and 50 percent on the maturity value), then, when the patients die, the buyers collect the full amount of insurance.

The AIDS sufferers are only too happy to take the money,

(10) for once they contract the illness, they typically lose their jobs or other sources of support. This way, they can at least have some ready cash when they need it. So, the entrepreneurs argue, they are doing the victims a favor while making a profit themselves. It is the American way.

(15) The fact that these entrepreneurs are making money out of mortality is brushed aside. Two companies, the *Times* reported, even offered a "menu" to the investors listing the available AIDS patients with such details as their current infections. The investor would then place his bet, as it were, by buying

(20) up the policy of the patient with the lowest life expectancy.

In the midst of recession, AIDS-insurance-policy trading has spawned no fewer than 25 new companies since 1988. It is a $100 million business.

Excerpted from an article by Shashi Tharoor from the *Indian Express*, New Delhi. By permission of the World Press Review.

1. Which of the following best describes the author's attitude toward the business he describes?

   **(1)** It mainly a way for AIDS victims to make "ready cash"
   **(2)** It is mainly a cruel product of the current American recession
   **(3)** It is typical of American business practice in all its forms
   **(4)** It exploits people in need for the sake of profit
   **(5)** It is a way for businessmen to do AIDS victims a favor

2. The author would probably agree with which of the following ideas?

   **(1)** AIDS victims deserve all the consequences of the disease.
   **(2)** AIDS victims should receive sufficient financial support when they lose their normal sources of income.
   **(3)** No life insurance policies should be sold at a discount no matter how desperate the policyholder is for money.
   **(4)** Federal insurance laws protect people from exploitation.
   **(5)** Ending the recession would help AIDS victims the most.

3. If someone involved in this insurance-buying business was a character in a fairy tale for children, he would be most similar to which of the following?

   **(1)** The wolf who dressed as her grandmother in order to eat Red Riding Hood
   **(2)** The boy whose nose kept growing every time he told a lie
   **(3)** One of Cinderella's mean. ugly sisters who pretended to be beautiful
   **(4)** The wicked stepmother who tortured her stepdaughter
   **(5)** The king whose touch turned everything into gold

Answers are on page 314.

# Applying What You Already Know

### Prereading Prompt

When you read an article about a volcano, you probably don't need the words *erupt* and *lava* defined. Most likely you know that *lava*, or hot, melted rock, *erupts* or becomes violently active when a volcano explodes. Every time you listen to someone or read something, you bring along information that you already know. On the GED you may be asked to apply what you already know. In this lesson you will learn how.

## Applying What You Already Know

The GED evaluates whether you can apply or use what you already know, not just restate this information. In Lesson 8, you learned one form a GED application question might take. In that type of question, you were given information and asked to show that you can apply it to a new situation.

Sometimes, though, you will be asked to apply information that you already know. Suppose you read a news article about crime in urban areas. You may not be as expert as the journalist, but you do have some information about this problem stored away in your mind. You have collected many facts and opinions based on what you have read in newspapers and magazines, seen on TV, found out from people, and perhaps even observed yourself. This stored information helps you more fully understand the ideas that are being presented in the article.

On the *Interpreting Literature and the Arts* section of the GED, you may find it useful to apply what you already know. When this happens, brainstorm everything you know about the purpose question before reading the passage. In this way, you will bring to mind all the many details you already know and be better able to answer the question. In this lesson you will learn about applying what you already know, just as you do every time you read a news article or book.

## Model Questions and Strategy

Below are sample questions about applying what you already know that you could find on the GED test. The questions are followed by a strategy you can use to find the answer.

- Which of the following do you think most likely happened next?
- What other details can you imagine about the situation?
- The situation in the passage is like which of the following?
- Which of the following is an example of the principle described in the passage?
- Which of the following ideas is one that would NOT fit into the passage you just read?
- Based on the general ideas described, what would happen in the following case?

Here is a strategy you can use to find the answer:

<u>Step 1:</u> Preview the question and figure out the topic.

<u>Step 2:</u> Brainstorm what you already know about the topic.

<u>Step 3:</u> Read the passage and examine the choices.

<u>Step 4.</u> Choose the best answer.

## Model Passage and Questions

Read the passage below and the question that follows it. Use the four-step strategy you have just learned to find the answer to the question.

### WHY DO PLANTS CHANGE AS YOU GO UP THE ROCKY MOUNTAINS?

Have you ever hiked or driven into the mountains? If you have, you probably noticed that the plants change as you go higher up a mountain. The kinds of trees and flowers that grow at the bottom are very different from those that grow
(5) high on a mountainside.

While hiking in the Rocky Mountains, you would see Douglas firs, ponderosa pines, buttercups, and columbines in the lower mountain areas. Higher in the mountains, there are different kinds of pines, spruces, and flowering plants like
(10) paintbrushes. If you climbed still higher in the Rockies, you would reach an area where there are no trees. Grasses and flowers grow close to the ground. Gradually even these plants disappear. At the mountaintops, only mosses and lichens grow on the rocks.

Excerpt from *Health Life Science*, Copyright ©1984. Reprinted by permission of D.C. Heath & Co.

Which of the following would a summer hiker be most likely to see upon arriving at a resort very high in the Rocky Mountains?

**(1)** sunflowers lining the walkways

**(2)** guests wearing sweaters

**(3)** employees wearing chains of orchids

**(4)** butterflies in the lobby

**(5)** signs listing low-altitude ear problems

<u>Step 1: Preview the question and figure out the topic.</u> As you skim the question and answer choices, you see that the question is about a resort high in the mountains.

<u>Step 2: Brainstorm what you already know about the topic.</u> Ask yourself: What do I already know about what happens when you go up in altitude? What happens to the temperature? What happens to the air and air pressure? What happens to the plants? What do I know about why these changes occur?

<u>Step 3: Read the passage and examine the choices.</u> After you read the passage, build a bridge of ideas between your knowledge of high altitudes and each of the choices. Ask yourself what you know about high altitudes and sunflowers, high altitudes and sweaters, high altitudes and orchids, high altitudes and butterflies, high altitudes and ear problems.

<u>Step 4: Choose the best answer.</u> You are probably aware that the temperature goes down as you rise in altitude. It makes sense that you might see guests wearing sweaters (2). (1) is wrong because you learned from the passage that flowers high up grow close to the ground; anyone who has seen a sunflower or a picture of one knows that they can grow far from the ground—higher than an adult's head. (3) is wrong because, as you may know, orchids are hot-climate flowers; you've probably seen them in the hot-house of plant stores. You know that butterflies are found where flowers are found, and you learned that flowers disappear high up in the Rockies, so (4) is wrong. You may have experienced "ear popping" as you drove up a mountain or rose in an airplane, but these problems are *high*-altitude, not *low*-altitude problems, so (5) is incorrect.

# Practice

Read the following excerpt and the question that follows it. Use the four-step strategy you have just learned to find the answer to the question.

## WHAT IS A METEOR?

Most people watching meteors will be satisfied if they see ten or twenty in an hour of watching. On special occasions, however, the meteors seem to come in droves. The most remarkable meteor shower I ever heard of was seen by a dis-
(5)    tinguished astronomer, Professor Denison Olmstead, of New Haven, Connecticut, on the night of November 12, 1833. He was watching the Leonids, which seem to come from directly overhead and race downward toward the horizon in all directions. He reported that meteors fell "like flakes of snow." He
(10)   estimated that he saw 240,000 meteors in nine hours that night.

From "Shooting Stars" from *This World of Wonder* by Hal Borland. Copyright ©1972, 1973 by Hal Borland. Reprinted by permission of Frances Collin Literary Agency.

Where would be the best place to watch a meteor shower?

**(1)** from a shopping mall
**(2)** from a city apartment building
**(3)** from a city skyscraper
**(4)** from a country hilltop
**(5)** from a well-lit airport

The answer is (4), from a country hilltop. You are probably aware that meteors are shooting stars. If you have ever looked at the stars or tried to look for meteors, you probably have noticed that the darker the sky and the more wide open the space, the better the visibility. As the passage tells you, meteors "race downward toward the horizon in all directions," so it makes sense that it is best to view them from a dark, open spot. As you know, shopping malls, city apartment buildings, city skyscrapers, and airports are lit up, so (1), (2), (3), and (5) are incorrect because the bright lights would interfere with viewing a meteor shower.

Items 1 and 2 refer to the following passage. Choose the best answer.

## HOW DOES THE OWL DEFEND ITSELF?

Deep in the forest, a screech owl sits perched on the limb of a tree. Suddenly the owl hears a noise and realizes that a predator is nearby. The frightened owl tries to camouflage itself by pulling in its feathers and staying very still. However,
(5) the owl still senses danger. As a last resort, the owl opens its eyes wide, snaps its beak, fluffs its feathers, and flaps its wings. The predator is frightened off by the owl's behavior.

From *Heath Life and Science*. Copyright ©1984. Reprinted by permission of D.C. Heath & Co.

1. The screech owl most likely uses the defenses described because it

   (1) cannot make noise
   (2) is not big or strong
   (3) has poor hearing
   (4) cannot fly
   (5) is an endangered species

2. Which of the following is an example of a behavior that serves the same function as the owl's feather-fluffing?

   (1) A spotted deer hides under a tree in sun-dappled shade as a mountain lion passes by.
   (2) A gray lizard suns itself on a gray rock and escapes the notice of a hawk.
   (3) A male seagull does a dance in the air around a female gulland attracts her as a mate.
   (4) A kingfisher builds a tunnel in the banks of a stream to hide its nest from enemies.
   (5) A kitten arches its back and hisses at a Great Dane who then crawls away with its tail between its legs.

Item 3 refers to the following passage. Choose the best answer.

### WHAT DO TEENS THINK IS "COOL"?

My host, a publisher, has no sooner finished his canapés than he pulls a photocopy from his pocket and, with a flourish of irritation, thrusts it toward me. It is a copy of a "test" that is going around among teens. "Are you cool?" the test
(5) asks. There are six questions. The third goes like this: "Wow! Someone wants to give you a present. Which would you choose: (a) a beautiful book; (b) a video game; (c) a camera?" My friend's index finger lunges at the answers: "Look, look here!" The questions are scored from one to three points. if
(10) you chose a video game, you are cool: You get three points. If you prefer a camera, you are not so cool: two points. But if you pick a book, you are really uncool: You only get one point, and you may never live it down. "Being cool," the test says, "is not really important to you."

Excerpted from "Reading is Not Cool" from *Le Figaro,* Paris , France.

3. A teenager who scored high on "the test" probably would want most to be
   (1) disliked by teachers
   (2) disliked by publishers
   (3) liked by other teens
   (4) given a present
   (5) smarter than other teens

Answers are on page 315.

# Analyzing Style

## Prereading Prompt

If you go someplace special, you probably think about what you want to wear to create the best impression. You might wonder which shoes, jewelry, and even hair style would look best. To make sure you achieved the result you wanted, you analyzed, or examined, each detail to see how it related to the overall effect you wanted. On the GED you may be asked to answer questions about how details help create a certain effect. You will learn how to answer such questions in this lesson.

## Key Words

**analysis**—careful examination of the parts that make up a whole

**style**—an author's particular way of writing

**sentence structure**—the way the words in a sentence are arranged

## Analyzing Style

When you *analyze* something, you examine all its parts to see what each one is and how they all fit together. The analysis questions on the *Interpreting Literature and Arts* section of the GED test your ability to understand why an author uses certain details or words to create a specific effect in a passage. Instead of looking at *what the author says or means* (comprehension), or *what else the author might say about a new situation* (application), analysis questions require you to look at *how the author says it and why*. In this lesson, we are going to analyze the author's **style**, an author's particular way of writing.

Style is created by word choice and **sentence structure**—the way the words in a sentence are arranged. Authors use different writing styles, such as formal or informal, simple or complex. Authors also write with various purposes in mind: to report, explain, persuade, or describe. In this lesson you will learn to analyze the style of a nonfiction passage by looking at the author's choice of words and use of detail.

On the GED, there are two types of questions that analyze style:

**(1)** those that present an aspect of style from a passage, such as the choice of words, and ask you to identify the effect of this word choice on the reader;

**(2)** those that present the overall effect of the style on the reader, such as a humorous effect, and ask you to identify how the effect was achieved.

Writers achieve certain effects in their work in various ways. A writer's choice of words, for example, will have a great effect on how the reader feels toward the subject matter. Words such as "aggressive," "unpleasant," and "ill-bred," suggest negative images, while "unfortunate," "old," and "vulnerable" create a sympathetic picture, for example.

To achieve a humorous effect, writers may present details that greatly exaggerate an idea, or details that are the opposite of what one might logically expect. To achieve a serious effect, writers might quote from well-known experts or include details about matters of life and death.

A writer might use many short, direct sentences to create a lively, dramatic effect, or even a sense of urgency. On the other hand, many long descriptive sentences may create a more neutral, less dramatic effect.

## Model Questions and Strategy

Below are some sample questions about analysis that you could find on the GED test. The questions are followed by a strategy you can use to find the answer.

• Why did the author include [certain details] in one paragraph?

• What does the inclusion of [a specific detail] tell you about the author's opinion?

• The reader gets a sense of [a specific effect] from which of the following details?

• Why is the first sentence effective in capturing the reader's attention?

Here is a strategy you can use to find the answers:

Step 1: Preview the question and the passage.

Step 2: Summarize the main idea of the passage.

Step 3: Think about why the author chose the particular words and details referred to in the question. Then predict the answer.

Step 4: Examine each choice.

Step 5: Choose the best answer.

Read the following excerpt and the question that follows it. Use the five-step strategy you have just learned to find the answer to the question.

### WHAT KIND OF MAN IS THE JAPANESE ARTIST KATSUSHIKA HOKUSAI?

Of all the great artists of Japan, the one Westerners probably like and understand best in Katsushika Hokusai. He was a restless, unpredictable man who lived in as many as a hundred different houses and changed his name at least thirty
(5)    times. For a very good artist, he acted at times like P.T. Barnum or a Hollywood producer with his curiosity and drive for novelty.

From "Hokusai: The Old Man Mad About Drawing" in *The Drawings of Hokusai* by Stephen Longstreet. Published by Borden Publishing Co. Alhambra, CA.

The author presented details about the artist's houses and name changes to

**(1)** confuse the reader by presenting puzzling details

**(2)** keep the reader from getting to know the subject too quickly

**(3)** show the reader that the writer dislikes his subject

**(4)** provide concrete examples of the artist's uniqueness

**(5)** illustrate how confused the artist is

<u>Step 1: Preview the passage and questions.</u> A quick look at the passage tells you that it is about a Japanese artist. Previewing the question reveals that it asks about the artist's houses and name changes.

<u>Step 2: Summarize the main idea of the passage.</u> Your summary might be something like this: Hokusai was a restless, curious, great artist of Japan.

<u>Step 3: Think about why the author chose the particular words and details in the passage.</u> Then predict the answer. How would the passage's effect on you have been different if the author hadn't told you about the artist's many houses and name changes? You probably wouldn't have had such a clear idea of why Hokusai was considered "restless" and "unpredictable." You might predict that these details are provided to make the word picture of the artist more vivid.

<u>Step 4: Examine each choice.</u> (1) seems wrong because the effect isn't to confuse you, but the opposite—to help you understand what the artist was like. Likewise, (2) seems to contradict what the author is trying to do; he is actually providing you with information to help you get to know the subject. (3) cannot be right because the writer seems to like writing about Hokusai, and to admire this "great" and "curious"—although eccentric—artist. While changing houses and names so often might be signs of confusion in some cases, the description of the artist's "drive for novelty" points to a love of change in Hokusai's case, so you can eliminate (5).

<u>Step 5: Choose the best answer.</u>

Choice (4)—to provide concrete examples of the artist's uniqueness—is the best match with your prediction: to make the word picture of the artist more vivid. Writers learn to include plenty of concrete details to make their writing more vivid; in this case, the striking details of a hundred houses and thirty names make it clear that Hokusai was unique.

## Practice

Read the following excerpt and the question that follows it. Use the strategy you have just learned to find the answer to the question.

### HOW DID THE CATTLE-KILLING AFFECT THE SPEAKER?

We always watched the killing [of cattle] with horror and curiosity, although we were never permitted to participate at that age. It seemed so sad and irrevocable to see the gushing blood when throats were cut, the desperate gasps for breath
(5) through severed windpipes, the struggle for and the rapid ebbing of life, the dimming and glazing of wide terrified eyes. We realized and accepted the fact that this was one of the procedures that were a part of our life on the range and that other lives had to be sacrificed to feed us. Throat-cutting,
(10) however, became a symbol of immediate death in our young minds, the ultimate horror, so dreadful that we tried not to use the word "throat."

Excerpt from *Rising from the Plains* by John McPhee. Copyright ©1965, 1986 by John McPhee. Reprinted by permission of Farrar, Straus & Giroux, Inc.

The reader gets a sense of horror from which detail?

**(1)** "although we were never permitted to participate at that age"
**(2)** "we realized and accepted the fact that this was one of the procedures that were a part of our life on the range"
**(3)** "desperate gasps of breath through severed windpipes"
**(4)** "other lives had to be sacrificed to feed us"
**(5)** "it seemed so sad and irrevocable"

(3) is the best answer. The description of the "desperate gasps of breath through severed windpipes" conveys the author's horror and anguish at seeing the cattle slaughtered for food. None of the other words or details suggest how throat-cutting became the "ultimate horror." (1) conveys a feeling of being left out, while (2) and (4) conveys a sense of resignation, an acceptance of the animals' fate. (5) creates a feeling of sadness and finality, not horror.

Items 1 through 3 refer to the passage that follows. Choose the one best answer to each item.

### HOW DO PEOPLE REACT IN LIFE-OR-DEATH SITUATIONS?

Feeling along the wall, Doug discovered a tiny groove into which he would press the tips of the fingers of his left hand. It might help him maintain balance as his weight began to shift from the lower ledge to the upper one. But there was within reach not even a lip of rock for
(5) his right hand. Just out of reach, however, was a substantial crevice, one that would hold several men. How could Doug reach it? I could not boost him, for my own balance was insecure. Clearly, Doug would have to jump to reach it—and he would have but one jump. Since he was standing on a ledge only a few inches wide, he would not expect to
(10) jump for his handhold, miss it, and land safely. A slip meant he would go hurtling down some 600 feet onto the rocks. After much discussion and indecision, Doug decided to take the chance and go up.

He asked me to do him a favor: If he failed and fell, I might still make it, since I was longer-legged; would I give certain messages to his
(15) family in that event? I nodded.

"Then listen carefully. Try to remember my exact words," he told me. "Tell Mother that I love her dearly. Tell her I think she is the most wonderful person in the world. Tell her not to worry—that I did not suffer. Tell Sister that I have been a mean little devil but I had no mal-
(20) ice towards her. Tell her I love her too—that some day I wanted to marry a girl as wholesome and cheery and good as she.

"Tell Dad I was brave and died unafraid. Tell him about our climb in full detail. Tell Dad I have always been very proud of him, that some day I had planned to be a doctor too. Tell him I lived a clean life, that I
(25) never did anything to make him ashamed—Tell Mother, Sister, and Dad I prayed for them."

Every word burned into me. My heart was sick, my lips quivered. I pressed my face against the rock so Doug could not see. I wept.

Excerpt from *Of Men and Mountains,* by William O. Douglas. Copyright © 1950, renewed 1978, by Sidney Davis, Trustee, William O. Douglas Trust. Published by HarperCollins.

1. The author creates an effect of suspense in the first paragraph by describing how Doug

    (1) had moved too far away from the narrator to be helped
    (2) had too much weight to keep his balance on his ledge
    (3) would have only one chance to move up from his ledge
    (4) could not land safely on the "substantial crevice"
    (5) had discovered a tiny groove along the edge of the wall

2. The author uses dialogue in the third paragraph to

    (1) make the passage more emotional by having Doug speak in his own words
    (2) show how afraid Doug is by using his own words
    (3) show how Doug has stopped making sense due to extreme stress
    (4) make the favor Doug asks perfectly clear
    (5) describe Doug as a person

3. Why is the last sentence an effective way to end the passage?

    (1) It is short, direct, and shows direct emotion, unlike most of the other sentences in the passage.
    (2) It makes the reader question the courage of the narrator.
    (3) It shows the narrator has not felt strong emotion until this moment.
    (4) It makes the reader question the narrator's motive for climbing
    (5) It shows the strong emotion Doug's words have created in the narrator.

Answers are on page 315.

# Analyzing Chronological Order and Order of Importance

## Prereading Prompt

If you ever bought a "do-it-yourself" kit and had to put something important together, you know the importance of chronological, or number, order. In chronological order, the first step is mentioned first, followed by the second step, and so on. Any other method of ordering the information would not help you put the item together. If you read an article about a proposed recycling plan, you would not be concerned about what happens first, next, and so on. Instead, you would probably want to know why you should support this plan.

Authors choose the most effective way to present their ideas. On the GED you may be asked to answer questions about the order of ideas in a passage. You will learn how to answer them in this lesson.

## Key Words

**chronological order**—items arranged in the order in which they take place

**persuasive writing**—writing that tries to convince you to see things in the way the writer sees them

## Analyzing Chronological Order and Order of Importance

How do writers decide on a structure for their ideas? Authors try to choose the most effective order to present their thoughts. The order they choose depends on their purpose in writing a specific passage. When they are writing to tell what happened, they usually use **chronological order**, items arranged in the order in which they take place. The details in biographies and diaries, for example, are usually arranged in chronological order. A news story, such as a report of a big traffic snarl, is also commonly organized in time order. The description of the steps in a process, such as how to make pizza, is often arranged chronologically as well.

Persuasive writing, writing that tries to convince you to see things as the writer sees them, often uses a different order. When the writer's purpose is to persuade, as in editorials or letters to the editor, items are often placed in **order of importance**, from most to least important.

Chronological order and order of importance are two of the most common ways to position ideas within a piece of writing.

Here are some sample questions about analyzing chronological order and order of importance that might appear on the Interpreting Literature and the Arts section of the GED.

- How does the arrangement of ideas reveal the author's purpose?
- The details in this passage are arranged to show _____?

## Model Strategy and Signal Words

Before you start thinking about *why* an author chooses a particular order for a given passage, you must figure out what order the writer is using. Here is a strategy you can use to tell chronological order from order of importance:

<u>Step 1</u>: Look for words that signal time order, such as the following:

| | |
|---|---|
| first, second, third, etc. | as soon as |
| before | when |
| after, afterwards | today, yesterday, tomorrow |
| finally, eventually | last week (month, year) |
| earlier | in the morning (at night, in the afternoon) |
| later | |
| while, meanwhile | at the beginning/at the end/in the middle of (a day, week, month) |
| next | |
| now | in the past, in the present, in the future |
| then | |
| during | subsequently |
| currently, at present | |

<u>Step 2:</u> Look for words that signal order of importance, such as the following:

| | |
|---|---|
| most (least, less, equally) important | also, in addition |
| best (main, primary) reasons | above all |
| another reason | finally |

<u>Step 3:</u> Ask yourself: "Is the writer's purpose to tell a story or to explain the steps in a process?" If so, this is probably time order.

<u>Step 4:</u> Ask yourself: "Is the writer's purpose to persuade that his or her opinion is correct?" If so, this is probably order of importance.

## Model Passage and Question

Read the following excerpt. Use the strategy you have just learned to tell whether the ideas are arranged in chronological order or in order of importance.

### WHY SHOULDN'T CATS HAVE TO BE ON LEASHES?

I object to the new requirement that cats be kept on leashes. First of all, cats do not bark or bite. Unlike many dogs, unleashed cats will not frighten or injure innocent pedestrians. Also, loose cats are not likely to make nuisances of
(5) themselves by digging up a neighbor's garden. Another reason for allowing cats to roam freely is that they simply cannot be trained to walk on a leash. My most serious objection to the new rule is that it denies cats their privilege to explore, a freedom we humans have no right to take away.

The writer's purpose is to persuade the reader that insisting on leashes for cats is a bad idea. The phrases *first of all*, *also*, *another reason*, and *my most serious objection* signal that the ideas have been arranged in order of importance, with the strongest reason last.

Read the passage below about Chief Joseph, and use the 4-step strategy you have just learned to answer the question about the order of ideas.

### WHY WILL CHIEF JOSEPH "FIGHT NO MORE"?

Tell General Howard I know his heart. What he told me before, I have in my heart. I am tired of fighting. Our chiefs are killed. Looking Glass is dead. Toohoolhoolzote is dead. The old men are all dead. It is the young men who say yes
(5) and no. He who led on the young men is dead. It is cold and we have no blankets. The little children are freezing to death. My people, some of them, have run away to the hills and have no blankets, no food; no one knows where they are—perhaps freezing to death. I want to have time to look for my children
(10) and see how many I can find. Maybe I shall find them among the dead. Hear me, my chiefs. I am tired; my heart is sick and sad. From where the sun now stands I will fight no more forever.

Excerpt from "I Will Fight No More Forever" by Chief Joseph.

The details in the passage are arranged to show

**(1)** the steps Chief Joseph wants to take to end the fighting
**(2)** which side is guilty
**(3)** different reactions of Chief Joseph's tribe
**(4)** the Chief's reasons for ending the fighting
**(5)** the sequence of events in the fighting

(4) is correct. The passage gives many reasons the Chief has for ending the fighting: "I am tired of fighting. Our chiefs are killed…. It is cold and we have no blankets. The little children are freezing to death… I want to have time look for my children…" Although Chief Joseph does not use the phrases that commonly signal order of importance, his purpose clues you in to the fact that he has chosen that order for his ideas. He is writing to persuade General Howard that it is time to stop fighting and that he will never fight the general again. Details about the horrors of war are arranged to convince General Howard that Chief Joseph truly intends to stop the bloodshed. Each detail is more moving than the one before, and he saves the most heartbreaking for last: "I want to have time to look for my children and see how many I can find. Maybe I shall find them among the dead."

(1) is incorrect because Chief Joseph does not propose how to end the fighting. Rather, he declares his reasons for wanting to "fight no more forever." (2) is incorrect because there is no mention of guilt or innocence. All the details give reasons for wanting to end the fighting, not anyone else's reactions. Choice (5) is incorrect because the details are not listed in chronological order, telling what happened first, next, and so on.

Items 1 to 3 refer to the following passage. Choose the one best answer to each item.

### WHAT HAPPENED WHEN THE *TITANIC* SANK?

Out of the dark she came, a vast, dim, white, monstrous shape, directly in the *Titanic*'s path. For a moment Fleet doubted his eyes. But she was a deadly reality, this ghastly *thing*. Frantically, Fleet struck three bells—*something dead*
(5) *ahead*. He snatched the telephone and called the bridge:

"Iceberg! Right ahead!"

The First Officer heard but did not stop to acknowledge the message.

"Hard-a-starboard!"

(10) Hichens strained at the wheel; the bow swung slowly to port. The monster was almost upon them now.

Murdoch leaped to the engine-room telegraph. Bells clanged. Far below in the engine-room those bells struck the first warning. Danger! The indicators on the dial faces swung
(15) around to "Stop!" Then "Full speed astern!" Frantically the engineers turned great valve wheels; answered the bridge bells...

There was a slight shock, a brief scraping, a small list to port. Shell ice—slabs and chunks of it—fell on the foredeck.
(20) Slowly the *Titanic* stopped.

Captain Smith hurried out of his cabin.

"What has the ship struck?"

Murdoch answered, "An iceberg, sir. I hard-a-starboarded and reversed the engines, and I was going to hard-a-port
(25) around it, but she was too close. I could not do any more. I have closed the water-tight doors."

Fourth Officer Boxhall, other officers, the carpenter, came to the bridge. The Captain sent Boxhall and the carpenter below to ascertain the damage.

(30) A few lights switched on in the first and second cabins; sleepy passengers peered through porthole glass; some casually asked the stewards:

"Why have we stopped?"

"I don't know, sir, but I don't suppose it is anything much."

From "R.M.S. Titanic" by Hanson W. Baldwin, *Appreciating Literature*, 1987, Macmillan.

1. The details in the passage are arranged to show

   (1) the sequence of events preceding the sinking of the ship
   (2) the people who were to blame for the collision
   (3) similarities among the officers aboard the ship
   (4) who mattered most to the author
   (5) the reasons ships should not travel through icy waters

2. The author's purpose is to enable readers to

   (1) understand the usual problems of winter sea travel
   (2) share perilous moments aboard ship
   (3) figure out who is to blame for the accident
   (4) understand how to pilot a ship
   (5) learn scientific facts about icebergs

3. The steward's answer—"I don't suppose it is anything much"—is an effective way to end the passage because it provides

   (1) relief from the mounting suspense by revealing that the ship has missed the iceberg
   (2) a surprise ending rather than the expected crash into the iceberg
   (3) a concise summary of the passage's main points
   (4) touching evidence of the victims' courage in the face of death
   (5) a chilling contrast with the approaching danger

Answers are on page 316.

# Analyzing Cause-and-Effect Order

## Prereading Prompt

Suppose you read this headline in the newspaper:
SUPERSTAR EJECTED FROM PLAYOFF GAME
What kind of information would you expect to find in
the article? Probably you would learn the causes for the
player's removal from the game and the effect his
removal had on the outcome of the game.

Some writers arrange information according to cause-
and-effect relationships. On the GED you may be asked
to answer questions that show you understand the causes and the effects in the writing. You will learn how in
this lesson.

## Key Words

**cause**—something that causes another
thing to happen

**effect**—something that happens as a
result of another thing; a result

## Analyzing Cause-and-Effect Order

In everyday life, you often try to find the **causes** or reasons for changes you
see. If a child starts crying, for example, you try to see what is causing the distress. You also try to predict the **effects** or results of many actions. When you
consider moving to a new place (cause), for instance, you think about how your
commuting, shopping, and socializing will be different (effect).

How do writers decide to use cause-and-effect order? In the last lesson you learned that writers often use time order to tell a story or give directions and order of importance to present an argument. Writers who want to trace how and why something happens often arrange their ideas in cause-and-effect order. For example, a science article about a recent hurricane might tell the causes for the storm, as well as its damaging effects. Likewise, an essay about the Vietnam War might outline some causes of the conflict and describe its effect on the people of the area.

You will find that a cause-and-effect relationship is often used by nonfiction writers to explain an event in a newspaper and in a manual to indicate how something should be done. Other nonfiction writers who are trying to persuade you to their way of thinking will convince you that something happened for specific reasons and had specific results.

You can identify causes by asking yourself: What could be behind this change? You can identify effects by asking yourself: What are the results of the action? To make cause-and-effect connections, use the facts in the passage, your background knowledge, and your imagination.

## Model Questions and Strategy

Here are some sample questions about cause-and-effect order that might appear on the *Interpreting Literature and the Arts* section of the GED.

- How does the structure of the passage reveal the author's purpose?
- The details in this passage are arranged to show _____?
- According to the passage, the effect of _____ is _____?
- According to the article, one reason for the _____ was _____?
- What is the main reason the author wants to _____?

Here is a strategy you can use to find the answer to cause-and-effect questions.

Step 1: Look for words that signal cause-and-effect order, such as the following:

| Cause Words | Effect Words |
|---|---|
| because | so |
| because of | then |
| since | as a result, as a result of |
| so that | therefore |
| | thus |
| | consequently |

Step 2: Eliminate choices that are not causes.

Step 3: Eliminate choices not supported by the passage.

Step 4: Choose the best answer.

# Model Passage and Question

Read the following excerpt. Use the strategy you have just learned to find the answer to the question.

## WHY QUIT DRINKING COFFEE?

I have decided to quit drinking coffee because I don't like what it does to my body. Coffee wakes me up in the morning, but I still feel drowsy all day if I work too hard before lunch. Coffee also stains my teeth. Consequently, my teeth are yellow from years of coffee drinking. Coffee makes my heart beat double-time. As a result, I feel nervous and jittery if I drink too much of it.

(5)

Which of the following phrases gives the main reason the writer wants to quit drinking coffee?

**(1)** Coffee is too expensive.

**(2)** She has been drinking too much of it.

**(3)** She feels that tea tastes better.

**(4)** Coffee upsets the writer's health and work habits.

**(5)** Coffee makes the writer drowsy.

Step 1: Look for words that signal cause-and-effect order. The phrases *because, so, consequently,* and *as a result* are clues that the ideas have been arranged in cause and effect order.

Step 2: Eliminate choices that are not causes. (5) is mentioned in the passage, but it does not explain the *cause* of her decision to quit drinking coffee.

Step 3: Eliminate choices not supported by the passage. While (1) and (3) may be true, but neither tea nor the cost of coffee is even mentioned in the passage. (5) confuses the statement in lines 2-3: "Coffee wakes me up in the morning, but I still feel drowsy all day if I work too hard in the morning."

Step 4: Choose the best answer. The correct answer is (4) because it is the main reason. Coffee makes her "drowsy" and causes her "heart [to] beat double-time." This upsets her health. As a result, she feels "nervous and jittery" if she drinks too much. This, in turn, upsets her work habits. As a summary of the paragraph's main points, (4) therefore is a detailed restatement of the topic sentence of the paragraph: "I have decided to quit drinking coffee because I don't like what it is doing to my body" (lines 1-2.) (2) is not the correct answer because the author never says how much coffee he or she is drinking, only that it has bad effects on her body.

# Practice

Read the following excerpt and choose the best answer to the question.

## WHAT KIND OF PERSON WAS WILMA RUDOLPH?

(5) After so many easy victories, using natural ability alone, I got a false sense of being unbeatable. But losing to those girls from Georgia, who knew every trick in the book, that was sobering. It brought me back down to earth, and it made me realize that I couldn't do it on natural ability alone, that there was more to track than just running fast. I also realized it was going to test me as a person—could I come back and win again after being so totally crushed by a defeat?

From *Wilma* by Wilma Rudolph and Bud Greenspan. Copyright ©1977 by Bud Greenspan. Used by permission of New American Library, a division of Penguin Books USA, Inc.

**1.** The details in the passage are arranged to show

    **(1)** the sequence of events in an important race

    **(2)** the reasons the author felt unbeatable

    **(3)** the effect that losing a race had on the author

    **(4)** the effects of solid training

    **(5)** the sequence of events preceding a race

(3) is correct because most of the details in the passage show what happened to Wilma Rudolph as a result of losing the race. She realized that she had had a "false sense of being unbeatable." She found that "losing...was sobering." She realized that she "couldn't do it on natural ability alone." She discovered that "there was more to track than just running fast" and that she was now going to be tested as a person to see if she could "come back and win."

(1) and (5) are incorrect because the details do not list the order of events. (2) is incorrect because most of the details are arranged to describe how she lost the feeling of being unbeatable *after* the race. Only the first sentence implies why she felt unbeatable ("After so many victories...") before the race with the girls from Georgia. (4) is incorrect because the details show the effects of losing a race, not the effects of solid training.

Items 1 through 3 refer to the passage that follows. Choose the one best answer to each item.

## WHAT IS IT LIKE TO WITNESS A FLOOD?

It was just this time last year that we had the flood. It was Hurricane Agnes, really, but by the time it got here, the weather bureau had demoted it to a tropical storm. I see by a
(5) clipping I saved that the date was June twenty-first, the solstice, midsummer's night, the longest daylight of the year; but I didn't notice it at the time. Everything was so exciting, and so very dark.

All it did was rain. It rained, and the creek started to rise.
(10) The creek, naturally, rises every time it rains; this didn't seem any different. But it kept raining, and that morning of the twenty-first, the creek kept rising.

That morning I'm standing at my kitchen window. Tinker Creek is out of its four-foot banks, way out, and it's still com-
(15) ing. The high creek doesn't look like our creek. Our creek splashes transparently over a jumble of rocks; the high creek obliterates everything in flat opacity...

Everything looks different. Where my eye is used to depth, I see the flat water, near, too near. I see trees I never noticed
(20) before, the black verticals of their rain-soaked trunks standing out of the pale water like pilings for a rotted dock. The stillness of grassy banks and stony ledges is gone; I see rushing, a wild sweep and hurry in one direction, as swift and compelling as a waterfall. The Atkins kids are out in their tiny
(25) rain gear, staring at the monster creek. It's risen up to their gates; the neighbors are gathering; I go out.

Excerpt from "The Flood" from *Pilgrim at Tinker Creek* by Annie Dillard. Copyright ©1974 by Annie Dillard. Reprinted by permission of HarperCollins Publishers, Inc.

1. The details in the passage are arranged to show

    (1) the reasons the flood occurred
    (2) the order of events before the flood
    (3) the different reactions of the neighbors to the flood
    (4) the long term effects of the flood on the residents
    (5) the effects of the flood on how things looked

2. The author changes from the past tense to the present tense in the third paragraph in order to

    (1) show how memory often distorts reality
    (2) point out similarities between floods of the past and present-day floods
    (3) let the reader share in the experience of witnessing the flood first-hand
    (4) demonstrate how a flood can happen anywhere, anytime
    (5) show the differences between what one remembers and what one is told

3. According to the last paragraph, the main effect of the flood was to

    (1) frighten the writer's neighbors
    (2) change the appearance of the landscape
    (3) create a tremendous noise
    (4) make people help each other
    (5) make the writer abandon her home

Answers are on page 316.

# Analyzing Tone

## Prereading Prompt

The words you use express not only ideas, but attitudes as well. Suppose you say, "This food is about as tasty as shoe leather." Your words express the idea that you dislike the food you are eating. They also reveal a sarcastic, or mocking, attitude, showing that you're making fun of something.

Your are probably an expert at understanding people's attitudes because you often make inferences about how they feel from what they say and how they say it. Writers, too, use words not only to express ideas, but also to show how they feel about their subjects. The tone of a piece of writing expresses the author's attitude toward his or her subject. On the GED you may be asked to answer questions about the author's attitude in a passage. You will learn how in this lesson.

## Key Words

**tone**—the words a writer uses to show his or her feelings. Some examples of tone are sarcastic, serious, humorous, angry, admiring, or matter-of-fact.

## Analyzing Tone

Writers choose specific words and phrases to create the tone of a piece of literature. Writers use different tones to communicate their ideas and to capture the reader's interest. The tone of a piece of writing depends on its purpose. Nonfiction writing can be objective (factual) or subjective (emotional). In objective articles, such as news stories, writers do not show their feelings about their topic. In subjective pieces, such as personal essays, writers do express their feelings in the tone of the article.

It is very important to recognize an author's tone. If you miss the tone, you may miss the point of what you are reading. To figure out the tone of a passage, think about the words and phrases the writer uses and the pictures they create in your mind. Look carefully at the details, too, for these will help reveal the author's tone.

## Model Questions and Strategy

Here are some sample questions about tone that might appear on the *Interpreting Literature and the Arts* section of the GED. They are followed by a strategy you can use to help find the answer.

• How does the author seem to feel about _____?
• Which of the following best describes the author's tone in this passage?

**Strategy:**

Step 1: Identify the topic of the passage.

Step 2: Ask yourself: What does the writer's choice of words and details reveal about his or her attitude toward the topic?

Step 3: Ask yourself: What is my reaction to the passage? How do I feel about what I just read?

Step 4: Choose the best answer.

Read the following excerpt. Use the strategy you have just learned to find the answer to the question.

## DOES ANYONE CARE IF A TREE DIES?

For a great tree death comes as a gradual transformation. Its vitality ebbs slowly. Even when life has abandoned it entirely it remains a majestic thing. On some hilltop a dead tree may dominate the landscape for miles around. Alone
(5) among living things it retains its character and dignity after death. Plants wither; animals disintegrate. But a dead tree may be as arresting, as filled with personality, in death as it is in life. Even its final moments, when the massive trunk lies prone and it has moldered into a ridge covered with mosses
(10) and fungi, it arrives at a fitting and noble end. It enriches and refreshes the earth. And later, as part of other green and growing things, it rises again.

From "The Death of a Tree" in *Dune Boy* by Edwin Way Teale. Copyright ©1943 by Dodd Mead. Used by permission of Mrs. Nellie D. Teale.

What words best describe the tone of the passage?

**(1)** lighthearted and humorous

**(2)** angry and confused

**(3)** sarcastic and bitter

**(4)** awed and respectful

**(5)** sorrowful and despairing

The correct answer is (4). The topic—the death of a tree—seems to fill the author with awe and wonder. While reading the words and details used to describe that death, the reader, too, feels respect. The author calls the tree "a majestic thing." Even when dead, it "dominates the landscape... Alone among living things it retains its character and dignity after death." In death, "it arrives at a fitting and noble end. It enriches and refreshes the earth." There are no details in the passage to support any of the other choices.

# Lesson 13 Exercise

Items 1 through 3 refer to the passage that follows. Choose the one best answer to each item.

### WHAT NEW UNDERSTANDING DOES THE AUTHOR GAIN WHILE ON A RAFT?

...The longer the voyage lasted, the safer we felt in our cozy lair, and we looked at the white-crested waves that danced past outside our doorway as if they were an impressive movie, conveying no menace to us at all. Even though the gaping
(5) wall was only five feet from the unprotected edge of the raft and only a foot and a half above the water line, yet we felt as if we had traveled many miles away from the sea and occupied a jungle dwelling remote from the sea's perils once we had crawled inside the door.
(10) Sometimes, too, we went out in the rubber boat to look at ourselves by night.... The world was simple—stars in the darkness.... We lived, and that we felt with alert intensity. We realized that life had been full for men before the technological age also—in fact, fuller and richer in many ways than the
(15) life of modern man. Time and evolution ceased to exist; all that was real and that mattered were the same today as they had always been and would always be.

From *Kon-Tiki: Across the Pacific by Raft* by Thor Heyerdahl. Copyright ©1950, 1960, 1984. Used by permission of the publisher, Prentice Hall Press/A division of Simon and Schuster, New York.

1. Which of the following best describes the author's tone in this passage?

   (1) reflective and meditative
   (2) bored and disappointed
   (3) critical and stern
   (4) playful and lively
   (5) objective and factual

2. Being at sea in the rubber boat under the stars makes the author feel

   (1) angry
   (2) weary
   (3) homesick
   (4) alive
   (5) safe

3. The details in the passage are arranged to show

   (1) the order of events after the raft capsized
   (2) the effects of the voyage on the author's thinking
   (3) the most important reasons for the author's fear
   (4) the steps to take when preparing for a long raft voyage
   (5) the reasons for the author's voyage by raft

Answers are on page 317.

# *CHAPTER 2*

In fiction, unlike nonfiction, the author creates characters, setting, and plot. These elements come from the author's imagination. One or more of these elements is not "real" in the sense that it is not an exact presentation of reality. Sometimes the setting or the characters can seem quite real. At other times, as in science fiction, these elements can be quite different from what you might encounter in the real world. A work of fiction becomes a work of literature when certain truths and insights give it lasting value.

Jack London                                          Credit: The Library of Congress

## Prereading Prompt

What keeps you reading a good story or watching a TV show? What makes you want to know how things will turn out? Maybe it's the series of fast-paced, hair-raising events. Maybe it's a character's interesting personality. Maybe it's the fascinating location. Understanding how these elements work to involve you and make an interesting story is important for answering GED questions. You will learn more about them in this chapter.

# FICTION

# What is Fiction?

Most people love a good story. The story might be about an orphan, a rich widow, a young gang, or even aliens from outer space. The events can be as chilling as near-death encounters with mobsters or as charming as two people falling in love. The settings can be as varied as a lake in Switzerland, an alley in Los Angeles, a castle in an ancient land, or a canal on Mars. Regardless of who does what, when, and where—a good story will fascinate you. You become involved and want to know why people do as they do, what will happen next, and how things will turn out in the end. While nonfiction is about reality, fiction is not. A good story lets you live for a short while in a world of someone else's creation—a world artfully imagined and skillfully crafted.

Fiction always tells a story. **Plot** is the sequence of events in that story. The plot is always told by the **narrator**, or storyteller. The **characters** are the people who take part in the events in the story. **Setting** is the time and place in which the events occur.

**Short stories** and **novels** are two of the most common forms of fiction. A short story is designed to be read in one setting and usually tells about one character and one major event. The novel takes longer to read and usually tells a more complex story with many characters.

## Key Words

**fiction**—works of literature that tell of imaginary characters and events

**short story**—a short form of fiction designed to be read in one sitting, usually about one main character and one major action

**novel**—a long form of fiction with a complex plot

91

# Literal Comprehension of Action

## Prereading Prompt

Have you ever watched a fast-paced, action-filled chase scene in a movie? If so, you were probably on the edge of your seat as you witnessed the thugs in the speeding get-away car try to outmaneuver the hotly pursuing police. Now suppose for a moment that at the end of the pursuit, all the people involved got out of their cars, shook hands, and went to the park for a quiet lunch. How would you feel? Probably you would be confused and disappointed. That's because the events did not logically follow each other. The action did not reach a believable conclusion.

On the GED you may be asked to answer questions that show you understand the logic of a story's action. You will learn how in this lesson.

## Key Words

**plot**—the sequence of events in a story

**conclusion**—the last event in a series of events

**action**—the series of happenings in a story

## Action

In fiction, as in the movies, the **plot** or sequence of events must occur in a logical fashion and proceed to a believable conclusion. Otherwise, the story will not make any sense. To understand a work of fiction, you must have a clear idea of the **plot**, the sequence of events in a story.

On the *Interpreting Literature and the Arts* section of the GED test, you may be asked to answer literal comprehension items about the action of the passage. As you learned in the Nonfiction section of this book (Lessons 1-4), literal comprehension items may require you to find specific details, restate information, or summarize the main idea of a passage. The strategy for finding specific details in a piece of fiction is the same as the one you learned to use on nonfiction.

## Model Questions and Strategy

Here are some sample questions that require you to restate or summarize the action in a fiction passage that might appear on the Interpreting Literature and the Arts section of the GED. They are followed by a strategy you can use to help find the answer.

- Which statement best summarizes the action of the passage?
- What is the main action of the passage?
- What action does the character take in the passage?

### Strategy:

Step 1: Briefly summarize the story in your mind.

Step 2: Identify the topic. Recall that the topic is a brief description of what the passage is about.

Step 3: Identify the main event(s). Ask yourself: Who is the main character? What are the main problems that arise and how does the main character react to them?

Step 4: Identify the main details. Ask yourself: What details are essential in making the author's point about the topic?

Step 5: State the topic in one sentence. Include information about the main events and details.

Step 6: Compare your summary with the answer choices. See which answer provides the closest match. Then pick the best answer.

Read the passage below. Use the strategy to find the answer that best summarizes the action of the passage.

### WHY IS THIS BOY OUT SO LATE AT NIGHT?

She was a large woman with a large purse that had everything in it but hammer and nails. It had a long strap and she carried it slung across her shoulder. It was about eleven o'clock at night, and she was walking alone, when a boy ran
(5) up behind her and tried to snatch her purse. The strap broke with the single tug the boy gave it from behind. But the boy's weight, and the weight of the purse combined caused him to lose his balance so, instead of taking off full blast as he had hoped, the boy fell on his back on the sidewalk, and his legs
(10) flew up. The large woman simply turned around and kicked him right square in his blue-jeaned sitter. Then she reached down, picked the boy up by his shirt front, and shook him until his teeth rattled.

From "Thank You, M'am," by Langston Hughes. Reprinted by permission of Harold Ober Associates, Inc. Copyright ©1958 by Langston Hughes. Copyright renewed 1986 by George Houston Bass.

What statement best summarizes the action of the passage?

**(1)** A woman with a large purse across her shoulder is walking at night, all alone.

**(2)** A boy falls down on the sidewalk, his legs flying up into the air.

**(3)** A woman's purse strap breaks with a single tug when grabbed from behind.

**(4)** A boy tries to rob a woman, but she catches him, kicks, and shakes him.

**(5)** A boy tugs at a woman's purse, breaks the strap, and then takes off full blast.

Step 1: Briefly summarize the story in your mind. Run through all the events that occurred. Can you feel the darkness? Do you hear the boy running up behind the woman? Do you see the purse snap off her shoulder as he grabs the strap from behind? Do you see him fall? Do you see her kick him, pick him up, and shake him?

Step 2: Identify the topic. From your mental summary, you will see that the passage is about purse-snatching.

Step 3: Identify the main event(s). Start by locating the main character. From running through the story in your mind, you know that the passage focuses on the woman. You can tell she is the main character by identifying the problem—what should she do when the boy tries to snatch her purse? How does she react to the problem? She solves it by "kicking him right square in his blue-jeaned sitter." Therefore, the main event concerns the woman's reaction to the attack.

Step 4: Identify the main details. No summary of the plot would be complete without mentioning the woman, the boy, the attempted robbery, and the boy's punishment. These are all important details that contribute to the author's main point: This woman is tough.

Step 5: State the topic in one sentence. Your sentence might look something like this: A woman grabs a boy who is trying to snatch her purse, kicks him, and shakes him.

Step 6: Compare your summary with the answer choices. (4) is closest to your summary. (1), (2), and (3) are incorrect because they each describe only one part of the action, not the events in the entire scene. (5) is incorrect because the boy did not take off full blast, as he had hoped.

Items 1 to 3 refer to the following passage. Choose the one best answer to each item.

### WHAT MISTAKES DID THIS MAN MAKE?

But before he could cut the strings, it happened. It was his own fault or, rather, his mistake. He should not have built the fire under the spruce tree. He should have built it in the open. But it had been easier to pull the twigs from the  brush
(5) and drop them directly on the fire. Now the tree under which he had done this carried a weight of snow on its boughs. No wind had blown for weeks, and each bough was fully freight- ed. Each time he had pulled a twig he had communicated a slight agitation to the tree—an imperceptible agitation, so far
(10) as he was concerned, but an agitation sufficient to bring about the disaster. High up in the tree one bough capsized its load of snow. This fell on the boughs beneath, capsizing them. This process continued, spreading out and involving the whole tree. It grew like an avalanche, and it descended
(15) without warning upon the man and the fire, and the fire was blotted out! Where it had burned was a mantle of fresh and disordered snow.

The man was shocked. It was as though he had just heard his own sentence of death. For a moment he sat and stared at
(20) the spot where the fire had been. Then he grew very calm. Perhaps the old-timer on Sulphur Creek was right. If he had only had a trailmate he would have been in no danger now. The trailmate could have built the fire. Well, it was up to him to build the fire over again, and this second time there must
(25) be no failure. Even if he succeeded, he would most likely lose some of his toes. His feet must be badly frozen by now, and there would be some time before the second fire was ready.

"To Build a Fire" by Jack London.

1. What is the main action of the passage?

   (1) A man is shocked to hear his death sentence delivered and then grows calm as he makes a plan.
   (2) A man learns that he will probably lose some of his toes in the extreme cold.
   (3) A man accidentally shakes a load of snow from a tree by pulling a twig out of the brush.
   (4) A man realizes that without a trailmate he must rebuild a fire in the snow by himself.
   (5) A man plans to stay alive by rebuilding a fire that was put out by snow falling from a tree.

2. Which of the following events is *not* part of the action?

   (1) The man had shaken the tree every time he pulled a bough from it.
   (2) An avalanche came roaring down the hill and destroyed the fire.
   (3) The fire is completely smothered by snow.
   (4) The man makes plans to rebuild the fire.
   (5) The man thinks about the advantages of having a companion along.

3. It was a mistake for the man to build the fire under the tree because

   (1) the fire came between him and the strings he needed to cut
   (2) it would have been easier to pull twigs in the open
   (3) spruce twigs did not burn as well as brush twigs
   (4) the fire was put out by snow falling from the tree
   (5) no wind had blown for weeks and his feet were frozen

Answers are on page 317.

# Literal Comprehension of Setting

## Prereading Prompt

You have probably gone to many events in your life—birthday parties, graduations, weddings, and funerals, to name a few. Each event took place at a specific time and place, and had its own special emotions associated with it. For example, you may have attended a rock concert on the evening of July 4, 1992, in an enormous outdoor stadium. Most likely, you felt excited, energized, and happy. You may have also attended a funeral in that year. Perhaps it took place on the morning of April 11 in a small room of a funeral parlor; then most likely you felt sad.

In fiction, just as in real life, events take place at certain times. Understanding how the time and the place contribute to the overall effect of a story is very important for answering GED questions. You will learn how in this lesson.

## Key Words

**atmosphere** or **mood**—the emotions associated with specific events in a story

**setting**—the time, place, and atmosphere of the events in a story

**time**—when the events in a story take place—the hour, day of the week, month of the year, or historical period

**place**—the location of the story

In fiction, as in real life, events take place in certain settings. **Setting** is the time and place of a story. **Time** refers to when the events take place—the hour of the day, the day of the week, month of the year, or the historical period. **Place** refers to the location of the story. Stories can occur in such vastly different places as an all-night diner in Iowa, a jungle in Africa, a spaceship heading toward Mars, or a boat in the middle of the Pacific Ocean. Setting helps create **atmosphere**, or the emotions associated with specific events in a story. A safari in Africa may evoke exhilaration and expectation, while the emotions associated with a plane disaster are grief and horror. By using details of time and place in this way, a writer can create a particular state of mind or feeling–a **mood**–in the reader.

In some longer works of fiction, the setting can change several times according to the action of the story. For instance, a novel may begin in the spring of one year and end during the winter of the next. Sometimes the setting is essential to the story. For example, a writer may decide that it is essential for a wedding to take place at home, rather than at City Hall, in order to convey an intimate feeling. At other times, setting is less important.

## Model Questions and Strategy

Here are some sample questions that require you to identify the setting or atmosphere in a fiction passage that might appear on the *Interpreting Literature and the Arts* section of the GED. They are followed by a strategy you can use to help find the answer.

- Which statement best describes the atmosphere (or mood) of the passage?
- The action takes place in _____ (where).
- The action/event takes place _____ (when).

### Strategy:

Step 1: Read the passage carefully.

Step 2: Look for details that directly state the time and place. Note the descriptive words that identify when and where the story is taking place.

Step 3: Identify the mood or feeling you get from the passage. Ask yourself: How does this passage make me feel? Summarize the feeling in a descriptive word. You might come up with something like "happy," "eerie," or "depressed," for example.

Step 4: Compare the details and feeling you identified with the answer choices. See which answer provides the closest match. Then pick the best answer.

## Model Passage and Question

Read the following passage. Use the strategy you have just learned to find the answer to the question.

### WHAT IS HAPPENING HERE?

"Keep her head up! Keep her head up!"
"Keep her head up, sir." The voices were weary and low.
This was surely a quiet evening. All save the oarsman lay heavily and listlessly in the boat's bottom. As for him, his
(5) eyes were just capable of noting the tall black waves that swept forward in a most sinister silence, save for an occasional subdued growl of a crest.

"The Open Boat," by Stephen Crane from The *Oxford Book of Short Stories*, chosen by V.S. Pritchett, Oxford University Press, 1981.

The action of the excerpt takes place

   **(1)** at night in a submarine at sea
   **(2)** at night on a motorboat on a lake
   **(3)** at dusk in a row boat on a noisy river
   **(4)** at evening in a motorboat at sea
   **(5)** at night in a rowboat at sea

<u>Step 1: Read the passage carefully.</u>

<u>Step 2: Look for details that directly state the time and place. Eliminate the answer choices that do not fit these details and choose the best answer.</u> The statement,"This was surely a quiet evening," in line 3 tells you the setting of time is evening. Since you are told that the water where the boat is has "tall black waves" that move in silence, the setting of place cannot be a noisy river (3). We are told that "the oarsman" is the only one sitting up in the boat, so the boat must be a rowboat; there is also no mention of a motor. Therefore, (2) and (4) are incorrect. If the oarsman is sitting up in the boat watching the waves sweep toward him, the boat cannot be a submarine. Therefore, (5) is the only answer that all the details support.

   Which of the following best describes the mood (or atmosphere) created in the excerpt?

   **(1)** gloomy
   **(2)** hopeful
   **(3)** peaceful
   **(4)** enthusiastic
   **(5)** happy

<u>Step 1:  Read the passage carefully.</u>

<u>Step 2: Identify the mood or atmosphere you get from details in the passage.</u> Phrases such as "heavily and listlessly," "sinister silence," and "subdued growl of a crest," and the description of men's voices as "weary and low" all suggest a gloomy, depressing mood or atmosphere.

<u>Step 3:  Compare the details and feeling you identified with the answer choices, Eliminate the answer choices that do not fit the mood or details.</u> Clearly none of the men in the boat are hopeful (2), or happy (5) if they are described as lying "heavily and listlessly in the boat's bottom" (line 4). Though the first line of the excerpt might sound enthusiastic at first, it is clear later that it expresses a fear that the boat will sink. Therefore (4) is wrong, The quiet of the evening (line 3) and the silence of the waves (lines 5-6) might suggest a peaceful atmosphere (3), but the waves are "tall, black waves" and the silence is "most sinister" (line 6). These details, with the others already mentioned, clearly suggest a gloomy atmosphere or mood (1).

## Lesson 2 Exercise

Items 1 through 3 refer to the passage that follows. Choose the one best answer to each item.

### WHY IS THIS YOUNG MAN AWAY FROM HOME?

There it was again, that sinister feeling in the pine shadows and a sense of something watching, waiting among the dense trees up ahead. This spruce valley was a dark, forbidding place even in the summer; now in the winter silence under
(5)  the blue-black trees was more than silence—it was like a spell. Queer, they had had to choose this place to lay their trapline, just a week before his father had come down with flu-pneumonia, leaving Gordon to cover the long line during the worst weeks of winter. He wouldn't have minded tenting
(10) the old line along the lake shore, but this haunted place—

Gordon Bent was sixteen, turning seventeen, already six feet tall and scantling thin. The first fuzz of beard showed like a faint gray lichen along his lean cheek. Timber-bred, he knew the woods and creatures as well as his father, and
(15) never before had he feared any of them. But something about this valley filled him with dread from the first.

It would have been all right but for the nights. The valley was a mile from home, so it took him two days to cover the trapline properly. So twice a week he had to make snow camp
(20) in the deep woods near the valley's head, sleeping out in the bark-covered, half-faced lean-to he and his father had set up for the storage of trapping gear.

Excerpt from "Accounts Settled," by Paul Annixter. Copyright ©1966 by Scholastic Magazines, Inc. Reprinted by permission of Scholastic, Inc..

1. What is the setting of the story?

   **(1)** a haunted house in the winter
   **(2)** a valley two days away from Gordon's home
   **(3)** a valley of spruce trees in the winter
   **(4)** a lean-to high in a spruce tree
   **(5)** a small but well-equipped cabin in a valley

2. What is the atmosphere of the story?

   **(1)** cheerful
   **(2)** menacing
   **(3)** panic-stricken
   **(4)** angry
   **(5)** calm and peaceful

3. In the main action of the passage, a teenage boy

   **(1)** stalks a wild animal through the forest
   **(2)** clears the faint gray lichen and timber from the forest floor
   **(3)** camps in the woods because his father is dying
   **(4)** tries to escape from a haunted forest
   **(5)** tends the traps alone because his father is ill

Answers are on page 318.

# Literal Comprehension of Characters

---

## Prereading Prompt

Have you ever gone on a blind date? If so, you know that a blind date is a social activity of two people who have never met before. The person who plans the date usually tells the two people about each other ahead of time. She may tell you that your date is a good-looking, well-dressed, intelligent, shy, generous person. Details such as these provide you with information to help you get to know the person. Finding out details about the characters in a story is very important for answering GED questions. You will learn how in this lesson.

---

### Key Words

**character**—any person in a story

**direct characterization**—a narrator's description of what a character is like

---

A **character** is any person in a story. Like real-life people, characters in fiction look, act, and feel certain ways. In fiction, authors usually provide many details about their characters so that readers get to know these characters well. Sometimes narrators tell you directly about a character. They might say, for example, "Willie was a quiet man," or "Matilda always showed great determination." These descriptions of what a character is like are called **direct characterization**.

On the Interpreting Literature and Arts section of the GED test, you may be asked literal comprehension questions about a character. Here are some sample questions that require you to identify a character's traits. They are followed by a strategy you can use to help find the answer.

## Model Questions and Strategy

- What words best describe the character?
- From what the character says in the excerpt, you know that [he or she] is _____
- From the character's action, you know that [he or she] is _____
- From what the character says and does in the excerpt, you know that [he or she] is _____

### Strategy:

Step 1: Read the passage carefully.

Step 2: Look for specific details that directly state how a character looks, feels, and acts. Look carefully at what the character says and what other characters in the passage say about that person. Note the descriptive words that identify the character's personality.

Step 3: Summarize the character's personality. Ask yourself: What picture do I get about this character from the details I found? What is this character like? Then summarize the character's traits. You might come up with something like "John is a selfish person," or "He is large and clumsy for his age," for example.

Step 4: Compare your summary with the answer choices. See which answer provides the closest match. Then pick the best answer.

## Model Passage and Question

Read the following passage. Use the strategy you have just learned to find the answer to the question.

### WHAT KIND OF MAN IS THIS?

That afternoon all the fellows followed Michael up the ladder to the roof of the old building and they sat with their legs hanging over the edge looking out at the whitecaps on the water. Michael was younger than some of them but he was
(5) much bigger, his legs were long, his huge hands dangled awkwardly at his sides and his thick black hair curled all over his head. "I'll stump you all to jump down," he said suddenly, and without thinking about it, he shoved himself off the roof and fell on the sawdust where he lay rolling around
(10) and laughing.

"The Runaway," by Morley Callaghan from The *Oxford Book of Short Stories*, chosen by V.S. Pritchett, Oxford University Press, 1981. Reprinted by permission of Barry Callahan.

From what Michael says and does in the passage, you know that he is

    **(1)** bold and impulsive

    **(2)** ugly and funny

    **(3)** thoughtful and impulsive

    **(4)** small and bullying

    **(5)** unathletic and cowardly

<u>Step 1: Read the passage carefully.</u>

<u>Step 2: Look for specific details that directly state how a character looks, feels, and acts.</u> Lines 4-7 has details about Michael's appearance: "Michael was younger than some of them but he was much bigger, his legs were long, his huge hands dangled awkwardly at his sides and his thick black hair curled all over his head." You know that he acts impulsively because he jumps from the roof "without thinking about it." He dares the other boys to jump—"I'll stump you all to jump down"—even though he is younger than they are.

<u>Step 3: Summarize the character's personality.</u> From the details you found about Michael's appearance and actions, you might come up with something like this: "Michael is daring and impulsive."and "Michael is big and awkward."

<u>Step 4: Compare your summary with the answer choices.</u> (1) is the correct choice. (2) is incorrect because nothing suggests that Michael is deformed or repulsive-looking; and although he laughs at his own actions, there are no details to suggest that he is a funny person. Eliminate (3) because he jumps "without thinking about it," which shows that he is *not* a thoughtful person. (4) is wrong because even though "Michael was younger than some of them ... he was much bigger." Also, no detail suggests that he is a bully. Finally, eliminate (5) because he leads the jump, which shows that he is neither cowardly nor unathletic.

Items 1 through 3 refer to the passage that follows. Choose the one best answer to each item.

### HOW DOES BARRY REACT WHEN HE SEES HIS OLD FRIEND?

Earlier, when Barry had left the house to go to the game, an overnight frost had still been thick on the roads, but the brisk April sun had soon dispersed it, and now he could feel the spring warmth on his back through the thick tweed of his
(5) coat. His left arm was beginning to stiffen up where he'd jarred it in a tackle, but it was nothing serious. He flexed his shoulders against the tightness of his jacket and was surprised again by the unexpected weight of his muscles, the thickening strength of his body. A few years back, he
(10) thought, he had been a small, unimportant boy, one of a swarming gang laughing and jostling to school, hardly aware that he possessed an identity. But time had transformed him. He walked solidly now, and often alone. He was tall, strongly made, his hands and feet were adult and heavy, the rooms in
(15) which all his life he'd moved had grown too small for him. Sometimes a devouring restlessness drove him from the house to walk long distances in the dark. He hardly understood how it had happened. Amused and quiet, he walked the High Street among the morning shoppers.
(20) He saw Jackie Bevan across the road and remembered how, when they were both six years old, Jackie had swallowed a pin. The flustered teachers had clucked about Jackie as he stood there, bawling, cheeks awash with tears, his nose wet. But now Jackie was tall and suave, his thick, pale hair
(25) sleekly tailored, his gray suit enviable. He was talking to a girl as golden as a daffodil.

"Hey, hey!" called Jackie. "How's the athlete, how's Barry boy?"

He waved a graceful hand at Barry.

(30) "Come and talk to Sue," he said.

Barry shifted his bag to his left hand and walked over, forming in his mind the answers he'd make to Jackie's questions.

"Did we win?" Jackie asked. "Was the old Barry Stanford
(35) magic in glittering evidence yet once more this morning? Were the invaders sent hunched and silent back to their hovels in the hills? What was the score? Give us an epic account, Barry, without modesty or delay. This is Sue, by the way."

From "Shaving," by Leslie Norris. Copyright ©1977 by Leslie Norris. Reprinted by permission of Gibbs Smith, publisher.

1. What words best describe Barry?

   (1) energetic and strong
   (2) smooth and silly
   (3) small and unimportant
   (4) weak and powerless
   (5) tall but delicate

2. What words best describe Jackie?

   (1) dark haired and quiet
   (2) friendly and clumsy
   (3) well-dressed and confident
   (4) solid and lonely
   (5) short and quiet

3. What is the story's setting?

   (1) at school on an April morning
   (2) during halftime at a football game
   (3) along High Street on a spring morning
   (4) along a street on a winter's evening
   (5) on a quiet street after a baseball game

Answers are on page 318.

# Inferring Action and Setting

### Prereading Prompt

As you watch the beginning of a movie, you probably make some guesses about what is taking place, and where. Actors don't usually reveal this kind of information in their opening lines. For example, suppose a movie opens with a shot of thousands of people on a hot, sunny day in an outdoor stadium waving banners that say, "Go Dolphins Go!" You might guess that the setting is Miami and that the Dolphins football team is about to play a game. Authors, like movie makers, don't always directly state all the details. Finding out how to infer this information in a passage of fiction is important for answering GED questions. You will learn how in this lesson.

Fiction writers, like screenwriters, do not always directly state what is happening, and where. They expect their readers will know these things from the details they give. For example, if you read a paragraph that includes words such as "pass," "high and wide," and "halfback," you can infer that the paragraph is about football. If you read about "commanders," trenches," and "enemy lines," you can infer that the passage is about war.

On the Interpreting Literature and Arts section of the GED test, you may be asked to infer the setting and the action of a passage. Below are some sample questions about setting and action. They are followed by a strategy you can use to help you find the answer.

# Model Questions and Strategy

- What does the character seem to be trying to do?
- What is the main action of the passage?
- Where does the action most likely take place?
- When does the action most likely take place?

### Strategy:

<u>Step 1:</u> Identify the topic of the passage. After you finish reading, ask yourself: What is the passage generally about?

<u>Step 2:</u> Look for details that help you imagine the scene. See if you can find clues about the time of year. Also, are there clues that tell you where the story takes place?

<u>Step 3:</u> Look for clues that suggest what the characters are doing. Ask yourself: What do they say? How do they interact with each other?

<u>Step 4:</u> Combine the details and clues to summarize the passage. In your summary, note what is happening, where, and when. Try to make your summary no more than one sentence long.

<u>Step 5:</u> Examine the answer choices and select the one that sounds the most like your statement. Then pick the best answer.

## Model Passage and Question

Read the following passage. See if you can infer what is taking place, and where.

### WHAT IS THIS WOMAN DOING?

There were any number of eights-and-a-half. In fact, there were more of that size than any other. Here was a light blue pair; there were some lavender, some all black and various shades of tan and gray. Mrs. Sommers selected a black pair
(5) and looked at them very long and closely. She pretended to be examining their texture, which the clerk assured her was excellent.

"A dollar and ninety-eight cents," she mused aloud. "Well, I'll take this pair." She handed the girl a five-dollar bill and
(10) waited for her change and for her parcel. What a very small parcel it was! It seemed lost in the depths of her shabby old shopping bag.

Excerpt from "A Pair of Silk Stockings," by Kate Chopin.

What is the main action of the passage?

**(1)** A woman is bargaining with a sales clerk about the price of a pair of stockings.

**(2)** A woman is examining the texture of some ties in various shades of tan and gray.

**(3)** A woman is buying a pair of black stockings in a store.

**(4)** A woman is trying to fit a shoe box into her shabby purse.

**(5)** A clerk is helping a woman decide which color stockings to buy.

The correct answer is (3). The woman is buying a pair of black stockings in a store. You can infer this from these details: she selected "a black pair" in size eight-in-a-half after examining their "texture"; she announced, "I'll take this pair"; she paid the clerk $1.98 for them; and the "parcel" is small enough to get lost in her bag. (1) is incorrect because the woman gives the clerk money but does not bargain at all. (2) is wrong because ties do not come in pairs, so she cannot be buying this item. (4) is incorrect because the woman has no trouble fitting the parcel in her bag. A shoe box would probably be too large to seem "lost in the depths of her shabby old shopping bag." Also, shoppers rarely examine the texture of a shoe. Rather, people look closely at how shoes are made or how they fit. (5) is wrong because the clerk does not help the woman with her decision.

Items 1 through 3 refer to the passage that follows. Choose the one best answer to each item.

### WHAT IS THIS MAN DOING?

The line rose slowly and steadily and then the surface of the ocean bulged ahead of the boat and the fish came out. He came out unendingly and water poured from his sides. He was bright in the sun and his head and back were dark pur-
(5) ple and in the sun the stripes on his sides showed wide and a light lavender. His sword was as long as a baseball bat and tapered like a rapier and he rose full length from the water and then re-entered it, smoothly, like a diver and the old man saw the great scythe-blade of his tail go under and the line
(10) commenced to race out.

"He is two feet longer than the skiff," the old man said. The line was going out fast but steadily and the fish was not panicked. The old man was trying with both hands to keep the line just inside of breaking strength. He knew that if he could
(15) not slow the fish with a steady pressure the fish could take out all the line and break it.

He is a great fish and I must convince him, he thought. I must never let him learn his strength nor what he could do if he made his run. If I were him I would put in everything now
(20) and go until something broke. But, thank God, they are not as intelligent as we who kill them; although they are more noble and more able.

1. The old man is trying to

    (1) race a whale
    (2) catch a fish
    (3) escape a shark
    (4) sail a ship
    (5) use a sword

2. The main action of the passage takes place

    (1) on the banks of a large river
    (2) on the shore of an island
    (3) on a boat in the ocean
    (4) under the water
    (5) on a dock

3. The animal is most likely a

    (1) shark
    (2) whale
    (3) striped bass
    (4) dolphin
    (5) swordfish

Answers are on page 319.

# Inferring the Narrative Point of View

## Prereading Prompt

Have you ever listened to friends talk about a baseball game they just played? One person, perhaps Amy, might comment, "It was fantastic!" while another, Joey, remarks, "Awful! The worst!" What accounts for these different points of view? You soon discover that Amy scored the winning home run, while Joey struck out three times. The way a story is told depends on the teller's point of view. Knowing how to find a story's point of view is very important for answering GED questions. You will learn how in this lesson.

## Key Words

**narrator**—the person telling the story. A narrator tells the story that the author has written, but is not the author.

**narrative point of view**—the point of view from which a story is told.

**third-person point of view**—the narrator is an observer and reporter of the events in the story and is not directly involved, saying *he* and *she* to tell what is taking place.

**first-person point of view**—the narrator tells the story and is directly involved in it, saying what "*I* did" and what "*I* said."

## Third-Person Point of View

Often in fiction, the story is told by the author as an all-knowing mind observing all the characters and events. In many works of fiction, however, the author tells the story through a single character's experience of the action. You may have to figure out who the narrator is and the point of view from which the story is told.

If the author completely takes the identity iof a character  and tells the story with the character's voice ("I went into the house to see her"), the story is told from a *first person point of view.*

If the author presents most of the action through one character's experience but also tells us things the character cannot know, the story is told from a **third person point of view**. In a third person point of view, the narrator refers to the main character as "he" or "she"—the third person pronouns, which give this type of narrative its name. This kind of narrator observes the story without being directly involved in them.  The third-person point of view enables the narrator to move beyond this main point of view character and tell us what other characters are doing and thinking. In the passage that follows from "The Good Deed" by Pearl S. Buck, the author reports the events as third person narrator.

> Mr. Pan was worried about his mother. He had been wor-
> ried about her when she was in China, and now he was wor-
> ried about her in New York, although he had thought that
> (5) once he got her out of his ancestral village in the province of
> Szechuen and safely away from the local bullies, who took
> over when the distant government fell, his anxieties would be
> ended. To this end he had risked his own life and paid out
> large sums of sound American money, and felt that day when
> (10) he saw her on the wharf, a tiny, dazed little old woman, in a
> lavender silk coat and black skirt, that now they would live
> happily together, he and his wife, their four small children
> and his beloved mother, in the huge safety of the American
> city.

From "The Good Deed," by Pearl S. Buck.  Reprinted by permission of Harold Ober Associates, Inc. Copyright ©1953 by Pearl S. Buck. Copyright renewed 1981.

## First-Person Point of View

Using this point of view makes the story more personal and direct because the narrator is directly involved in the story, referring to himself or herself as "I." Even though a first-person narrator cannot enter the minds of all the characters as a third-person narrator can, the narrator can still reveal a great deal about the characters by giving details about how they think and feel. The following excerpt from Mark Twain's novel *The Adventures of Huckleberry Finn* is narrated in the first-person point of view by Huck Finn himself. See what information Huck reveals about himself and his friends.

You don't know about me without you have read a book by the name of *The Adventures of Tom Sawyer* ; but that ain't no matter. That book was made by Mr. Mark Twain, and he told the truth, mainly. There was things which he stretched, but (5) mainly he told the truth. That is nothing. I never seen anybody but lied one time or another, without it was Aunt Polly, or the widow, or maybe Mary. Aunt Polly—Tom's Aunt Polly, she is—and Mary, and the Widow Douglas is all told about in that book, which is mostly a true book, with some stretchers, (10) as I said before.

Excerpt from *The Adventures of Huckleberry Finn* by Mark Twain.

On the Interpreting Literature and the Arts section of the GED test, you may be asked to infer the narrator of a piece of fiction. Below are some sample questions about the narrator. They are followed by a strategy you can use to help you find the answer.

## Model Questions and Strategy

- Who is telling the story?
- What is storyteller's point of view?
- Who tells about the action in this passage?

**Strategy:**

<u>Step 1:</u> Identify the topic of the passage. After you finish reading, ask yourself: What is the excerpt telling me about?

<u>Step 2:</u> Look for details that help you identify the narrator. Try to "hear" the narrator's voice as you read. What does the voice sound like? To whom does it belong?

<u>Step 3:</u> Look for clues that identify point of view. Ask yourself: Does the storyteller use the pronouns "he" and "she"? Does the storyteller report on what is happening and what is being said without directly taking part? If so, this story is told from the third-person point of view. If not, ask yourself: Does the storyteller refer to "I," "me," or "we"? Does the storyteller give his or her name? If so, this story is told from the first-person point of view.

<u>Step 4:</u> Decide from which point of view is told and look for the choice that best matches your decision. Then pick the best answer.

# Model Passage and Question

Read the following passage. See if you can identify the storyteller's point of view.

## WHO IS TELLING THIS STORY?

I was getting along fine with Mama, Papa-Daddy and Uncle Rondo until my sister Stella-Rondo just separated from her husband and came back home again. Mr. Whitaker! Of course I went with Mr. Whitaker first, when he first appeared (5) here in China Grove, taking "Pose Yourself" photos, and Stella-Rondo broke us up. Told him I was one-sided. Bigger on one side than the other, which is a deliberate, calculated falsehood: I'm the same. Stella-Rondo is exactly twelve months to the day younger than I am and for that reason (10) she's spoiled.

From "Why I Live at the P.O." by Eudora Welty, from *A Curtain of Green and Other Stories*, copyright ©1941, 1969 by Eudora Welty. Reprinted by permission of Harcourt Brace Jovanovich, Inc.

Who tells you about China Grove?

**(1)** Stella-Rondo

**(2)** Uncle Rondo

**(3)** Papa-Daddy

**(4)** an unnamed, third-person narrator

**(5)** Stella Rondo's older sister

The correct answer is (5). You can infer this from two details. In the first sentence, you learn that the narrator "was getting along fine with Mama, Papa-Daddy and Uncle Rondo until my sister Stella-Rondo just separated from her husband...." This tells you that the narrator is Stella-Rondo's sister. The last sentence tells you that "Stella-Rondo is exactly twelve months to the day younger than I am," so you know that the narrator is older than Stella-Rondo. (1), (2), and (3) are incorrect because these characters are being described by the narrator; they are not telling the story. (4) is incorrect because the narrator refers to herself as "I," so the story is told by a first-person narrator.

Items 1 through 3 refer to the passage that follows. Choose the one best answer to each item.

### WHAT ARE THESE PEOPLE ABOUT TO DO?

Mr. Graves opened the slip of paper and there was a general sigh through the crowd as he held it up and everyone could see that it was blank. Nancy and Bill, Jr., opened theirs at the same time, and both beamed and laughed, turning
(5) around to the crowd and holding their slips of paper above their heads.

"Tessie," Mr. Summers said. There was a pause, and then Mr. Summers looked at Bill Hutchinson, and Bill unfolded his paper and showed it. It was blank.

(10) "It's Tessie," Mr. Summers said, and his voice was hushed. "Show us her paper, Bill."

Bill Hutchinson went over to his wife and forced the slip of paper out of her hand. It had a black spot on it, the black spot Mr. Summers had made the night before with the heavy
(15) pencil in the coal-company office. Bill Hutchinson held it up, and there was a stir in the crowd.

"All right, folks," Mr. Summers said. "Let's finish quickly."

Although the villagers had forgotten the ritual and lost the original black box, they still remembered to use stones. The
(20) pile of stones the boys had made earlier was ready; there were stones on the ground with the blowing scraps of paper that had come out of the box. Mrs. Delacroix selected a stone so large she had to pick it up with both hands and turned to Mrs. Dunbar. "Come on," she said. "Hurry up."

(25) Mrs. Dunbar had small stones in both hands, and she said, gasping for breath, "I can't run at all. You'll have to go ahead and I'll catch up with you."

The children had stones already, and someone gave little Davy Hutchinson a few pebbles.

(30) Tessie Hutchinson was in the center of a cleared space by now, and she held her hands out desperately as the villagers moved in on her. "It isn't fair," she said. A stone hit her on the side of her head.

Old Man Warner was saying, "Come on, come on, every-
(35) one." Steve Adams was in the front of the crowd of villagers, with Mrs. Graves beside him.

"It isn't fair, it isn't right," Mrs. Hutchinson screamed, and then they were upon her.

1. Who tells about the action in the passage?

   (1) Mr. Graves
   (2) Mr. Summers
   (3) Mrs. Hutchinson
   (4) an unnamed first-person narrator
   (5) an unnamed outside observer

2. What statement best summarizes the action of the passage?

   (1) Villagers wait to see who has the marked paper and begin throwing stones at Tess.
   (2) Villagers crowd together as they collect rocks to make a clearing in the village.
   (3) Villagers watch as Mr. Graves holds up a blank paper, and Tessie holds back her marked one.
   (4) Villagers show each other their empty papers, and Mrs. Hutchinson proudly holds up her marked one.
   (5) Village boys make a pile of stones, and Mr. Summers makes a black spot on a slip of paper.

3. According to Mrs. Hutchinson, it "isn't fair" (lines 32 and 37) that

   (1) Steve Adams was in the front of the crowd of villagers next to Mrs. Graves
   (2) she had not been given a chance to collect stones with the boys earlier
   (3) Mr. Summers had put a black spot on a piece of paper the night before
   (4) she was going to be stoned for having the paper with the black spot
   (5) she was not allowed to take part in the ritual because she showed her paper last

Answers are on page 319.

# Inferring Character

## Prereading Prompt

If you see a man in a three-piece suit and highly polished shoes carrying a briefcase as he walks up to the courthouse, you might reasonably infer that he is a lawyer. If you overhear him saying, "I've worked on this case for no money. I believe the guy's innocent," you might infer that the lawyer is a principled, dedicated man. You have inferred certain things about this person by his dress, speech, and actions. In fiction, just as in real life, the personality of a character is revealed through speech, actions, thoughts, and feelings. You also get to know a character from what a third-person narrator and other characters say about him or her. Knowing how to infer details about characters is important in answering GED questions. You will learn how in this lesson.

## Key Words

**indirectly**—not stated

In Chapter 2, Lesson 3, you learned about direct characterization—direct description of a character by the narrator. In this lesson you will study indirect characterization—ways an author describes a character's personality by clues within the story. These clues include descriptions of the character's appearance, behavior, or background, what other characters say about the character, and how other characters react to the character. Below are two excerpts in which the authors reveal character traits indirectly. Read each passage carefully. Then see what conclusions you can draw about the personalities of characters and narrators based on the clues provided.

## HOW WOULD YOU DESCRIBE THE NARRATOR?

Please, God, let him telephone me now. Dear God, let him call me now. I won't ask anything else of You, truly I won't. It isn't very much to ask. It would be so little to You, God, such a little, little thing. Only let him telephone now. Please, God.
(5) Please, please, please.

"A Telephone Call" from *The Portable Dorothy Parker* by Dorothy Parker. Copyright ©1928, copyright renewed 1956 by Dorothy Parker. Used by permission of Viking Penguin, a division of Penguin Books USA, Inc.

From the narrator's actions, you can infer that she is a deeply dependent— almost desperate—person. You might also conclude that she believes in prayer.

### WHAT KIND OF PERSON IS FELD?

Feld was a little disappointed because he thought of accountants as bookkeepers and would have preferred "a higher profession." However, it was not long before he had
(5) investigated the subject and discovered that Certified Public Accountants were highly respected people, so he was thoroughly content as Saturday approached.

From "The First Seven Years," from *The Magic Barrel* by Bernard Malamud. Copyright ©1950. 1955, 1958 and renewed 1986 by Bernard Malamud. Reprinted by permission of Farrar, Straus & Giroux, Inc.

From the third-person narrator's descriptions of Feld's thoughts and actions, you can infer that Feld puts a great emphasis on appearance and what others think. He is not an independent thinker, so he accepts other people's views as his own.

## Inferring What Characters are Like

On the Interpreting Literature and the Arts section of the GED test, you may be asked to draw inferences about characters. Below are three sample questions.

• Which of the following best describes the narrator?

• From lines 00-00, which of the following can be inferred about the character?

• The character's actions in lines 00-00 show that she is _____ (descriptive words).

Here's a strategy you can use to collect clues for forming an impression of what a character or narrator is like.

### Strategy

<u>Step 1:</u> Ask yourself: How does the character look, speak, and act?

<u>Step 2:</u> Ask yourself: What do I know of the character's thoughts?

<u>Step 3:</u> Ask yourself: How do others react to the character?

<u>Step 4:</u> Put together all the descriptive details to form a mental picture of the character.

Read the following passage. Use the strategy you have just learned to find the answer to the question.

### HOW DOES THIS CHARACTER VIEW HIMSELF?

So we walk up Amsterdam Avenue to the Washington and *Gorilla, My Love* playin, they say, which suit me just fine, though the "my love" part kinda drag Big Brood some. As for Baby Jason, shoot, like Grandaddy say, he'd follow me into
(5) the fiery furnace if I say come on. So we go in and get three bags of Havmore potato chips which not only are the best potato chips but the best bags for blowin up and bustin real loud so the matron come trottin down the aisle with her chunky self, flashin that flashlight dead in your eye so you
(10) can give her some lip, and if she answer back and you already finish seein the show anyway, why than you just turn the place out. Which I love to do, no lie. With Baby Jason kickin at the seat in front, egging me on, and Big Brood mumblin bout what fiercesome things we goin to do. Which
(15) means me. Like when the big boys come up on us talkin bout Lemme a mickel. It's me that hide the money. Or when the bad boys in the park take Big Brood's Spaudeen way from him. It's me that jump on they back and fight a while. And it's me that turns out the show if the matron get too salty.

From *Gorilla, My Love* by Toni Cade Bambara,Copyright ©1960, 1963, 1964, 1965, 1970, 1972 by Toni Cade Bambara. Reprinted by permission of Random House, Inc.

What kind of person is the narrator?

**(1)** a romantic person who falls in love

**(2)** a wiseguy who gets into trouble

**(3)** a thief who steals money and brags about it

**(4)** a truant who skips school to go to the movies

**(5)** a moneylender who jokes rather than fights

The correct answer is (2). The first-person narrator tells the reader about the things that he does: "blowin up and bustin" potato chip bags during a movie, giving the matron "some lip," and disrupting the movie if the matron "get too salty." He also explains how he hides money and jumps and fights "bad boys in the park." All these details suggest an arrogant leader who makes trouble. (1) is incorrect because the narrator does not fall in love. On the contrary, he is annoyed about the "My Love" part of the movie at this stage of his life. (3) is wrong because the narrator does not steal money; rather, he hides money. Eliminate (4) because there are no details to suggest that the narrator skips school to go to the movies. (5) is wrong on two counts. First, the narrator hides money so that he will not have to lend it to the big boys. Second, he does indeed "fight a while."

Items 1 to 3 refer to the following passage. Choose the one best answer to each item.

### WHAT KIND OF WOMAN IS MRS. TONY ROBERTS?

Mrs. Tony Roberts is the pleading woman. She just loves to ask for things. Her husband gives her all he can take and scrape, which is considerably more than most wives get for their housekeeping, but she goes from door to door begging
(5) for things.

She starts at the store. "Mist' Clarke," she sing-songs in a high keening voice, "gimme lil' piece uh meat tuh boil a pot uh greens wid. Lawd knows me an' mah chillen is so hongry! Hits uh SHAME! Tony don't fee-ee-eee-ed me!"

(10) Mr. Clarke knows that she has money and that her larder is well stocked, for Tony Roberts is the best provider on his list. But her keening annoys him and he rises heavily. The pleader at his elbow shows all the joy of a starving man being seated at a feast.

(15) "Thass right Mist' Clarke. De Lawd loveth de cheerful giver. Gimme jes' a lil' piece 'bout dis big (indicating the width of her hand) an' de Lawd'll bless yuh."

She follows this angel-on-earth to his meat tub and super-intends the cutting, crying out in pain when he refuses to
(20) move the knife over just a teeny bit mo'.

Finally, meat in hand, she departs, remarking on the meanness of some people who give a piece of salt meat only two-fingers wide when they were plainly asked for a handwide piece. Clarke puts it down to Tony's account and resumes his
(25) reading. With the slab of salt pork as a foundation, she visits various homes until she has collected all she wants for the day. At the Piersons for instance: "Sister Pierson, plee-ee-ease gimme uh han'ful uh collard greens fuh me an' mah po' chillen! ...'Deed, me an' mah children is so hongry. Tony
(30) doan' fee-ee-eed me!"

Excerpt from *The Eatonville Anthology* by Zora Neale Hurston. Reprinted by permission of Zora M. Goins, Clifford Hurston, Winifred Hurston Clark, Edgar Hurston, Sr., Lucy Hurston Hogan and Barbara Hurston Lewis.

1. Which of the following best describes Mrs. Roberts?

   (1) solemn and religious
   (2) determined and conniving
   (3) meek and timid
   (4) cheerful and self-sufficient
   (5) carefree and honest

2. How does Mrs. Roberts feel about Mr. Clarke?

   (1) She feels that he is stingy.
   (2) She thinks that he is generous.
   (3) She feels that he is a cheerful giver.
   (4) She thinks that he is an angel on earth.
   (5) She thinks that he reads too much.

3. The word "keening" in line 7 means

   (1) complaining
   (2) happy
   (3) groaning
   (4) whispering
   (5) scraping

Answers are on page 320.

# Inferring Theme

## Prereading Prompt

Have you ever read about someone who tried to commit a crime, failed, and was then sentenced to many years in jail? If so, after having read the details, you may have commented, "Crime doesn't pay." These words gave your opinion about this social issue. You have different beliefs and opinions about various aspects of life.

Authors use characters and their struggles to communicate their own beliefs about life. Knowing how to find the theme, or underlying idea, of a story is very important in answering GED questions. You will learn how in this lesson.

## Key Words

**theme**—the main subject or idea expressed in fiction. It usually expresses a general statement about life.

## Inferring the Theme of a Passage

The main subject or most important idea in a work of fiction is called its **theme**. For example, the theme of one of your favorite novels might be *You can't keep a good person down* or *True love will endure*. Sometimes the author states the theme outright, but more often you will have to infer it from the details in the work. In previous lessons you learned how to infer the action, setting, and characterization in a story. These three elements help to create the theme. Looking for details about these elements of a work of fiction can help you infer the theme. Another way to infer the theme is to figure out the conflict, or struggle, in a story. This conflict can be internal (within a character) or external (between characters, between a character and nature, or between a character and society).

On the Interpreting Literature and the Arts section of the GED, you may be asked to infer the theme or themes of a passage. Below are several sample questions you might find on the exam:

- What message is implied by the passage?
- What is the author saying about _____ (bravery, love, etc.)?
- Which of the following themes is NOT implied by the passage?
- The passage indicates the author's belief that _____.
- What lesson or truth is the author trying to teach the reader?

### Strategy

<u>Step 1:</u> Identify the topic of the passage: What is it generally about?

<u>Step 2:</u> Identify the main idea of the passage. What is the author's main point about the topic?

<u>Step 3:</u> Look for clues to why the author has written this story, with this main point. Ask yourself: Has the character learned something or changed? A lesson learned or a change is often a clue to theme. Ask yourself: Are certain facts or words or descriptions repeated? Repetition is often a clue to theme. Ask yourself: Do any of the characters' comments seem striking for one reason or another? A character's comments can be a clue to the theme.

<u>Step 4:</u> Put together the clues and answer this question: What message or truth about people and their nature does the author want me to remember after I have finished reading this piece?

<u>Step 5:</u> Look at the answer choices in the GED question and choose the one that best matches the theme you have gathered.

Read the following passage. Use the strategy you have just learned to see if you can find the theme.

### HOW DOES THIS WOMAN VIEW LIFE?

She was two. Old enough for nursery school they said, and I did not know then what I know now—the fatigue of the long day, and the lacerations of group life in the kinds of nurseries that are only parking places for children.

(5)   Except that it would have made no difference if I had known. It was the only place there was. It was the only way we could be together, the only way I could hold a job.

From "I Stand Here Ironing," from *Tell Me A Riddle* by Tillie Olsen. Copyright ©1956, 1957, 1960, 1961 by Tillie Olsen. Used by permission of Delacorte Press/Seymour Lawrence, a division of Bantam Doubleday Dell Publishing Group, Inc.

What theme is implied by this passage?

**(1)** Sometimes ordinary people must make painful sacrifices for the sake of their families.

**(2)** Children should be in nursery school at age two because they need and enjoy living in a group.

**(3)** No nursery schools are good places for children because children suffer from being simply parked.

**(4)** Mothers should not work because their children will not be cared for in nursery school.

**(5)** Authorities state that a child who is two years of age is old enough to go to nursery school.

From the details that describe this woman's thoughts and feelings, you can infer that she feels badly about having to put her daughter in a nursery school. She did not realize "the fatigue of the long day" in nursery school or the "lacerations of group life in the kinds of nurseries that are only parking places for children." But she had no choice: "It was the only way we could be together, the only way I could hold a job." From these details, you can infer the theme is (1): Sometimes ordinary people must make painful sacrifices for the sake of their families. (2) is incorrect because the details show how badly the narrator feels about having put her daughter in nursery school at age two: the day was too long for the child and the narrator did not realize the "lacerations of group life in the kinds of nurseries that are only parking places for children." (3) is a poor choice because you cannot assume from the passage that *all* nursery schools are bad, only that this one is terrible because it is a "parking place" for children. (4) is wrong because the passage gives details about this *one* person who had to work for the sake of her family's survival, not about whether mothers should or should not work. (5) is incorrect because the passage states that "they"—experts or authorities—say two-year-olds are old enough for nursery school (line 1), but this is clearly only a detail, not the main idea.

### HOW CAN YOU SURVIVE IN FREEZING COLD?

When all was ready, the man reached in his pocket for a second piece of birch bark. He knew the bark was there, and, though he could not feel it with his fingers, he could hear its crisp rustling as he fumbled for it. Try as he would, he could
(5) not clutch hold of it. And all the time, in his consciousness, was the knowledge that each instant his feet were freezing. This thought tended to put him in a panic, but he fought against it and kept calm. He pulled on his mittens with his teeth, and threshed his arms back and forth, beating his
(10) hands with all his might against his sides. He did this sitting down, and he stood up to do it; and all the while the dog sat in the snow, its wolf brush of a tail curled around warmly over its forefeet, its sharp wolf ears pricked forward intently as it watched the man. And the man, as he beat and threshed
(15) his arms and his hands, felt a great surge of envy as he regarded the creature that was warm and secure in its natural covering.

"To Build a Fire" by Jack London.

1. The passage indicates the author's belief that

   **(1)** human being and animals are much alike
   **(2)** human beings are smarter than animals
   **(3)** animals are smarter than human beings
   **(4)** animals are better equipped to live in nature
   **(5)** human beings easily master natural difficulties

Item 3 refer to the passage that follows. Choose the best answer.

## HOW DO THESE MEN FEEL ABOUT THE GULLS?

Canton-flannel gulls flew near and far. Sometimes they sat down on the sea, near patches of brown seaweed that rolled over the waves with a movement like carpets on a line in a gale. The birds sat comfortably in groups, and they were
(5) envied by some in the dinghy, for the wrath of the sea was no more to them than it was to a covey of prairie chickens a thousand miles inland. Often they came very close and stared at the men with black, beadlike eyes. At these times they were uncanny and sinister in their unblinking scrutiny, and
(10) the men hooted angrily at them, telling them to be gone. One came, and evidently decided to alight on the top of the captain's head. The bird flew parallel to the boat, and did not circle, but made short sidelong jumps in the air in chicken fashion. His black eyes were wistfully fixed upon the captain's
(15) head. "Ugly brute," said the oiler to the bird. "You look as if you were made with a jackknife." The cook and the correspondent swore darkly at the creature. The captain naturally wished to knock it away with the end of the heavy painter, but he did not dare do it, because anything resembling an
(20) emphatic gesture would have capsized this freighted boat; and so, with his open hand, the captain gently and carefully waved the gull away. After it had been discouraged from the pursuit the captain breathed easier on account of his hair, and others breathed easier because the bird struck their
(25) minds at this time as being somehow gruesome and ominous.

From "The Open Boat" by Stephen Crane.

2. According to lines 7-10 and 22-25, the men in the boat regard the gulls as

   (1) a sign that some kind of help is on its way
   (2) an indication that the sea is getting calmer
   (3) a natural part of sea life, as chickens are part of a farm
   (4) an interesting change in their depressing situation
   (5) an indication that they might not survive their situation

3. The atmosphere of the passage is

   (1) calm
   (2) tense
   (3) hopeful
   (4) joyous
   (5) sad

Answers are on page 320.

# Inferring Figurative Language

## Prereading Prompt

Sometimes you say things that you don't expect to be taken literally, or word for word. For example, you might say, "I'm so hungry I could eat a bear," or "This fog is like pea soup." Expressions such as these create strong pictures in people's minds. Writers, too, use words to create mental pictures. They use figures of speech, or **figurative language**, to help create these mental images. Knowing how to go beyond the literal meaning of such language is very important for answering GED questions. You will learn how in this lesson.

## Key Words

**figurative language**—words and phrases used to express meanings other than the literal, or actual meaning

**simile**—a comparison, using the words *like* or *as*, of two unlike things, such as *your hands are like ice*

**metaphor**—a comparison of two unlike things without the words *like* or *as*, such as *your hands are ice cubes*

## Figurative Language

**Figurative language** are words and phrases that express a meaning other than their literal, or actual meaning. Authors use figurative language to express their ideas in vivid and imaginative ways which makes their writing fresh and exciting.

There are many different kinds of figurative language. Two of the most common are **similes** and **metaphors**. Both compare unlike things in order to make you look at these objects in new ways. Often, one object in the comparison is used to illuminate the other. A **simile** uses *like* or *as* to make comparisons, as in this example:

*His snores are like thunder.*

By comparing snoring to thunder, the writer emphasizes how loud the snores are. Here is a longer simile from John Updike's story, "The Slump." As you read, see how the simile makes you feel about baseball.

> And I'd go out and the stadium mumble would scoop at me
> and the grass seemed too precious to walk on, like emeralds,
> and by the time I got into the cage I couldn't remember if I
> batted left or right.

From "The Slump" from *Museums and Women* by John Updike. Copyright ©1972. Published by Random House.

In this example, the narrator compares a baseball field to emeralds, precious green jewels. The simile implies that baseball is so awe-inspiring that one feels almost overwhelmed by it.

A **metaphor** also makes comparisons, but without using *like* or *as*. Here is an example:

*John is a bull in a china shop.*

The meaning of the sentence must be inferred; it cannot be taken literally. The metaphor does not mean that John is running loose in a shop where china is sold. Instead, the metaphor implies that a person named John is clumsy. Here is a longer metaphor from Eudora Welty's story, "A Worn Path." As you read, see what picture the metaphor gives you about the woman and her style of walking.

> She was very old and small and she walked slowly in the
> dark pine shadows, moving a little from side to side in her
> steps, with the balanced heaviness and lightness of a pendu-
> lum in a grandfather clock.

Excerpt from "A Worn Path," by Eudora Welty. in *A Curtain of Green and Other Stories*. Copyright ©1941, renewed 1969 by Eudora Welty. Reprinted by permission of Harcourt Brace & Co.

In this metaphor, the author compares the woman's way of walking with the movement of a pendulum in a grandfather clock. The metaphor helps you picture the particular way this very old woman walks—swaying from side to side in a way that is heavy and light at the same time.

On the Interpreting Literature and Arts section of the GED test, you will sometimes be asked to interpret the meaning of figurative language. You will not be required to know the name of the figure of speech in the question. Here are some sample questions about figurative speech. They are followed by a strategy you can use to help you find the answer.

## Model Questions and Strategy

On the Interpreting Literature and the Arts section of the GED, you may be asked to infer the meaning of figurative language. Here are several sample questions you may find on the exam.

- What does the author suggest about _____ by comparing it with _____?
- Why does the speaker compare a _____ with a _____?
- What does the expression in line 00 mean?
- The phrase _____ is used to suggest _____?
- By comparing _____ (a person) with a _____ (object), the speaker is emphasizing which of the person's qualities?

Here is a strategy to use for finding the answers to such questions:

### Strategy:

<u>Step 1:</u> Identify the two things that are being compared.

<u>Step 2:</u> Figure out how the two things are alike. Ask yourself: What do these things have in common?

<u>Step 3:</u> Identify the person, place, object, or thing that is central to the comparison. Ask yourself: Which part of the comparison is most important? Why?

<u>Step 4:</u> In your own words, tell what the comparison stresses about the central object. Ask yourself: Why did the author make this comparison?

<u>Step 5:</u> Look at the answer choices and pick the one that best matches your statement.

# Practice

Read the following passage. Use the strategy you have just learned to figure out what the comparison means.

### WHAT MENTAL PICTURE DO YOU FORM OF THIS SCENE?

She followed the track, swaying through the quiet bare fields, through the little strings of trees silver in their dead leaves, past cabins silver from weather, with the doors and windows boarded shut, all like old women under a spell sit-
(5) ting there. "I walking in their sleep," she said, nodding her head vigorously.

Excerpt from "A Worn Path," by Eudora Welty. in *A Curtain of Green and Other Stories.* Copyright ©1941, renewed 1969 by Eudora Welty. Reprinted by permission of Harcourt Brace & Co.

In lines 3-5, the author compares the cabins to old women to suggest

   **(1)** that old women need to look after themselves
   **(2)** that the buildings are about to collapse
   **(3)** that old women are often in a trance
   **(4)** that the cabins are timeworn and still
   **(5)** that old women often sit remembering in the fields

The correct answer is (4). By comparing boarded up cabins to old women under a spell, the author emphasizes that the old cabins are closed and entirely still. (1) is incorrect because there is no suggestion that women should look after themselves, and (2) is incorrect because no detail suggests that the buildings are about to fall down or go to pieces. (3) is not correct because the comparison is made to emphasize something about the cabins, not about the women. Besides, there is no evidence that such trances are common, just that they are similar in stillness to boarded-up cabins. Similarly, (5) is incorrect because the speaker is suggesting something about cabins, not old women. Also, the speaker does not suggest anything about the behavior of old women in general.

Items 1 through 3 refer to the passage that follows. Choose the one best answer to each item.

## HOW DOES THIS LIFEGUARD FEEL ABOUT DEATH?

Here the cinema of life is run backwards. The old are the first to arrive. They are idle, and have lost the gift of sleep. Each of our bodies is a clock that loses time. Young as I am, I can hear in myself the protein acids ticking; I wake at odd
(5) hours and in the shuddering darkness and silence feel my death rushing towards me like an express train. The older we get, and the fewer the mornings left to us, the more deeply dawn stabs us awake. The old ladies wear wide straw hats and, in their hats' shadows, smiles as wide, which they
(10) bestow upon each other, upon salty shells they discover in the morning-smooth sand, and even upon me, downy-eyed from my night of dissipation. The gentlemen are often incongruous; withered white legs support brazen barrel chests, absurdly potent, bustling with white froth. How these old
(15) roosters preen on their 'condition'! With what fatuous expertness they swim in the icy water always, however, prudently parallel to the shore, at a depth no greater than their height.

From "Lifeguard," by John Updike, from *Pigeon Feathers and Other Stories*. Copyright ©1961 by John Updike. Reprinted by permission Alfred A. Knopf, Inc.

1. In line 3, the narrator compares "our bodies" to "clocks" that lose time to suggest that

   (1) people rise early in the summer
   (2) people sleep later as they grow older
   (3) protein acids are like odd hours
   (4) our days alive are numbered
   (5) life is endless

2. The phrase "like an express train" is used to suggest

   (1) comfort and ease
   (2) speed and inevitability
   (3) predictability and sameness
   (4) modern times
   (5) the difference between the beach and a city

3. The descriptive details of the passage indicate the author's belief that

   (1) old people waste their energy pretending to be happy and healthy
   (2) the beach is a good place for old people to go
   (3) how young you feel matters more than how old you are
   (4) time stops for no one regardless of how young you are
   (5) swimming builds the body and clears the mind

Answers are on page 321

# Applying Themes And Details

## Prereading Prompt

When you leave a movie theater, do you ever think about the events and wonder what you would have done in a similar situation? For example, you might have thought, "If I were that guy, I would have told my daughter about my past. It's better that she find out those things from me than from the CIA." An effective movie is one in which you become involved in the story and think about how the story ideas might be expanded. You might ask yourself what situation in your own life would be most like a situation in a novel you are reading. On the GED you may be asked to take information from a passage and use it in another situation. You will learn how in this lesson.

## Applying Ideas Found in Fiction

In Lessons 8 and 9 in Chapter 1, you learned about applying ideas from nonfiction pieces to new situations. You have probably already had experience asking your own application questions about fiction, too. For example, have you ever found yourself daydreaming about a novel, imagining what the main character would do or think if he or she had your job or your lover? To take attitudes which are responses to one situation and connect them with another situation is to *apply* them. Any time you stop to wonder, "But what if..." you are asking an application question. You are trying to predict how information would "transfer" to a different situation.

# Model Questions and Strategy

On the Interpreting Literature and the Arts section of the GED test, you may be asked to apply ideas from one situation in a work of fiction to a new situation. Here are some sample questions of this kind that you might find on the exam:

- Which of the following would the character be most/least likely to do?
- What do you think would most likely happen after the point at which the story ends?
- Which of the following situations is most similar to the one in the passage?
- Which of the following details about the character would the author be most likely to add?

In Chapter 1, you practiced answering test items by building a "bridge of ideas" between information in the nonfiction passage and information in the answer choices. Applying ideas from fiction requires a similar strategy. Follow these steps:

## Strategy

Step 1: Preview the question and figure out the topic.

Step 2: Brainstorm what you already know or can figure out about the topic. Ask yourself: What are the characters like? How do they act and think? What problems do they face? How are they likely to act?

Step 3: Examine the choices. Try to predict the answer. See if you can build a bridge of ideas between your knowledge of the characters and each of the choices. Ask yourself: Based on my mental picture of the characters, how would I imagine the character acting in a new situation?

Step 4: Choose the best answer. Ask yourself: Which bridge of ideas is the strongest and best balanced?

Read the following passage. Use the strategy above to apply what you learn about Laurie from the passage to a new situation dealing with the teacher.

### HOW HAS LAURIE CHANGED?

The day my son Laurie started kindergarten he renounced corduroy overalls with bibs and began wearing blue jeans with a belt; I watched him go off the first morning with the older girl next door, seeing clearly that an era of my life was (5) ended, my sweet-voiced nursery-school tot replaced by a long-trousered, swaggering character who forgot to stop at the corner and wave goodbye to me.

Excerpt from "Charles" from *The Lottery*. Copyright ©1948, 1949 by Shirley Jackson; copyright renewed 1976, 1977 by Laurence Hyman, Barry Hyman, Mrs. Sarah Weber, and Mrs. Joanne Schnurer, reprinted by permission of Farrar, Straus, and Giroux, Inc.

What would Laurie be most likely to do when the kindergarten teacher asks him his name?

**(1)** slump down in his seat with a shy expression

**(2)** answer his name with confidence

**(3)** run out of the room in terror

**(4)** start to cry with loud sobs

**(5)** answer playfully with someone else's name

The correct answer is (2). Think about how Laurie left home in the morning with confidence, without crying or even needing to wave goodbye to his mother. You can predict that he would act with confidence in the new situation as well. The strongest bridge of ideas connects your mental image of Laurie confidently striding off to school to him later confidently giving the teacher his name. Of course, people do not always behave consistently in different situations. However, remember that on the GED test, you must make the best guess that you can from the evidence in the passage.

It would seem uncharacteristic for Laurie to grow shy, run away in fear, or cry in one new situation (talking to the teacher) because he has not acted that way in another new situation (heading to school the first day). Therefore, you can eliminate (1), (3), and (4). Since there is no evidence that Laurie is a trickster, (5) is also unlikely.

# Lesson 9 Exercise

Items 1 through 3 refer to the passage that follows. Choose the one best answer to each item.

### HOW DO THE PARENTS REACT TO THE CHILDREN'S FIGHTING?

Nine times out of ten, Francis would be greeted with affection, but tonight the children are absorbed in their own antagonisms. Francis has not finished his sentence about the plane crash before Henry plants a kick in Louisa's behind.
(5) Louisa swings around, cursing. Francis makes the mistake of scolding Louisa for bad language before he punishes Henry. Now Louisa turns on her father and accuses him of favoritism. Henry is always right; she is persecuted and lonely; her lot is hopeless. Francis turns to his son, but the boy
(10) has justification for the kick—she hit him first; she hit him on the ear, which is dangerous. Louisa agrees with this passionately. She hit him on the ear, and she *meant* to hit him on the ear, because he messed up her china collection. Henry says that this is a lie. Little Toby turns away from the wood
(15) box to throw in some evidence for Louisa. Henry claps his hand over little Toby's mouth. Francis separates the two boys but accidentally pushes Toby in the wood box. Toby begins to cry. Louisa is already crying. Just then Julia Weed comes into part of the room where the table is laid. She is a pretty, intel-
(20) ligent woman, and the white in her hair is premature. She does not seem to notice the fracas. "Hello, darling," she says serenely to Francis. "Wash your hands, everyone. Dinner is ready." She strikes a match and lights the six candles in this vale of tears.

From "The Country Husband," by John Cheever, Copyright ©1954 by The New Yorker Magazine, Inc. Reprinted by permission of Alfred A. Knopf, Inc.

1. What would Julia be most likely to do if the children started to fight in a store?

   (1) yell at them publicly
   (2) spank them immediately
   (3) leave them with a quiet good-bye
   (4) ignore their arguing and continue shopping
   (5) take them home quietly and send them to bed without supper

2. Which scene most likely occurs the next time Francis comes home from work?

   (1) Louisa locks the door on her father and laughingly refuses to let him in.
   (2) Henry runs up to his father and plants a kick in Francis's behind.
   (3) Toby shakes his father's hand warmly and asks how his day was.
   (4) Louisa, Henry, and Toby hug their father and tell him their news all at once.
   (5) The children argue and fight while Julia calmly lights the candles.

3. The effect of Francis upon the children is most similar to the effect of

   (1) a clumsy bear falling on top of a hive of bees
   (2) a can of cat food upon hungry cats
   (3) a rock star upon a group of fans
   (4) a returning soldier upon the soldier's family
   (5) a prankster's false alarm upon the fire company

Answers are on page 321.

# Applying the Author's Attitude

## Prereading Prompt

Suppose a homeless person asks you for some money. You decide to keep walking and not pay any attention. Now imagine that the person continues to follow you, asking again and again for money. What do you do? One thing you might do is think about how someone you admire might have acted in a similar situation. For example, you might say to yourself, "What would Martin Luther King, Jr. or Eleanor Roosevelt, or even Bill Cosby, have done in such a situation?" Thinking about another's attitude and then applying it to a new situation is similar to what you may be asked to do on the GED. This lesson will show you how.

## Key Word

**attitude**—how a person thinks, acts, or feels about something

## Figuring Out the Author's Attitude

In Lessons 7 and 8 of Chapter 1, you learned how to figure out the opinion of a nonfiction author and how to apply that opinion to new situations. Fiction writers, too, inject their attitudes—their personal feelings and beliefs–into their writing. As with nonfiction, it is vital that you understand how authors feel about the characters and situations they create. Otherwise, you miss the point of the story.

Suppose you read about a young narrator with a love of adventure. The narrator also enjoys occasionally rebelling against authority. An application question might be: What kinds of books would the narrator most enjoy reading? You might guess that he would like adventure stories, especially those in which the main character defies the law. Stories about Robin Hood would probably be perfect for him.

Any time you stop to say, "I wonder what the author would say about…" you are asking an application question about the author's attitude. You are trying to predict how information would "transfer" into a new situation, just as you did in the last lesson on details and theme.

Below are several sample questions on applying the author's attitude that you could find on the Interpreting Literature and the Arts section of the GED test:

## Model Questions and Strategy

On the Interpreting Literature and the Arts section of the GED, you may be asked to apply the author's attitude to some new situation. Here are some sample questions you may find on the exam.

- What would the author probably think about _____ (topic)?
- Which of the following opinions would the author be most likely to express?
- Which of the following arguments would the author be most likely to defend?
- With which of the following statements would the author most likely agree?

### Strategy

The strategy for finding the answer to these types of questions is similar to the one you learned in Lesson 8 of Chapter 1:

<u>Step 1:</u> Preview the passage and questions. Notice that for this type of question, you cannot read the passage for an answer. You usually cannot predict the answer before looking at the choices, either.

<u>Step 2:</u> Summarize the main idea of the passage. Ask yourself: What is the author's opinion of the main idea? Remember that you are focusing on the author's opinions—not your own. Remember, too, that the author is NOT the narrator and the narrator's attitudes are not necessarily the author's.

<u>Step 3:</u> Think about the details that support the main idea. Ask yourself: What do these details suggest about the author's feelings and beliefs? What is the message or theme that the author wants to share with you?

<u>Step 4:</u> Examine each choice. Ask yourself: Where can I build the most complete bridge of ideas? To which choice can I transfer the most ideas from the passage?

# Practice

Read the following passage about a group of people working together in the Arctic. Use the four-step strategy to answer the question after it.

## WHAT MATTERS MOST TO THESE PEOPLE?

(5) Our camaraderie came from our enthusiasm for the work and from exhilaration with the landscape, the daily contact with sea birds, seals, and fish. We rarely voiced these things to each other; they surfaced in a word of encouragement or understanding around rough work done in unending dampness or cold. Our mutual regard was founded in the accomplishment of our tasks and was as important to our survival as the emergency gear stowed in a blue box forward of the steering console.

Excerpt from *Arctic Dreams*, by Barry Lopez. Copyright ©1986 by Barry Holstun Lopez. Reprinted by permission of Charles Scribners Sons, an imprint of Macmillian Publishing.

If the author wanted to describe similar feelings in a different setting, about which of the following would he most likely write?

**(1)** traveling on a spacecraft

**(2)** playing a game of singles tennis

**(3)** engaging in a boxing match

**(4)** acting in a play

**(5)** writing a novel

The correct answer is (1). The author expresses his feelings about the value of "shared enthusiasm for the work," as well as the importance of accomplishing tasks. Both of these are necessary, the author suggests, in order to feel camaraderie and respect for others, whose survival is linked to your own. Similarly, in space travel, your survival depends on how well you and your fellow fliers accomplish the necessary tasks. (2) and (3) are incorrect because in singles tennis and in boxing, players do not feel a sense of camaraderie with their opponents. Rather, each player acts alone in order to win and is not concerned with the survival of a team of people. (4) is also incorrect; although acting may produce a feeling of camaraderie among actors, this feeling does not come from having been in a life-and-death situation where crucial survival-related tasks were accomplished. (5), writing a novel, again, is a solitary pastime in which one person's feeling of respect for another does not come into play.

Items 1 through 3 refer to the passage that follows. Choose the one best answer to each item.

### WHAT VALUES ARE IMPORTANT TO THIS WOMAN?

"You ain' no reg'lar bag-toter, is you?"

"Ma'am?"

"You talk too good."

"Well, I only do this in vacationtime. I'm still in school."

(5)    "You is. What you aimin' to be?"

"I'm studying medicine."

"You is?" She beamed. "Aimin' to be a doctor, huh? Thank the Lord for that. That's what I always wanted my David to be. My granchile hyeh in New York. He's to meet me hyeh

(10) now."

"I bet you'll have a great time."

"Mussn't bet, child. That's sinful. I tole him 'fore he left home, I say, 'Son, you the only one o' the chillun what's got a chance to amount to sump'm. Don't th'ow it away. Be a

(15) preacher or a doctor. Work yo' way up and don' stop short. If the Lord don' see fit for you to doctor the soul, then doctor the body. If you don' get to be a reg'lar doctor, be a tooth-doctor. If you jes' can't make that, be a foot-doctor. And if you don't get that fur, be a undertaker. That's the least you must

(20) be. That ain' so bad. Keep you acquainted with the house of the Lord. Always mind the house o' the Lord—whatever you do, do like a church steeple: aim high and go straight.' "

"Did he get to be a doctor?"

"Don' b'lieve he did. Too late startin', I reckon. But he's

(25) done succeeded at sump'm. Mus' be at least a undertaker, 'cause he started sendin' the homefolks money, an' he come home las' year dressed like Judge Pettiford's boy what went off to school in Virginia. Wouldn't tell none of us 'zackly what he was doin', but he said he wouldn' never be happy till I

(30) come and see for myself. So hyeh I is." Something softened her voice. "His mammy died befo' he knowed her. But he was always sech a good child—" The something was apprehension. "Hope he *is* a undertaker."

From "Miss Cynthie," by Rudolph Fisher. Copyright ©1933 by the author.

1. If the author were to meet the grand-mother, which of the following opinions would he be most likely to express?

   (1) I dislike her because she is unedu-cated.
   (2) I mistrust her because she seems apprehensive.
   (3) I resent her because she asks too many questions.
   (4) I respect her because she seems friendly and caring.
   (5) I admire her because I share her beliefs.

2. Which of the following topics would the author be most likely to include in another discussion between the two characters?

   (1) politics
   (2) religion
   (3) marriage
   (4) travel
   (5) crime

3. Which of the following statements would the author be most likely to defend?

   (1) If you don't go to college, you'll never be successful.
   (2) If you want a good job, go to a big city.
   (3) Whichever career you choose, do the best you can at it.
   (4) Go into medicine–that's where the money is.
   (5) Choose a career that will let you see the world.

Answers are on page 322.

# Analyzing the Author's Purpose and Tone

## Prereading Prompt

If you've ever played on a sports team, you know that before an important game the coach brings all the players together and gives a pep talk. He or she tells you in a serious, maybe even dramatic, way how important it is for you to play your best. Her tone reflects her feelings about the game: She wants you to win–very badly. On the other days, the coach might have a lighter, more playful tone. She simply wants you to get out on the field and enjoy yourselves. To fit the purpose of the piece of writing, skillful authors, like successful coaches, can change their tone. On the GED you may be asked to answer questions about an author's purpose and tone. You will learn how in this lesson.

## Key Words

**tone**—a way of writing that shows the author's or character's attitude through a choice of words

**purpose**—in literature, the reason for writing, such as to inform, persuade, or entertain

## Analyzing the Author's Purpose and Tone

In Lesson 13 of Chapter 1, you studied the author's tone in nonfiction. You learned to recognize various tones, such as humorous, sarcastic, mournful, angry. You also learned how important it is to identify the tone of a piece of writing to understand fully what the author is saying.

Understanding the author's tone in a piece of fiction is just as important. As with nonfiction, the tone of a fictional piece can help you better understand the author's purpose in writing the piece. Is the story meant to entertain you? Or, is it designed to inform you about something or persuade you that a particular opinion is correct?

Read the following excerpt from Damon Runyon's short story "Blood Pressure." As you read, try to "hear" the tone and figure out the author's purpose.

> "A nervous man such as you with a blood pressure away up in the paint cards must live quietly," Doc Brennan says. "Ten bucks, please," he says.
>
> (5) Well, I am standing there thinking it is not going to be so tough to avoid excitement the way things are around this town right now, and wishing I have my ten bucks back to bet it on Sun Beau in the fourth race at Pimlico the next day, when all of a sudden I look up, and who is in front of me but Rusty Charley.

Excerpt from "Blood Pressure," by Damon Runyon. From *Guys and Dolls* by Damon Runyon. Copyright ©1932, by Damon Runyon. By permission of Sheldon Abend, American Play Service, New York.

Informal words such as "Doc" and "bucks" help create the informal tone. The doctor's casual attitude and the character's desire to bet the money he paid the doctor on the horses add humor. This informal, humorous tone tells you that the author's purpose is to entertain.

# Model Questions and Strategy

On the Interpreting Literature and Arts section of the GED test, you may be asked to analyze the author's purpose and tone. In previous lessons in analysis, you learned that all analysis items require you to think about the relationship of author, reader, and writing. To answer these items, you look carefully at how authors express themselves and their reasons for writing. Here are several possible questions about purpose and tone in fiction that could appear on the GED.

- Which of the following best describes the author's tone in this passage?
- Which of the following best describes the author's purpose in telling this story?
- Which of the following details contributes to the _____ (tone) of this passage?
- How is the tone at the end of the passage different from the tone at the beginning?

## Strategy

Here is a strategy you can use to find the answer to these types of questions:

Step 1: Ask yourself about the writer. What does the writer's choice of particular words and details reveal about the writer's attitude? What is the author's purpose in describing the character's problem: To entertain? to inform? to describe? to persuade?

Step 2: Ask yourself about the speaker: As I "listen" to the speaker, what tone of voice do I imagine? Does that tone change?

Step 3: Put your impressions about all these things together with the test question into a statement about the tone and purpose of the piece.

Step 4: Look at the answer choices in the GED question and choose the one that best matches your statement.

# Practice

Look at the passage below. Use the strategy to find the purpose and tone of the piece.

### WHY DOES THIS WOMAN FEEL AS SHE DOES?

Well, she could just hear Cornelia telling her husband that Mother was getting a little childish and they'd have to humor her. The things that most annoyed her was that Cornelia thought she was deaf, dumb, and blind. Little hasty glances
(5) and tiny gestures tossed around her and over her head saying, "Don't cross her, let her have her way, she's eighty years old," and she sitting there as if she lived in a thin glass cage. Sometimes Granny almost made up her mind to pack up and move back to her own house where nobody could remind her
(10) every minute that she was old. Wait, wait, Cornelia, till your own children whisper behind your back!

From "The Jilting of Granny Weatherall," by Katherine Ann Porter in *Flowering Judas and Other Stories*. Copyright ©1930 and renewed 1958 by Katherine Anne Porter. Reprinted by permission of Harcourt, Brace and Co.

What is the purpose and tone of the passage?

**(1)** The purpose is to show the meanness of Cornelia; the tone is sarcastic.

**(2)** The purpose is to show how little very old people understand; the tone is mocking.

**(3)** The purpose is to show a woman's feelings about being old; the tone is angry.

**(4)** The purpose is to show a woman's feelings about her daughter's husband; the tone is regretful.

**(5)** The purpose is to show how children don't understand their parents; the tone is humorous.

The correct answer is (3). The old woman shows her feelings about being old. She is angry, as is shown by her thinking about packing up and leaving, her reaction to Cornelia treating her as if she were "deaf, dumb, and blind", and especially by the last sentence. (1) is incorrect; although the old woman feels that Cornelia is mean, the main focus of the passage is on how the woman feels about being old. The tone is not sarcastic, since the old woman states exactly how she feels. (2) is incorrect because the woman obviously understands everything going on around her. Although she might feel that her daughter is making fun of *her*, the tone is angry, not mocking. (4) is wrong because the old woman simply mentions her daughter's husband once in connection with what the daughter says to him, not to show how she feels toward him. The old woman does not feel regretful because she is not feeling sad about something she has done in the past; her feeling is anger at her daughter. Even though this passage shows this woman feels she is not understood by her daughter, (5) is not correct because the old woman only uses the word "humor" to describe how her daughter and daughter's husband treat her: That is, they pretend to agree with her while really believing she is "a little childish" (line 2). There is nothing humorous in the tone of the passage.

Items 1 through 3 refer to the passage that follows. Choose the one best answer to each item.

## WHY DOES THE ENGINEER FEEL AS HE DOES?

Every day for more than twenty years, as the train approached this house, the engineer had blown on the whistle, and every day, as soon as she heard this signal, a woman had appeared on the back porch of the little house and waved to
(5) him. At first she had a small child clinging to her skirts, and now this child had grown to full womanhood, and every day she, too, came with her mother to the porch and waved....

He felt for them and for the little house in which they lived such tenderness as a man might feel for his own children,
(10) and at length the picture of their lives was carved so sharply in his heart that he felt that he knew their lives completely, to every hour and moment of the day, and he resolved that one day, when his years of service should be ended, he would go and find these people and speak at least with them whose
(15) lives had been so wrought into his own.

That day came. At last the engineer stepped from a train onto the station platform of the town where these two women lived. His years upon the rail had ended. He was a pensioned servant of his company, with no more work to do. The engi-
(20) neer walked slowly through the station and out into the streets of the town. Everything was as strange to him as if he had never seen this town before. As he walked on, his sense of bewilderment and confusion grew. Could this be the town where he had passed ten thousand times? Were these the
(25) same houses he had seen so often from the high windows of his cab? It was all as unfamiliar, as disquieting as a city in a dream, and the perplexity of his spirit increased as he went on....

And instantly, with a sense of bitter loss and grief, he was
(30) sorry he had come. He knew at once that the woman who stood there looking at him with a mistrustful eye was the same woman who had waved to him so many thousand times. But her face was harsh and pinched and meager; the flesh sagged wearily in sallow folds, and the small eyes peered
(35) at him with timid suspicion and uneasy doubt. All the brave freedom, the warmth, and the affection that he had read into her gesture vanished in the moment that he saw her and heard her unfriendly tongue....His heart, which had been brave and confident when he looked along the familiar vista
(40) of the rails, was now sick with doubt and horror....

From "The Far and the Near" by Thomas Wolfe from *Death to Morning*. Copyright ©1935 by International Magazines Co., Inc. renewed 1963 by Paul Gitlin. Reprinted by permission of Charles Scribners Sons, an imprint of Macmillian Publishing Company.

1. The tone of the second paragraph is

   (1) humorous and witty
   (2) fearful and gloomy
   (3) rude and angry
   (4) sympathetic and hopeful
   (5) sarcastic and bitter

2. The tone of the last paragraph is

   (1) mistrustful
   (2) humorous
   (3) sad
   (4) angry
   (5) sarcastic

3. The purpose of the passage is to

   (1) describe a town and its people
   (2) inform us about a railroad engineer's work
   (3) entertain with stories about travel
   (4) describe a person's changing emotions
   (5) persuade readers to value past experiences

Answers are on page 322.

# Analyzing Style

## Prereading Prompt

Ask four people to dance to the same music, and each does it a different way. Invite four friends to a party, and each will make his or her entrance differently. Tell two basketball players to take a shot, and one might do it with grace and ease while the other does it awkwardly and with difficulty. Everyone has a unique sense of style. Authors, too, have their own personal writing styles. On the GED you may be asked to answer questions about an author's style. You will learn how in this lesson.

## Key Words

**style**—the particular way a writer expresses himself or herself

## Analyzing an Author's Style

Since style is an author's characteristic way of writing, different authors have different writing styles. Some writers use many descriptive words and details, while others use few. Some writers use long, complex sentences, while others use short, simple sentences. Some writers use a lot of figurative language, while others do not. In short, style is the way in which the author's expression of an idea reflects his or her personality. Compare these two examples.

In the falling quiet there was no sky or earth, only snow lifting in the wind, frosting the window glass, chilling the rooms, deadening and hushing the city.

Excerpt from *Miriam* by Truman Capote. Copyright by Truman Capote. Reprinted by permission of Random House, Inc.

These Seven Commandments would now be inscribed on the wall; they would form an unalterable law by which all the animals on Animal Farm must live forever.

Excerpt from Animal Farm  by George Orwell.

The two examples are approximately the same length. Notice, however, the difference in their style. The first example includes many descriptive words and phrases such as "falling quiet," "frosting the window glass," "deadening and hushing the city." The second example, in contrast, has only two descriptive words: "seven" and "unalterable." The author of the first passage also used many more details and implied comparisons. In addition, there are four commas separating ideas in the first passage. The author of the second passage, in contrast, did not use any commas. Rather, he joined two complete sentences with a semicolon. The style of the first sentence seems to appeal to the imagination; the second, to the intellect.

## Model Questions and Strategy

On the Interpreting Literature and the Arts section of the GED, you may be asked questions about an  author's style. Here are some sample questions you may find on the exam.

- Which of the following best describes the author's style?
- Why is the opening/closing sentence particularly effective?
- What is the effect of using _____ (a certain detail) in line 00.
- What is the effect of ending the passage with such a short/long sentence?
- What effect is created by beginning the first three sentences with the word _____?

### Strategy:

Step 1: Preview the questions, noticing any that ask about style. Then read the passage for content.

Step 2: As you read the passage, ask yourself: How does this style go with the content of the passage? That is: What is the effect of this style on the meaning of the passage? For example, how does it help create a mood that goes with the action , or give you a clearer image of the action, of the main character, or of the narrator?

Step 3: Look at the answer choices in the question about style. Ask yourself: How does my idea of the author's style explain the effect the question asks about?

Step 4: Choose the best answer—the answer choice that best describes the effect  the question asks about.

NOTE: The question may ask about a particular part of the passage. If you feel you don't remember this part well enough, quickly check back to the lines mentioned and then choose the best answer.

## Practice

Read the following passage. Use the strategy above to answer the question.

### HOW DOES THE NARRATOR REALLY FEEL?

True!–nervous–very, very dreadfully nervous I had been and am; but why *will* you say that I am mad? The disease had sharpened my senses—not destroyed—not dulled them. (5) Above all was the sense of hearing acute. I heard all things in the heaven and in the earth. I heard many things in hell. How, then, am I mad? Hearken! and observe how healthily— how calmly I can tell you the whole story.

Excerpt from "The Tell-Tale Heart," by Edgar Allan Poe.

How does the style reveal the narrator's state of mind?

**(1)** Long sentences with figurative language reveal a happy narrator.

**(2)** Long, repetitious sentences reveal a bored narrator.

**(3)** Short, jerky sentences reveal a jittery narrator.

**(4)** Complex sentences reveal a tired narrator.

**(5)** Highly descriptive sentences reveal a calm narrator.

The style of the passage–short, jerky sentences–indicates that the narrator feels jittery or nervous. The correct answer, then, is (3). (1) is not correct because there are not many long sentences, there is no use of figurative language, and the narrator does not seem happy at all. (2) is incorrect because the narrator seems extremely excited, not bored, as indicated by the exclamation points, the many dashes, and the short sentences. (4) is incorrect because most of the sentences are simple, not complex, and the narrator seems amazingly alert, not tired at all. (5) is incorrect because the narrator is not speaking "calmly" at all, despite his claim in the last line. The sentences are straightforward and not highly descriptive. Suppose the writer had used long, smooth sentences without interruptions, repetitions, questions, and exclamations. In that case, you might conclude that the speaker really *was* as calm as he says.

# Lesson 12 Exercise

Items 1 through 3 refer to the passage that follows. Choose the one best answer to each item.

## WHAT KIND OF PERSON IS THIS NARRATOR?

I don't have much work to do around the house like some girls. My mother does that. And I don't have to earn my pocket money by hustling; George runs errands for the big boys and sells Christmas cards. And anything else that's got to get
(5) done, my father does. All I have to do in life is mind my brother Raymond, which is enough.

Sometimes I slip and say my little brother Raymond. But as any fool can see he's much bigger and he's older, too. But a lot of people call him my little brother cause he needs looking
(10) after cause he's not quite right. And a lot of smart mouths got lots to say about that, too, especially when George was minding him. But now, if anybody has anything to say to Raymond, anything to say about his big head, they have to come by me. And I don't play the dozens or believe in stand-
(15) ing around with somebody in my face doing a lot of talking. I much rather just knock you down and take my chances even if I am a little girl with skinny arms and a squeaky voice, which is how I got the name Squeaky. And if things get too rough, I run. And as anybody can tell you, I'm the fastest
(20) thing on two feet.

There is no track meet that I don't want to win the first-place medal. I used to win the 20-yard dash when I was a little kid in kindergarten. Nowadays, it's the 50-yard dash. And tomorrow I'm subject to run the quarter-meter relay all by
(25) myself and come in first, second, and third. The big kids call me Mercury cause I'm the swiftest thing in the neighborhood. Everybody knows that—except two people who know better, my father and me. He can beat me to Amsterdam Avenue with me having a two fire-hydrant headstart and him running
(30) with his hands in his pockets and whistling. But that's private information. Cause can you imagine some 35-year-old man stuffing himself into PAL shorts to race little kids? So as far as everyone's concerned, I'm the fastest and that goes for Gretchen, too, who has put out the tale that she is going to
(35) win the first-place medal this year. Ridiculous. In the second place, she's got short legs. In the third place, she's got freckles. In the first place, no one can beat me and that's all there is to it.

1. The author uses informal language to

   (1) show that the race is important to the narrator
   (2) reveal the narrator to the audience in her own words
   (3) reveal that the narrator is confused
   (4) inform us about the life of an athlete
   (5) make us feel sympathy for the narrator's weakness

2. The last sentence is an effective way to end the excerpt because it

   (1) creates suspense about when the race will be
   (2) makes makes the reader wonder about the meaning of the passage
   (3) provides a startlingly new image of the narrator
   (4) sums up the narrator's feelings about herself
   (5) shows the narrator is basically insecure

3. The narrator's language reveals that she is

   (1) self-confident and boastful
   (2) rude and disrespectful
   (3) polite and shy
   (4) angry and bitter
   (5) snobbish and deceitful

Answers are on page 322.

# Analyzing Structure

## Prereading Prompt

If you were explaining to a friend how to bake an apple pie, you would probably tell him what to do first, next, and so on. If, on the other hand, you were trying to explain what an apple pandowdy is, you might compare it to an apple pie, pointing out similarities and differences. Authors, too, choose the most effective way of presenting their ideas. They choose the structure that they feel will help make their message clearest. On the GED you may be asked to answer questions about the structure of a piece of writing. You will learn how in this lesson.

## Key Word

**structure**—the way a piece of writing is organized

## What is Structure?

Like a speaker, a writer has to decide which ideas to present first, which to put last, and which to place in the middle. As you saw in Lessons 11 and 12 in the Nonfiction section of this book, there are several different ways to organize a piece of writing. Three of these are: organization by time (chronological); organization by cause and effect; and organization by comparison and contrast. Authors choose the **structure**, or way of arranging ideas, that they feel will help make their message clearest. In other words, the structure they choose depends on their purpose in writing.

## Chronological Order

### WHY IS MRS. TAYLOR AWAKE SO EARLY?

Mrs. Taylor got out of bed at five o'clock that morning. This was an hour ahead of her usual time. She moved around her attic room quietly, making herself her morning cup of tea on the hot plate. She dressed so as not to disturb her landlady,
(5) Mrs. Connell, on the floor below.

After she had drunk her tea and eaten a slice of toast, she washed her cup and saucer in some water she had gotten from the bathroom the evening before. She then put them away on her "kitchen" shelf in the clothes closet. She tiptoed
(10) down the steep stairs to the bathroom and washed her face and hands.

When she returned to her room, her 76-year-old face shone with the excitement of the day.

From "A Trip for Mrs. Taylor," by Hugh Garner, from *Hugh Garner's Best Stories*. Copyright ©1963 by Hugh Garner. By permission of McGraw-Hill Ryerson Ltd., Canada.

The author describes the details in chronological order to dramatize the fact that Mrs Taylor does everything in strict order. In this way, the structure serves another purpose—revealing Mrs. Taylor's personality. We see that she likes routine, order, and neatness. If the writer had used a different structure, his purpose—to tell a story about an orderly woman—would not have been served as well.

## Cause and Effect

### WHY IS THIS MAN UPSET?

I was lecturing recently, and one of my stops was Flagstaff, Arizona, which is about 7,000 miles above sea level.

As soon as I got out of the plane, I smelled something peculiar.

(5) "What's that smell?" I asked the man who met me at the plane.

"I don't smell anything," he replied.

"There's a definite odor that I'm not familiar with," I said.

"Oh, you must be talking about the fresh air. A lot of people
(10) come out here who have never smelled fresh air before."

"What's it supposed to do?" I asked suspiciously.

"Nothing. You just breathe it like any other kind of air. It's supposed to be good for your lungs."

"I've heard that story before." I said. "How come if it's air,
(15) my eyes aren't watering?"

"Your eyes don't water with fresh air. That's the advantage of it. Saves you a lot in paper tissues."

I looked around and everything appeared crystal clear. It was a strange sensation and made me feel very uncomfortable.

Because the air is not polluted, the narrator thinks it smells "peculiar"; because his eyes are not watering, he thinks it might not even be air. The narrator's belief that air is always polluted makes the effects of clean air seem unnatural to him. In this way, the author organizes the narrator's thoughts according to a cause-and-effect relationship that is illogical, in order to make a humorous comment about the way people have become accustomed to pollution.

## Comparison and Contrast

### HOW DOES EILEEN FEEL ABOUT THE DOG AND HER FATHER?

She came out the side door, with the dog tugging at his leash. The worn leather grip jerked her hand and she said in a hushed, embarrassed voice: "Stop that, you know better! 
(5) Stop that!" The dog was vain and partly bald. She never thought of him as an animal, but as an extension of her father, whose dog he was. Indeed, the dog resembled his master. Both had vague mottled skin, liverish and brown as if camouflaged, and their eyes were watery with alertness. It 
(10) seemed to Eileen that their ears, though of different shapes and colors, had in common an unclear, intangible quality of *intensity*—they both heard everything, heard whispers not meant for their ears and words not spoken aloud, heard even the echoes of words that should have faded away.

The author compares and contrasts the dog and Eileen's father, showing how they are the same and different from each other. The similarities are all negative features, such as: "Both had vague mottled skin, liverish and brown as if camouflaged, and their eyes were watery with alertness." This comparison/contrast structure helps the author achieve her purpose: to show how negatively Eileen feels about both the man and the dog.

# Model Questions and Strategy

On the Interpreting Literature and the Arts section of the GED, you may be asked questions about the structure of passages. Here are some sample questions you may find on the exam.

- How are the details in this passage organized?
- The details in this passage are arranged to show _____?
- Which of the following best describes the ways most of the details in this passage are organized?
- What does the arrangement of ideas in this passage indicate about the author's purpose (or opinion)?
- Which of the following best explains the effect of putting the details about _____ and _____ side-by-side?
- Which of the following best explains why the author chose to put the detail about _____ at the end of the passage rather than at the beginning?

In Lessons 11 and 12 of Chapter 1 you learned about words nonfiction authors commonly use when connecting ideas within different structures. Fiction authors use the same signal words when arranging their ideas. Therefore, you may want to review these lessons to refresh your memory about words that signal chronological order, organization by cause and effect, and organization by order of importance.

## Strategy

Here is a strategy you can use to answer questions about structure, after previewing those questions:

Step 1: Summarize the passage in your own words to identify its topic.

Step 2: Identify the structure of the passage.

Step 3: Identify the author's purpose. Ask yourself: Why did the author place the details in this order and not in another order? How does this arrangement help make the meaning clear? How does this arrangement suit the author's purpose?

Step 4: Predict the answer to the test question.

Step 5: Compare your prediction to the answer choices and choose the answer that best matches your prediction.

# Practice

Read the following passage. Use the strategy to answer the question about the structure of the passage.

## WHAT IS HAPPENING HERE?

He pulled on high leather boots and put on heavy gloves. He stuffed the spaces between pants and boots, gloves and arms, shirt and neck, with gasoline-soaked rags. With close-fitting goggles, he shielded his eyes. Finally, he plugged his
(5) nose and ears with cotton. The men poured gasoline over his clothes.

An old Indian came up to him. He had, he said, a salve with an odor that kept ants away. He smeared the boss's boots and gloves and face with the ointment. Then he gave
(10) him a gourd full of a bitter medicine–"For their poison," he said. Leiningen drank it down.

With a bound, he leaped over the trench. He was among the ants.

Behind him, the ring of flame blazed high again. Leiningen
(15) ran. He *must* get through.

Not until he reached the halfway point did he feel ants under his clothes. He struck at them, scarcely conscious of their bites. He reached the dam. The wheel was thick with ants. They flowed over his hands, arms, and shoulders.
(20) Before he had turned the wheel once, the swarm had covered his face. Straining madly, he turned and turned.

From "Leiningen Versus the Ants" by Carl Stephenson. Reprinted by permission of Ann Elmo Agency Inc.

How does the arrangement of ideas reveal the author's purpose?

**(1)** By stating the cause for the invasion of the ants, the author gives important information about the effects of these insects.

**(2)** By giving details in chronological order, the author builds suspense.

**(3)** By comparing the old Indian and Leiningen, the author shows how different the two leaders are from each other.

**(4)** By giving details in chronological order, the author shows how Leiningen and others can save themselves in times of crisis.

**(5)** By showing the cause for the Indian's aid, the author shows the value of the Indian's medicine.

The correct answer is (2). The author's purpose is to tell a suspenseful story.

By putting the details in chronological order, he builds suspense. Each detail makes the reader want to read on and find out what happens next. As Leiningen smears on the salve—will the ointment keep the ants away? As he starts running among the ants—will Leiningen make it to wherever he is going? As he gets to the wheel and the ants attack—will he survive? (1), (3), (4), and (5) are all incorrect because they misstate the author's purpose. The author's main reason for writing the story is not to give important information about ants (1), to show the differences between the men (3), to give general instruction on coping during disasters (4), or to convince you that Indian medicine is valuable (5). Furthermore, (1), (3), and (5) are incorrect because they contain false statements about the content and arrangement of ideas in the passage. (1) is incorrect because the details do not reveal the cause of the ants' invasion, nor do they give any valuable information about these insects. (3) is incorrect because the author does not compare the Indian and Leiningen. (5) is incorrect because the author does not give the cause for the Indian's help, nor does the author make a statement about the value of Indian medicine.

Items 1 to 3 refer to the following passage. Choose the one best answer to each item.

## WHY IS THIS WOMAN UPSET?

During dinner she slipped into a moody depression which gave Dexter a feeling of uneasiness. Whatever petulance she uttered in her throaty voice worried him. Whatever she smiled at—at him, at a chicken liver, at nothing—it disturbed him that her smile could have no root in mirth, or even in amuse-
(5) ment. When the scarlet corners of her lips curved down, it was less a smile than an invitation to a kiss.

Then, after dinner, she led him out on the dark sun-porch and deliberately changed the atmosphere.

"Do you mind if I weep a little?" she asked.
(10) "I'm afraid I'm boring you," he responded quickly.

"You're not. I like you. But I've just had a terrible afternoon. There was a man I cared about, and this afternoon he told me out of a clear sky that he was poor as a church-mouse. He'd never even hinted before. Does this sound horri-
(15) bly mundane [ordinary]?"

"Perhaps he was afraid to tell you."

"Suppose he was," she answered. "He didn't start right. You see, if I'd thought of him as poor—well, I've been mad about loads of poor men, and fully intended to marry them all. But
(20) in this case, I hadn't thought of him that way, and my interest in him wasn't strong enough to survive the shock. As if a girl calmly informed her fiance that she was a widow. He might not object to widows, but—"

"Let's start right," she interrupted herself suddenly. "Who
(25) are you anyhow?"

For a moment Dexter hesitated. Then:

"I'm nobody," he announced. "My career is largely a matter of futures."

"No," he said frankly. "I'm probably making more money
(30) than any man my age in the Northwest. I know that's an obnoxious remark, but you advised me to start right."

From "Winter Dreams" by F. Scott Fitzgerald from *All the Sad Young Men*. Copyright © 1922 by Metropolitan Publishing, renewed 1950 by Frances Scott Fitzgerald Lanahan. Reprinted with permission of Charles Scribner's Sons, an imprint of Macmillan Publishing Co.

1. The author lists the things the woman smiled at in a series (lines 3-4) to emphasize the fact that she

   (1) is having a nervous breakdown
   (2) is not amused but angry at the narrator
   (3) is not amused but sad about something
   (4) is letting the narrator know she thinks he is "a nobody"
   (5) is a widow who is nervous about new relationships

2. The narrator's description of himself in lines 28-32 contrasts with the man the woman describes in lines 13-15 in which of the following ways?

   (1) The narrator is rich and calls himself "a nobody" while the other man was poor and made the woman think he was not.
   (2) The narrator is dishonest and the other man was honest.
   (3) The other man disappointed the woman and the narrator makes her happy.
   (4) The other man was young and poor and the narrator is old and rich.
   (5) The other man could not "survive the shock" of the woman rejecting him; the narrator is surviving the shock.

3. In lines 28-32, the narrator contradicts himself. The best explanation for this behavior is which of the following?

   (1) He wants "to start right" but does not want to boast about his wealth.
   (2) He wants to get away from the woman but be polite about it.
   (3) He wants "to start right" by impressing her even if he has to tell a lie.
   (4) He tells her a lie about his age but then tells her his true age.
   (5) He tells her his career has no future but then admits it does.

Answers are on page 323.

# Analyzing Characters and Action

## Prereading Prompt

Suppose you have an after-school job and your boss tells you that you are fired. What might you do—scream? punch the wall? cry? go home and clean your house? go on a buying spree? sleep? Different people react to the same situation in different ways. A shy, quiet person, for example, might not even ask the boss for an explanation. Instead, he or she might simply go to sleep after hearing the bad news. An angry person might scream at the boss or get into a fight later in the day. Just as real people react to situations in certain, often predictable, ways, so do fictional characters. Authors try to create characters who say and do things that real people might do, given a similar set of circumstances and similar personality traits. On the GED you may be asked to analyze why a character says or does what he or she did. You will find out how in this lesson.

## Analyzing Characters and Action

To analyze characters and figure out why they act as they do, you need to pay attention to how they get along with other characters. In the brief passage below, a character named Della sells her hair. As you read, ask yourself: Why would Della take such an action? How must she feel about Jim?

## WHY DID DELLA SELL HER HAIR?

"Jim, darling," she cried, "don't look at me that way. I had my hair cut off and sold it because I couldn't have lived through Christmas without giving you a present. It'll grow out again—you won't mind, will you? I just had to do it. My hair (5) grows awfully fast. Say 'Merry Christmas!' Jim, and let's be happy. You don't know what a nice—what a beautiful, nice gift I've got for you."

From "The Gift of the Magi," by O. Henry.

Della sold her hair in order to get enough money to buy Jim a present. From the details, you can infer the characters' relationship: Della is in love with Jim. She believes in showing her love by giving him a special present at Christmas. Another person might not have done what Della did. She might not have felt that giving a special gift at Christmas is as important as, say, spending a quiet evening together watching a favorite movie.

## Model Questions and Strategy

On the Interpreting Literature and Arts section of the GED test, you may be asked to analyze why a character takes a certain action. Below are several sample questions about characters and their actions that you can be asked on the GED. These questions are followed by a strategy you can use to help you answer these test items.

• Why does the character do (feel, say) what he (or she) does?

• What can you tell about the character's personality from his (or her) actions?

• What does the character's reaction show you about his (or her) relationship with another character?

### Strategy

Step 1: Summarize the passage in your own words.

Step 2: Identify the character's main traits. Ask yourself: What are the characters like? Look closely at the details about speech, dress, thought, and action in the passage. What do these details tell you about the characters? From this information, form a mental picture of each character.

Step 3: Figure out the relationships between the characters. Note the words and gestures that the characters exchange: This will help you analyze their relationships.

Step 4: Identify the reasons for the character's actions. Ask yourself: Why are the characters like this? Gather any information you can from what the author tells you about the characters' pasts. Pay close attention to what happens right before and after the action in question.

Step 5: Predict the answer to the test question.

Step 6: Select the choice that best matches your prediction.

# Practice

Read the following passage about a husband and a wife. Use the strategy above to answer the question about the characters and action.

## WHY DO THESE CHARACTERS FEEL AS THEY DO?

Norma Jean works at the Rexall drugstore, and she has acquired an amazing amount of information about cosmetics. When she explains to Leroy the three stages of complexion care, involving creams, toners, and moisturizers, he thinks
(5) happily of other petroleum products—axle grease, diesel fuel. This is a connection between him and Norma Jean. Since he has been home, he has felt unusually tender about his wife and guilty over his long absences. But he can't tell what she feels about him. Norma Jean has never complained about his
(10) traveling; she has never made hurt remarks, like calling his truck a "widow-maker." He is reasonably certain she has been faithful to him, but he wishes she would celebrate his permanent homecoming more happily. Norma Jean is often startled to find Leroy at home, and he thinks she seems a little disap-
(15) pointed about it. Perhaps he reminds her too much of the early days of their marriage, before he went on the road. They had a child who died as an infant, years ago. They never speak about their memories of Randy, which have almost faded, but now that Leroy is home all the time, they some-
(20) times feel awkward around each other, and Leroy wonders if one of them should mention the child. He has the family that they are waking up out of a dream together—that they must create a new marriage, start afresh. They are lucky they are still married. Leroy has read that for most people losing a
(25) child destroys the marriage—or else he heard this on *Donahue*. He can't always remember where he learns things anymore.

From "Shiloh" from *Shiloh and Other Stories* by Bobbie Ann Mason. Copyright ©1982 by Bobbie Ann Mason. Reprinted by permission of HarperCollins Publishers.

One possible reason for Norma Jean and Leroy's feeling of awkwardness around each other is that

**(1)** They are not used to being at home together, and this reminds them of their early days together and the death of their son.

**(2)** They are interested in totally different things and can't share their interests.

**(3)** Norma Jean makes nasty remarks about Leroy's truck, and Leroy is slowly losing his memory.

**(4)** Their marriage is about to fall apart, and they must start all over trying to make it work.

**(5)** Neither one can remember any details about the death of their son Randy.

The correct answer is (1). The two characters feel awkward around each other because they are not used to being together and have never gotten over the death of their son. According to lines 19-21, "they sometimes feel awkward around each other, and Leroy wonders if one of them should mention the child." (2) is incorrect because even though Norma Jean and Leroy do have different interests—she is interested in cosmetology and he in "other petroleum products"—the narrator suggests that this really is a "connection" between them. (3) is wrong because the narrator says that Norma Jean does not make nasty remarks about Leroy's truck or his absence. Whether or not Leroy is losing his memory is not an issue. Eliminate (4) because there are no details to show that their marriage is about to fall apart, or that they are trying to patch it up. Finally, (5) is not correct because the memories of their son "have almost faded," so they *can* still remember some details. Further, this fact simply adds information; it does not suggest a cause for their feeling awkward in each other's presence.

# Lesson 14 Exercise

Items 1 through 3 refer to the passage that follows. Choose the one best answer to each item.

### WHAT CAUSES ANNE TO BECOME UPSET?

When she got home the next morning at eleven, she surprised Mrs. Davenport asleep in front of a TV game show. The woman was befuddled and distraught, and Anne felt sorry for her, waking up in front of so many strange televisions, in so
(5) many strange houses. For the first time, she saw Mrs. Davenport as old and vulnerable and unfortunate rather than aggressive and unpleasant and ill-bred. She lied and said she didn't have the right change and gave Mrs. Davenport an extra five dollars.

(10) "We'll straighten it out next time," said Mrs. Davenport, quickly folding the money and pushing it into her purse, as if she expected Anne to change her mind.

Anne went into the kitchen to make herself a cup of coffee. She saw a pad of lined notepaper that Mrs. Davenport had
(15) left and thought that she should put it in a drawer so that children wouldn't use it. A slip of paper fell out of the pad onto the floor. She picked it up. It was written on, and she didn't want to read it, but she saw her own name. Her name riveted her; she couldn't keep her eyes away.

(20) "This one's such a slob," the letter said. "Just to test her last week, I left a cookie behind the door of the playroom. Well, it's still there. I'm leaving it there to see how long it takes her to get around to it."

Anne ran up the stairs as if she had been shot out of a can-
(25) non. She opened the door of the playroom. The room was a mess: pieces of puzzles, crayons, blocks, naked dolls were sprawled around the floor. She looked behind the door. There it was, a chocolate chip cookie, covered with dust and hair. She remembered that she had just given Mrs. Davenport an
(30) extra five dollars. How had she allowed that woman in her house, with her children, even for a moment? She picked up the cookie, and crushing in it the palm of her hand she walked to the telephone.

1. One the basis of lines 5-9, the best explanation of Anne's behavior is that

   (1) she likes Mrs, Davenport more than she ever has and wants to show her affection
   (2) she thinks Mrs. Davenport has no place to sleep and needs money to rent a room
   (3) she feels guilty about disliking Mrs. Davenport because she feels sympathy for her
   (4) she is confused when she gets home and is surprised to find Mrs. Davenport asleep in her house
   (5) she is an upper-class woman who thinks she ought to share her wealth with poor people

2. Anne's reaction to finding a cookie behind the door (lines 29-35) shows that Anne is

   (1) a neat housekeeper
   (2) a person oversensitive to criticism
   (3) a young woman hostile to older women
   (4) an unhappily married woman
   (5) a mother overprotective of her children

3. When Anne goes to the telephone (lines 31-33), which of the following is she most likely to do?

   (1) tell Mrs. Davenport she feels sorry for her and promise to pay her better wages
   (2) admit to Mrs. Davenport that she has shortcomings as a housekeeper and ask her advice
   (3) tell Mrs. Davenport to mail the five dollars back to her or she will call the police
   (4) tell Mrs. Davenport that her conduct is unacceptable and that she is out of a job
   (5) accuse Mrs. Davenport of telling lies about her and the way she treats her children

Answers are on page 324

# CHAPTER 3

Drama is a type of literature that tells a story through two basic elements: dialogue and stage directions. Much of the story that is told in the play appears in the form of dialogue, or conversation among the characters. The stage directions are the playwright's instructions about how the play should be performed. In this chapter, you will take a closer look at the interpreting skills you already use to experience dramatic works. You will see how the reading skills you've studied in earlier chapters can apply to the study of plays, and how understanding the skills of playwrights can make dramatic works even more fun and rewarding to watch.

A Scene from *Hamlet*

## Prereading Prompt

You have probably spent many hours watching television shows and movies. If the show is good, you become involved in the characters' lives and cheer the "good guys" and boo the "bad guys." The enjoyment you experience comes from watching the action as it takes place. Seeing a live performance in a theater can be even more exciting. That's because plays take place right before your eyes in live action. You are so close to what is taking place that you are almost a part of the action. How do writers of dramatic literature make it seem as if you are experiencing the action in real life? Understanding their skills can help you enjoy plays and films even more. It can also help you answer questions on the GED test.

# DRAMA

## What is Drama?

Drama, like fiction, is a type of literature. The two are alike in many ways. Drama and fiction both have setting, plot, characters, theme, conflict, and dialogue. They are both creations of the writer's imagination, even though a dramatic work might seem quite realistic. There is, however, one major difference between drama and fiction. Drama is written to be performed. One or more actors appear in each scene. It is the words and the actions of those actors that you study when you read a dramatic script.

The author of a drama that is intended to be performed on a stage in front of a live audience is called a **playwright**. The playwright divides his or her work, known as the **play**, into major sections, known as **acts**. An act may be divided into several smaller sections, known as **scenes**. The written version of the play is called the **script**. Drama might be written for film and be called a **screenplay** or for television and be called a **teleplay**. Each kind of drama can be appreciated for its beauty both on the printed page and in performance.

When you read dramatic literature, try to "see" and "hear" what is taking place. The sharper your image of the action, the better you will be able to understand the drama.

### Key Words

**drama**—a type of literature that tells a story through the speech and actions of the characters in the story

**playwright**—the author of a play

**play**—a work of drama, intended to be performed

**script**—the written version of the play

# Literal Comprehension of Dialogue

## Prereading Prompt

Have you ever overhead a conversation that went something like this?

FIRST PERSON: Oh? You're kidding. Really? The Smiths?

SECOND PERSON: Yessirree. Alice said they were moving to Alaska—in two weeks!

FIRST PERSON: But they've lived here all their lives.

SECOND PERSON: I guess it had something to do with Fred's losing his job at the factory.

FIRST PERSON: Not again!

From these brief remarks you've learned a number of things: the Smiths are moving to Alaska, they had lived in one place all their lives, Fred has lost his job recently, and this isn't the first time he has lost his job.

Whenever people talk to each other, they exchange information. Some information is stated directly, as in the above example. On the GED, you may be asked to answer questions about information stated directly in a play. You will learn how in this lesson.

## Key Words

**dialogue**—the words spoken by the characters in a play

## Dialogue

Since drama is written to be acted, it looks different on the page from other types of literature. In drama, much of the story is in the form of **dialogue**, the words spoken by the characters in a play. The dialogue often explains past events, describes current happenings, and reveals hopes for the future. When you read a drama, you will see a character's name next to the line of dialogue to let you know who is speaking.

In the Fiction section of this book, you learned that one of the ways in which fictional characters interact is through dialogue. Drama depends on dialogue far more than fiction does. That's because playwrights do not include long descriptive passages in their work, as novelists do. As a result, when description is needed in a play, the playwright must provide it in some other way. Some playwrights will include a narrator, a character who provides the necessary details. The narrator may be a character in the play, or a voice from offstage. More often, however, the playwright uses dialogue to provide the details.

Imagine, for example, that one scene of a play is set in a dark, mysterious forest. The playwright will describe the setting in stage directions; but if he or she wants to emphasize the air of mystery, he or she probably will have a character say something about it. Likewise, if the audience needs to know about the events that happened before the play opens, the playwright will have one or more of the characters mention these events in dialogue.

When reading a play, try to imagine how an actor might say the character's words. For example, if a character is a nasty, gruff man, the actor would most likely speak in a loud, angry voice. By using your imagination in this way, you will make the play come alive.

In the Interpreting Literature and Arts section of the GED test, you may be asked literal comprehension questions about dialogue. These questions test your ability to understand information directly stated in the passage. Some literal interpretation questions direct you to a specific line or place in the passage. This helps you know approximately where to look for the answer. Remember: to answer literal interpretation questions you do not have to "read between the lines"; the answer will be stated directly in the passage.

Below are some sample literal interpretation questions about drama that you could find on the GED test. They are followed by a strategy you can use to help find the answer.

## Model Questions and Strategy

- According to line _____ , why did _____ happen?
- According to the passage, which of the following is true?
- As used in the passage, what does the term _____ mean?
- Which of the following details is stated in the passage?
- Which of the following lines of dialogue show _____ (how one character feels about another character, why the characters are angry at each other, what the relationship is between the characters, and so on)?

### Strategy:

Step 1: Read the purpose question and the items following the passage. Keep these questions in mind as you read the passage.

Step 2: Summarize the passage in your own words.

Step 3: Look at the item. Make a prediction before you look at the choices. If a line reference is given, look at the line and the surrounding lines for the answer. If there is no line reference, look through the passage for key words from the question. For example, if the question asks, "What is the relationship between Eva and Ned?" look for the words "Eva" and "Ned." The relationship will most likely be defined nearby.

To identify a character's lines, look for each time his or her name appears on the left in capital letters. Any italicized words after the character's name are stage directions.

## Model Passage and Question

Read the following passage. Use the strategy you have just learned to find the answer to the question.

### WHY IS MARSHA ANGRY AT KARL?

*Karl, wearing a heavy jacket and a cap with ear-muffs, enters and shuts the door quickly. Marsha, seated at the kitchen table, watches him. He leans a spade covered with dirt against the wall by the door. Without looking at her, he takes off his work gloves and stuffs* (5) *them in the pockets of his jacket.*

KARL: Well, it's finished.

MARSHA: You didn't take long.

KARL: It wasn't a big hole.

(*Marsha sets down her coffee cup with a sharp clatter and glares at* (10) *him. He looks at her and then turns, takes off his cap and hangs it on a hook on the wall.*)

KARL: He wasn't a big dog.

MARSHA: You hardly stepped outside before you're back.

KARL: What did you want me to do—sing a hymn over him? The (15)  ground's hard this time of year.

MARSHA: The ground's not the only thing that's hard this time of year. You must've barely covered him.

KARL: You watched me from the window, didn't you?  You saw how deep I dug—up to my knees.

(20) MARSHA: I should've taken him to the animal hospital.

KARL: Too late for that now.

MARSHA: I mean to cremate [burn a body to ashes], instead of letting you bury him!

KARL: Listen: don't blame yourself—or me. You think you (25)  should've taken him before, when he got sick. He was seventeen years old. I miss him just as much as you do. He was old, that's all.

MARSHA:  I feel old.

Which of the following details is stated in the passage?

**(1)** Marsha and Karl are two old people who live on a farm.

**(2)** Karl has not dug the dog's grave deep enough to cover the dog's body.

**(3)** The dog was too big for Karl to bury properly.

**(4)** Marsha is angry with Karl because he did not sing a hymn over the dog's body.

**(5)** The dog's grave is a small, knee-deep hole.

(5) is the correct answer. Karl makes two statements about the size of the dog's grave that he has dug: "It wasn't a big hole" (line 8) and "You saw how deep I dug—up to my knees" (lines 18-19). Choice (5) is a restatement of these two details. (1) is incorrect because the dialogue of the passage does not state how old Karl and Marsha are or whether they live on a farm or not. In the last line Marsha says "I feel old," but that does not mean that she *is* old. The fact that Karl digs a grave near enough to the house for Marsha to watch him as he digs may suggest that they live in the country, but the passage does not state this; their house might be in a small town, or even in a city. Marsha says to Karl in line 17 "You must've barely covered him," but Karl contradicts her by saying that the grave is "up to my knees." For her to say he "must've" barely covered the dog's body with dirt suggests that she did not actually see how deep the grave was, and that she is accusing Karl of not covering the body because he did not take long to dig the grave. Therefore, (2) is wrong. Karl says "He wasn't a big dog" (line 12) and Marsha does not contradict him, so (3) is also incorrect. Marsha does not say that Karl should have sung a hymn over the dog's grave; Karl's comment in line 14 is his way of saying that Marsha is making unreasonable criticisms of the way he buried their dog.

Items 1 through 3 refer to the passage that follows. Choose the one best answer to each item.

**HOW DO THESE TWO SONS FEEL ABOUT THEIR MOTHER'S TASTE?**

LEE: I never realized the old lady was so security-minded.

AUSTIN: How do you mean?

LEE: Made a little tour this morning. She's got locks on everything. Locks and double-locks and chain locks and—What's she got
(5)  that's so valuable?

AUSTIN: Antiques I guess. I don't know.

LEE: Antiques? Brought everything with her from the old place, huh. Just the same crap we always had around. Plates and spoons.

(10) AUSTIN: I guess they have personal value to her.

LEE: Personal value. Yeah. Just a lota' junk. Most of it's phony anyway. Idaho decals. Now who in the hell wants to eat offa' a plate with the State of Idaho starin' ya' in the face. Every time ya' take a bite ya' get to see a little bit more.

(15) AUSTIN: Well it must mean something to her or she wouldn't save it.

LEE: Yeah, well personally I don't wann' be invaded by Idaho when I'm eatin'. When I'm eatin' I'm home. Ya' know what I'm sayin'? I'm not driftin', I'm home. I don't need my thoughts swept off to
(20)  Idaho. I don't need that!

From *True West*, by Sam Shepard, in *Sam Shepard Seven Plays.* By permission of Bantam Books, a division of Bantam, Doubleday, Dell Publishing Group, Inc.

1. What line of dialogue shows that Austin understands his mother's feelings about the objects in her house?

   **(1)** "I never realized the old lady was so security-minded."
   **(2)** "Antiques, I guess."
   **(3)** "I guess they have personal value to her."
   **(4)** "Most of it's phony anyway."
   **(5)** "Just the same crap we always had around."

2. Lee has just discovered that his mother cares about

   **(1)** buying expensive furniture
   **(2)** the safety of the things in her house
   **(3)** Idaho
   **(4)** refurnishing her home
   **(5)** eating healthful food

3. What lines of dialogue tell you that Lee does not like his mother's antiques?

   **(1)** "I never realized the old lady was so security-minded."
   **(2)** "Made a little tour this morning. She's got locks on everything."
   **(3)** "Just a lota' junk. Most of it's phony anyway."
   **(4)** "Well it must mean something to her or she wouldn't save it."
   **(5)** "When I'm eatin' I'm home. Ya' know what I'm sayin'? I'm not driftin', I'm home."

Answers are on page 324.

# Literal Comprehension of Stage Directions

## Prereading Prompt

Have you ever tried to take a family photograph? If so, you may have found yourself saying things like this: "Sara, move a little to the left. Henry, bend down a bit. Now, everyone smile! Bertha! I said smile and say "Cheese." Okay, everyone. Stay still. Perfectly still. Click! Hooray! We did it!"

Directions such as these help everyone know what to do in order to have a successful family photo. Playwrights, like photographers, need to give directions to insure their plays will be performed as they intended. On the GED, you may have to answer questions about the stage directions in a play. You will learn how in this lesson.

## Key Words

**stage directions**—instructions in a play telling actors where and how to move, and describing the setting

**setting**—where and when the action of the play takes place

## Stage Directions

Playwrights use stage directions to show a character's tone of voice, expressions, gestures, and actions. Stage directions guide the director, the actors, and the designers on ways to bring a play "to life" in performance. They also guide you, the reader, as you bring the script of a play to life in your imagination.

Stage directions also describe the setting in time and place of a scene, as in the following excerpt:

*The set [setting] is the large sun porch/family room of a prosperous southern Missouri farmhouse built around 1860.*

*We see the wide doors to a hallway upstage, and a stairway going up. At one side doors open to a porch that wraps around most or all of the house. In Act II this porch, with the living room in the background, will be facing the audience.*

Excerpt from *Fifth of July* by Lanford Wilson. Copyright ©1978 by Lanford Wilson. Reprinted by permission of Hill and Wang, a division of Farrar, Straus & Giroux.

Play careful attention to stage directions because they can help you imagine what would be happening on stage if you saw the play being performed.

In the Interpreting Literature and Arts section of the GED test, you may be asked literal comprehension questions about stage directions in a play. These questions test your ability to understand information directly stated in the passage. Below are some sample literal interpretation questions that you may be asked about stage directions, along with a strategy you can use to help find the answer.

## Model Questions and Strategy

• Which of the following details is stated in the stage directions?

• What stage directions reveal the following actions: (for example: how the two characters look at each other, how they feel about each other, and so forth)?

### Strategy:

Step 1: Read the purpose question and the items following the passage. Keep these in mind as you read the passage. As you read, pay special attention to the stage directions, looking for key words from the items following the passage. Try to visualize what is taking place in the passage.

Step 2: Read each item again and try to make a prediction before looking at the choices. Eliminate any choices that do not seem to fit.

Step 3: Look back to the passage to find the answer. Remember that the answer will be directly stated in the passage.

Step 4: Check the answer you picked to make sure that the words convey a similar thought to the one asked for in the question. Rephrase the answer to make sure that it means the same as the words in the passage.

## Model Passage and Question

Read the following passage. Use the strategy to help you find the answer to the question about stage directions.

### ARE THESE TWO MEN FRIENDS?

*The General and his wife take their seats in the first row, the General directly in front of Cherdyakov.*

CHERDYAKOV *(leans over to the General)*: Good evening, General.

(5) GENERAL: *(turns, looks at Cherdyakov coldly)*: Hmm?... What? Oh yes. Yes. Good evening. *(The General turns front again, looks at his program.)*

CHERDYAKOV: Permit me, sir. I am Cherdyakov... Ivan Ilyitch. This is a great honor for me, sir.

GENERAL: *(turns coldly)*: Yes.

(10) CHERDYAKOV: Like yourself, dear General, I too serve the Ministry of Public Parks... That is to say, I serve you, who is indeed himself the Minister of Public Parks. I am the Assistant Chief Clerk in the Department of Trees and Bushes.

GENERAL: Ahh, yes. Keep up the good work... Lovely trees and (15) bushes this year. Very nice.

Excerpt from *The Sneeze* from *The Good Doctor.* by Neil Simon. By permission of Random House,

What stage direction reveals the General's disinterest in Cherdyakov?

**(1)** *leans over to the General*

**(2)** *turns coldly*

**(3)** Hmmm.

**(4)** *The General and his wife take their seats in the first row, the General directly in front of Cherdyakov.*

**(5)** Ahh, yes. Keep up the good work.

The correct response is (2). The words *turns coldly* are stage directions in line 9. You know they are stage directions because they are in italics within parentheses. They describe the action taken by the General to show he is not interested in speaking with Cherdyakov. (1) is incorrect; although it is a stage direction, it does not indicate the General's disinterest. Rather, it shows Cherdyakov's interest in speaking with the General. (3) and (5) cannot be correct because they are not stage directions; they are lines of dialogue. (4) is not correct because although the sentence is a stage direction, it does not reveal the General's attitude toward Cherdyakov. It simply tells how these people take their seats.

Items 1 through 3 refer to the passage that follows. Choose the one best answer to each item.

### HOW DOES LAURA FEEL ABOUT OPENING THE DOOR?

AMANDA *(calling)*: Laura, sweetheart! The door!

*(Laura stares at it without moving.)*

JIM: I think we just beat the rain.

(5) TOM: Uh-huh. *(He rings again, nervously. Jim whistles and fishes for a cigarette.)*

AMANDA *(very, very gaily)*: Laura, that is your brother and Mr. O'Connor! Will you let them in, darling?

*(Laura crosses to the kitchenette door.)*

LAURA *(breathlessly)*: Mother—you go to the door!

(10) *(Amanda steps out of the kitchenette and stares furiously at Laura. She points imperiously at the door.)*

LAURA: Please, please!

AMANDA *(in a fierce whisper)*: What is the matter with you, you silly thing?

(15) LAURA *(desperately)*: Please, you answer it, *please*!

AMANDA: I told you I wasn't going to humor you, Laura. Why have you chosen this moment to lose your mind?

LAURA: Please, please, please, you go!

AMANDA: You'll have to go to the door because I can't!

(20) LAURA *(despairingly)*: I can't either!

AMANDA: *Why?*

LAURA: I'm *sick*!

AMANDA: I'm sick too,—of your nonsense! Why can't you and your brother be normal people? Fantastic whims and behavior! *(Tom*

(25) *gives a long ring.)* Preposterous goings on! Can you give me one reason—*(She calls out lyrically.)* Coming! Just one second!—why you should be afraid to open a door? Now you answer it, Laura!

LAURA: Oh, oh, oh…*(She returns through the portieres, darts to the Victrola, winds it frantically and turns it on.)*

(30) AMANDA: Laura Wingfield, you march right to that door!

LAURA: *Yes—yes, Mother!*

1. Which of the following details is stated in the stage directions?

   (1) Jim and Tom just beat the rain.
   (2) Tom rings the bell for a long time.
   (3) Amanda answers the door.
   (4) Laura answers the door.
   (5) Amanda turns on the phonograph.

2. According to lines 9-14, Amanda's attitude Laura's behavior is one of

   (1) fear
   (2) anger
   (3) happiness
   (4) surprise
   (5) sympathy

3. Which of the following best describes Laura's attitude toward the arrival of her brother and Mr. O'Connor?

   (1) excitement
   (2) delight
   (3) anger
   (4) fear
   (5) impatience

Answers are on page 324.

# Inferring Motivation and Previous Events

## Prereading Prompt

Do you know anyone who has ever watched a trial? If so, you know that the prosecutors try to provide as much evidence as they can to help prove the defendant committed the crime. They give details about the person's past actions and behavior. They include statements from witnesses that link the person to the crime. They also suggest possible motives, or reasons, that the person may have had for committing the crime, such as the need for money. Playwrights, like lawyers, know the value of including information about why a person might do something. These kinds of details help create believable pictures of what is or has taken place. Knowing how to find details about a character's motivation is very important for answering GED questions. You will learn how in this lesson.

## Key Words

**motivation**—in drama, the reason for a character's behavior

## Motivation

The reason for a character's behavior is called **motivation**. The character's personality along with the circumstances presented in the play helps determine the character's motivation.

You know from Lessons 1 and 2 that playwrights sometimes convey details about characters directly through dialogue and stage directions. However, you will find that playwrights also give this information indirectly. Often, the playwright cannot tell the audience directly about a character's motivation as a writer of fiction might; rather, the playwright must show it indirectly through the words and actions of the characters. As we watch the action of the play unfold, we infer the characters' motivations.

As with fiction, these inferences consist of putting together details to find an unstated conclusion. For example, imagine that a character in a scene suddenly bursts into tears. What would be a logical reason for such behavior? What details were provided? Perhaps someone's death was mentioned, and the character feels overwhelming grief. Maybe the scene takes place in a courtroom, and the character has been found innocent. In this case, these might be tears of relief.

As you read a script, pay particular attention to dialogue and the characters' reactions to each other. Look for reasonable motivations for the actions in the play.

## Previous Events

In Lesson 1 you learned that characters often provide descriptive and background information in their dialogue. The playwright will sometimes state these details directly. In other cases, though, the playwright will prefer merely to suggest these details. For example, one character's comments that the other character should honor his parents' memory implies that the character's parents have died.

In the Interpreting Literature and Arts section of the GED test, you may be asked inference questions about motivation and past events in a play. These questions test your ability to understand information indirectly stated in the passage. Below are some sample questions about inference that you may be asked, along with a strategy you can use to help find the answer.

## Model Questions and Strategy

- What can you infer about [a character] from his or her mention of _____ in line 00?
- What can you conclude from the statement in lines 00-00 about [a character's] personality?
- What must have happened just before this passage?
- From the details given, what events must have recently taken place?

### Strategy:

Step 1: Read the question and the passage. Then, reread the question and the choices in turn. As you read, pay special attention to the details. Try to form a mental picture of what is taking place in the passage.

Step 2: Eliminate any choices that do not seem to fit.

Step 3: Look for clues in the passage to find the answer. Clues can be directly stated and refer to things that took place in the past. They can also be details about how one character views another. In addition, clues can be provided in the stage directions. For example, these might show how one character treats another physically.

Step 4: Make a prediction before you select the answer. Then examine each choice in turn.

Step 5: Choose the one best answer. To check it, reword the question in light of the answer and see if it makes sense.

## Model Passage and Question

Read the following passage. Use the strategy above to help you find the answer to the inference question about previous events.

### WHY IS FRANCES CALLING FELIX?

OSCAR: *Will you forget Frances!* We'll get our own pots. Don't drive me crazy before you move in. *(The phone rings. Oscar picks it up quickly.)* Hello? Oh, hello, Frances!

FELIX *(Stops cleaning and starts to wave his arms wildly. He whis--*
(5) *pers screamingly)*: I'm not here! I'm not here! You didn't see me. You don't know where I am. I didn't call. I'm not here. I'm not here.

OSCAR *(Into the phone)*: Yes, he's here.

FELIX *(Pacing back and forth)*: How does she sound? Is she wor--
(10) ried? Is she crying? What is she saying? Does she want to speak to me? I don't want to speak to her.

OSCAR *(Into the phone)*: Yes, he is.

FELIX: You can tell her I'm not coming back. I've made up my mind. I've had it there. I've taken as much as she has. You can
(15) tell her for me if she thinks I'm coming back, she's got another think coming. Tell her. Tell her.

OSCAR *(Into the phone)*: Yes! Yes, he's fine.

FELIX Don't tell her I'm fine! You heard me carrying on before. What are you telling her that for? I'm not fine.

(20) OSCAR *(Into the phone)*: Yes, I understand, Frances.

FELIX *(Sits down next to Oscar)*: Does she want to speak to me? Ask her if she wants to speak to me? . . .

FELIX: She didn't want to speak to me?

OSCAR: No!

(25) FELIX: Why did she call?

OSCAR: She wants to know when you're coming over for your clothes. She wants to have the room repainted.

From the details given, what event must have recently taken place?

    **(1)** Frances and Felix redecorated their house

    **(2)** Oscar asked Frances to marry him

    **(3)** Felix and Frances have recently separated

    **(4)** Oscar and Felix just met

    **(5)** Felix forgot to take his clothes on vacation

The correct answer is (3). Felix says, "You can tell her I'm not coming back. I've made up my mind. I've had it there. I've taken just as much as she has. You can tell her for me if she thinks I'm coming back she's got another think coming." These words suggest that he left the home he shared with Frances. (1) cannot be correct; although Frances says she wants to have the room repainted, there is no suggestion that the two of them recently redecorated their house together. Since Frances wants him to come for his clothes, instead of simply moving them to another room herself, you can infer that she wants him to stay out of the house for good. (2) is not correct because Oscar is only having a phone conversation with Frances, who has called to give Felix a message. Nothing Oscar says suggests that he has any romantic interest in Frances, let alone that he has just asked her to marry him. (4) is also incorrect: it does not seem likely that the two men have just met, since Frances is calling Oscar's home thinking that she will find Felix there. Therefore, they must have known each other for some time. (5) is incorrect because it is implied that Felix has either been kicked out of his home or left, not that he is on a vacation.

Items 1 through 3 refer to the passage that follows. Choose the one best answer to each item.

### WHY HAVEN'T THESE CHARACTERS
### SEEN EACH OTHER IN A LONG TIME?

(INTERIOR: LIVING ROOM. *Mac enters. His daughter, Sue Anne, is there.*)

SUE ANNE: Do you recognize me?

MAC: Yes, I do....

(5) SUE ANNE: You've changed. You don't look like your pictures any more.

MAC: Don't I? Well, who knows when the last picture of me was taken. It doesn't make a whole lot of difference about this, but I did try to get in touch with you. I wrote you a few letters. Did
(10) you ever get them?

SUE ANNE: No.

MAC: Well, your mama didn't have to give them to you. Courts gave her complete jurisdiction. Quite rightly, I guess, considering my state at the time.

(15) SUE ANNE: I told Mama I was coming here. She told me she'd have me arrested if I did. Then Harry reminded her that I'm eighteen now and I don't have to mind anybody. Mama says you tried to kill her once.

MAC: I did.

(20) SUE ANNE: Why did you try to kill her?

MAC: Well, she got me mad some way. I was drunk.... I don't know. It was one of those things.

SUE ANNE: Someone told Mama the other night you were the best country-Western singer they ever heard.

(25) MAC: Oh.

SUE ANNE: Mama threw a glass of whiskey right in her face. She said they were just saying that to spite her. You think you will ever sing again?

MAC: Oh, I think about it once in a while.... Will you have some
(30) supper with us?

SUE ANNE: No, thank you. I can't. I have a date tonight. Plays in Mama's band. We have to sneak around 'cause Mama don't like him. Would you like to meet him? He'd like to meet you.

MAC: Oh, I don't think that's such a good idea. I really wouldn't
(35) want your mama to think we was ganging up on her behind her back.

From *Tender Mercies*, a screenplay by Horton Foote. Copyright ©1986 by Horton Foote. Published by Grove Press. Reprinted by permission of Lucy Kroll Agency for the author.

1. What can you infer about Mac and Sue Anne's mother's relationship?

   (1) They are still fighting about custody rights over Sue Anne.
   (2) When married, they were very close and loving, having sung in the same band.
   (3) They didn't get along well and got divorced.
   (4) Their marriage was ruined by alcoholism, and only Sue Anne's mother has stopped drinking.
   (5) They still talk with each other about Sue Anne although they are divorced.

2. What event occurred recently to suggest that Sue Anne's mother is still angry at Mac?

   (1) Sue Anne's mother divorced Mac.
   (2) Sue Anne's mother reacted violently to a compliment about Mac's music.
   (3) Sue Anne's mother refused to sing any of the songs that Mac wrote.
   (4) Sue Anne's mother tried to kill Mac.
   (5) Sue Anne's mother did not give Sue Anne the letters Mac wrote to his daughter.

3. Which of the following details is stated in the passage?

   (1) Sue Anne's mother left Mac because of his drinking.
   (2) Sue Anne's mother is a great country-and-western singer.
   (3) Mac is a devoted father.
   (4) Sue Anne did not tell anyone she was meeting Mac.
   (5) Mac once tried to kill Sue Anne's mother.

Answers are on page 325.

# Inferring Setting and Mood

## Prereading Prompt

Suppose a character is fixing his tie, looking in the mirror over a dresser, and saying, "This is my lucky day. I'm going to get that job!" Then he clicks his heels and dashes off the stage. From his words and actions you can infer that he is feeling hopeful, confident, and energetic. You can also infer that he is at home, most likely in his bedroom.

On the GED, you may have to answer questions about the setting and mood of a passage. You will learn how in this lesson.

## Key Words

**mood**—a particular state of mind or feeling in a character; also, the atmosphere surrounding an event

## Setting

Sometimes when you read an excerpt from a play, the stage directions will clearly explain the setting. Other times, however, the setting may not be directly stated. In these instances, you will have to infer the setting from the characters' dialogue and actions. If two characters are ordering Italian food from a waiter and drinking wine, you might infer that the setting is an Italian restaurant.

When you are asked inference questions about the setting of a play on the GED test, ask yourself, "What details tell me where the characters are now?" or "When is the action taking place?"

## Mood

Have you ever read something that touched you deeply and left you feeling thoughtful long after? Has a play, movie, or television show seemed so funny to you that later you felt good just thinking about it? If so, then you were reacting to the mood of the drama.

Playwrights, like other kinds of writers, try to involve the emotions of the audience through the plot. For example, watching a marriage, the fixing up of a house, an anniversary party, or the birth of a child would probably make the audience feel joyful. On the other hand, a suspenseful play might have a mysterious or menacing atmosphere.

The actions that characters in a play take can also create an emotional response. For instance, suppose one character consistently hurts others without feeling any sense of wrongdoing. In this case, when the man is hurt by another, the audience would probably not feel sad. Most characters don't state directly how they feel. You have to infer their emotional state from the things they say and do.

In the Interpreting Literature and Arts section of the GED test, you may be asked inference questions about the mood and setting in a play. When this happens, ask yourself, "How do I feel after having read this excerpt? How do the characters seem to feel? What specific words and actions reveal their feelings?"

Below are some sample inference questions on setting and mood that you may be asked on the GED test.

## Model Questions

- Where (or when) does the action take place?
- What mood is suggested by lines ____?
- What mood is suggested by the passage as a whole?
- What can you infer about _____(a character) from lines 00-00?

# Model Passage and Question

Read the following passage. See if you can figure out the answer to the inference question about previous events.

## WHAT HAS STANLEY DONE?

STELLA (*In bedroom, a bit above and to right of Stanley*): She hasn't got her job. What will she do?

STANLEY (*Turning to Stella*): She's not stayin' here after Tuesday. You know that, don't you? Just to make sure, I bought her tick-
(5)　et myself. A bus ticket! (*Fumbles in his breast pocket to show Stella ticket.*)

STELLA: In the first place, Blanche wouldn't go on a bus.

STANLEY: She'll go on a bus and like it.

STELLA: No, she won't, no, she won't, Stanley!

(10) STANLEY: *She'll go!* Period! P.S.—She'll go *Tuesday*!

STELLA (*Slowly*): What'll—she—do? What on earth will she—*do*?

STANLEY: Her future is mapped out for her.

STELLA: What do you mean? (*Grabs Stanley's arm. Blanche sings in bathroom.*)

(15) STANLEY (*Frees himself from her grip. Goes to bathroom door, pounding on it.*) Hey, canary bird! Toots! Get OUT of the BATHROOM!
(*Stella moves close to right of Stanley. Door opens. Blanche emerges with a gay peal of laughter. Steam rises from bathroom.*)

BLANCHE (*Stepping into bedroom. Carries hairbrush.*): Oh, I feel so
(20)　good after my long, hot bath, I feel so good and cool and—rested!
(*Crosses to left center. Stanley goes into bathroom, slamming door shut, which arrests Blanche's crossing.*)

STELLA (*Sadly and doubtfully, crossing into living room.*): Do you,
Blanche? (*Picks up extra candles by cake and stuffs them into
(25)　little candle box.*)

BLANCHE (*Brushing hair vigorously*): Yes, I do, so refreshed! A hot
bath and a long, cool drink always gives me a brand new outlook on life! (*Looks at bathroom door, then at Stella.*) Something
has happened. What is it?

STELLA (*Turning away quickly*): Why, nothing has happened,
(30)　Blanche.

BLANCHE (*Pausing in center of bedroom, facing Stella*): You're lying!
Something has!

How do you think Stella feels at the end of the excerpt?

**(1)** refreshed and hopeful

**(2)** rested and happy

**(3)** eager and energetic

**(4)** superior and detached

**(5)** anxious and upset

The correct answer is (5). Stella knows that Stanley wants to kick Blanche out—he has brought her a bus ticket home. Stella is anxious and upset because Blanche hasn't got a job or plans for the future. "What will she do?" Stella cries, "What'll—she—do? What on earth will she—*do*?" Blanche's forced exit from Stella's home will surely make Blanche very unhappy, and Stella's knowing this would make her anxious (since she knows something that Blanche doesn't) and upset. (1) is incorrect because "refreshed" describes Blanche as she comes out of the bathroom, not Stella. (2) is incorrect for the same reason—it describes Blanche, not Stella: in line 20, Blanche says "rested!," and according to the stage directions, *"Blanche emerges with a gay peal of laughter."* Eliminate (3) and (4) because there are no details to suggest that Stella had these responses. Rather than being eager or energetic, Stella seems to have been slowed down by what Stanley has just told her. The pauses in her comment—"What'll—she—do? What on earth will she—*do*?"—suggest her weariness. In the same way, there is nothing to suggest that Stella feels superior and detached (4), since she is involved in the conflict between Stanley and Blanche; she grabs Stanley's arm and feels sad and doubtful (line 23) when he is rude to Blanche and slams the bathroom door.

Items 1 through 3 refer to the passage that follows. Choose the one best answer to each item.

## WHY IS THE COUPLE DIVIDING UP THE FURNITURE?

ALICIA *(Distributing the tags among the furniture)*: Let's see—this sofa is yours—Bill—*(a Bill tag)* This chair's mine—Alicia—*(an Alicia tag)* You did say I could have it, didn't you?

BILL: Help yourself.

(5) ALICIA: This table is yours—Bill—this small sofa is mine—Alicia— that chair is yours—Bill. Oh, I've already tagged that—this chair is mine—Alicia's—somehow it's more feminine. That pretty well divides up the furniture.... Now the paintings. *(She goes to an interesting painting—is about to tag it with her name)* I would

(10) like to have this one, if you don't mind, Bill.

BILL: Suits me.

ALICIA: Now, Bill, you're sure?—I mean, that you don't want it? Of course I love it, but then you love it, too.

BILL: Now, Sweetie, you saw it first—I remember very clearly.

(15) Paris, '53. What was the name of the restaurant? Chez Something.

ALICIA: Nico.

BILL: Chez Nico. Too much to eat, too much to drink, too much for this painting.

(20) ALICIA: Listen, I wanted to go back to the hotel and sleep. It was you that wanted to go to art galleries.

BILL: Yes, but you never can just look. You always have to buy, don't you? That acquisitive streak of yours.

ALICIA: If it weren't for that acquisitive streak of mine, we wouldn't

(25) have so many lovely things.

BILL: And by the same token, we wouldn't have to pin on so many lovely labels.

ALICIA: I didn't exactly collect things for that purpose, you know. In my naive way, I thought we were going to spend our lives

(30) together.

BILL: Oh, you poor little abandoned bride!

ALICIA: Really! You have the most extraordinary way of—*(She gains control of herself)* Bill, we agreed we're not going to argue. This whole thing is to be what is known as amicable—a civilized

(35) divorce. Up to now we've divided everything fairly, and avoided argument.... Now! Do you want the picture? Because if you do, take it.

1. What is the setting of this excerpt?

   **(1)** a French restaurant
   **(2)** a furniture store
   **(3)** a court of law
   **(4)** an art gallery
   **(5)** a living room

2. What mood is implied in lines 20-31?

   **(1)** hopeful
   **(2)** sad
   **(3)** angry
   **(4)** happy
   **(5)** peaceful

3. What can you infer about the marriage between Alicia and Bill?

   **(1)** It ended because of Bill's acquisitive streak.
   **(2)** It was seldom marked by argument.
   **(3)** It may survive a long time.
   **(4)** It lasted for several years.
   **(5)** It was broken up by another woman.

Answers are on page 325.

# Applying Attitudes in Drama

Prereading Prompt

Have you ever watched a TV show and been able to predict what the character was going to do in a certain situation, even though you had never seen the episode before? If so, you are applying information you already know about the character's personality to a new situation. In a similar way, after reading a play in which a character shows great appreciation for his family, you might imagine that this character would favor agencies that provide "big brothers and sisters" to children who need a sense of belonging to a family.

On the GED, you may be asked to apply a character's or the playwright's attitude to a new situation. You will learn how in this lesson.

## Applying Characters' Attitudes

One test of the effectiveness of a dramatic work is the degree of audience involvement. There are many different ways audience members can become involved. One way is to root for a character, hoping that whatever he or she does will turn out for the best. Another way is to think about the characters' personalities and philosophies and apply them to a new situation.

In Tennessee Williams' play *Summer and Smoke*, a woman named Alma comes to tell a young doctor named John that she has stopped resisting her love for him and now has a very different attitude toward life from the one she had the summer before, when she rejected his sexual advances. Read the following dialog and try to put Alma's view of life into your own words.

ALMA: You've gone back to calling me "Miss Alma" again.

JOHN: We never really got past that point with each other.

ALMA: Oh yes we did. We got so close that we almost breathed together!

(5) JOHN (*with embarrassment*): I didn't know that.

ALMA: No? Well, I did, I knew it. (*Her hand touches his face tenderly.*) You shave more carefully now? You don't have those little razor cuts on your chin that you dusted with gardenia talcum....

JOHN: I shave more carefully now.

(10) ALMA: So that explains it! (*Her fingers remain on his face, moving gently up and down it like a blind person reading Braille. He is intensely embarrassed and gently removes her hands from him.*) Is it—impossible now?

JOHN: I don't think I know what you mean.

(15) ALMA: You know what I mean, all right! So be honest with me. One time I said "no" to something. You may remember the time and all that demented howling from the cock fight? But now I've changed my mind, or the girl who said "no," she doesn't exist anymore, she died last summer—suffocated in smoke from (20) something on fire inside her. No, she doesn't live now, but she left me her ring— You see? The one you admired, the topaz ring set in pearls.... And she said to me when she slipped this ring on my finger, "Remember I have died empty-handed, and so make sure that your hands have *something in them*!" (*She* (25) *drops her gloves. She clasps his head again in her hands.*) I said "What about pride?"—She said,"Forget about pride, whenever it stands between you and what you must have!" And then I said, "But what if he doesn't want me?" I don't know what she said then. I'm not sure whether she said anything or not—her lips (30) stopped moving—Yes, I think she stopped breathing. (*He gently removes her craving hands from his face.*) No! (*He shakes his head in dumb suffering.*) Then the answer is "no"!

Alma's basic view is that people should satisfy their desires or they will end up "empty-handed" and die of "something on fire inside"—the emotions they have not expressed. If you were to apply this philosophy to other situations, you might expect Alma to tell someone with an unsatisfying job to quit and someone in an unsatisfying relationship to break it off. Applying her attitude to reading matter, you would judge her to prefer stories of romantic passion. Applying her attitude a political situation, you would predict that she would favor individual rights over laws that forbid people to do things. Because you know Alma's attitude toward life, you can apply her point of view to other situations she might encounter.

## Applying the Playwrights' Attitudes

The attitudes of the playwright are suggested by stage directions and by details in the dialogue. For example, in the excerpt from *Summer and Smoke* the playwright dramatizes the theme of the play by having Alma say "the girl who said 'no' she doesn't exist any more, she died last summer—suffocated in smoke from something on fire inside her. No, she doesn't live now, but she left me her ring—." For Alma to talk about herself as two people, one dead, one alive, makes the conflict in her between self-expression and self-denial a life-and-death matter. The playwright dramatizes the tragedy of unfulfilled emotion even more by showing us, in the stage directions, that while Alma openly expresses her feelings and repeatedly touches him, the young doctor no longer desires her and cannot respond. If someone asked you to apply the author's basic attitude toward life in this scene to some other situation you would guess he would advise people to act on their feelings honestly and to disregard any attitudes that hold them back from self-expression.

On the Interpreting Literature and Arts section of the GED test, you may be asked application questions about the author's or characters' attitudes in drama. As you learned in previous lessons, application items test your ability to understand main ideas and details from one situation and apply this information in a new context.

Below are sample application questions you might find about drama on the GED test, and a strategy to use to find the answer.

## Model Questions

- What would the playwright probably think about_____?
- Would the playwright be likely to agree with the idea that _____?
- Which of the following would the character be most (least) likely to do?
- The situation in the passage is like which of the following?
- What other details can you imagine about the characters and situation?

### Strategy:

Step 1: Read the passage carefully. As you read, keep the purpose questions and items following the passage in mind.

Step 2: Summarize the situation in the passage. Ask yourself: "What is the 'old' situation? How will it help me understand the 'new' situation?" Read for information that will help you build a "bridge" of ideas between the new situation in the item and the old situation in the passage.

Step 3: Make a prediction about the new situation based on the specific details from the old situation.

Step 4: Compare your prediction with the answer choices. See which answer provides the closest match. Then pick the best answer.

## Model Passage and Question

Read the following passage. Use the strategy you have just learned to find the answer to the question.

## HOW DOES KINO FEEL ABOUT HIS LIFE?

KINO: Father, are we not very unfortunate people to live in Japan?

FATHER: Why do you think so?

KINO: The volcano is behind our house, and the sea is in front.
When they work together to make earthquake and big wave, we
(5)     are helpless. Always, many of us are lost.

FATHER: To live in the presence of death makes us brave and
strong. That is why our people never fear death. We see it too
often, and we do not fear it. To die a little sooner or a little later
does not matter. But to live bravely, to love life, to see how
(10)    beautiful the trees are and the mountains—yes, and even the
sea—to enjoy work because it produces food—in these we are
fortunate people. We love life because we live in danger. We do
not fear death, for we understand that death and life are neces
sary to each other.

(15) KINO: What is death?

FATHER: Death is the great gateway.

KINO: The gateway… where?

From *The Big Wave*, by Pearl S. Buck. Copyright ©1958 by the author. Reprinted by permission of Harold Ober Associates Inc.

If Kino's father was a leader of a country during a time of danger, which of the following actions would he probably NOT take?

**(1)** argue that the crisis is really an opportunity

**(2)** order the people to move to a new territory

**(3)** encourage the people to work hard

**(4)** produce a movie about heroes from national history

**(5)** ask religious leaders to give sermons on life after death

The correct answer is (2). Everything that Kino's father says is a reason for staying in their home between a volcano and the sea, a dangerous location because of volcanic eruptions and the "big wave." Faced with a national crisis, therefore, Kino's father as a leader would not recommend moving his people to a new territory. He admits to Kino that they live in a dangerous place but he argues that "To live in the presence of death makes us brave and strong" (lines 6-7); therefore, he probably would argue that a national crisis was really an opportunity (1). With Kino, he argues that "we are fortunate people" to be able to produce food even in a dangerous place, so he probably would encourage people to work hard as a way of enjoying life during a national crisis (3). Since he argues that "to live in the presence of death makes us brave and strong" (lines 16-17), he would be likely to celebrate examples of courage during a time of danger—for instance, in a movie about national heroes (4). In line 16 he says that "death is the great gateway," which suggests that he believes in life after death. Since this is part of an argument against Kino's fear of death from the dangers near their home, it is likely that he would urge religious leaders to reduce everyone's fear of death by preaching about life after death,

Items 1 through 3 refer to the passage that follows. Choose the one best answer to each item.

**WHAT HAS HAPPENED TO KEN
AND HOW DOES HE FEEL ABOUT IT?**

MRS. BOYLE: We can't just stop treatment, just like that.

KEN: Why not?

MRS. BOYLE: It's the job of the hospital to save life, not to lose it.

KEN: The hospital's done all it can, but it wasn't enough. It wasn't
(5)   the hospital's fault; the original injury was too big.

MRS. BOYLE: We have to make the best of the situation.

KEN: No. "We" don't have to do anything. I have to do what is to be
done and that is to cash in the chips.

MRS. BOYLE: It's not unusual, you know, for people injured as you
(10)   have been, to suffer with this depression for a considerable
time before they begin to see that life is possible.

KEN: How long?

MRS. BOYLE: It varies.

KEN: Don't hedge.

(15) MRS. BOYLE: It could be a year or so.

KEN: And it could last the rest of my life.

MRS. BOYLE: That would be most unlikely.

KEN: I'm sorry, but I cannot settle for that.

MRS. BOYLE: Try not to dwell on it. I'll see what I can do to get you
(20)   started on some occupational therapy. Perhaps we could make
a start on the reading machines.

KEN: Do you have many books for those machines?

MRS. BOYLE: Quite a few.

KEN: Can I make a request for the first one?

(25) MRS. BOYLE: If you like.

KEN: "How to be a sculptor with no hands."

MRS. BOYLE: I'll be back tomorrow with the machine.

KEN: It's marvelous you know.

MRS. BOYLE: What is?

(30) KEN: All you people have the same technique. When I say some
thing really awkward you just pretend I haven't said anything
at all. You're all the bloody same...Well, there's another outburst. That should be your cue to comment on the light-shade
or the color of the walls.

(35) MRS. BOYLE: I'm sorry if I have upset you.

From *Whose Life is it Anyway?* by Brian Clark. Reprinted by permission of Judy Daish, Ltd., London.

1. From Ken's point of view, his situation is most similar to which of the following?

   **(1)** a customer being refused service in a restaurant

   **(2)** a sculptor who has been given the wrong kind of stone to work with

   **(3)** a student who has failed a reading exam

   **(4)** an unhappy child no one will listen to

   **(5)** an old man whose family has deserted him

2. What would Mrs. Boyle probably *never* say to a friend?

   **(1)** Where there's life, there's hope.

   **(2)** One day at a time.

   **(3)** Where there's a will, there's a way.

   **(4)** Throw in the towel.

   **(5)** Don't give up the ship.

3. Which of the following best describes Ken's mood?

   **(1)** resigned

   **(2)** hopeful

   **(3)** philosophical

   **(4)** calm

   **(5)** angry

Answers are on page 326.

# Analyzing the Theme

## Prereading Prompt

Some people take a great many risks in life. They may feel that taking risks develops courage and that courage is very important in becoming independent and strong. A risk-taking person in a play might embody this theme: People who take risks turn out to be courageous, independent, and successful. The theme of a play is conveyed by many details—the characters' dialogue and actions, the plot, the title, the setting, and the mood.

On the GED, you may have to answer questions about the theme in a play. You will learn how in this lesson.

## Key Words

**title**—the name of a piece of literature

**theme**—i the underlying truth about life in a work of literature

## Analyzing the Theme

From previous lessons, you know that the theme of a literary work is the underlying truth about life that is expressed. As you learned in regard to fiction, the theme of an imaginative work of literature is often the same as the author's attitude toward the action. Through their characters, writers show you the conflict in the story and portray emotions on stage to make you feel their point of view. Thus, writers use their characters to express their ideas and opinions about many aspects of life. The characters' actions also show the writer's feelings about different issues. By putting together the characters' words, action, and gestures, you can come to understand some of the themes of the work.

For example, Willy Loman, the main character in Arthur Miller's play *Death of a Salesman*, says this:

> WILLY: The street is lined with cars. There's not a breath of fresh air in the neighborhood. The grass don't grow any more, you can't raise a carrot in the back yard. They should've had a law against apartment houses. Remember those two beautiful elm
> (5) trees out there? When I and Biff hung the swing between them?
>
> LINDA: Yeah, like being a million miles from the city.
>
> WILLY: They should've arrested the builder for cutting those down. They massacred the neighborhood. *(Lost)* More and more I think of those days, Linda.

From *Death of a Salesman* by Arthur Miller. Copyright ©1949, renewed 1977 by Arthur Miller. Used by permission of Viking Penguin, a division of Penguin Books USA, Inc.

Willy's words and his manner of speaking suggest his feeling that life was better in the past. In this passage, Miller's theme is that no one in today's world seems to care about the quality of life.

On the Interpreting Literature and Arts section of the GED test, you may be asked analysis questions about the theme of a dramatic work. When this happens, think about the words, gestures, and actions of the characters. Put all the details together to form a statement about life. For example, suppose the main character of a play has dinner each night with his family, takes his family on an annual vacation, watches his children play sports and perform in plays, and always has time to discuss important issues with his family. In the play, his children become well-adjusted, happy, and successful people. One theme of the play might be that the family unit is central to having a healthy society. Here are some sample questions that require you to analyze a play's theme.

## Model Questions

- What statement about life do (the character's) words and actions suggest?
- Which statement summarizes the play's theme?
- What statement about life is the author making in this play?
- What is the author's purpose in writing the play?
- What is the main conflict in the play?

# Model Passage and Question

Read the following passage. See if you can figure out the answer to the analysis question about theme.

## WHY IS WILLY UPSET?

WILLY: I know it when I walk in. They seem to laugh at me.

LINDA: Why? Why would they laugh at you? Don't talk that way, Willy. *(Willy moves to the edge of the stage. Linda goes into the kitchen and starts to darn stockings.)*

(5) WILLY: I don't know the reason for it, but they just pass me by. I'm not noticed.

LINDA: But you're doing wonderful, dear. You're making seventy to a hundred dollars a week.

WILLY: But I gotta be at it ten, twelve hours a day. Other men—I

(10) don't know—they do it easier. I don't know why—I can't stop myself—I talk too much. A man oughta come in with a few words. One thing about Charley. He's a man of few words, and they respect him.

LINDA: You don't talk too much, you're just lively.

(15) WILLY: *(smiling)*: Well, I figure, what the hell, life is short, a couple of jokes. *(To himself)* I joke too much! *(The smile goes.)*

LINDA: Why? You're—

WILLY: I'm fat. I'm very—foolish to look at, Linda. I didn't tell you, but Christmas time I happened to be calling on F.H. Stewarts,

(20) and a salesman I know, as I was going in to see the buyer I heard him say something about—walrus. And I—I cracked him right across the face. I won't take that. I simply will not take that. But they do laugh at me. I know that.

From *Death of a Salesman* by Arthur Miller. Copyright ©1949, renewed 1977 by Arthur Miller. Used by permission of Viking Penguin, a division of Penguin Books USA, Inc.

Which of the following best expresses the theme of the passage?

**(1)** Most women are less concerned with money than men are.

**(2)** Lack of self-respect can torture men with doubts.

**(3)** A sense of humor can cure most painful doubts.

**(4)** People avoid talking about painful truths.

**(5)** People are products of their pasts.

The correct response is (2). Everything Willy says indicates that he feels people do not respect him: "They seem to laugh at me" (line 1) he says: "they pass me by. I'm not noticed," he says in lines 5-6. In lines 9-13 he condemns himself for being too talkative and says his friend Charley is "a man of few words, and they respect him." He tells his wife that when he heard a salesman comment on his weight sarcastically (lines 20-22), he "cracked him right across the face." As soon as he feels better about himself in lines 15-16 for being "lively," he says "I joke too much! (*The smile goes.*)" Therefore, (3) cannot be correct. Since Willy does nothing but brood over painful truths about himself, (4) is wrong. (5) is incorrect because no details suggest that the way Willy is today is any different from the way he has always been, and neither he nor his wife mention the past. Although Linda, his wife, is not tormented as Willy is about his status as a salesman, she is the one who mentions how much he earns a week in lines 7-8; so (1) is also not supported by details in the dialogue.

Items 1 through 3 refer to the passage that follows. Choose the one best answer to each item.

## WHY IS CHRIS ANGRY?

MOTHER: Altogether! *(To Chris, but not facing him)* Your brother's alive, darling, because if he's dead, your father killed him. Do you understand me now? As long as you live, that boy is alive. God does not let a son be killed by his father. Now you see,
(5) don't you? Now you see. *(Beyond control, she hurries up and into the house.)*

KELLER *(Chris has not moved. He speaks insinuatingly, questioning ly)*: She's out of her mind.

CHRIS *(in a broken whisper)*: Then...you did it? ...

(10) KELLER *(afraid of him, his deadly insistence)*: What's the matter with you? What the hell is the matter with you? ...

CHRIS: I want to know what you did, now what did you do? You had 120 cracked engine-heads, now what did you do?

KELLER: If you're going to hang me, I—

(15) CHRIS: I'm listening. God Almighty, I'm listening!

KELLER *(Their movements now are those of subtle pursuit and escape. Keller keeps a step out of Chris's range as he talks)*: You're a boy, what could I do? I'm in business, a man is in business; 120 cracked, you're out of business; you got a
(20) process, the process don't work you're out of business; you don't know how to operate, your stuff is no good; they close you up, they tear up your contracts, what the hell's it to them? You lay 40 years into a business and they knock you out in five minutes; what could I do, let them take 40 years, let them take
(25) my life away? *(His voice cracking.)* I never thought they'd install them. I swear to God. I thought they'd stop 'em before anybody took off.

CHRIS: Then why'd you ship them out?

KELLER: By the time they could spot them I thought I'd have the
(30) process going again, and I could show them they needed me and they'd let it go by. But weeks passed and I got no kickback, so I was going to tell them.

CHRIS: Then why didn't you tell them?

KELLER: It was too late. The paper, it was all over the front page,
(35) 21 went down, it was too late....

CHRIS: God in heaven, what kind of a man are you? Kids were hanging in the air by those heads. You know that!

1. Which of the following statements summarizes the major theme of the passage?

   (1) Work is the most important element of a person's life.
   (2) Anger does nothing to solve a problem.
   (3) People should do whatever they feel is best.
   (4) People have responsibility to others.
   (5) Making plane parts is a difficult business.

2. Which of the following words best describes Chris's attitude toward his father?

   (1) respect
   (2) amazement
   (3) indifference
   (4) sorrow
   (5) contempt

3. What might Chris do if his country were at war?

   (1) finish his education first, then enlist in the armed forces
   (2) refuse to join the armed forces
   (3) go into some kind of business that would help those fighting
   (4) become a spy
   (5) become a pilot

Answers are on page 326.

# Analyzing the Effect of Language and Gesture

## Prereading Prompt

In most conversations, you neither yell nor whisper. You speak in a "normal" tone of voice. At other times, you may speak very softly or very loudly. If you scream, "Get out of my room this minute!" and raise your fist, you make the point that you are angry. Your tone of voice and your gestures express your feelings.

On the GED, you may have to answer questions about the effects of language and gesture. You will learn how in this lesson.

## Key Words

**gestures**—movements that characters make indicated in stage directions

## Analyzing the Effect of Language

When you read a play, you can tell how the words are to be spoken only if such information is given in the stage directions. For example, if the stage directions say *with indifference*, you know that the character will speak without a great display of emotion. These stage directions help convey the intended *tone*, or manner of expression. Possible tones include angry, sad, confused, sweet, and nasty, for example.

The style of language used by characters adds meaning to the play. The characters' speech should fit their background, age, education, and so on. For example, to show highly educated people, the playwright might have the characters discuss complex philosophical concepts using sophisticated vocabulary. On the other hand, to show working class people in an American city, the playwright might use the informal, conversational language we hear in the following passage from Arthur Miller's *A View from the Bridge*. (The play is set in Brooklyn, New York; the bridge in the title is the Brooklyn Bridge; and Eddie is a longshoreman, or dockworker.)

> EDDIE: Catherine? *She turns to him.* I was just tellin' Beatrice... if you wanna go out, like... I mean I realize maybe I kept you home too much. Because he's the first guy you ever knew, y'know? I mean now that you got a job, you might meet some
> (5) fellas, and you get a different idea, y'know? I mean you could always come back to him, you're still only kids, the both of yiz. What's the hurry? Maybe you'd get around a little bit, you grow up a little more, maybe you'll see different in a couple of months. I mean you be surprised, it don't have to be him.
>
> (10) CATHERINE: No, we made up already.
>
> EDDIE (*with increasing anxiety*): Katie, wait a minute.
>
> CATHERINE: No, I made up my mind.

From *A View from the Bridge* by Arthur Miller. Copyright ©1955,1957, renewed 1983, 1985 by Arthur Miller. Used by permission of Viking Penguin, a division of Penguin Books USA, Inc.

## Analyzing the Effect of Gesture

You know that playwrights use a number of different techniques to convey their ideas. To bring their characters to life, they use gestures as well as language. These gestures are important because they give you hints about a character's personality and feelings. For instance, a stage direction that says *covers her mouth as she giggles* might suggest that the character is shy. When you read a play, pay attention to the stage directions to see what gestures the characters are using and what these actions reveal about their motives, attitudes, and feelings.

Since plays are meant to be performed, to grasp the fullest meaning you should try to imagine the characters on a stage as you read. Imagining the characters' movements, tone of voice, and facial expressions can help you more fully understand and appreciate a play.

On the Interpreting Literature and Arts section of the GED test, you may be asked analysis questions about the effects a playwright achieves through language and gestures. Below are some sample questions along with a strategy you can use to help find the answer.

## Model Questions

- What effects does (a gesture, tone of voice, style of language) have on (a certain character)?
- What does the playwright's choice of words tell you about the character?
- What does the playwright's choice of words tell you about the mood (or atmosphere) of the play?
- What tone does a character's voice take in lines 00-00?

## Strategy

Step 1: Read the passage carefully. Pay special attention to the stage directions. Keep the purpose question and items in mind as you read.

Step 2: Summarize what you have read. Try to imagine how the characters look and speak.

Step 3: Return to the item and make a prediction about the answer. Ask yourself these questions: What does this (style of language, gesture, way of speaking) suggest? For example, pounding on a desk would indicate anger, whereas giving someone a hug might suggest warmth and love. How has the playwright used language to convey his or her ideas? For instance, a character who speaks very formally might be highly educated, while a character who uses incorrect grammar and poor sentence structure might be uneducated.

Step 4: Compare your summary with the answer choices. See which answer provides the closest match. Then pick the best answer.

## Model Passage and Question

Read the following passage. See if you can figure out the answer to the analysis item.

**WHAT KIND OF PERSON IS MAMA?**

RUTH: I got to go in. We need the money.

MAMA: Somebody would of thought my children done all but starved to death the way they talk about money here late. Child, we got a great big old check coming tomorrow.

(5) RUTH: *(Sincerely, but also self-righteously)*: Now that's your money. It ain't got nothing to do with me. We all feel like that—Walter and Bennie and me—even Travis.

MAMA: *(Thoughtfully, and suddenly very far away)*: Ten thousand dollars—

(10) RUTH: Sure is wonderful.

MAMA: Ten thousand dollars.

RUTH: You know what you should do, Miss Lena? You should take yourself a trip somewhere. To Europe or South America or someplace—

(15) MAMA *(Throwing up her hands at the thought)*: Oh, child!

RUTH: I'm serious. Just pack up and leave! Go on away and enjoy yourself some. Forget about the family and have yourself a ball for once in your life—

MAMA *(drily)*: You sound like I'm about ready to die. Who'd go with
(20)  me? What I look like wandering 'round Europe by myself?

RUTH: Shoot—these here rich white women do it all the time. They don't think nothing of packing up their suitcases and piling on one of them big steamships and—swoosh!—they gone, child.

MAMA: Something always told me I wasn't no rich white woman.

What does the stage direction *(Thoughtfully, and suddenly very far away)* suggest about Mama?

> **(1)** that she is used to having a lot of money
>
> **(2)** that she is a dreamer
>
> **(3)** that she can't quite believe the money is coming
>
> **(4)** that she is about to go on a trip
>
> **(5)** that she might be losing her mind

The correct answer is (3). A stage direction that shows someone first being thoughtful and then speaking as if far away implies that the character feels that the subject of her thoughts and words are unreal to her. This suggestion is strengthened when he repeats the words "Ten thousand dollars." It is obvious that Mama is not used to having so much money. (1) is not correct because "*suddenly very far away*" suggests that the character is not used to saying words like "ten thousand dollars," let alone having that amount of money. If she were, she wouldn't say the words as if she were far away. (2) is not correct because the stage directions say that she is "thoughtful"; therefore, she is not a dreamer. In fact, Mamma's realistic character is dramatized by her practical question in line 20 about the trip Ruth proposes that Mama take to "Europe or South America or someplace—" (lines 14-15). (4) is not correct because the words "*suddenly very far away*" suggest a feeling of disbelief, as if one were in a dream. The words do not suggest that anyone is, in fact, going away. (5) is not correct because anyone who is thoughtful is not about to lose her mind.

Items 1 through 3 refer to the passage that follows. Choose the one best answer to each item.

### WHY IS TOM WORRIED ABOUT LAURA?

TOM: Just one little warning, Mother. I didn't tell him anything about Laura. I didn't let on that we had dark ulterior motives. I just said, "How about coming home for dinner some time?" and he said, "Fine," and that was the whole conversation.

(5) AMANDA: I bet it was, too. I tell you, sometimes you can be as eloquent as an oyster. However, when he sees how pretty and sweet that child is, he's going to be, well, he's going to be very glad he was asked over here to have some dinner. *(Sits in arm chair.)*

(10) TOM: Mother, just one thing. You won't expect too much of Laura, will you?

AMANDA: I don't know what you mean. *(Tom crosses slowly to Amanda. He stands for a moment, looking at her. Then—)*

TOM: Well, Laura seems all those things to you and me because
(15) she's ours and we love her. We don't even notice she's crippled any more.

AMANDA: Don't use that word.

TOM: Mother, you have to face the facts; she is, and that's not all.

AMANDA: What do you mean "that's not all"? *(Tom kneels by her*
(20) *chair.)*

TOM: Mother—you know that Laura is very different from other girls.

AMANDA: Yes, I do know that, and I think that difference is all in her favor, too.

(25) TOM: Not quite all—in the eyes of others—strangers—she's terribly shy. She lives in a world of her own and these things make her seem a little peculiar to people outside the house.

AMANDA: Don't use that word peculiar.

TOM: You have to face facts.—She is.

(30) AMANDA: I don't know in any way she's peculiar. *(Music cue 12, till curtain. Tom pauses a moment for music, then—)*

TOM: Mother, Laura lives in a world of little glass animals. She plays old phonograph records—and—that's about all—*(Tom rises slowly, goes quietly out the door right, leaving it open, and*
(35) *exits slowly up the alley. Amanda rises, goes on to fire-escape landing right, looks at moon.)*

AMANDA: Laura! Laura! *(Laura answers from kitchen right.)*

LAURA: Yes, Mother.

AMANDA: Let those dishes go and come in front! *(Laura appears*
(40) *with dish towel. Gaily.)* Laura, come here and make a wish on the moon! ...

LAURA: What shall I wish for, Mother?

AMANDA: *(Her voice trembling and her eyes suddenly filling with*
(45)    *tears.)* Happiness! And just a little bit of good fortune! *(The*
*stage dims out.)*

From *The Glass Menagerie*, by Tennessee Williams. Copyright ©1945 by Tennessee Williams and Edwina D. Williams and renewed 1973 by Tennessee Williams. Reprinted by permission of Random House, Inc.

1. Amanda does not like Tom to use the words "crippled" and "peculiar" when discussing his sister. What does this suggest about Amanda?

    (1) She is trying to improve Tom's vocabulary.
    (2) She regards Tom as an intruder.
    (3) She is trying hard to face up to reality.
    (4) She is avoiding reality.
    (5) She is an intolerant person.

2. What attitude does Tom express toward Laura in lines 25-27?

    (1) angry
    (2) resentful
    (3) sympathetic
    (4) humorous
    (5) sarcastic

3. What do the stage direction *"Her voice trembling and her eyes suddenly filling with tears"* suggest about Amanda?

    (1) that she is a fool
    (2) that she is a hypocrite
    (3) that she sincerely wants the most for her children
    (4) that she will do anything to get what she wants
    (5) that she is a crybaby

Answers are on page 327.

# CHAPTER 4

**Poetry** is very old. It began with the earliest music and dance. People sang and danced to express their feelings about life. Today, most poems are not sung, but they are meant to be read aloud. Poetry is a special way of expressing thoughts and emotions in which each word's meaning counts a great deal.

Maya Angelou                                    Credit: AP/Wide World Photos

## Prereading Prompt

Have you ever said to a friend, "I'm as hungry as a bear?" If so, there may be "a touch of the poet" in you, and you may not know it!

Have you ever walked along the street singing these words by Aretha Franklin?

Think
Think about what you're trying to do to me
Think
Let your mind go
Let yourself be free

From "Think" by Aretha Franklin and Theodore R. White. Copyright by the composers. Reprinted by permission of Theodore R. White.

If you enjoy singing lyrics like these, you may love poetry and not know it. Finding the techniques poets use to express emotions and communicate ideas in fresh, interesting ways is a useful skill that will take the mystery out of poetry. It will also help you enjoy the poetry that you read. Knowing how to do this is very important for answering GED questions. You will learn how in this lesson.

# POETRY

## What is Poetry?

Poetry is one way of expressing thoughts and emotions. A poet, like a composer, uses rhythm and sound to express emotions and communicate ideas. However, composers use musical techniques to write their songs, while poets use literary techniques to write their poems.

One important literary technique used by poets is **rhyme**, or the repetition of similar or identical sounds. Rhyming words usually come at the end of their lines, as in the following example from "Otto," by Gwendolyn Brooks:

> It's Christmas day. I did not get
> The presents I hoped for. Yet
> It is not nice to frown or fret.

Excerpt from "Otto" by Gwendolyn Brooks from *Bronzeville Boys and Girls*. Copyright ©1956 by Gwendolyn Brooks Blakely. Reprinted by permission of the author.

Another important technique used by poets is **rhythm,** the pattern of stressed and unstressed sounds. In these lines by A. E. Housman, we have put the heavy sounds in capital letters and underlined them to show the pattern of stressed syllables. As you read these lines, consider how the rhythm helps express this part of the poem's meaning:

> When I was ONE-and-TWENty
>   I HEARD a WISE man SAY,
> "Give CROWNS and POUNDS and GUINeas,
>   But NOT your HEART aWAY."

From "A Shropshire Lad" fron *The Collected Poems of A.E. Houseman*. Copyright ©1967 by Robert Symons. Used by permission of Henry Holt & Co.

Poets also use other techniques to help create strong mental pictures in their readers' minds. By using a heavy beat to emphasize a word or by making a comparison so that you see something from a different angle, poets are able to express ideas and emotions in fresh, original ways. Read (or sing) these lyrics by Burt Bacharach and Hal David to see if you agree:

> If you see me walkin' down the street
> And I start to cry
> Each time we meet
> Walk on by
> Walk on by.

Excerpt from "Walk on By". Copyright ©1964 (renewed) New Hidden Valley Music & Casa David. All rights reserved. Used by permission of Warner/ChappellMusic, Inc.

## Key Words

**rhyme**—the pattern of similar sounds in a poem, usually appearing at the ends of lines

**rhythm**—a pattern of stressed and unstressed sounds in poetry

# Literal Comprehension of Poetry

## Key Words

**narrative poetry**—poetry that tells a story, with plot, characters, and dialogue

**lyric poetry**—poetry that expresses a thought or an intense emotion through images

## The Form of Poetry

No doubt you have noticed that poems look different from other forms of literature. Their form—the arrangement of words—sets poetry apart from prose. Poems are almost always written in **lines**. Unlike the lines of sentences, poetic lines have a specific number of words to create poetic effects such as rhythm and rhyme. Poetic lines are arranged in groups called **stanzas**, unlike the sentences in prose, which are arranged in paragraphs.

Because of their unique form, poems can usually be read quickly. Just as you experience a burst of flavor when you bite into a juicy piece of fruit, reading a poem will give you a quick burst of meaning and sensation. When you step back and think about a poem you have read, however, you may see a deeper meaning in the poem.

## Finding Main Ideas and Details in Poems

Even though poems have a different form from other types of writing, they still have main ideas and details like nonfiction, fiction, and drama. Poets often select sensory details to help you grasp their main ideas more fully. These details appeal to your sight, taste, touch, smell, and hearing. Poets also arrange their ideas in specific ways to convey their ideas.

There are basically two types of poems: **narrative** and **lyric**. **Narrative poems** tell a story. Like novels and short stories in fiction, narrative poems have plots, characters, setting, and dialogue. Below is an excerpt from the narrative poem "Casey at the Bat." As you read, see if you can follow the story.

### HOW IS THE BASEBALL GAME GOING?

#### Casey at the Bat

The outlook wasn't brilliant for the Mudville nine that day;
The score stood two to four, with but an inning left to play.
So, when Cooney died at second, and Burrows did the same,
A sickly silence fell upon the patrons of the game.
(5)  A straggling few got up to go, leaving there the rest,
With that hope that springs eternal within the human breast,
For they thought, "If only Casey could get a whack at that,"
They'd put up even money now, with Casey at the bat.

From "Casey at the Bat," by Ernest L. Thayer.

This brief excerpt gives you specific details about the setting (a baseball stadium), characters (the Mudville Nine), and the plot (who will win the game). You do not have to infer these details; they are stated directly.

**Lyric poems**, in contrast, are usually short and express a thought or an intense emotion. Below is a lyric poem called "I Shall Not Care" by Sara Teasdale. As you read it, see if you can identify the emotion the poet conveys.

### HOW DOES THE POET FEEL?

#### I Shall Not Care

When I am dead and over me bright April
Shakes out her rain-drenched hair,
Tho' you should lean above me broken-hearted,
I shall not care.

(5)

I shall have peace, as leafy trees are peaceful
When rain bends down the bough,
And I shall be more silent and cold-hearted
Than you are now.

"I Shall Not Care" from *Collected Poems of Sara Teasdale* by Sara Teasdale. Copyright ©1937 Macmillian Publishing Company. Reprinted with permission of the publisher.

In this poem the speaker expresses a deep feeling of hurt and resentment by describing herself as dead and buried in the springtime of the year. At first, we think the speaker is the hard-hearted one, who says she "shall not care" about her lover's "broken-hearted" grief. The second stanza, however, states the poet's real meaning—that only if she were dead would she be as "silent and cold-hearted" as her lover is now. Much of the poem's power comes from the sharp change of feeling between the two stanzas—from the apparent sadness and indifference in the first stanza to the real bitterness suddenly revealed in the last line.

## Model Questions and Strategy

On the Interpreting Literature and Arts section of the GED test, you may be asked questions about the literal meaning of a poem. Below are several sample questions about poetry that you can be asked on the GED. These questions are followed by a strategy you can use to help you answer these test items.

- The poet tells about _____?
- What is the main idea of this poem?
- How does the title reveal the meaning of the poem?

### Strategy

Step 1: Look at the poem's title. The title will often tell you what the poem will be about. For example, you would expect a poem with the title "Casey at the Bat" to be about a specific baseball player at a specific game, and it is. Likewise, the title "I Shall Not Care" reveals the mood the poem will express.

Step 2: Look for the stated main idea. Many poets express their ideas in clear, straightforward language. In "I Shall Not Care," for example, the poet expresses the main idea directly: "When I am dead... [although] you should lean above me broken-hearted... I shall have peace... And I shall be more silent and cold-hearted/Than you are now."

Step 3: Look for details that support the stated main idea. Ask yourself: What details back-up the main idea I found?

Step 4: Predict the answer to the test question.

Step 5: Select the choice that best matches your prediction.

## Model Passage and Question

The question below is based on the poem "Richard Cory" by E. A. Robinson. Read the poem and see if you can find the answer to the literal question about it.

### WHAT DOES THE POET TELL YOU ABOUT RICHARD CORY?

#### Richard Cory

Whenever Richard Cory went down town,
We people on the pavement looked at him:
He was a gentleman from sole to crown,
Clean favored, and imperially slim.

(5)  And he was always quietly arrayed,
And he was always human when he talked;
But still he fluttered pulses when he said,
"Good-morning," and he glittered when he walked.

And he was rich—yes, richer than a king—
(10) And admirably schooled in every grace:
In fine, we thought that he was everything
To make us wish that we were in his place.

So on we worked, and waited for the light,
And went without the meat, and cursed the bread;
(15) And Richard Cory, one calm summer night,
Went home and put a bullet through his head.

"Richard Cory," by Edwin Arlington Robinson from *The Children of the Night*.

The poet tells about Richard Cory's

**(1)** personality, appearance, and death

**(2)** work habits and his dreams of death

**(3)** wealth and behavior and the resentment they caused in town

**(4)** wealth and how the rich and poor were different in town

**(5)** wealthy appearance and actual poverty

The correct answer is (1). The poet gives specific details about Richard Cory's personality: he was "a gentleman from sole to crown" and "always human when he talked." His appearance is described as "Clean favored, and imperially slim" and "quietly arrayed." His death is described as well: "And Richard Cory, one calm summer night/Went home and put a bullet through his head." (2) is incorrect; although the poem does describe Richard Cory's going to town, we are not told anything about his work habits, nor are we told any of his dreams. (3) is false because the townspeople did not seem to resent his riches; rather, they envied him. Eliminate (4) because we are not told about any of the differences between rich and poor; we only learn that Richard Cory was rich and most of the others in town were not. Finally, (5) is wrong because no detail in the poem presents the idea that Richard Cory is actually poor despite his rich appearance.

Items 1 through 3 refer to the poem that follows. Choose the one best answer to each item.

### WHAT DO YOU DO WHEN A GOOD MAN DIES?

#### Lament

Listen, children:
Your father is dead.
From his old coats
I'll make you little jackets;
(5) I'll make you little trousers
From his old pants.
There'll be in his pockets
Things he used to put there,
Keys and pennies
(10) Covered with tobacco;
Dan shall have the pennies
To save in his bank;
Anne shall have the keys
To make a pretty noise with.
(15) Life must go on,
And the dead be forgotten;
Life must go on,
Though good men die;
Anne, eat your breakfast;
(20) Dan, take your medicine;
Life must go on;
I forget just why.

1. What is the main idea expressed in the poem?

   (1) A good man who has died should be remembered by everyone.
   (2) Family life should continue in spite of a father's death.
   (3) Small children should obey their mother as a way of remembering their dead father.
   (4) The dead often leave things of little value behind.
   (5) It's important to tell children when a death occurs.

2. How does the speaker try to get her children to go on with life?

   (1) She buys new jackets and trousers for them.
   (2) She gives them presents.
   (3) She makes sure they are well-fed and in good health.
   (4) She throws away the dead man's clothing.
   (5) She throws a party, with noisemakers.

3. How does the title of the poem reveal its literal meaning?

   (1) The title suggests that the poem will be about a feeling of sorrow or grief.
   (2) The title suggests that the poem will tell about people who forget why they feel sad.
   (3) The title suggests that the poem will tell a story about death in a family.
   (4) The title is the opposite of what the poem is about.
   (5) The title reveals the main emotion of the poem, anger.

Answers are on page 327.

# Inferring Theme and Point of View

## Prereading Prompt

Suppose you see a movie in which a poor child grows up to become the President of the United States. What are your thoughts as you leave the theatre? Perhaps you think, "If the character in the movie could do it, I can too," or "In America, anything is possible." Both these ideas could be the themes, or main ideas, of the movie. Although these ideas are never directly stated in the movie, they are revealed through the unfolding of events.

Poems, like movies, also have themes. The theme sometimes appears throughout a poem in various statements and images. At other times, the poet does not introduce the theme until late in the poem. To discover the unstated theme of a poem, look at the events that take place in the poem, as well as the title. These will give you clues about what statement the poet is making about life.

On the GED, you may be asked to infer the theme and point of view of a poem. You will learn how in this lesson.

## Inferring Theme

As you will recall from Fiction Lesson 7, the **theme** of a literary work is the main idea that it expresses. The theme will be a general idea about life and experience. Do not confuse theme with **subject**, the main topic. For example, the subject of a poem might be love, while the theme could be "Love conquers all."

Below is a poem called "How Heavy the Days" by Hermann Hesse. As you read this poem, see if you can identify its subject and theme.

**HOW DOES THE POET FEEL ABOUT LOVE?**

**How Heavy the Days**

How heavy the days are.
There's not a fire that can warm me,
Not a sun to laugh with me,
Everything bare,
(5) Everything cold and merciless,
And even the beloved, clear
Stars look desolately down,
Since I learned in my heart that
Love can die.

"How Heavy the Days," by Hermann Hesse from *Poems by Herman Hesse* translated by James Wright. Copyright ©1970 by James Wright. Reprinted by permission of Farrar, Straus & Girioux and Jonathan Cape, Ltd.

The subject of this poem is love. The theme is that the world looks depressing to someone who is no longer loved.

## Inferring Point of View

In poetry as in fiction the author's meaning is often stated indirectly. Often you have to infer the point of view of the speaker of the poem just as you often have to infer the attitudes of the narrator in a story or a novel. The speaker in the poem—the "I"—may be the poet or a character whose personality the poet is adopting as a role, the way an actor will take on the identity of a character in a movie. Just as you infer a character's attitudes from what he or she says and does, so you can infer the attitudes of the speaker in a poem by putting together direct statements of meaning to figure out the unstated point of view.

As you read "Housecleaning" by Nikki Giovanni, ask yourself two questions: (1) What is the subject of the poem?; and (2) What is the speaker's attitude toward the subject?

**HOW DOES THE SPEAKER MEAN BY "HOUSECLEANING"?**

**Housecleaning**

i always liked house cleaning
even as a child
i dug straightening
the cabinets
(5) putting new paper on
the shelves
washing the refrigerator
inside out
and unfortunately this habit has
(10) carried over and i find
i must remove you
from my life

"Housecleaning," by Nikki Giovanni from *The Women and the Men* Copyright ©1970,1974, 1975. Used by permission of William Morrow & Co.

In the last two lines, we discover that the subject of the poem is not literally housecleaning but the speaker's relationship with her lover—or ex-lover. By "housecleaning" the speaker means "getting rid of her lover."

What can you infer from the comparison between literal housecleaning and her behavior toward her lover? Her implied meaning is that her lover made her life messy and dirty in some way. Since "even as a child" the speaker liked to have things orderly and clean she "unfortunately" "must remove you [the lover]/from my life." The attitude of the speaker toward the poem's subject, therefore, is one of determination—a determination to keep her life in order.

## Model Questions and Strategy

On the Interpreting Literature and Arts section of the GED test, you may be asked inferential questions about the theme or point of view in a poem. Below are two sample questions about poetry that you can be asked on the GED. These questions are followed by a strategy you can use to help you answer these test items.

• What is the theme of this poem?

• The speaker in this poem is _____?

• How does (the speaker of the poem) feel about (a topic or event in the poem)?

• The (speaker of the poem) says/does (some statement/some action) because he/she thinks _____

### Strategy

<u>Step 1:</u> Read the poem carefully, keeping the purpose question and items in mind.

<u>Step 2:</u> If you are asked a question about the theme, summarize the main idea in your own words. Ask yourself: What is the subject of this poem? What is the speaker's attitude about this subject?

<u>Step 3:</u> Try to predict the answer to the test question.

<u>Step 4:</u> Select the choice that best matches your prediction.

# Model Passage and Question

Read the passage below. Then answer the inference question that follows.

## HOW DOES THE SPEAKER VIEW THE HARLEM NIGHT?

### Harlem Night Song

Come,
Let us roam the night together
Singing.

I love you.

(5)  Across
The Harlem roof-tops
Moon is shining.
Night sky is blue.
Stars are great drops
(10) Of golden dew.

Down the street
A band is playing.

I love you.

Come,
(15) Let us roam the night together
Singing.

Excerpt from "Harlem Night Song " from *Selected Poems* by Langston
Hughes. Copyright ©1926 by Alfred A Knopf and Langston Hughes and
renewed 1945 by Langston Hughes. Reprinted by permission of Random.
House, Inc.

What is the implied theme of the poem?

**(1)** Love makes you feel like running away from the world around you.

**(2)** Harlem nights are filled with loud music and people roaming the streets.

**(3)** Love makes you feel happy and full of life.

**(4)** Some invitations are not worth accepting.

**(5)** People who have nothing to do get into trouble.

The correct answer is (3). The poet invites the person he loves to "roam the night together/singing." Twice he declares "I love you." He wants the person he loves to see the moon, sky, and stars with him, and to hear the band. He is in a joyful, expansive mood. (1) is incorrect because the speaker does not suggest that being in love makes him want to run away. On the contrary, he invites the person he loves to come with him and experience the Harlem night. (2) is incorrect because the speaker says that a band is playing—not that it is loud. Further, nowhere does the speaker state that anyone besides himself and his lover is roaming the streets. (4) is wrong because the speaker's invitation seems to be one that most people would want to accept. There is nothing expressed in the poem that seems negative. Eliminate (5) because the speaker is in love and has observed many things that he wants to share with the person he loves. He is not without things to do, and there is no hint of trouble.

# Lesson 2 Exercise

Item 1 refers to the poem that follows. Choose the best answer.

## HOW DOES THE SPEAKER FEEL ABOUT LOVE?

**Brown Penny**

I whispered, 'I am too young.'
And then, 'I am old enough';
Wherefore I threw a penny
To find out if I might love.
(5) 'Go and love, go and love, young man,
If the lady be young and fair.'
Ah, penny, brown penny, brown penny,
I am looped in the loops of her hair.

O love is a crooked thing.
(10) There is nobody wise enough
To find out all that is in it,
For he would be thinking of love
Till the stars had run away
And the shadows eaten the moon.
(15) Ah, penny, brown penny, brown penny,
One cannot begin it too soon.

"Brown Penny" by William Butler Yeats from *The Poems of W.B. Yeats: A New Edition* edited by Richard J. Finneran (New York: Macmillan, 1983). Reprinted with permission of Macmillan Publishing Company.

1. Which of the following best describes the speakers attitude toward love in the poem?

   **(1)** excited and confident
   **(2)** angry and proud
   **(3)** hesitating and eager
   **(4)** sad and disappointed
   **(5)** carefree and happy

Items 2 and 3 refer to the following poem. Choose the best answer

**HOW DOES THE SPEAKER FEEL ABOUT POLITICS?**

### Politics

*'In our time the destiny of man presents its meaning*
*in political terms.'*—Thomas Mann

How can I,that girl standing there.
My attention fix
On Roman or on Russian
Or on Spanish politics?
(5)   Yet here's a travelled man that knows
What he talks about,
And there's a politician
That has read and thought,
And maybe what they say is true
(10)   Of war and war's alarms,
But O that I were young again
And held her in my arms!

"Politics" by William Butler Yeats from *The Poems of W.B. Yeats: A New Edition*
edited by Richard J. Finneran. Copyright ©1940 by Georgie Yeats, renewed
1968 by Bertha Georgie Yeats, Michael Butler Yeats, and Anne Yeats. Reprinted
with permission of Macmillan Publishing Company.

2. The implied speaker of the poem is

(1) a politician
(2) a young man
(3) Thomas Mann
(4) an older man
(5) a world traveller

3. The theme of the poem is best expressed by which of the following?

(1) Politicians want to interfere with love, so we must keep it a secret from them if we want to be happy.
(2) Finding your true love is the best way to gain the happiness that the politicians are always promising to give everyone.
(3) Politics may be the most important force in life, but love has the strongest meaning for people of all ages.
(4) In a world controlled by war and terror, love is the only solution to the conflicts between people.
(5) In times of crisis, love is an irresponsible impulse that should not distract us from serious problems.

Answers are on page 328.

# Inferring the Meaning of Figurative Language

## Prereading Prompt

Every day you make comparisons. You might say, "I'm as cold as ice," or "You're as busy as a bee." These comparisons are not original. Nevertheless, they serve to get across the idea that you want to express.

Poets, too, use comparisons and other forms of figurative language to convey their ideas. However, they try to be as original as possible. On the GED, you may be asked to answer questions about the meaning of figurative language such as comparisons. You will learn how in this lesson.

## Key Words

**figurative language**—words that are not used as exact representations of their meaning

**simile**—a comparison of two different things that uses *as* or *like*

**metaphor**—a comparison of unlike things which says that one *is* the other

**personification**—describes something nonhuman as if it were human

**symbol**—an object that represents not only itself but a much larger idea

# Inferring the Meaning of Figurative Language

Poetry is different from other types of writing because it relies on **figurative language**, words that are not used as exact representations of their meaning, to convey the poet's thoughts. You learned about **similes** and **metaphors**, two kinds of figurative language, in Lesson 8 of the Fiction section of this book. A simile, you will recall, compares two different things by saying that one is *as* or *like* the other. Here is a simile from the poet Langston Hughes:

> What happens to a dream deferred?
> Does it dry up
> Like a raisin in the sun?

From *The DreamKeeper and Other Poems* by Langston Hughes. Copyright ©1932 by Alfred A. Knopf, Inc. and renewed 1960 by Langston Hughes. Reprinted by permission of the publisher.

A *metaphor* compares unlike things by saying one *is* the other. This metaphor is by the poet William Ernest Henley:

> I am the captain of my soul.

Similes and metaphors are most helpful in giving brief, intense descriptions. Thus they are especially suited to poetry, a form of writing that greatly depends on condensed language.

Another type of figurative language that is often used in poetry is **personification**, describing something nonhuman in human terms, for example, "The sky weeps." Obviously, the sky cannot weep, but the poet is treating something nonhuman, the sky, as if it were human. This example also makes the sky sound as if it had feelings, a human trait.

Often, poets use **symbols** in their poems. A **symbol** is an object that represents not only itself but also an idea that is much broader in scope. This country's flag is a familiar example of a symbol. It represents the United States of America, its government, its people, and so on. In that sense, the United States flag is a symbol: It represents an idea that is greater than itself. A poet can use a symbol throughout a poem and thereby explore its many different meaning.

On the Interpreting Literature and Arts section of the GED test, you may be asked to interpret figurative language in a poem. Use this strategy to help you answer these questions:

Step 1: Read the poem carefully, keeping the purpose question and items in mind.

Step 2: If the question is about a comparison, try to visualize what is being compared. By picturing the ideas in your mind, you will be better able to understand the poem's meaning.

If the question is about personification, ask yourself: "What human qualities are being described? What do they reveal about the object?"

If the question is a symbol, ask yourself: "What does this symbol stand for? How is it described?"

# Model Passage and Question

Read the following poem. Then try to figure out the answer to the question, which asks you to interpret figurative language.

## WHERE IS THE POET GOING

### The Road Not Taken

Two roads diverged in a yellow wood,
And sorry I could not travel both
And be one traveler, long I stood
And looked down one as far as I could
(5) To where it bent in the undergrowth;

Then took the other, as just as fair,
And having perhaps the better claim,
Because it was grassy and wanted wear;
Though as for that, the passing there
(10) Had worn them really about the same,

And both that morning equally lay
In leaves no step had trodden back.
Oh, I kept the first for another day!
Yet knowing how way leads on to way,
(15) I doubted if I should ever come back.

I shall be telling this with a sigh
Somewhere ages and ages hence:
Two roads diverged in a wood, and I—
I took the one less traveled by,
(20) And that has made all the difference.

"The Road Not Taken," by Robert Frost.

The road is a symbol for
**(1)** love
**(2)** life
**(3)** paths in the woods
**(4)** highways
**(5)** death

The correct choice is (2). The poet sees two roads in the woods and chooses the one less traveled, which has made all the difference in his life. We, too, travel down many roads in our lives. We make many choices and they make "all the difference." (1) is incorrect because there are no details that suggest love, no mention of people's feelings towards each other, of doing things together, of sharing life. (3) is incorrect because the question asks about a *symbol*. A path cannot be a symbol for a road since a symbol is something that represents an idea that is broader in scope than the literal meaning. (4) is incorrect because, once again, highways cannot be symbols for roads. (5) is incorrect because the poet travels down one road, thinks about his choice, wonders if he will try the other one one day, and then sums up his actions. These details in no way imply death; rather they suggest choice and life.

# Lesson 3 Exercise

Items 1 through 3 refer to the poem that follows. Choose the one best answer to each item.

**SHOULD PEOPLE SHARE THEIR FEELINGS WITH EACH OTHER?**

**Any Human to Another**

The ills I sorrow at
Not me alone
Like an arrow,
Pierce to the marrow,
(5) Through the fat
And past the bone.

Your grief and mine
Must intertwine
Like sea and river,
(10) Be fused and mingle,
Diverse yet single,
Forever and forever.

Let no man be so proud
And confident,
(15) To think he is allowed
A little tent
Pitched in a meadow
Of sun and shadow
All his little own.

(20) Joy may be shy, unique,
Friendly to a few,
Sorrow never scorned to speak
To any who
Were false or true.

(25) Your every grief
Like a blade
Shining and unsheathed
Must strike me down.
Of bitter aloes wreathed,
(30) My sorrow must be laid
On your head like a crown.

1. What words suggest that joy is like people?

   (1) proud and confident
   (2) shining and unsheathed
   (3) diverse yet single
   (4) fused and mingle
   (5) shy, unique, friendly to a few

2. What idea is expressed in the third stanza?

   (1) People cannot live without other people.
   (2) People should live in tents.
   (3) Be confident and proud.
   (4) Try to find a place for yourself that is quiet and peaceful.
   (5) Some people like living alone.

3. In the last two lines, the poet suggests

   (1) feeling sorry for yourself is not useful
   (2) sharing sorrow is honorable
   (3) people should wear crowns
   (4) royalty never feels pain
   (5) friends should share only their joys

Answers are on page 328.

# Applying Ideas in Poetry

Prereading Prompt

A person who believes in the benefits of exercise would also probably eat and drink healthfully. You can make reasonable assumptions about what people might do in new situations based on what they have done in the past. A person who dislikes loud music would probably not attend a rock concert. A person who loves reading biographies of movie stars would probably see a great many films each year. Knowing how to take information from one situation and use it in a new context is very important for answering GED questions. You will learn how in this lesson.

## Applying Themes and Details

Most poetic themes are universal in application. That means that they are themes that many people can identify with. As a result, it is often not difficult to "translate" the ideas of a poem into a new setting.

The first step in answering an application item about theme or detail is to determine what the poet is saying. Then, apply that idea to the new setting. If a poet speaks of the beauty of an untouched landscape, for example, you might assume that he or she would be in favor of strong environmental controls.

Read this stanza from a poem about words. As you read, think about what attitude the poet has towards words.

> I love bright words, words up and singing early;
> Words that are luminous in the dark, and sing;
> Warm lazy words, white cattle under trees;
> I love words opalescent, cool, and pearly,
> Like midsummer moths, and honeyed words like bees,
> Gilded and sticky, with a little sting.

The idea behind these lines is that words can be beneficial and beautiful and yet potentially harmful, too. An application of that principle might be to look for something else that is beneficial and beautiful and yet potentially harmful at the same time. The poet could express the same thought in words such as these:

> rain-filled words like summer storms/Brief and refreshing, with lightning sparkling words like waterfalls/Majestic and thundering, crashing to the rocks below

## Applying the Poet's Attitude

Recognizing the poet's attitude means thinking about both the theme of the poem and the details that support the idea. Sometimes the poet's attitude is clearly expressed as the theme of the poem; at other times, you must make inferences. If the poet makes use of a speaker, it is important to distinguish between the speaker's attitude and the poet's attitude.

If a theme of a poem is love for language, you can apply the poet's attitude to situations apart from poetry. You can assume, for example, that if the poet were a teacher, he or she would be likely to teach a course on the history of English which would explore the development of language rather than a course on marine biology which probably would be a very factual discussion of sea life.

## Model Passage and Question

Read the following poem. See if you can find the answer to the application item.

**ACCORDING TO THE POET, WHAT SHOULD CAUSE SORROW?**

**If There Be Sorrow**

If there be sorrow
let it be
for things undone...
undreamed
(5)    unrealized
       unattained
to these add one:
Love withheld...
...restrained

"If There Be Sorrow" from *I Am a Black Woman* by Mari Evans published by William Morrow & Co., 1970 by permission of the author.

What advice might the poet give to a son or daughter who wants to sail across the Atlantic alone?

**(1)** Wait until you are older.

**(2)** Do it immediately.

**(3)** Try to find something to do that is less risky.

**(4)** Don't be so unrealistic. You could never do that!

**(5)** Go to school instead.

The correct answer is (2). The poem's underlying message is that sorrow comes from not doing things, not realizing and attaining one's dreams. Therefore, the poet would most likely advise her child to follow his or her dream. (1) is incorrect because, as the first six lines suggest, sorrow comes from not trying to attain one's dreams. (3) is incorrect because the poet does not discuss which dreams someone should follow. The implication of the poem is that if you can dream it, you should try to attain it. (4) is incorrect because the poet is saying that sorrow comes from not following one's dreams—which may or may not be realistic. The main idea of the poem is that to avoid sorrow, one should dream and try to reach one's dreams. (5) is incorrect because nowhere is it suggested that one should do anything other than try to realize one's dreams.

Items 1 through 3 refer to the poem that follows. Choose the one best answer to each item.

### WHAT ADVICE DOES THIS SON HAVE FOR HIS FATHER?

#### Do Not Go Gentle Into That Good Night

Do not go gentle into that good night,
Old age should burn and rave at the close of day;
Rage, rage against the dying of the light.

Though wise men at their end know dark is right,
(5) Because their words had forked no lightning they
Do not go gentle into that good night.

Good men, the last wave by, crying how bright
Their frail deeds might have danced in a green bay,
Rage, rage against the dying of the light.

(10) Wild men who caught and sang the sun in flight,
And learn, too late, they grieved it on its way,
Do not go gentle into that good night.

Grave men, near death, who see with blinding sight
Blind eyes could blaze like meteors and be gay,
(15) Rage, rage against the dying of the light.

And you, my father, there on the sad height,
Curse, bless, me now with your fierce tears, I pray,
Do not go gentle into that good night.
Rage, rage against the dying of the light.

1. If the attitude the poet expresses in the title of the poem were applied to the situation of an AIDS patient, the poet most likely would say which of the following statements to the patient?

   (1) "Hang on through your dark night of suffering until science finds a cure."
   (2) "Be gentle with your doctors; they are doing all they can."
   (3) "Keep yourself in a gentle sleep to avoid the worst of the pain."
   (4) "Look forward to the 'good night of death' as a relief from your pain."
   (5) "Keep struggling against the night of your early death."

2. Which of the following do you think the speaker would LEAST like to hear his father say?

   (1) I know that I am dying and I hate it.
   (2) I am at peace knowing that soon I'll meet my maker.
   (3) There's so much of the world I haven't seen!
   (4) I want to accomplish so much more!
   (5) How dare you tell me how to live and die!

3. With which of the following ideas would the poet most likely agree?

   (1) most people who suffer bring their misfortunes on themselves.
   (2) Old age should be devoted to calm reflection on one's whole life.
   (3) Protesting against human suffering expresses strength of character.
   (4) Human beings are too blind to understand their situations.
   (5) No human beings are really gentle or courageous.

Answers are on page 329.

# Analyzing Structure and Rhyme in Poetry

## Prereading Prompt

Have you ever brought something into your room in order to change how the room looks or feels? For example, you may have brought flowers to give a warmer effect, or you may have taken away all the knickknacks to create a less cluttered look. Poets, too, make certain choices based on the effect they want to create. They might vary the line length and have few rhymes in a poem to create a jarring, unpredictable effect. They might make each line the same length and have many rhyming words to create a soothing, more inviting effect.

Knowing how to analyze structure and rhyme in poetry is important for answering GED questions. You will learn how in this lesson.

## Key Words

**stanza**—a group of lines forming a unit in a poem

**rhyme**—pattern of similar sounds in a poem usually found at the end of lines

# Effects of Structure in Poetry

The lines of a poem can be arranged in a number of different ways; for example, the lines can be arranged a a single, unbroken block of lines. That might create an effect of unified, powerful thought and feeling, such as you might experience listening to a strong vocalist singing a series of lines in a song in one extended breath. On the other hand, the lines might be arranged in **stanzas**, groups of lines that form separate units within a poem. Stanzas, therefore, correspond to paragraphs in prose, which group sentences into units. The number and arrangement of lines in a stanza help create the effect of the poem, along with the statements and images in the lines, Different kinds of stanzas can have different effects, and the same kind of stanza can be used different ways for different effects. Read the following poem by Wallace Stevens and ask yourself how the stanza form helps create the effect of the poem.

### WHAT DOES THE SPEAKER FEEL IN THE PARK?

#### Vacancy in the Park

March...Someone has walked across the
    snow.
Someone looking for he knows not what.

It is like a boat that has pulled away
(5)  From the shore at night and disappeared.

It is like a guitar left on a table
By a woman, who has forgotten it.

It is like the feeling of a man
Come back to see a certain house.

(10)  The four winds blow through the rustic arbor,
Under its mattress of vines.

The structure of this poem reinforces the effect of the images—an effect of sadness and loneliness. Each stanza uses a different image to create this effect—someone walking across snow, "looking for he knows not what,"a boat disappearing into the night, a guitar left forgotten (and, it is implied, silent) on a table, man coming back to a "certain house" (suggesting a home he has left or lost, or that is empty), winds blowing through a wooden framework covered with vines (an arbor) in a "rustic" place (a place in the country) with no one around. The stanzas reinforce the effect of loneliness because they do not—as a single block of lines might—build up momentum and power among their lines. Each stanza begins and ends as a simple, flat statement; each one stands apart from the other. The lack of any rhymes at the ends of the lines to provide emphasis or to connect one line with another, or to connect one stanza with another, underlines the sense of aloneness and sadness even more.

# Effects of Rhyme in Poetry

The **rhyme scheme**, the repetition of similar sounds, also adds to the effect of a poem. Rhyming words appear most often at the end of lines. To figure out the rhyme scheme, readers can label each rhyming sound with a letter. The sound of the last word in the first line is labeled A. The end-of-line words that rhyme with it are also labeled A. The first different end-of-line word is labeled B. End-of-line words that rhyme with B are also labeled B, and so on. When the letters are listed according to the order of the lines of the poem, the rhyme scheme becomes clear. In the following poem, the rhyme scheme is A, B, A, B. As you read the following poem, ask yourself what effect the rhyme scheme has in expressing the poem's meaning.

### HOW DOES THE SOUL REACT TO THE WORLD?

**The Soul selects her own society–**

The Soul selects her own Society—
Then—shuts the Door—
On her divine Majority—
Obtrude no more—

(5) Unmoved—she notes the Chariots—pausing—
At her low Gate—
Unmoved—an Emperor be kneeling
Upon her Mat—

I've known her—from an ample nation—
(10) Choose One—
Then—close the Valves of her attention
Like Stone—

"The Soul selects her own society" by Emily Dickinson. Reprinted by permission of the publishers and Trustees of Amherst College from *The Poems of Emily Dickinson*, Thomas H. Johnson, ed., Cambridge, Mass.; The Belnap Press of Harvard University Press, Copyright ©1951, 1955, 1979, 1983 by the President and Fellows of Harvard College.

The stanza form and rhyme scheme of this poem help express its theme. The theme is stated directly in the first two lines, which tell us that the soul "selects her own Society—/Then—shuts the door—" Once the soul has selected whoever she wants to live with her ("her own Society") and has shut the door on the the rest of the world, we should not put ourselves forward ("obtrude") to be accepted as part of her "divine Majority" of selected ones.

The other two stanzas of the poem illustrate and dramatize this meaning. Most of the A lines present images of worldly power and glory (chariots, emperors, "ample nations"); in contrast, each B line expresses the soul's rejection of worldly power and glory. The stanza form and the rhyme scheme reinforce this contrast. The longer A lines all have rhyme words that end with unaccented syllables which create a rise in voice and an unemphatic, light effect.

By contrast, the very short B lines end with one-syllable, strongly accented words that produce an emphatic effect. The poet intensifies the effect of these lines in the last stanza by shortening them to two strongly accented words each. She intensifies the effect of her B-rhymes in the last two stanzas by using inexact rhymes: She rhymes "gate" with "mat" and "one" with "stone." In this way, the poet ends the rhyme-scheme of each stanza with an especially hard, flat sound, to express the soul's hard, emphatic rejection of the world.

## Model Questions and Strategy

On the Interpreting Literature and Arts section of the GED test, you may be asked to analyze a poem's structure and rhyme. Below are several sample questions about these topics that you can be asked on the GED. These questions are followed by a strategy you can use to help you answer these test items.

• Why is the final line an effective conclusion to the poem?

• How is the last stanza an effective conclusion to the poem?

• Why does the speaker  include the line "_____"?

### Strategy

Use this strategy to help you answer these questions:

<u>Step 1:</u> Read the purpose question, the item following the poem, and the poem itself.

<u>Step 2:</u> Think about the overall effect of the poem. Ask yourself: What is the poem's main idea? What is the main emotion expressed in the poem? How do I feel after reading the poem?

<u>Step 3:</u> Look at the arrangement of lines and the rhyme. Ask yourself: How do these techniques contribute to the overall effect of the poem?

<u>Step 4:</u> Predict the answer. Then see which of the items match your prediction. Select the best match.

## Model Passage and Question

Read the following poem. See if you can find the answer to the analysis question.

### HOW DOES THE SPEAKER FEEL ABOUT HER LOVER?

**Where Have You Gone?**

Where have you gone
with your confident
walk with
your crooked smile

(5) why did you leave
me
when you took your
laughter
and departed

(10) are you aware that
with you
went the sun
all light
and what few stars

(15) there were?

where have you gone
with your confident
walk your
crooked smile the

(20) rent money
in one pocket and
my heart
in another...

"Where Have You Gone," by Mari Evans from *I Am a Black Woman* published by William Morrow & Co. , 1970, by permission of the author.

Why is the last stanza an effective conclusion to the poem?

**(1)** It reveals that the speaker never loved her lover.

**(2)** It reveals that the speaker regards the whole relationship humorously now.

**(3)** It makes us realize the speaker is mostly concerned about her lost money.

**(4)** It suggests the speaker intends to take revenge on her lover.

**(5)** It reveals another reason for the speaker's suffering.

Choice (5) is the correct answer. The last stanza creates a striking effect by revealing that the speaker is suffering not only because her lover has left her but also because he has stolen her rent money. The effect of shock and pain—a certain kind of bitter comedy—is made more intense by the almost exact repetition of the first lines of the poem ("Where have you gone/with your confident/walk with/your crooked smile") just before the poet adds "the rent money." Repeating the first images in the poem lets us see the lover's confidence and smile in a different, negative light and understand the meaning of the word "crooked." Despite the element of humor in this surprise ending, it is clear that the speaker does not regard her experience humorously (2) because she asks the same sad question of the lover ("where have you gone") in the last stanza that she asks in the first lines. For her to say in the last stanza that he has taken "the rent money/in one pocket and/my heart/in another" shows that (1) and (3) cannot be true; her pain comes from the fact that she still loves him and his theft shows how little he cares for her. Nothing in the poem, however, suggests that she intends to take revenge (4).

Items 1 through 3 refer to the poem that follows. Choose the one best answer to each item.

### WHAT DOES THE MOTHER TELL HER SON?

**Mother to Son**

Well, son, I'll tell you:
Life for me ain't been no crystal stair.
It's had tacks in it,
And splinters,
(5) And boards torn up,
And places with no carpet on the floor—
Bare.
But all the time
I'se been a-climbin' on,
(10) And reaching' landin's,
And turnin' corners,
And sometimes goin' in the dark
Where there ain't been no light.
So boy, don't you turn back.
(15) Don't set you down on the steps
'Cause you finds it's kinder hard.
Don't you fall now—
For I'se still goin', honey,
I'se still climbin',
(20) And life for me ain't been no crystal stair.

1. Why is the single word description in line 7 an effective conclusion for the images in lines 3-7?

   (1) It makes the other images seem exaggerated.
   (2) It contrasts with the effect of the other images.
   (3) It suggests an image similar to a "crystal stair."
   (4) It suggests that the speaker's struggle is almost over.
   (5) It emphasizes the poverty suggested by the images.

2. The poet repeats the statement in line 2 in the last line to

   (1) stress the contrast between the image of the "crystal stair" and the images of life in the poem
   (2) suggest that the speaker believes she will be rewarded in heaven for her struggle
   (3) contrast the speaker's present condition with her past
   (4) suggest that religious faith is what has kept the mother going all these years
   (5) express the mother's belief that the son's life will be easier than hers has been

3. The lack of a rhyme scheme and the irregular lengths of the lines help to characterize the speaker as

   (1) impatient and irritable
   (2) plain-spoken and down-to-earth
   (3) long-suffering and defeated
   (4) dominant and demanding
   (5) warm-hearted and optimistic

Answers are on page 329.

# Analyzing Sound Repetition in Poetry

## Prereading Prompt

Have you ever noticed that the words in titles of many television shows begin with the same letters? Here are some examples:

| The Brady Bunch | Reading Rainbow |
| Sesame Street | L.A. Law |
| Sanford and Son | Candid Camera |

The titles of many movies also have words beginning with the same letter, such as *Driving Miss Daisy, Baby Boom*, and *Dirty Dancing*. The reason many writers use sound repetition is because it suggests certain ideas or emotions that enhance the meaning of the words. For example, a stream of *b's* might suggest a lively feeling, as if someone were bounding along, as in upbeat "Brady Bunch."

Poets, like song lyricists and movie and TV writers, know that their choice of words creates certain moods or tones. Both the kinds of sounds and the number of times certain sounds are repeated add to the effect of the poem.

On the GED, you may be asked to answer questions about sound repetition in poetry. You will learn how in this lesson.

## Key Words

**alliteration**—repetition of consonant sounds that appear at the beginning of words
**assonance**—repetition of vowel sounds in words

## Effects of Sound in Poetry

You know that a poem can create a mood through its presentation of images, especially through similes and metaphors. A poem can also create a mood through its pattern of sounds, both the types of sounds and the way they are repeated.

One way to repeat sounds is rhyme. Another common method is **alliteration,** the repetition of a consonant sound that comes at the beginning of words. Here is an example of alliteration from "We Real Cool" by Gwendolyn Brooks. Notice the alliterative pairs: lurk/late, strike/straight, sing/sin, and jazz/June.

**We Real Cool**
**The Pool Players Seven at the Golden Shovel**
We real cool.  We
Left school.  We
Lurk late.  We
Strike straight.  We
(5) Sing sin.  We
Think gin.  We
Jazz June.  We
Die soon.

"We Real Cool" from *Blacks* by Gwendolyn Brooks. Copyright ©1991 by the author. Published by Third World Press, Chicago, 1991.

The repetition of vowel sounds, or **assonance,** can also be found in the *i* sounds in *sing, sin, thin,* and *gin* in "We Real Cool." The poet purposely repeats both kinds of sounds to suggest a feeling or tone. The brisk "i" sounds create a fast-moving, crisp pace that echoes the pool players' boasting. This tone also underscores the irony at the heart of the poem. The players think they are cool, but the poet and her audience know they are foolish because they "Think gin" and will "Die soon."

Poets can also repeat certain words—and their sounds—to strengthen a point. In "We Real Cool," the word *we* is repeated seven times. This shows the strength of the bond between the pool players.

In the Interpreting Literature and Arts section of the GED test, you may be asked to analyze the effect of sound repetition in poetry. Use this strategy to help you answer these questions:

### Strategy

Step 1: Read the purpose question, the item following the poem, and the poem itself.

Step 2: Locate the sound or words that are being repeated. Ask yourself: What effect does this repetition create? For example, many "s" or "z" sounds might suggest a feeling of anger, while many "oo" sounds (as in *flew* and *true*) might suggest a feeling of contentment.

Step 3: Predict the answer. Then see which of the items match your prediction. Select the best match.

## Model Passage and Question

Read the following poem. See if you can find the answer to the analysis question.

### WHAT KIND OF BIRD IS THE EAGLE?

#### The Eagle

He clasps the crag with crooked hands;
Close to the sun in lonely lands,
Ring'd with the azure world, he stands.
The wrinkled sea beneath him crawls;
(5) He watches from his mountain walls,
And like a thunderbolt he falls.

"The Eagle" by Alfred, Lord Tennyson.

What effect does the hard *c* sounds in the first two lines create?

**(1)** soothing

**(2)** mysterious

**(3)** lazy

**(4)** melodic

**(5)** harsh

The correct response is (5). A hard *c* sound creates a harsh, discomforting, and even disagreeable sound. (1) is incorrect because a hard *c* sound is not soothing like the *sh* sound as in *sharing, shelter, shell* and *shaded*. The sound of hard *c* is in the description of the first two lines does not suggest mystery (2). Rather, it sharpens our picture of the eagle grasping the sharp rocks with his claws—all the physical details of this action involve sharp, hard objects and the hard *c* sounds make the action more vivid. (3) is incorrect because a lazy sound would be a sound that slowed one's speech, like an often-repeated *l* sound, as in *lulling, lustrous, luxurious*, and *lordly*. A melodic sound is one that is pleasing to the ear, as in the *w* sounds of *wishing, waiting*, and *whispering*; so (4) is not correct either.

Items 1 through 3 refer to the poem that follows. Choose the one best answer to each item.

## HOW DOES THE POET FEEL ABOUT THE FOXES?

### Four Little Foxes

Speak gently, Spring, and make no sudden sound;
For in my windy valley, yesterday I found
New-born foxes squirming on the ground—
    Speak gently.

(5)  Walk softly, March, forbear the bitter blow;
Her feet within a trap, her blood upon the snow,
The four little foxes saw their mother go—
    Walk softly.

Go lightly, Spring, oh, give them no alarm;
(10)  When I cover them with boughs to shelter them from harm,
The thin blue foxes suckled at my arm—
    Go lightly.

Step softly, March, with your rampant hurricane;
Nuzzling one another, and whimpering with pain,
(15)  The new little foxes are shivering in the rain—
    Step softly.

"Four Little Foxes" from *Slow Smoke* by Lew Sarett. Copyright ©1953 by Lew Sarett.

1. The poet uses the *b* sound in the second stanza to help the reader emotionally experience

  (1) the dangers of fox hunting
  (2) the mechanism of fox traps
  (3) the pains of animal motherhood
  (4) the cruelty of trapping animals
  (5) the ability of animals to escape traps

2. The repeated *s* sounds in the first line help to create a tone that expresses the poet's

  (1) happiness for the little foxes
  (2) fear of grown-up foxes
  (3) protectiveness about the little foxes
  (4) recognition that the little foxes are dying
  (5) excitement that he has caught another fox

3. In lines 15–16, the *i* sounds in "nuzzling," "whimpering," "little," and "shivering," together with the images in the lines, help express the speaker's feeling toward the little foxes. His feeling is one of

  (1) depression
  (2) delight
  (3) hope
  (4) pity
  (5) contempt

Answers are on page 329.

# CHAPTER 5

Critics and reviewers are experts in the field of commentary. They have opinions about their subject and know how to support their opinions with their in-depth knowledge.

Broadway Theatre District          Credit: N.Y. Convention & Visitors Bureau

## Prereading Prompt

People often have different opinions about such things as movies, books, music, plays, and paintings. One person might value action and special effects in a movie, while another might value humor, music, and a strong story line. Writers of commentary carefully write their reviews to try to convince their audience to see things their way. Figuring out how they do that is important for answering GED questions. You will learn more about their techniques in this chapter.

# COMMENTARY ON THE ARTS

## What is Commentary on the Arts?

Commentary is a type of nonfiction prose about literature and other kinds of creative works. Commentary has three main purposes:

1. to **summarize**, or provide information about art
2. to **analyze**, or show how a work of art achieves a particular effect
3. to **evaluate**, or make judgments about the value of art

### About Which Arts is Commentary Written?

*Art* is sometimes defined as "the production of something beautiful." The arts, then, are the ways in which people (artists) create things of beauty to give pleasure to an audience (readers, viewers, and so on).

Some people write their opinions about various forms of art for a living. These people are called **critics** or reviewers. They might review literary arts (novels, poems, plays in script form, and so on); visual arts (painting, drawing, sculpture, for example); and performing arts (music, dance, films, stage plays, and television).

The most common type of commentary of the arts is the **review**. A review is an opinion that is offered about a particular work of art. Reviewers generally include the standards by which they judged the art work.

On the Interpreting Literature and the Arts section of the GED, you can expect about 25 percent of the items to be questions about commentaries on the arts. You will *not* be required to know anything in advance about the art forms that these questions cover. To help you prepare, this chapter will focus on some of the elements that critics use in developing their ideas.

### Key Words

**commentary**—a written opinion about literature and other kinds of creative works

**standards**—a set of ideas about what makes something good or bad

# How Do Reviewers Support Their Opinions?

## Prereading Prompt

Suppose you see a wonderful play and decide to tell your friends that they must see it. They ask you why. To convince them, you might mention the fantastic acting, mysterious plot, beautiful scenery, and exotic costumes—any details that will help prove your point. By doing so, you have become a critic expressing an opinion and backing it up with specific details. Finding out how to do this is very important for answering GED questions. You will learn how in this lesson.

## Key Words

**opinions**—statements reflecting the writer's beliefs or values but that cannot be proven true

**facts**—statements that can be proven to be true

## Reviews

Most critics write their opinions rather than speaking them. These written opinions are called **reviews**, and present the author's opinions about a particular work of art. Reviews are the most familiar form of commentary on the arts, and can be found in nearly all newspapers and magazines. Critics usually begin their reviews by describing the content of the work of art. To review a movie or play, for example, a critic might begin by retelling the story and describing the characters and setting. Then, they will evaluate the strengths and weaknesses of the work of art to convince the reader that their opinion is valid. To reinforce their opinions, critics include facts as well as the standards by which they evaluated the work of art.

Since critics want readers to understand their opinions easily, they most often state their views directly rather than imply them. Sometimes, they state their main idea early in the review and use the rest of the space to explain their reasons for supporting this opinion. Other times, critics present their opinions further on in the review. In this instance, main idea and supporting details are arranged in one of two ways:

- as a conclusion from several broad statements, or
- as a contrast to ideas presented early in the review.

Therefore, you cannot assume that the critic's main idea will always be the first statement in the review. If you cannot find the main idea in the first sentence, look further on for an idea that is a conclusion or contrast to what the critic says in the first few lines.

## Supporting Details

To persuade people to accept their views, critics must do more than simply state opinions. They must defend, support, or prove them. In commentary, it is especially important that the author give factual details to support the main idea. **Facts** are statements that can be proved true. Critics use facts like these:

- quotations from experts in the field
- statistics
- comparisons to similar works that have already been judged
- references to details in the work of art

An **opinion**, in contrast, is a statement reflecting the writer's beliefs or values but that has not or cannot be proven true. For example, the critic who says of a movie, "This was one of the most exciting action films of the year," would not be offering convincing support by adding, "My friends liked it a lot." Opinions should not be supported with other opinions; rather, they should be supported by facts. In this case, the critic might use statistics showing how many people have gone to see this movie compared to how many people saw other action movies this week.

On the Interpreting Literature and Arts section of the GED test, you may be asked literal comprehension questions about commentaries. Below are several model questions, along with a strategy you can use to find the answer to these types of questions.

## Model Questions

- Which of the following statements best expresses the main idea of this passage?
- Which of the following statements best expresses the critic's impression of the _____(book, movie, play, and so forth)?
- The author of this passage wants the reader to conclude that_____(the work of art) is _____?
- Which of the following details is used to support the critic's opinion?
- Which of the following facts was used in the review?

**Strategy**

<u>Step 1:</u> Read the purpose question, the items following the passage, and then the passage itself.

<u>Step 2:</u> Ask yourself, "What is the critic's general opinion of the work?" Look for a sentence that directly states the critic's opinion.

<u>Step 3:</u> Look for facts that help support the opinion you found.

## Model Passage and Question

Read the following passage and question. Use the strategy you have just learned to help you find the answer to the literal comprehension question.

### IS THIS BOOK ENJOYABLE?

**SPARKY! By Sparky Anderson with Dan Ewald. (Prentice Hall, $18.95)** George (Sparky) Anderson has managed in the major leagues since 1970. He is the only manager to win more than 800 games with two different teams and to
(5) win a World Series in both leagues. Mr. Anderson also suffered a physical and emotional breakdown in May 1989, which he says was brought on by the daily stress of managing in the big leagues. This episode and his subsequent recovery are candidly discussed by Mr. Anderson, the manag-
(10) er of the Detroit Tigers, and his collaborator, Dan Ewald, the Tigers' public relations director, in "Sparky!" The book, however, is not merely a chronicle of a man's self-discovery and return to health; it is a fine baseball book filled with anecdotes and insights. Mr. Anderson's style is as direct and
(15) down-to-earth as a hard, clean slide into second…. "Sparky!" gives us not only a vivid portrait of baseball's most successful manager but also a refreshing view of a guy who has his head screwed on right.

Excerpted from Michael Lichtenstein, "Sparky!" *The New York Times Book Review*, April 15, 1990.© 1990 *The New York Times*. Reprinted with permission.

The author of the review wants the readers to conclude that the book

    **(1)** is a detailed analysis of the nervous breakdown of a major league manager

    **(2)** will be of interest mainly to Detroit Tigers' fans

    **(3)** consists of anecdotes about baseball and insights about the game

    **(4)** is a colorful look at a great baseball manager

    **(5)** is a gossipy look at well-known baseball players

The correct answer is (4). The last sentence says, "'Sparky!' gives us not only a vivid portrait of baseball's most successful manager but also a refreshing view of a guy who has his head screwed on right." In other words, the book presents a colorful view of this great baseball manager, who also seems to be a person who has his priorities in order. (1) and (3) are incorrect because the review states that the book "is not merely a chronicle of a man's self-discovery and return to health; it is (also) a fine baseball book filled with anecdotes and insights." (2) is incorrect; although Sparky Anderson was "the manager of the Detroit Tigers," nowhere in the review is it stated or implied that fans of that team would be the people mainly interested in reading about this remarkable man. (5) is also incorrect; although the book does include some anecdotes about famous baseball players and managers, the author of the review mentions this as only one part of the book. The most important part seems to be the "chronicle of a man's self-discovery and return to health" (lines 12-13).

Items 1 through 3 refer to the review that follows. Choose the one best answer to each item.

### IS *THE GAME* WORTH SEEING?

Leon Hunter, a hot-shot black advertising executive, is called in to mastermind the New York mayoral campaign of Carl Rydell, who is white, conservative and bigoted. To the consternation of his friends, Leon accepts, but for private rea-
(5) sons that only another chess player as shrewd and far-sighted as Leon could see.

In the hands of more adroit filmmakers, "The Game" might have been a savagely funny satire of politics, racism and the Manhattan game of dog-eat-dog. No one connected with "The
(10) Game," however, seems to have had a clue about how a movie is put together.

"The Game" is a first feature by Curtis Brown...a former advertising executive who later became a successful photographer, specializing in advertising and fashion work.

(15) Mr. Brown knows his milieu. He has a sense of humor, but "The Game" is hopelessly amateurish in the writing, the direction and, with a couple of exceptions, the performances. The film dawdles over unnecessary details and skimps on the important ones. The story, based on a clever idea, is so wit-
(20) lessly composed that it brings laughs in the wrong places....

Mr. Brown plays Leon with a kind of malevolent reticence that is quite good. Vanessa Shaw is also effective as a former Black Panther who is making good on Madison Avenue. Everybody else seems to have egg on his face.

Excerpted from Vincent Canby, "Black Mastermind for a Bigoted Candidate," *The New York Times*, April 27, 1990. Copyright ©1990 *The New York Times*. Reprinted with permission.

1. Which of the following statements best describes the critic's impression of the movie?

   (1) The movie has excellent acting.
   (2) The movie lacks basic skills in film-making.
   (3) The story is clever and creates many laughs.
   (4) First-time filmmakers can be highly successful.
   (5) The film is loosely based on David Dinkins' successful campaign for mayor of New York.

2. The main purpose of the second paragraph is to

   (1) summarize the movie's plot
   (2) give examples of how the movie is funny
   (3) provide the reviewer's opinion
   (4) give background on people involved in the movie
   (5) describe the setting

3. Which of the following details is used to support the writer's opinion of the film?

   (1) It is odd for a black advertising executive to work for a political candidate who is white and bigoted.
   (2) The writer-director covers three topics—politics, racism, and advertising—in one film.
   (3) The way the film emphasizes details produces more laughter than the director planned.
   (4) The writer-director had two different careers in advertising before he made his film.
   (5) The main character's motivation is a secret, long-range plan of action.

Answers appear on page 330.

# Inferring Bias and Objectivity

## Prereading Prompt

Some people like loud music; others prefer soft. Some people enjoy fast-paced, action-filled movies that are scary; others prefer slower-paced romantic films. Knowing the qualities that people like in literature, music, and art is important. This way, when someone makes a suggestion about what you might want to see, read, or do, you immediately know the basis for the recommendation. Then you can make an intelligent choice for yourself. Inferring the basis of a critic's opinion is a skill that will help you read commentaries with more insight. Finding out how to do this is very important for answering GED questions. You will learn how in this lesson.

## Key Words

**bias**—a personal opinion for or against something or someone; a preference

**objectivity**—the state of not being influenced by one's own opinions; using factual support and recognized standards

## Bias

Writers of commentary usually have a background of special training and experience in evaluating the arts. They already have general opinions about what they like or dislike in art, and those opinions will color their consideration of the subject at hand. These background opinions form a critic's **bias**, a personal attitude for or against someone or something.

As you read commentary, you should be aware of the critic's bias. If, when reviewing a movie, a critic states, "the chase scenes were unnecessarily violent and totally unbelievable," you can conclude that the critic feels too much violence is not justified in movies and that he or she likes movies that are not based on fantasy or on extreme situations. You may feel very differently about what makes a good movie. Knowing the critic's bias, then, will help you judge reviews and form your own opinion about the worth of what is being discussed.

## Objectivity

As you have seen, good commentary depends heavily upon factual support of the critic's opinion. The more that this support is based on recognized standards for quality in the arts, the more objective it is considered to be. A commentary that begins, "My own view is..." signifies to the reader that what follows is the author's opinion and not fact. Nevertheless, even though the author is not objective, he or she may still have a valid point to make if the review goes on to explain why the author believes his or her opinion is correct. You can judge the validity of the point by examining how the views are supported— mostly by facts, or mostly by opinions.

On the Interpreting Literature and Arts section of the GED test, you may be asked inferential comprehension questions about bias and objectivity in commentary. Here is a strategy you can follow to help you answer these questions.

### Strategy

<u>Step 1:</u> Read the purpose question, the items following the passage, and then the passage itself.

<u>Step 2:</u> Look in the passage for key words from the question. Close by these words, you should find clues to the answer. For example, if a question asks about a critic's opinion on "form in painting," look for the word "form" in the review. Read the sentences near the one in which "form" appears.

<u>Step 3:</u> Make a judgment about what the reviewer is saying about the topic. In this case, decide what the critic is saying about form.

<u>Step 4:</u> Read over the answer choices to see if your response is most similar to one of them. Select the choice closest to your response.

# Model Passage and Question

Read the following passage and question. Use the strategy you have just learned to help you find the answer to the inferential comprehension question about bias and objectivity.

### DID THE CRITIC ENJOY THE BALLET?

The dancing was polished—and fresh—in the program presented by the New York City Ballet on Wednesday night at the New York State Theatre. But the star of the evening was George Balanchine, who was represented by three of his best-
(5)  known ballets.

"Allegro Brillante" is a sunny, bouncing gallop through its Tchaikovsky score. Balanchine once said the piece contained everything he knew about classical ballet, in 13 minutes. But although it includes a good deal of demanding virtuoso danc-
(10)  ing, nothing looked forced or even challenging in this plotless outpouring of dance.

Excerpted from Jennifer Dunning, "Balanchine's Virtuosity Concentrated," *The New York Times*, April 27, 1990. ©1990 *The New York Times*. Reprinted with permission.

What can you assume the author thinks about the role of plot in ballets?

**(1)** All ballet should have a clear plot.

**(2)** Plot is a necessary ingredient in classical ballet, but it is not necessary in more modern pieces.

**(3)** Having a plot is not essential to having a fine ballet.

**(4)** Plotless ballets should be no longer than 13 minutes.

**(5)** Plot in ballet demands virtuoso dancing.

Choice (3) is correct. The review of "Allegro Brillante" is favorable. You know this because the reviewer uses such positive terms as "polished," "fresh," "sunny," "bouncing gallop," and "triumph." In the only sentence with the word "plotless," the reviewer states, "But although it includes a good deal of demanding virtuoso dancing, nothing looked forced or even challenging in this plotless outpouring of dance." Therefore, the fact that this dance has no plot does not detract from its brilliance. Plot, then, is not an important ingredient in dance according to this reviewer. (1) is incorrect because the reviewer does not imply that all ballets should have clear plots. The importance of plot in all ballet is never discussed. (2) is incorrect because the reviewer does not state what ingredients classical ballets should have in contrst to those that modern ballets should have. (4) is incorrect because no statement suggests that all plotless ballets should be no longer than 13 minutes. The passage only quotes Balanchine's praise for this one plotless ballet that is 13 minutes long. (5) is likwise incorrect; although "Allegro Brillante," a plotless ballet, demanded virtuoso dancing, that does not mean that all plotless ballets demand the same kind of dancing.

Items 1 through 3 refer to the review that follows. Choose the one best answer to each item.

## DOES MUSIC HAVE MEANING?

My own belief is that all music has an expressive power, some more and some less, but that all music has a certain meaning behind the notes and that meaning behind the notes constitutes, after all, what the piece is saying, what the piece
(5) is about. This whole problem can be stated quite simply by asking, "Is there meaning to music?" My answer to that would be, "Yes." And "Can you state in so many words what the meaning is?" My answer to that would be, "No." Therein lies the difficulty.

(10) Simple-minded souls will never be satisfied with the answer to the second of these questions. They always want music to have a meaning, and the more concrete it is the better they like it. The more the music reminds them of a train, a storm, a funeral, or any other familiar conception the more expres-
(15) sive it appears to be to them. This popular idea of music's meaning—stimulated and abetted by the usual run of musical commentator—should be discouraged wherever and whenever it is met. One timid lady once confessed to me that she suspected something seriously lacking in her apprecia-
(20) tion of music because of her inability to connect it with anything definite. This is getting the whole thing backward, of course.

Still, the question remains. How close should the intelligent music lover wish to come to pinning a definite meaning to any
(25) particular work? No closer than a general concept, I should say. Music expresses, at different moments, serenity or exuberance, regret or triumph, fury or delight. It expresses each of these moods, and many others, in a numberless variety of subtle shadings and differences. It may even express a state
(30) of meaning for which there exists no adequate word in any language. In that case, musicians often like to say that it has only a purely musical meaning. They sometimes go farther and say that *all* music has only a purely musical meaning. What they really mean is that no appropriate word can be
(35) found to express the music's meaning and that, even if it could, they do not feel the need of finding it.

Excerpted from *What To Listen for in Music* by Aaron Copland. Copyright ©1957, 1985 Estate of Aaron Copland. Reprinted by permission.

1. In the second paragraph of the review, the critic reveals a bias?

   (1) against timid people
   (2) against people who believe that music should have a clear meaning
   (3) against people who can't connect with music
   (4) against people who are simple-minded
   (5) against people who believe that music should not have concrete meaning

2. How do you know that the critic is offering his opinion and not an entirely objective commentary?

   (1) He discusses popular ideas of musical commentators and others.
   (2) He discusses the meaning of music to different people.
   (3) He begins with the words "My own belief is that…."
   (4) He concludes by summing up what musicians think about the meaning of music.
   (5) He gives facts about how different people view music.

3. Which of the following statements best expresses the main idea of the passage?

   (1) A piece of music has no specific meaning.
   (2) Music usually has a concrete meaning.
   (3) Music can always be summed up in words.
   (4) People who can't use words, can't appreciate music.
   (5) The meaning of music often cannot be stated in words.

Answers appear on page 330.

# Applying Main Ideas, Details, and the Author's Attitude

## Prereading Prompt

Does your aunt like to hike in the woods? If so, you can assume that she probably enjoys watching nature programs on TV. Does your uncle dislike loud music? If so, he probably wouldn't want to attend rock concerts. By knowing how a person reacts in one situation, you can make predictions about how he or she will react in certain other situations. The same principle is true when you read commentaries. By knowing how the author feels about certain subjects, you can make predictions about how he or she will feel about certain other situations.

On the GED, you might be asked to apply main ideas, details, or the author's attitudes to new situations, and some of these will concern commentary on the arts. You will learn how to do this in this lesson.

## Applying Main Ideas and Details

As you have learned earlier in this book, one way in which you can judge the clarity of an author's ideas is to apply them to new situations. The same method can be used to judge commentary. For example, if a reviewer enjoys a film because of its many scenes of foreign lands, you might predict that the reviewer would enjoy traveling. Another reviewer might feel that ballets should have strong plots. On this basis, you should predict that this reviewer would enjoy books with clear plots as well.

In Lesson 2, you read a passage by Aaron Copland, an American composer, about music. You might apply the main idea of that passage to the advertising industry. Imagine that an advertising company is trying to think of phrases to describe a new perfume. Would the Copland agree that this is a suitable approach to advertising perfume? Probably not, since his main point is that nonverbal expression, such as music, cannot be described adequately in words. He might agree, however, that it is sensible for perfume manufacturers to advertise their products by including samples in the mail or in magazines. In this way, people could respond to the perfumes individually, without trying to describe their characteristics, since this is the way Copland thinks people should experience music.

## Applying the Author's Attitude

To determine the author's attitude in commentary, you should first determine the author's bias as well as his or her opinion. For example, think about the critic who wrote the review of "The Game" in Lesson 1. In that review, the author's bias leans in favor of a strong style that satirizes "politics, racism, and the Manhattan game of dog-eat-dog." Would this critic endorse a serious book that tries to flatter people in power? Possibly, but not likely. Since the reviewer criticized the movie for a story that "is so witlessly composed that it brings laughs in the wrong places," you could probably predict that the reviewer would be more enthusiastic about a book that pokes fun at politicians, racists, or power brokers.

On the Interpreting Literature and Arts section of the GED test, you may be asked application questions about the main idea, details, and the author's attitude in a piece of commentary. To help you answer these questions, read the model questions and strategy that follows.

## Model Questions

- Which of the following would the author be most/least likely to do?
- What would the author probably think about _____?
- Which of the following topics would the author be most/least likely to approve?
- The situation in the passage is like which of the following?

### Strategy

Step 1: Read the question. Then read the passage with the question in mind. Ask yourself: "What is the 'old' situation that will help me understand the 'new' one?" Try to find information that will help you build a "bridge" of ideas between the new situation in the item and the old situation in the passage.

Step 2: Make a prediction about the answer from the evidence you found in the passage.

Step 3: Examine all the choices. Narrow them down until you are satisfied that your answer is the best possible choice.

# Model Passage and Question

Read the following passage and the question. Use the strategy you have just learned to help you find the answer to the application question.

## WHAT ARE THE DIFFERENT OPINIONS OF SYLVESTER STALLONE?

While [Sylvester] Stallone has been captivating audiences and wooed by the motion picture industry for more of his movies, he's made a career of appalling critics who have labeled his films, among other things, "stupid," "boring," and
(5) "empty." Why, then, in the estimation of those who have made a study of his career, is Mr. Stallone so popular with his public? What makes him unique, and what will be his significance, if any, in film history?

...In the process of returning movies to more traditional
(10) values, Mr. Stallone has, of course, gained detractors. Objections to the violence of Rambo, or the portrayal of the Soviets in "Rocky IV" are well known. Others are not. "What bothers me is the exaggeration of the characters he creates," said Douglas Kellner, professor of psychology at the
(15) University of Texas.... "It was possible to be a John Wayne, but it's impossible to be a Rocky or a Rambo. There's been virtually nothing this unreal in the whole history of American hero films. It's pure escapism, whose great appeal illustrates just how frustrated a lot of people are."
(20) Others criticize Mr. Stallone's politics. Daniel Czitrom, associate professor of history at Mount Holyoke College, says that beneath the muscles and violence is "an appeal to sheer male power.... In some ways, Stallone represents a kind of denial of the social and political upheaval of the 60's."

Excerpted from Steven D. Stark, "Ten Years Into the Stallone Era: What It, Uh, All Means," *The New York Times*, February 22, 1987. Copyright ©1987 *The New York Times*. Reprinted with permission.

The author would probably predict that if Stallone were president, he would

**(1)** lose his popularity with the voters

**(2)** deal realistically with issues in his speeches

**(3)** use discussion to resolve conflicts

**(4)** favor rights for women and minorities

**(5)** stress the need for a strong defense

(5) is the correct answer. The author says that Stallone's movies stress "muscles and violence" and "an appeal to sheer male power" (lines 22-23). Stallone as president therefore would not resolve conflicts by discussion (3) rather than by force, or favor women's rights (4). Favoring minority rights (4) also would give people with little power more power to stand up against such force. As for (1), lines 1-8 tell us that Stallone is very popular and lines 18-19 indicate his wide public support. If his movies are "unreal" (line 17) and "pure escapism" (line 18), he is not likely as a president to deal with issues realistically (2).

# Lesson 3 Exercise

Items 1 through 3 refer to the review that follows. Choose the one best answer to each item.

## DOES THE CRITIC APPROVE OF THIS NOVEL?

This intriguing novel gives the reader a double-whammy for his or her money. The first whammy is a blood-and-guts World War II adventure full of the boom of exploding shells, the arm-around-the-shoulder comradeship of soldiers under
(5) fire, and the repeated use of a four-letter word, whether the circumstance calls for it or not. The second part, which takes place in the 1980's, is a mystery caper: to discover the real father of Ulick, the son of an eccentric Canadian soldier named Hugo Burke. Why the importance of who's Papa? Well,
(10) because Ulick was born some 12 months after Hugo was reported killed in battle. It is vital to know the truth of Ulick's parentage because he is the heir apparent to head of the fabulously rich Burke Foundation dedicated to providing "facilities for study and research into all aspects of the internation-
(15) al communist conspiracy." The author, Anthony McCandless, was a Royal Marine Commando officer in Yugoslavia and Italy during World War II, and his brilliant reconstruction of his experiences illuminates and authenticates the war sequences. He is less successful in the search for the father's identity;
(20) here, he continually trips over his own feet in unraveling a complicated and mind-boggling series of take-it-on-faith implausible events. The revelation is not made until six pages before the end of the novel, but the journey to the startling conclusion is full of derring-do that is handled with appropri-
(25) ate jauntiness.

1. Which of the following television programs do you think the critic would most likely enjoy?

   (1) a soap opera about a woman who unknowingly marries the man who killed her father
   (2) a a rags-to-riches story about a poor boy who becomes wealthy through a series of fantastic "lucky breaks"
   (3) a mystery set during the Russian Revolution and based on the actual diaries of a Russian soldier
   (4) a story about a time traveler who meets and falls in love with his great-grandmother as a young woman
   (5) a comedy about a series of chance events that result in the marriage of twin sisters to twin brothers

2. If the critic was a writing teacher, which of the following statements would he most likely make to his students?

   (1) Write about mystery because that will intrigue your audience.
   (2) Write about familiar things because they will be most illuminating.
   (3) Write about war because everyone likes to read about blood-and-guts.
   (4) Write about rich people because everyone is interested in how they live their lives.
   (5) Write about complicated things because everyone likes a mind-boggling story.

3. The critic remarks upon "the repeated use of a four-letter word, whether the circumstances call for it or not" (lines 5-6) to reveal

   (1) how the author involves the reader in the action
   (2) the author's flair for realistic dialogue
   (3) his own distaste for unnecessary obscene language in books
   (4) his own preference for long words and complicated sentences
   (5) how the author creates a lack of sympathy for the soldiers in the story

Answers appear on page 331.

# Analyzing Commentary

## Prereading Prompt

Have you ever tried to convince friends to see certain movies with you, read certain books you enjoyed, or watch a television series that you like? If you were successful in convincing your friends, you are probably skilled in the art of persuasion—and you may not even know it. You have presented your opinion clearly, supported it effectively, and summarized it neatly. Finding out how to structure an argument and then use effective diction is a very important skill that will help you understand the commentary you read. Knowing how to analyze these elements is important in answering questions on the GED. You will learn how in this lesson.

## Key Words

**diction**—the choice of words an author uses to suit his or her purpose and audience

Commentary is enjoyable in part because of the way authors structure their arguments. The most common structure for an argument is (1) *opinion*, (2) *support*, and (3) *conclusion*. In Lesson 1, you learned that reviewers structure their arguments several ways. Recall that an opinion need not come at the beginning of the argument. Remember, too, that the most effective support for an argument comes from facts rather than from opinions. The conclusion, then, should be a generalization or a restatement of the original point.

Here is a brief example of the elements in the structure of an argument:

| | |
|---|---|
| *Opinion* | *The Unsolved Murder in the Desert* was spellbinding and thoroughly enjoyable. |
| *Support* | It is well written. (opinion) |
| | It has been on the *New York Times* Best Seller List for 51 weeks. (fact) |
| | The plot is believable and fast-paced.(opinion) |
| | It was given superb reviews by critics in the *New York Times*, *Chicago Sun-Times*, and *Boston Globe*. (fact) |
| *Summary* | Buy a copy of this book. You won't be able to put it down. |

As you read commentary, notice how the parts of the argument fit together. If they fit in a sensible way, the argument is most likely valid. If you do not agree with the critic's conclusion, you should be able to think of a well-structured argument to support your view.

## Diction

Critics often use specific language, called **diction**, to reinforce the point they are making. **Diction** is the choice of words that an author uses to suit his or her purpose and audience. For example, to appeal to experts in the field, a critic may use words that are understood only by readers who already know a great deal about the subject being discussed. To appeal to a more general audience, on the other hand, the critic might use informal, everyday language. In each case, the diction helps gain the readers' confidence and prepare them to better accept the critic's opinion. Diction may be used in other ways, as well.

**Wordplay.** Wordplay often takes an image from the subject matter or from the title of a work and gives it a new twist of meaning—for example, "New *Airplane* Sequel Crash-lands," where the image of flying suggested by the movie's title is used to describe the artistic failure of its sequel. Humor is usually the effect of wordplay, and its effectiveness depends on how well it communicates the writer's meaning to his or her audience.

**Descriptive Language.** Critics select their adjectives and adverbs with care to persuade their readers to accept their opinions. Therefore, you should look closely at the descriptive language to see how the critic judges the work of art. Adjectives like "brilliant" and "superb," for example, show the review is favorable; while "pretentious" and "unfocused" tell you it is negative.

On the Interpreting Literature and Arts section of the GED test, you may be asked to analyze the structure of an argument or the author's use of diction in commentary. To find an answer about the structure, look for the author's opinion, supporting details, and the summary. Be sure you are clear about whether the details are facts or opinions. To find an answer about diction, first look for the word or words in question. Then try to figure out what effect they are intended to have on the audience. If the diction is easy to understand, for example, the review is probably intended for a general audience. On the other hand, if the diction is highly technical, the review is most likely intended for experts in that field.

Read the following passage and the question and try to figure out the answer to the analysis question.

### IS *"E" FOR ELVIS* WORTH READING?

*"E" IS FOR ELVIS: An A-to-Z Illustrated Guide to the King of Rock and Roll.* By Caroline Latham and Jeannie Sakol (NAL, $19.95) "E" is also for enormous: Elvis Presley, a man of enormous talent and enormous excess, has inspired
(5) books of enormous ambition (Greil Marcus's "Mystery Train"), enormous contempt (Albert Goldman's "Elvis"), and enormous triviality (too many to single out just one). "'E' is for Elvis" is among the most trivial of all, yet it's not without a certain goony charm. The book is organized as an alphabeti-
(10) cal listing of notable people, events and items in Presley's life. Caroline Latham and Jeannie Sakol's concept of notable, however, may differ from yours and mine: "Crazy," for example, is one entry under "C." What's that? Why, "it's one of the nicknames frequently used for Elvis Presley by members of
(15) his entourage." Oh. But wait, on the same page there's an entry for George Cukor. What's the great film director's Elvis connection? He apparently spent one day on the set of a Presley movie and is quoted as saying of the rock idol: "He can do anything! He would be a dream to direct. His comedy
(20) timing is faultless." ...Presley is in many respects the culmination of this century's popular culture, and cannot be summarized, contained or even dismissed by a book as foolish and harmless as "'E' is for Elvis."

Excerpted from Ken Tucker, "'E' Is For Elvis: An Illustrated Guide to the King of Rock and Roll," *The New York Times Book Review*, May 13, 1990. © 1990 The New York Times. Reprinted with permission.

The last sentence in this review serves to

**(1)** encourage people to buy this book

**(2)** show that the book might be popular

**(3)** suggests that Elvis was foolish and harmless

**(4)** stress that today's popular culture is worthless

**(5)** make the reviewer's position about the book clear

The correct answer is (5). The final sentence summarizes the reviewer's opinion of the book. (1) is incorrect because the reviewer is not encouraging people to read the book by labelling it "foolish and harmless." As for (2), lines 6-9 tell us that there are a great many trivial Elvis books, which suggests trivial Elvis books are very popular, and says this book is "among the most trivial." However, the last sentence says nothing to suggest this book will be popular; so (2) is wrong. (3) is incorrect because the author states that the book, not Elvis, is foolish and harmless. (4) is incorrect because the reviewer states that this century's popular culture "cannot be summarized, contained or even dismissed by a book as foolish and harmless as *"E" is for Elvis.*" The culture itself, therefore, is not worthless.

# Lesson 4 Exercise

Items 1 through 3 refer to the review that follows. Choose the one best answer to each item.

## WHY IS THIS MOVIE ENJOYABLE?

Life must get lonely when it's lived in the shadow of an indestructible 20-year-old hit. The mind must begin to play strange tricks. What other explanation can there be for *Star Trek IV: The Voyage Home*, a large, lavish, and absolutely sin-
(5) cere mass-market entertainment about saving the whales?...

Then again, it isn't the rationality of the *Star Trek* series that has made it lovable. It's the nuttiness, which is in extremely good supply this time. *Star Trek IV*...starts out on a dangerously high-tech note, with lots of the electronic gad-
(10) getry and scientific gibberish that the Enterprise crew seems to hold so dear. It begins to look as if this film may remain as impenetrable as some of the earlier ones have been. Then, lo and behold, all the talk about war and the planet Klingon, which took up most of the less lively *Star Trek III: The Search*
(15) *for Spock*, gives way to a discussion of the whale, its enemies, and its future.

It seems that a visiting space probe is planning to destroy the planet Earth unless it can continue its chats with the mighty humpback, even though the species has become
(20) extinct... So it's off to 1986 to round up some whales, build a giant fish tank and race back to the 23rd century in time to save the world. Simple!

There's something rather touching about the sight of the same old Enterprise crew on the streets of San Francisco,
(25) searching for whales and trying to remember where they parked....

Mr. Nimoy directed this *Star Trek* installment, and indeed he should probably direct all of them. His technical expertise leaves much to be desired...but his sincerity is unmistakable,
(30) and it counts for a lot. The technical minutiae, the solemn silliness and the preachy tone occasionally sounded here... are all essential to the *Star Trek* mystique. Whatever it is, it seems durable beyond anyone's wildest dreams. And Mr. Nimoy, by injecting some levity this time, has done a great
(35) deal to assure the series' longevity.

1. Judging from the author's diction, this review is probably intended mainly for

   (1) serious students of filmmaking
   (2) average film-viewing audiences
   (3) people under 20 years of age
   (4) technically expert filmmakers
   (5) scientists

2. What is the structure of this commentary?

   (1) opinion followed by summary
   (2) support, opinion, summary
   (3) summary followed by opinion
   (4) opinion, support, summary
   (5) support, summary, opinion

3. What is the reviewer's opinion of the *Star Trek* movie?

   (1) It is boring and incomprehensible.
   (2) It is enjoyable because of its craziness.
   (3) It is scientifically unsound and meaningless.
   (4) It is expert and impressive.
   (5) It is simple but disturbing.

Answers appear on page 331.

# PRACTICE ITEMS

These practice items are like the actual GED test in length and difficulty, but unlike the GED, they are grouped according to types of literature: nonfiction, fiction, drama, poetry, and commentary. This grouping helps you focus on one content area at a time. Your results will help you determine which skills you have mastered and which you should study further.

There are several ways you can use the Practice Items. First, after you have finished a chapter, you can work through those Practice Items that correspond to the same type of literature you just studied. Or, you can save all the Practice Items until you have completed all the chapters in the book. Third, you may wish to use the Practice Items as a practice GED test. To do this, complete all the Practice Items in one sitting. Since the actual GED is 65 minutes long, allow yourself the same amount of time. This will give you an idea how you will do on the actual Literature and the Arts test. Regardless of how you use the Practice Items, they will help you gain valuable experience with GED-type questions.

Score your answers to the Practice Items by checking the answer key on page 333. Read through the explanation even if you answered the item correctly. This will reinforce your knowledge of literature and help you develop your test-taking skills. After you score your work, fill in the Performance Analysis Chart on page 282. The chart will help you determine which skills and areas you know best, and direct you to the parts of the book where you can review areas in which you need additional review.

# Practice Items

**Directions:** Choose the one best answer to each question.

### Nonfiction

*Items 1 to 4 refer to the following passage.*

### WHAT MAKES KELLY UNUSUAL?

I never meant to say anything about this, but the fact is that I have never met a dog that didn't have it in for me. You take Kelly, for instance. He's a wire-haired
(5) fox terrier and he's had us for three years now. I wouldn't say that he was terribly handsome but he does have a very nice smile. What he doesn't have is any sense of fitness. All the other dogs in the neigh-
(10) borhood spend their afternoons yapping at each other's heels or chasing cats. Kelly spends his whole day, every day, chasing swans on the millpond. I don't actually worry because he will never catch one. For
(15) one thing, he can't swim. Instead of settling for a simple dogpaddle like everybody else, he has to show off and try some complicated overhand stroke, with the result that he always sinks and has to be fished
(20) out. Naturally, people talk, and I never take him for a walk that somebody doesn't point to him and say, "There's that crazy dog that chases swans."

Another thing about that dog is that he
(25) absolutely refuses to put himself in the other fellow's position. We have a pencil sharpener in the kitchen and Kelly used to enjoy having an occasional munch on the plastic cover. As long as it was just a nip
(30) now and then, I didn't mind. But one day he simply lost his head and ate the whole thing. Then I had to buy a new one and of course I put it up high out of Kelly's reach. Well, the scenes we were treated
(35) to—and the sulking! In fact, ever since, he has been eating things I know he doesn't like just to get even. I don't mean things like socks and mittens and paper napkins, which of course are delicious. Lately
(40) he's been eating plastic airplanes, suede brushes, and light bulbs. Well, if he wants to sit under the piano and make low and loving growls over a suede brush just to show me, okay. But frankly I think he's
(45) lowering himself.

1. What does the author mean when she says that Kelly doesn't have "any sense of fitness" (line 8)?

    **(1)** Kelly is badly out of shape.
    **(2)** Kelly constantly gets into fights.
    **(3)** Kelly eats light bulbs.
    **(4)** Kelly doesn't act like a normal dog.
    **(5)** Kelly doesn't know how to swim.

2. The author's description of Kelly sitting under the piano with a suede brush is an example of her idea that dogs

    **(1)** like leather
    **(2)** are always hungry
    **(3)** have it in for her
    **(4)** are often mistreated
    **(5)** can feel sad

3. Because of the way Kelly acts at the millpond (lines 11-20), you can conclude that he

    **(1)** dislikes the company of other dogs
    **(2)** doesn't learn from experience
    **(3)** is good at catching swans
    **(4)** doesn't like to chase animals
    **(5)** is becoming a better swimmer

**4.** What is the tone of this passage?

   **(1)** angry
   **(2)** bitter
   **(3)** sad
   **(4)** resentful
   **(5)** playful

*Items 5 to 9* refer to the following passage.

### HOW DOES THIS MAN FEEL ABOUT HIS TRUCK?

I do not own a horse. I am attached to a truck, however, and I have come to think of it in a similar way. It has no name; it never occurred to me to give it a name. It
(5) has little decoration; neither of us is partial to decoration. I have a piece of turquoise in the truck because I had heard once that some of the southwestern tribes tied a small piece of turquoise in a
(10) horse's hock to keep him from stumbling. I like the idea. I also hang sage in the truck when I go on a long trip. But inside, the truck doesn't look much different from others that look just like it on the outside.
(15) I like it that way. Because I like my privacy.

For two years in Wyoming I worked on a ranch wrangling horses. The horse I rode when I had to have a good horse was a
(20) quarter horse and his name was Coke High. This name came with him. At first I thought he'd been named for the soft drink. I'd known stranger names given to horses by whites. Years later I wondered if
(25) some deviant Wyoming cowboy wise to cocaine had not named him. Now I thing he was probably named after a rancher, an historical figure of the region. I never asked the people who owned him for fear
(30) of spoiling the spirit of my inquiry.

We were running over a hundred horses on this ranch. They all had names. After a few weeks I knew all the horses and the names too. You had to. No one knew how
(35) to talk about the animals or put them in order or tell the wranglers what to do unless they were using the names—Princess, Big Red, Shoshone, Clay.

My truck is named Dodge. The name
(40) came with it. I don't know if it was named after the town or the verb or the man who invented it. I like it for a name. Perfectly anonymous, like Rex for a dog or Old Paint. You can't tell anything with a name
(45) like that.

Excerpted from "My Horse" by Barry Lopez. Copyright ©1975 by Barry Lopez. Reprinted by permission of Sterling Lord Literistic, Inc.

**5.** How has the author decorated his truck?

   **(1)** with turquoise and sage
   **(2)** with an animal skin
   **(3)** like a Western ranch
   **(4)** not at all
   **(5)** in a homey way

**6.** According to the author, how are Coke High and the truck similar?

   **(1)** Neither has a cowboy name.
   **(2)** Both came with their own names.
   **(3)** Both are named after men.
   **(4)** Both have unusual names.
   **(5)** Neither has a real owner.

**7.** Why didn't the author ever find out the origin of his horse's name?

   **(1)** He wasn't interested.
   **(2)** The owners wouldn't tell him.
   **(3)** He was too busy keeping track of the other horses' names.
   **(4)** If he knew, he wouldn't be able to wonder about it anymore.
   **(5)** If he knew, he would have to change Coke High's name.

**8.** If the author were to buy a motorcycle, which of the following would he be most likely to do?

   **(1)** give it a name
   **(2)** repaint it
   **(3)** add chrome fixtures
   **(4)** leave it the way it came
   **(5)** join a motorcycle club

**9.** Why does the author include the discussion of horses in the middle of talking about his truck?

- **(1)** because he is writing whatever comes into his mind
- **(2)** in order to suggest how he feels about names
- **(3)** in order to suggest he is not white
- **(4)** because he knows more about horses than he does about trucks
- **(5)** in order to interest his readers in horses

## Fiction

*Items 10 to 13 refer to the following passage.*

### HOW DOES GRUBER DEAL WITH HIS TENANT?

Gruber mopped his brow with a large yellowed handkerchief.

"Listen, my friend, you're gonna make lots of trouble for yourself. If they catch
(5) you in here you might go to the workhouse. I'm only trying to advise you."

To his surprise Kessler looked at him with wet, brimming eyes.

"What did I did to you?" he bitterly
(10) wept. "Who throws out of his house a man that he lived there ten years and pays every month on time his rent? What did I do, tell me? Who hurts a man without reason? Are you a Hitler or a Jew?" He was
(15) hitting his chest with his fist.

Gruber removed his hat. He listened carefully, at first at a loss what to say, but then answered: "Listen, Kessler, it's not personal. I own this house and it's falling
(20) apart. My bills are sky high. If the *tenants don't take care* they have to go. You *don't take care* and you fight with my janitor, so you have to go. Leave in the morning, and I won't say another word. But if you don't
(25) leave the flat, you'll get the heave-ho again. I'll call the marshall."

"Mr. Gruber," said Kessler, "I won't go. Kill me if you want it, but I won't go."

Ignace hurried away from the door as
(30) Gruber left in anger. The next morning, after a restless night of worries, the landlord set out to drive to the city marshal's office. On the way he stopped at a candy store for a pack of cigarettes, and there
(35) decided once more to speak to Kessler. A thought had occurred to him: he would offer to get the old man into a public home.

He drove to the tenement and knocked
(40) on Ignace's door.

"Is the old gink still up there?"

"I don't know if so, Mr. Gruber." The janitor was ill at ease.

"What do you mean you don't know?"
(45) "I didn't see him go out. Before, I looked in his keyhole but nothing moves."

"So why didn't you open the door with your key?"

"I was afraid," Ignace answered ner-
(50) vously.

"What are you afraid?"

Ignace wouldn't say.

Excerpt from "The Mourners" from *The Magic Barrel* by Bernard Malamud. Copyright ©1950, 1955, 1958, and renewed 1986 by Bernard Malamud. Reprinted by permission of Farrar Straus & Giroux.

**10.** Why is Kessler being evicted from his apartment?

- **(1)** He has not paid his rent.
- **(2)** The building is going to be torn down.
- **(3)** Kessler is a bad tenant.
- **(4)** Kessler and Gruber have had a personal disagreement.
- **(5)** Kessler is Jewish.

**11.** Gruber's actions throughout the passage indicate that

- **(1)** he probably has some sympathy for Kessler's situation
- **(2)** he wanted to get rid of Kessler for some time
- **(3)** Ignace has good reason to be afraid of Gruber
- **(4)** Kessler was correct in calling Gruber a "Hitler"
- **(5)** he cares only about making money

**12.** Ignace's nervousness at the end of the passage (lines 41-52) is probably a sign of his fear that

**(1)** Gruber will evict him, too.

**(2)** Kessler will not be accepted in the public home.

**(3)** Kessler might be dead.

**(4)** Gruber will allow Kessler to stay, after all.

**(5)** Kessler has already gone to the workhouse.

**13.** If, in this story, Gruber were an employer instead of a landlord, which of the following statements might Kessler have made?

**(1)** "Why won't you hire me? I have the right experience."

**(2)** "Why don't you resign? You'll only cause trouble if you stay."

**(3)** "Why didn't I get that promotion? You know how hard I work!"

**(4)** "Why am I letting you go? You're always starting arguments in the office."

**(5)** "How can you fire me? I'm your own brother!"

*Items 14 to 18* refer to the following passage.

### IN WHAT WAYS IS HETTY PENNEFATHER A GYPSY?

Her name was Hetty, and she was born with the twentieth century. She was seventy when she died of cold and malnutrition. She had been alone for a long time....
(5) Her four children were now middle-aged, with grown children. Of these descendants one daughter sent her Christmas cards, but otherwise she did not exist for them. For they were all respectable people, with
(10) homes and good jobs and cars. And Hetty was not respectable. She had always been a bit strange, these people said, when mentioning her at all.

When Fred Pennefather, her husband
(15) was alive and the children just growing up, they all lived much too close and uncomfortable in a council flat.... The Pennefathers were good tenants, paying their rent, keeping out of debt; he was a
(20) building worker, "steady," and proud of it. There was no evidence then of Hetty's future dislocation from the normal, unless it was that she very often slipped down for an hour or so to the platforms
(25) where the locomotives drew in and ground out again. She liked the smell of it all, she said. She liked to see people moving about, "coming and going from all those foreign places." She meant
(30) Scotland, Ireland, the North of England. These visits into the din, the smoke, the massed swirling people were for her a drug, like other people's drinking or gambling. Her husband teased her, calling her
(35) a gypsy. She was in fact part-gypsy, for her mother had been one, but had chosen to leave her people and marry a man who lived in a house. Fred Pennefather liked his wife for being different from the run of
(40) the women he knew, and had married her because of it, but her children were fearful that her gypsy blood might show itself in worse ways than haunting railway stations. She was a tall woman with a lot of
(45) glossy black hair, a skin that tanned easily, and dark strong eyes. She wore bright colors, and enjoyed quick tempers and sudden reconciliations. In her prime she attracted attention, was proud and hand-
(50) some. All this made it inevitable that the people in those streets should refer to her as "that gypsy woman." When she heard them, she shouted back that she was none the worse for that.

Excerpt from "An Old Woman and Her Cat" by Doris Lessing from *The Story of a Non-Marrying Man*. Copyright ©1972 The Doris Lessing Trust. Reprinted by permission of Jonathan Cloves, Ltd. London, on behalf of the Doris Lessing Trust.

**14.** Why have Hetty's children failed to stay in touch with her?

**(1)** They feel that Hetty is not respectable enough.

**(2)** They resent Hetty for wasting their inheritance money.

**(3)** They feel that Hetty neglected them when they were young.

**(4)** They blame Hetty for the death of their father.

**(5)** They blame Hetty for their early life of poverty.

**15.** Hetty's "dislocation from the normal" (line 22) refers to her

   **(1)** move to the suburbs of London
   **(2)** odd habits
   **(3)** love of foreign countries and cultures
   **(4)** exceptional beauty
   **(5)** death at the age of seventy

**16.** Which of the following pairs of words best describes Hetty?

   **(1)** confused and afraid
   **(2)** steady and hardworking
   **(3)** insane and dangerous
   **(4)** ugly and frightening
   **(5)** strong-minded but odd

**17.** Hetty's feelings about visiting railway stations are most like

   **(1)** a child's feelings about going to the movies
   **(2)** a child's feelings about his or her parents
   **(3)** a dieter's feelings about exercise
   **(4)** a smoker's feelings about cigarettes
   **(5)** an actor's feelings about a script

**18.** What do Hetty's shouts to the people in the street suggest about her?

   **(1)** She is ashamed of her gypsy blood.
   **(2)** She is proud of her gypsy blood.
   **(3)** She is as crazy as her children think she is.
   **(4)** Her husband was wrong about her.
   **(5)** She is trying to embarrass her children.

## Drama

*Items 19 to 22 refer to the following passage.*

### WHAT CONFESSION DOES WILLIE MAKE TO HIS WIFE?

LINDA, *hearing Willy outside the bedroom, calls with some trepidation:* Willy!

WILLY: It's all right. I came back.

LINDA: Why? What happened? *Slight*
(5) *pause.* Did something happen, Willy?

WILLY: No, nothing happened.

LINDA: You didn't smash the car, did you?

WILLY, *with casual irritation*: I said nothing happened. Didn't you hear me?

(10) LINDA: Don't you feel well?

WILLY: I'm tired to the death. The flute has faded away. He sits on the bed beside her, a little numb. I couldn't make it. I just couldn't make it, Linda.

(15) LINDA, *very carefully, delicately*: Where were you all day? You look terrible.

WILLY: I got as far as a little above Yonkers. I stopped for a cup of coffee. Maybe it was the coffee.

(20) LINDA: What?

WILLY, *after a pause*: I suddenly couldn't drive any more. The car kept going off onto the shoulder, y'know?

LINDA, *helpfully*: Oh. Maybe it was the
(25) steering again. I don't think Angelo knows the Studebaker.

WILLY: No, it's me, it's me. Suddenly I realize I'm goin' sixty miles an hour and don't remember the last five minutes.
(30) I'm—I can't seem to—keep my mind to it.

LINDA: Maybe it's your glasses. You never went for your new glasses.

WILLY: No, I see everything. I came back
(35) ten miles an hour. It took me nearly four hours from Yonkers.

LINDA, *resigned:* Well, you'll just have to take a rest, Willy, you can't continue this way.

(40) WILLY: I just got back from Florida.

LINDA: But you didn't rest your mind. Your mind is overactive, and the mind is what counts, dear.

**19.** In this passage, why is Willy upset?

   **(1)** He realizes that his car isn't working properly.

   **(2)** He has wrecked his car.

   **(3)** He has a serious physical illness.

   **(4)** He fears that he is losing control.

   **(5)** He doesn't know how to make Linda understand him.

**20.** In the early part of this passage (lines 1-5), it is apparent that

   **(1)** Willy is unusually late getting home.

   **(2)** Linda is more worried about the Studebaker than she is about Willy.

   **(3)** Linda is concerned about seeing Willy home so soon.

   **(4)** Willy has been drinking.

   **(5)** Willy and Linda have had an argument.

**21.** Which of the following words best characterizes Linda?

   **(1)** enthusiastic

   **(2)** foolish

   **(3)** supportive

   **(4)** irritable

   **(5)** irresponsible

**22.** Why does the author use dashes when Willy says, "I'm—I can't seem to—keep my mind to it" (lines 30-31)?

   **(1)** to indicate Willy's speech problem

   **(2)** to suggest that Willy has had a stroke

   **(3)** to emphasize Willy's confusion

   **(4)** to show that Linda won't let Willy speak

   **(5)** to lead up to the idea that a Florida vacation is not restful

*Items 23 to 26 refer to the following passage.*

## WHY DID THE VISITOR WANT TO SEE MAMA?

MAMA: Well—this all the packing got done since I left out of here this morning. I testify before God that my children got all the energy of the dead. What time
(5) the moving men due?

BENEATHA: Four o'clock. You had a caller, Mama. *(She is smiling, teasingly)*

MAMA: Sure enough—who?

BENEATHA: *(Her arms folded saucily)* The
(10) Welcoming Committee. (WALTER *and* RUTH *giggle)*

MAMA: *(Innocently)* Who?

BENEATHA: The Welcoming Committee. They said they're sure going to be glad
(15) to see you when you get there.

WALTER: *(Devilishly)* Yeah, they said they can't hardly wait to see your face. *(Laughter)*

MAMA: *(Sensing their facetiousness)* What's
(20) the matter with you all?

WALTER: Ain't nothing the matter with us. We just telling you 'bout the gentleman who came to see you this afternoon. From the Clybourne Park Improvement
(25) Association.

MAMA: What he want?

RUTH: *(In the same mood as* BENEATHA *and* WALTER*)* To welcome you, honey.

WALTER: He said they can't hardly wait. He
(30) said the one thing they don't have, that they just *dying* to have out there is a fine family of colored people! *(To* RUTH *and* BENEATHA*)* Ain't that right!

RUTH AND BENEATHA: *(Mockingly)* Yeah! He
(35) left his card in case—*(They indicate the card, and* MAMA *picks it up and throws it on the floor—understanding and looking off as she draws her chair up to the table on which she has put her plant
(40) and some sticks and some cord)*

MAMA: Father, give us strength. *(Knowingly—and without fun)* Did he threaten us?

BENEATHA: Oh—Mama—they don't do it
(45) like that any more. He talked Brotherhood. He said everybody ought learn how to sit down and hate each

other with good Christian fellowship. *(She and* WALTER *shake hands to ridicule* (50) *the remark)*

MAMA: *(Sadly)* Lord, protect us...

RUTH: You should hear the money those folks raised to buy the house from us. All we paid and then some.

(55) BENEATHA: What they think we going to do—eat 'em?

RUTH: No, honey, marry 'em.

MAMA: *(Shaking her head)* Lord, Lord, Lord ...

**23.** Which of the following best describes what is happening in this passage?

**(1)** The family is discussing how good it is to be welcome in a new community.

**(2)** Mama is trying to convince her children to move to a new community.

**(3)** The children are warning Mama that they will not really be welcome in their new home.

**(4)** The Welcoming Committee is threatening the family.

**(5)** The family is deciding not to move.

**24.** How do the stage directions help to make the meaning of the passage clear?

**(1)** They dramatize the seriousness of the situation.

**(2)** They emphasize Mama's wisdom in dealing with family problems.

**(3)** They reveal the innocence of Walter, Beneatha, and Ruth.

**(4)** They contrast what the children say and what the Welcoming Committee really meant.

**(5)** They reveal an unstated conflict between Mama and Walter.

**25.** What causes Mama to say "Father, give us strength" and "Lord protect us ..." (lines 41 and 51)?

**(1)** She needs to set an example for her children.

**(2)** She is saddened when she understands what her children are saying.

**(3)** She wants to give thanks for her new good neighbors.

**(4)** She wants to pray for her family's physical safety.

**(5)** She is angry at her children's rude behavior.

**26.** To which of the following people or groups would the Clybourne Park Improvement Association be most likely to extend a similar welcome?

**(1)** a family from Great Britain

**(2)** a retired businessman from Arizona

**(3)** a half-way house for recovering drug abusers

**(4)** a new minister from the Midwest

**(5)** the family of a major-league baseball player

**Poetry**

*Items 27 to 30* refer to the following song lyrics.

## WHY DOES THE POET APPRECIATE HIS FATHER?

An only child, alone and wild—
    A cabinetmaker's son:
His hands were meant for different work
    And his heart was known to none.
(5) He left his home and went his lone
    And solitary way,
And he gave to me a gift I know
    I never can repay

I thank you for the music
(10)     And your stories of the road;
I thank you for the freedom
    When it came my time to go.
I thank you for the kindness
    And the times when you got tough—
(15) And, Papa, I don't think I've said
    "I love you" near enough.

The leader of the band is tired,
    And his eyes are growing old,
But his blood runs through my instrument,
(20)     And his song is in my soul.
My life has been a poor attempt
    To imitate the man—
I'm just a living legacy
    To the leader of the band.

**27.** Who is described as being "alone and wild" (line 1) as a child?

  **(1)** the speaker
  **(2)** the cabinetmaker
  **(3)** the speaker's father
  **(4)** the speaker's son
  **(5)** the speaker's grandfather

**28.** In which of the following ways is the son different from his father?

  **(1)** The father left his home; the son did not.
  **(2)** The father never said "I love you"; the son always did.
  **(3)** The father was an obedient child; the son was not.
  **(4)** The father had no talents; the son has.
  **(5)** The father chose a career different from his own father's; the son chose his father's career.

**29.** Which of the following is NOT one of the "gifts" the son is thankful for?

  **(1)** a love of music
  **(2)** tales about travelling
  **(3)** freedom to make his own decisions
  **(4)** parental discipline
  **(5)** the love of working with wood

**30.** By using the words "just a living legacy" (line 23), the poet is emphasizing the idea that the speaker

  **(1)** has become an excellent musician
  **(2)** resents the band leader
  **(3)** is a complete failure
  **(4)** will inherit his father's money
  **(5)** feels he will never be as good as his father

*Items 31 to 35* refer to the following poem.

## WHAT IS IT THAT REFUSES TO BE DESTROYED?

from *Still I Rise*

You may write me down in history
With your bitter, twisted lies,
You may trod me in the very dirt
But still, like dust, I'll rise.

...

(5) You may shoot me with your words,
You may cut me with your eyes.
You may kill me with your hatefulness,
But still, like air, I'll rise.

...

Out of the huts of history's shame
(10) I rise
Up from a past that's rooted in pain
I rise
I'm a black ocean, leaping and wide,
Welling and swelling I bear in the tide.

(15) Leaving behind nights of terror and fear
I rise
Into a daybreak that's wondrously clear
I rise
Bringing the gifts that my ancestors gave,
(20) I am the dream and the hope of the slave.
I rise
I rise
I rise.

Excerpted from AND STILL I RISE.by Maya Angelou. Copyright ©1978 by Maya Angelou. Reprinted with permission of the author and Random House, Inc.

**31.** How is history described in this poem?
   **(1)** as full of injustices
   **(2)** as being as wide as a black ocean
   **(3)** as dusty and dull
   **(4)** as something to be proud of
   **(5)** as well-written and truthful

**32.** Which of the following best describes what the speaker of this poem says she represents?
   **(1)** a group of historians
   **(2)** the future of the black race
   **(3)** the product of imagination
   **(4)** abused women
   **(5)** waves in the ocean

**33.** Which of the following would make the best title for this poem?
   **(1)** Dark Nights Ahead
   **(2)** We Shall Overcome
   **(3)** Giving Up
   **(4)** Rewriting History
   **(5)** My Glorious Past

**34.** The poet uses the phrase "a daybreak that's wondrously clear" (line 17) to
   **(1)** describe the weather forecast
   **(2)** encourage the reader to get an early start
   **(3)** contrast the past with a future full of hope
   **(4)** explain why she is an early riser
   **(5)** illustrate what she means by "history's shame"

**35.** Why does the poet repeat "I rise" three times at the end of the poem?

**(1)** to bring herself good luck

**(2)** to make the poem sound like a gospel song

**(3)** to suggest that the speaker is going to heaven

**(4)** to give the poem a surprise ending

**(5)** to suggest an ongoing and unstoppable process

## Commentary

*Items 36 to 40 refer to the following passage.*

### WHY IS THE SOCRATES SCULPTURE PARK A SPECIAL PLACE?

The recent opening of the Socrates Sculpture Park in Long Island City, Queens, has awakened dreams. There are a handful of outdoor sites in New York City where
(5) sculpture has been exhibited with some regularity during the summer months, but there has not been any place in which quality large-scale sculpture could be seen all year round. Now there is....
(10) According to a brochure for the sculpture park, the project is "dedicated to Socrates in his search for the truth." The driving force behind the park is Mark di Suvero, whose large steel works feed off
(15) architecture, and who has a rare capacity to mobilize people from different walks of life.... Di Suvero was instrumental in leasing the land from the city for five years, and in raising the $200,000 that has been
(20) spent so far in clearing and landscaping the grounds and assembling the first show. The park is still raw, and there is no sense yet of a clear guiding vision, but its very existence is remarkable, and its
(25) potential is almost unlimited....

The park is a realization of a dream. For years di Suvero has been committed to using his resources to help other sculptors and to create a more active role for
(30) sculpture in the community. Sculptors like Scott Pfaffman and Paul Pappas worked on the grounds. Di Suvero handled the crane. Young people from a nearby housing project were instrumental in
(35) getting the park into shape.

But herein lies a danger. Although it is much too early to make a judgment, the park feels like an early 1970's democratic free-for-all—like a project that believes it
(40) can get by on general good will and cooperation. Because there is no sense of hierarchy, there is also no sense that anyone has decided exactly what the park should look like, and the first show is not coher-
(45) ent. The landscaping of the park, like the present installation, seems arbitrary. What is missing is the sense of a touch, clearly defined guiding vision....

The park will probably organize two
(50) shows a year. It is considering an international sculpture show on Minimalism. In the distant future it may also organize an open competition. There is some talk that the park will be the site of the 1989
(55) Whitney Biennial. Clearly there is a great need of a place where sculpture can not only make friends but also influence people—where all the thoughts, feelings and information rumbling within it can be
(60) released.

Excerpt from "di Suvero's Dream of a Sculpture Park..." by Michael Brenson. Copyright ©1986 by The New York Times Company. Reprinted with permission.

**36.** What was Mark di Suvero's major contribution to the building of the Socrates Sculpture Park?

**(1)** He operated the crane.

**(2)** He donated a huge sculpture.

**(3)** He organized the planning and financing.

**(4)** He supplied the steel.

**(5)** He planned several future shows.

**37.** According to the review, what dream was fulfilled by the creation of the park?

**(1)** New York City's goal of selling the land to raise money

**(2)** the start of outdoor sculpture exhibitions

**(3)** Socrates' hope that people would remember him

**(4)** the desire of Long Island sculptors for a place to work

**(5)** the desire to support sculptors and connect people with sculpture

**38.** What does the reviewer mean when he refers to the park as raw (line 22)?

   **(1)** The sculpture exhibited there is exposed to the weather.

   **(2)** The sculpture exhibited there is considered crude.

   **(3)** The park was opened to the public too early.

   **(4)** The clearing of the land was done cheaply.

   **(5)** The "look" of the park still needs some work.

**39.** The reviewer uses the words "herein lies the danger" (line 36) to

   **(1)** suggest that an outdoor park can be dangerous

   **(2)** introduce what he sees as the park's main weakness

   **(3)** warn the park might decay

   **(4)** advise against building more sculpture parks

   **(5)** imply that the park will not be popular

**40.** To which of the following would the reviewer most likely give similar approval?

   **(1)** a "hands-on" science museum

   **(2)** a film about Abraham Lincoln

   **(3)** a televised panel discussion about Socrates

   **(4)** a book of photographs of famous bronze sculptures

   **(5)** a novel about a famous art theft

*Items 41 to 45* refer to the following passage.

### HOW DOES JESSICA FLETCHER SOLVE MYSTERIES?

Clearly, "Murder, She Wrote" does not dabble in flashiness or special effects.... In general, the mystery show is considerably different from the standard police
(5) show, which tends to specialize in screeching tires and shoot-outs. Going back to the rules established by Arthur Conan Doyle for Mr. Holmes, the good mystery is more cerebral in its approach
(10) to solutions. This is certainly true of the amateur sleuth, who is not even likely to carry a gun. Jessica Fletcher of "Murder, She Wrote" is a writer of mysteries and, supposedly, goes about solving cases in
(15) her spare time, whenever that might be. If she bears more than a passing resemblance to the very British Miss Marple, there is good reason. Messrs. Levinson, Link and Fischer developed the character
(20) after watching a TV movie starring Helen Hayes as the Agatha Christie character. But unlike Miss Christie's terribly proper and sedate heroine, or Miss Hayes' fluttery version of the character, Miss [Angela]
(25) Lansbury's Jessica is a no-nonsense, practical woman who is honest enough to exclaim "Oh, good Lord!" when taken by surprise.

Needless to say, even "Murder, She
(30) Wrote" gets to dabble in some violence as each script is obliged to come up with at least one murder victim. But just about always, the actual murder isn't seen. The victim is always being "discovered" after
(35) the fact. And Jessica herself is a model of nonviolence. Nevertheless, the show can flirt with the fact of violence in most of its attention-grabbing aspects. Last Sunday's episode, for example, took place in a small
(40) Southern town as the peripatetic Jessica visited an old friend, a teacher and fellow mystery writer, played, with perhaps a hint of a wink by Mr. [Craig] Stevens of "Peter Gunn." With the local rednecks get-
(45) ting drunker and rowdier after the murder of one of their friends, Jessica confessed that the atmosphere in this town was "terrifying, it feels as if it's about to explode." Before long, the sheriff, a black man
(50) (Dorian Harewood), was facing a nasty crowd waiting to lynch the jailed suspect, who was, of course, innocent. But the sheriff managed to defuse the situation, while Jessica, her efficiency undimin-
(55) ished, set about exposing the real murderer. Great art? Hardly. Good entertainment, the electronic equivalent of a good read? You bet. And not a gratuitous bit of cheap "action" footage in the entire hour.

**41.** What is the reviewer's opinion of "Murder, She Wrote"?

(1) It requires concentrated thought by the viewer.
(2) It is very dull.
(3) It is fun.
(4) It is not worth watching.
(5) It is an excellent example of television as art.

**42.** The term "cerebral" (line 9) is most probably the opposite of

(1) physical
(2) thoughtful
(3) ordinary
(4) no-nonsense
(5) efficient

**43.** According to the reviewer, a major difference between Jessica Fletcher and Miss Marple is that

(1) Miss Marple is more violent
(2) Jessica Fletcher is sillier
(3) Jessica Fletcher is more proper
(4) Jessica Fletcher is more down-to-earth
(5) Miss Marple is more intelligent

**44.** The way in which the reviewer retells a recent episode of "Murder, She Wrote" indicates that he found the plot to be

(1) predictable but entertaining
(2) terrifying and violent
(3) original and shocking
(4) unbelievable but comical
(5) confusing and disturbing

**45.** Which of the following kinds of programs would the reviewer be LEAST likely to enjoy?

(1) a knowledge-based quiz program
(2) a well-produced comedy special
(3) a live broadcast of a jazz performance
(4) a disaster movie
(5) a discussion of current events

Answers are on page 333.

# Practice Items

## Performance Analysis Chart

**Directions:** Circle the number of each item that you got correct on the Practice Items. Count how many items you got correct in each row; count how many items you got correct in each column. Write the amount correct per row and column as the numerator in the fraction in the appropriate "Total Correct" box. (The denominators represent the total number of items in the row or column.) Write the grand total correct over the denominator, **45**, at the lower right corner of the chart. (For example, if you got 40 items correct, write 40 so that the fraction reads 40/**45**.)

| Item Type | Nonfiction (page 14) | Fiction (page 90) | Drama (page 168) | Poetry (page 210) | Commentary (page 246) | TOTAL CORRECT |
|---|---|---|---|---|---|---|
| **Literal Comprehension** | 2, 5 | 10. 14, 15 | 23 | 29, 31, 32 | 36, 37, 42, 43 | **/13** |
| **Inferential Comprehension** | 1, 3, 6, 7 | 11, 12 | 19, 20, 25 | 27, 28 | 38, 41 | **/13** |
| **Application** | 8 | 13, 17 | 26 | 33 | 40, 45 | **/7** |
| **Analysis** | 4, 9 | 16, 18 | 21, 22, 24 | 30, 34, 35 | 39, 44 | **/12** |
| **TOTAL CORRECT** | **/9** | **/9** | **/8** | **/9** | **/10** | **/45** |

# PRACTICE TEST

As with the actual Interpreting Literature and the Arts Test, the types of literature on the following Practice Test are not grouped together. For example, you may begin with a poem, then have a commentary, a piece of fiction, then another poem. This arrangement of items requires you to "switch gears" between different types of literature as you work. This Practice Test is also the same length as the actual GED, 45 items, and as challenging. Taking the Practice Test will help you know what to expect when you take the actual Interpreting Literature and Arts Test.

You can use the Practice Test in two different ways. First, take it to get valuable hands-on test-taking experience. To do this, take the Practice Test under GED test conditions. Complete the test in one sitting within the 65-minute time limit. If you would rather, you can take the Practice Test in sections. For instance, you can plan to complete ten items a day or a quarter of the test at a time. Even though this method does not simulate the actual GED testing situation, it can give you an idea of your strengths and weaknesses.

When you have completed the Practice Test, use the answer key on page 339 to score your results. Read the information in the answer key even if you answered the item correctly. These explanations will help you reinforce your knowledge of literature and improve your test-taking skills. Then use the Performance Analysis Chart at the end of the test to identify the areas where you can use additional review and direct you to the parts of the book where you can review specific topics.

# Practice Test

**Directions**: Choose the one best answer to each question.

*Items 1 to 4* refer to the following passage.

### HOW WELL DOES THE BOY UNDERSTAND HIS PARENTS?

...As time went on I saw more and more how he managed to alienate Mother and me. What made it worse was that I couldn't grasp his method or see what
(5) attraction he had for Mother. In every possible way he was less winning than I. He had a common accent and made noises at his tea. I thought for a while that it might be the newspapers she was interested in,
(10) so I made up bits of news of my own to read to her. Then I thought it might be the smoking, which I personally thought attractive, and took his pipes and went around the house dribbling into them till
(15) he caught me. I even made noises at my tea, but Mother only told me I was disgusting. It all seemed to hinge around that unhealthy habit of sleeping together, so I made a point of dropping into their
(20) bedroom and nosing round, talking to myself, so that they wouldn't know I was watching them, but they were never up to anything I could see. In the end it beat me. It seemed to depend on being grown-
(25) up and giving people rings, and I realized I'd have to wait.

But at the same time I wanted him to see that I was only waiting, not giving up the fight. One evening when he was being
(30) particularly obnoxious, chattering away well above my head, I let him have it.

"Mummy," I said, "do you know what I'm going to do when I grow up?"

"No, dear," she replied. "What?"
(35) "I'm going to marry you," I said quietly.

Father gave a great guffaw out of him,
but he didn't take me in. I knew it must only be pretense. And Mother, in spite of everything, was pleased. I felt she was
(40) probably relieved to know that one day Father's hold on her would be broken.

"Won't that be nice?" she said with a smile.

"It'll be very nice," I said confidently,
(45) "because we're going to have lots and lots of babies."

"That's right, dear," she said placidly. "I think we'll have one soon, and then you'll have plenty of company."
(50) I was no end pleased about that because it showed that in spite of the way she gave in to Father, she still considered my wishes.

1. Why does the boy take his father's pipes (lines 12-13)?

   **(1)** He wants to try smoking.
   **(2)** He thinks the pipes are attractive.
   **(3)** He wants to get even with his father by destroying them.
   **(4)** He wants to gain his mother's favor.
   **(5)** He wants his father to think that he is grown up.

2. What does the boy decide to wait for?

   **(1)** his father's death
   **(2)** being old enough to marry his mother
   **(3)** telling his mother he will marry her
   **(4)** his parents to come out of the bedroom
   **(5)** the next beating from his father

**3.** Which word best summarizes the boy's feelings toward his father?

   **(1)** indifference
   **(2)** jealousy
   **(3)** fear
   **(4)** admiration
   **(5)** hatred

**4.** Why does the author tell this story from the child's point of view?

   **(1)** to make the story easy to read
   **(2)** to teach parents how to handle their children
   **(3)** to make the descriptions in the story more interesting
   **(4)** to surprise the reader with the child's intelligence
   **(5)** to point out the humor in the situation

*Items 5 to 9 refer to the following passage.*

### WHAT DOES TEVYE WANT FROM GOD?

*The exterior of Tevye's house,* TEVYE *enters, pulling his cart. He stops, and sits on the wagon seat, exhausted.*

(5) TEVYE: Today I am a horse. Dear God, did you have to make my poor old horse lose his shoe just before the Sabbath? That wasn't nice: It's enough you pick on me, Tevye, bless me with five daughters, a life of poverty. What have you got
(10) against my horse? Sometimes I think when things are too quiet up there, You say to Yourself: Let's see, what kind of mischief can I play on my friend Tevye?"

GOLDE: (*Entering from house*) You're finally
(15) here, my breadwinner.

TEVYE: (*To heaven*) I'll talk to You later.

GOLDE: Where's your horse?

TEVYE: He was invited to the blacksmith's for the Sabbath.

(20) GOLDE: Hurry up, the sun won't wait for you. I have something to say to you. (*Exits into house.*)

TEVYE: As the Good Book says, "Heal us, O Lord, and we shall be healed." In
(25) other words, send us the cure, we've got the sickness already. (*Gestures to the*

*door.*) I'm not really complaining—after all, with Your help, I'm starving to death. You made many, many poor peo-
(30) ple. I realize, of course, that it's no shame to be poor, but it's no great honor either. So what would have been so terrible if I had a small fortune?

   ["If I Were a Rich Man"]
(35)    If I were a rich man
   Daidle deedle daidle
Digguh digguh deedle daidle dum,
  All day long I'd biddy biddy bum,
   If I were a wealthy man.

(40)   Wouldn't have to work hard,
   Daidle deedle daidle
Digguh digguh deedle daidle dum,
  If I were a biddy biddy rich
Digguh digguh deedle daidle man.

(45) I'd build a big, tall house with rooms by the dozen
  Right in the middle of the town,
A fine tin roof and real wooden floors below.
(50) There would be one long staircase just going up,
  And one even longer coming down,
  And one more leading nowhere just for show.

(55) I'd fill my yard with chicks and turkeys and geese
And ducks for the town to see and hear,
Squawking just as noisily as they can.
And each loud quack and cluck and gobble and honk
(60) Will land like a trumpet on the ear,
  As if to say, here lives a wealthy man.
   (*Sighs.*)

**5.** What does Tevye mean when he says "Today I am a horse (line 4)?

   **(1)** God had turned him into a horse.
   **(2)** He wishes he were a horse.
   **(3)** He had to take his horse's place.
   **(4)** He feels embarrassed.
   **(5)** He has just been to the blacksmith's.

6. Which of the following statements is true of Tevye?

   (1) He has a no home.
   (2) He is very sick.
   (3) He knows things will improve soon.
   (4) He doesn't believe in God.
   (5) He is poor.

7. What is suggested about Tevye's character by the way he speaks?

   (1) He has a sense of humor about his life.
   (2) He is always finding fault with himself.
   (3) He gives up quickly when things go wrong.
   (4) He is a very calm person.
   (5) He is impatient and violent.

8. What does the author intend by including the song at the end of the passage (lines 34-63)?

   (1) to criticize Golde
   (2) to give an example of what Tevye would do with money
   (3) to explain how Tevye really lives
   (4) to change the setting
   (5) to compare Tevye to poor people

9. What will Tevye probably do if Golde starts to nag him?

   (1) yell back at her
   (2) try to apologize
   (3) make fun of her
   (4) start to cry
   (5) make a humorous appeal to God

*Items 10 to 14 refer to the following passage.*

**WHAT IS A SHELL GAME?**

Watching the snow fall made me think about a lot of things. I thought about what Dad had said the night before. He knew he would already have left for work when I got up that morning, so he gave
(5) me his good-bye speech the night before. I never used to listen to Dad when he talked to me—I never thought he had anything to say worth listening to—but I
(10) always used to make believe I was listening to him. But that night, I didn't even pretend I was thinking about what he said.

Dad started telling me that it would be a
(15) long time before I would see the streets of New York City again. And that maybe when I got back, I would appreciate them enough to stop all that goddamn stealing and stay home like somebody with some
(20) sense. He talked on and on like that. Then he said something. Dad asked me if I remembered when I used to get up every Sunday morning to go out and watch Mr. Jimmy win money from people who were
(25) dumb enough to go hunting for a pea that wasn't there. I told him I remembered. Then he asked me if I knew what a fool was. I said a fool was somebody stupid. Dad said I was right, but there was more
(30) to it than that. He said it takes a stupid person to keep looking for something that is never there. Dad told me to go into the kitchen and get a black-eyed pea.

When I came back with the pea, Dad
(35) had set up the card table and was sitting at it with three half nutshells in front of him. I gave him the pea, and Dad started switching the shells around the way Mr. Jimmy used to do. It looked like Dad was
(40) doing it real slow, and I was sure I knew where the pea was all the time. I never knew Dad could do that trick, and even then I was sure he was doing it too slow. When Dad stopped sliding the nutshells
(45) around, he told me to pick up the one I thought the pea was under. We did this ten times. Each time, I was sure the pea was under the shell I picked up. Ten times I picked the wrong shell. After I made that
(50) last wrong pick, Dad looked at me and just kept shaking his head for a little while. Then he said, "That's jis what you been doin' all your life, lookin' for a pea that ain't there. And I'm mighty 'fraid
(55) that's how you gon end your whole life, lookin' for that pea."

Excerpted from Claude Brown, *Manchild in the Promised Land.* Copyright ©1965 by Claude Brown. Reprinted with permission.

**10.** To whom is Dad referring when he talks about "a fool" (lines 26-31)?

    **(1)** Mr. Jimmy

    **(2)** himself

    **(3)** his son

    **(4)** an uneducated person

    **(5)** New Yorkers

**11.** What is the boy who is telling the story probably about to do?

    **(1)** move to California

    **(2)** enlist in the army

    **(3)** begin college

    **(4)** go to reform school

    **(5)** become a magician

**12.** Which of the following opinions concerning welfare would Dad be most likely to agree with?

    **(1)** Instead of relying on welfare, people should work to support themselves.

    **(2)** the government has a responsibility to take care of the nation's poor.

    **(3)** There is too much corruption in the welfare system.

    **(4)** Accepting welfare is a disgrace.

    **(5)** People on welfare will never be able to support themselves.

**13.** Which of the following ideas would Dad probably think is best illustrated by the shell game?

    **(1)** Gamblers are usually skillful.

    **(2)** Success is just a matter of luck.

    **(3)** Games are the spice of life.

    **(4)** People are usually dishonest.

    **(5)** People should set realistic goals for themselves.

**14.** How does the author suggest that he started paying attention to what his father had to say?

    **(1)** by saying he used to "make believe"

    **(2)** by saying his father "talked on and on"

    **(3)** by saying "then he said something"

    **(4)** by believing his father was playing the game too slowly

    **(5)** by picking the right shell

*Items 15 to 19* refer to the following passage.

## WHAT GOOD THING HAS PUBLIC TELEVISION DONE THIS YEAR?

Television can do interesting things when it has to; public television can do some of the most interesting things of all. As it happens, public television is having a
(5) very interesting season, although, as is often the case in public television, our attention is deflected by other things. "The Africans" attracts attention because it is denounced by the National Endowment
(10) for the Humanities. A literacy campaign on public television attracts attention through its own self-promotion. At the same time, observers note, public television has no smashing new dramatic
(15) series. Where is this season's "Jewel in the Crown"? Public television seems to be off to an abysmal year.

In fact, this is not so; the season would be a success if it offered nothing more
(20) than "The Story of English." The nine-part series is public television at its best, a reflection of the original reasons the system was conceived.

    ...

"The Story of English" has been a
(25) delight to the eye and the ear since it started, even though its topic—the growth and dissemination of the English language—is the stuff of which dry, dusty seminars can be made. Tomorrow night's
(30) episode, "Black on White," traces the evolution of black American English from the West Coast of Africa 300 years ago to our cities today. It visits, among other places, the Sea Islands of Georgia, where Gullah
(35) is spoken. Gullah is the form of English— or the "variety" of English, as the series calls it—that first was spoken by African slaves.

The program's special mark of distinc-
(40) tion here is that it does not treat either Gullah or the people who speak it as espe-

cially quaint or anachronistic. Gullah has a logic, syntax and history of its own. Later, the program visits Philadelphia, the (45) home, says Robert MacNeil, the host and co-author of the series, of some "ghetto Homers." He is talking here about rap, a form of musicalized speech that I have always thought of as deficient in the mer- (50) its of either music or speech. The program persuades me I was wrong. Rap has something to offer. "The Story of English" fulfills the Carnegie Commission's old mandate about giving us a "fuller awareness of (55) the wonder and vitality of the arts" and leading us down new roads. The series is a triumph.

Excerpted from John Corry, "A Season That Fulfills The Aims Of Public Television". Copyright ©1987 by The New York Times Company. Reprinted by permission.

**15.** What is the author's opinion of "The Story of English"?

   **(1)** It is popular only because it is self-promoting.

   **(2)** It is important and interesting.

   **(3)** It is important but dry and dusty.

   **(4)** It is interesting, but not as interesting as "The Africans."

   **(5)** It causes viewers to lose interest quickly.

**16.** According to the reviewer, what is the purpose of this public television series?

   **(1)** to teach viewers how to speak Gullah

   **(2)** to lead viewers to a new awareness about language

   **(3)** to explain relationships between blacks and whites

   **(4)** to teach literacy

   **(5)** to provide a smashing dramatic series

**17.** When Robert MacNeil refers to "ghetto Homers" (lines 46-49), he is talking about

   **(1)** baseball players

   **(2)** Philadelphia television personalities

   **(3)** street musicians

   **(4)** co-authors of the series

   **(5)** English teachers

**18.** What effect did the episode "Black on White" have on the reviewer?

   **(1)** It taught him to appreciate black American English.

   **(2)** It convinced him that he was right about rap music.

   **(3)** It made him want to go to the Sea Islands

   **(4)** It caused him to lose interest in public television.

   **(5)** It encouraged him to become an historian.

**19.** The author of this review would most probably praise public television for broadcasting

   **(1)** a series featuring funny sports "bloopers"

   **(2)** a show exploring artists' contributions to culture

   **(3)** a musical-variety show

   **(4)** a televised presidential address

   **(5)** a comedy about life along the Sea Islands

*Items 20 to 23* refer to the following poem.

## HOW DOES THE POET FEEL ABOUT HER "OWN DEAR LOVE"?

### LOVE SONG

My own dear love he is strong and bold
    And he cares not what comes after.
His words ring sweet as a chime of gold
    And his eyes are lit with laughter.
(5) He is jubilant as a flag unfurled—
    Oh, a girl, she'd not forget him.
My own dear love, he is all my world—
    And I wish I'd never met him.

My love, he's mad, and my love, he's fleet,
(10)     And a wild young wood-thing bore him!
The ways are fair to his roaming feet,
    And the skies are sunlit for him.
As sharply sweet to my heart he seems
    As the fragrance of acacia.
(15) My own dear love, he is all my dreams—
    And I wish he were in Asia.

My love runs by like a day in June,
    And he makes no friend of sorrows,
He'll tread his galloping rigadoon
(20)     In the pathway of the morrows.
He'll live his days where the sunbeams start,
    Nor could storm or wind uproot him.
My own dear love, he is all my heart—
    And I wish somebody'd shoot him.

"Love Song" by Dorothy Parker. Copyright ©1944 by the author. Reprinted with permission of Viking Penguin, Inc.

**20.** Which of the following does the speaker believe is true about her lover?

- **(1)** He is attractive to women.
- **(2)** He is almost never happy.
- **(3)** He is perfect in every way.
- **(4)** He is very patriotic.
- **(5)** He is too serious about the future.

**21.** The last two lines in each stanza set up a contrast that is intended to

- **(1)** express deep tragedy
- **(2)** make the reader laugh
- **(3)** make the reader cry
- **(4)** illustrate the nature of true love
- **(5)** touch the lover's heart

**22.** What does the poet suggest about the speaker's lover by saying, "a wild young wood-thing bore him" (line 10)?

- **(1)** His mother was crazy.
- **(2)** He grew up in the woods.
- **(3)** He is bored by anything to do with nature.
- **(4)** He seems as carefree as a wild animal.
- **(5)** He is very shy.

**23.** If this poet were to take the same approach in another poem, which of the following would be the most likely subject?

- **(1)** child abuse
- **(2)** raising teenage children
- **(3)** the death of a beloved parent
- **(4)** coping with cancer
- **(5)** the assassination of Martin Luther King, Jr.

*Items 24 to 27* refer to the following passage.

## WHAT HAS HAPPENED DURING THE NIGHT?

She sat up stiffly, staring out at the dawn. The train was rushing through a region of bare hillocks huddled against a lifeless sky. It looked like the first day of
(5) creation. The air of the car was close, and she pushed up her windows to let in the keen wind. Then she looked at her watch: it was seven o'clock, and soon the people about her would be stirring. She slipped
(10) into her clothes, smoothed her disheveled hair and crept to the dressing room. When she had washed her face and adjusted her dress she felt more hopeful. It was always a struggle for her not to be cheerful in the
(15) morning. Her cheeks burned deliciously under the coarse towel and the wet hair about her temples broke into strong upward tendrils. Every inch of her was full of life and elasticity. And in ten hours they
(20) would be home!

She stepped to her husband's berth: it was time for him to take his early glass of milk. The window shade was down, and in the dusk of the curtained enclosure she
(25) could just see that he lay sideways, with his face away from her. She leaned over him and drew up the shade. As she did so she touched one of his hands. It felt cold....
(30) She bent closer, laying her hand on his arm and calling him by name. He did not move. She spoke again more loudly; she grasped his shoulders and gently shook it. He lay motionless. She caught hold of his
(35) hand again: it slipped from her limply, like a dead thing. A dead thing?

Her breath caught. She must see his face. She leaned forward, and hurriedly, shrinkingly, with a sickening reluctance of
(40) the flesh, laid her hands on his shoulders and turned him over. His head fell back; his face looked small and smooth; he gazed at her with steady eyes.

Excerpted from Edith Wharton, *A Greater Inclination*. Reprinted by permission of Charles Scribner's Sons.

**24.** Which of the following best explains what happens in this passage?

  **(1)** A woman meets her husband on a train.

  **(2)** A woman wakes up on a train and then wakens her husband.

  **(3)** A woman murders her husband on a train trip.

  **(4)** A woman wakes up on a train and finds her husband is dead.

  **(5)** A woman wakes up on a train and discovers that her husband has gotten motion-sick.

**25.** Which of the following best describes the woman in the beginning of this passage?

  **(1)** exhausted from worry

  **(2)** lonely and lifeless

  **(3)** afraid of going home

  **(4)** cranky from sleeplessness

  **(5)** more and more happy as she wakes up

**26.** Which of the following is the most logical assumption that can be made about the couple's relationship?

  **(1)** The woman does not like to be left alone.

  **(2)** The woman has a much more cheerful nature than her husband does.

  **(3)** The husband is often away from home on business.

  **(4)** The woman and her husband are newlyweds.

  **(5)** The husband has been ill for some time.

**27.** Which of the woman's actions suggests that she is used to taking care of the man?

  **(1)** looking at her watch

  **(2)** thinking about his glass of milk

  **(3)** drawing up the shade

  **(4)** touching his hand

  **(5)** calling his name

*Items 28 to 31* refer to the following passage.

## WHAT LESSONS HAS MRS. CHAPIN LEARNED IN HER LIFE?
### Elizabeth Chapin, 75

*She was born in Chicago and has lived in the same house since 1908. A widow, her children married, she keeps a tidy place; a blooming geranium garden is in the back yard.*

Don't cut off nice things of the past. Why are they tearing down these old land-marks, the buildings, the trees? I don't call that progress. We must have some-
(5) thing to build our life on, and our own ideals. I don't say foggy memories, no. Why do we tear down the water tower? I agree it's a monstrosity, but it's Chicago. It was a thing of beauty in its time. Is it
(10) because we've never been anywhere? Other countries seem to want them and hold them and retain them and be proud of them....

The automobile, what could you do
(15) without it? In another few generations, people will have no legs, we won't need them. I take this dog for a walk every day. Walk a few blocks to the bakery shop. I have known people who live around the
(20) corner from the bakery, who take their car to get there. People are amazed when I tell them I don't pass a day that I don't walk three, four miles. It just wouldn't occur to me. There's so much to see, to observe,
(25) while you're walking. What happens to us that we don't see these things? When I take the dog for a walk, I see things. People's eyes are closed, with a film over them, or what is it?
(30) Mothers don't take their children any-where. Do something. Lady downstairs, I said put on your hat and I'll take you to Lincoln Park. I took another woman to the Art Institute. She hadn't been there in
(35) thirty-five years. These things are in our hands and we don't use them. I don't understand it. A month or so doesn't go by when I don't go to the Art Institute, maybe for an hour or so. It refreshes your
(40) mind again. It's provocative.

Excerpted from Studs Terkel, *Division Street: America*. Copyright ©1967 by Studs Terkel. Reprinted by permission of the author and Random House, Inc.

**28.** What is Mrs. Chapin's basic opinion of people?

**(1)** People are afraid to take long walks in the city.

**(2)** People are too slow to appreciate progress.

**(3)** People often tear down historical monuments.

**(4)** People don't appreciate the beauty around them.

**(5)** People don't understand art.

**29.** What can you conclude from Mrs. Chapin's comment, "Other countries seem to want them and hold them and retain them and be proud of them...." (lines 11-13)?

**(1)** The buildings in other countries are more beautiful than the ones in America.

**(2)** The water tower should be sold for display in another country.

**(3)** Other countries show their appre-ciation of the past by taking care of historical buildings and land-marks.

**(4)** People in other countries tend to live in the past.

**(5)** America is the most progressive country in the world.

**30.** What does Mrs. Chapin mean when she refers to a visit to the Art Institute as "provocative" (line 40)?

**(1)** The Art Institute displays contro-versial paintings.

**(2)** It is a good way for mothers to spend a day with their children.

**(3)** It makes her think about what she sees.

**(4)** The Art Institute is ignored by most Chicago residents.

**(5)** The Art Institute can be appreciat-ed best in hour-long visits.

**31.** Which of the following details from the author's introduction shows that Mrs. Chapin lives according to her opinions?

**(1)** Mrs. Chapin lives in Chicago.

**(2)** Mrs. Chapin was born in Chicago.

**(3)** Mrs. Chapin is a widow.

**(4)** Mr. Chapin has seen her children marry.

**(5)** Mrs. Chapin has a geranium garden.

*Items 32 to 35* refer to the following passage.

### WHAT CIRCUMSTANCES HAVE BROUGHT JEFF TO HIS DECISION?

"You ain't scairt, is you, Jeff?"

"Nah, baby," he said trembling. "I ain't scairt."

"Remember how we planned it, Jeff. We
(5) gotta do it like we said. Brave-like."

Jeff said nothing more. For an instant there was light in his cavernous brain. The great chamber was, for less than a second, peopled by characters he knew
(10) and loved. They were simple, healthy creatures, and they behaved in a manner that he could understand. They had quality. But since he had already taken leave of them long ago, the remembrance did not
(15) break his heart again. Young Jeff Patton was among them, the Jeff Patton of fifty years ago who went down to New Orleans with a crowd of country boys to the Mardi Gras doings. The gay young crowd, boys
(20) with candy-striped shirts and rouged-brown girls in noisy silks, was like a picture in his head. Yet it did not make him sad. On that very trip Slim Burns had killed Joe Beasley—the crowd had been
(25) broken up. Since then Jeff Patton's world had been the Greenbriar Plantation. If

there had been other Mardi Gras carnivals, he had not heard of them. Since then there had been no time; the years
(30) had fallen on him like waves. Now he was old, worn out. Another paralytic stroke (like the one he had already suffered) would put him on his back for keeps. In that condition, with a frail blind woman to
(35) look after him, he would be worse off than if he were dead.

Suddenly Jeff's hands became steady. He actually felt brave. He slowed down the motor of the car and carefully pulled off
(40) the road. Below, the water of the stream boomed, a soft thunder in the deep channel. Jeff ran the car onto the clay slope, pointed it directly toward the stream and put his foot heavily on the accelerator.
(45) The little car leaped furiously down the steep incline toward the water. The movement was nearly as swift and direct as a fall. The two old black folks, sitting quietly side by side, showed no excitement. In
(50) another instant the car hit the water and dropped immediately out of sight.

A little later it lodged in the mud of a shallow place. One wheel of the crushed and upturned little Ford became visible
(55) above the rushing water.

Excerpted from "A Summer Tragedy" by Arna Bontemps. Copyright ©1933 by Arna Bontemps. Reprinted by permission of Harold Ober Associates, Inc.

**32.** In this passage, Jeff and his wife

**(1)** travel to New Orleans

**(2)** plan their future

**(3)** lose their car

**(4)** end their lives

**(5)** return to the Greenbriar Plantation

**33.** Early in the passage (lines 6-25), Jeff thinks about

**(1)** the pleasures of his youth

**(2)** his fear of the future

**(3)** his wife's disabilities

**(4)** the wickedness of his past

**(5)** the wisdom of his decision

**34.** Which of the following best describes the way Jeff thinks of himself in the present?

  **(1)** simple and healthy
  **(2)** young and gay
  **(3)** active and strong
  **(4)** old and tired
  **(5)** frail and blind

**35.** According to the passage, when did Jeff become brave?

  **(1)** when he was young
  **(2)** after Joe Beasley was killed
  **(3)** while he was at Greenbriar
  **(4)** after the car hit the water
  **(5)** after he had thought about his past and present

*Items 36 to 40* refer to the following poem.

### WHO SHOULD BE WARM IN BED?
#### Lone Vigil

"Why do you wait in the cold half-light,
  Who should be warm in bed?"

"The children walk in the garden;
  I must go there instead.
(5) Out of the dusk, along the stones,
  Their soundless feet draw near;
And tenderly I call them,
  By the three names we hold dear."

"Why do you say the children come,
(10) The sons we know were slain?
They are long dead and buried—
  How can they walk again?
Little the comfort left to us
  When the wind wails in the thatch.
(15) Put out the failing candle
  And fasten every latch."

"Aye, they are laid in a foreign soil;
  Yet, weary and heartsore
As lonely moths they follow
(20) The gleam from the northern door
You may lie down to sleep and rest
  Who only know them dead;
But my children walk in the garden;
  I will go there instead."

**36.** In what way does the poet show that there are two speakers in this poem?

  **(1)** by naming each speaker
  **(2)** by setting up the stanzas as questions and answers enclosed in quotation marks
  **(3)** by identifying one as father and one as mother
  **(4)** by indenting every other line
  **(5)** by setting the conversation in the garden

**37.** The speaker in the second and fourth stanzas wants to go to the garden because

  **(1)** her children are waiting there for her
  **(2)** her children's ghosts are haunting the garden
  **(3)** she knows her children are still alive
  **(4)** she wants to remember her children as if they were alive
  **(5)** she can't accept the idea that her sons have died

**38.** The speaker in the first and third stanzas doesn't

  **(1)** believe his children are dead
  **(2)** understand why his partner wants to walk in the garden at night
  **(3)** care about how his wife feels
  **(4)** know for certain that his children are dead
  **(5)** want to stay in bed

**39.** What does the poet mean when she says that "As lonely moths they follow/The gleam from the northern door" (lines 19-20)?

  **(1)** The outdoor lights are attracting moths.
  **(2)** Moths don't take the place of children.
  **(3)** The sons' spirits would like to come home.
  **(4)** The sons have turned into moths.
  **(5)** The moths, like the sons, will die soon.

**40.** Which of the following groups of people would probably be most emotionally affected by this poem?

**(1)** parents who had lost a child in a war

**(2)** believers in an afterlife

**(3)** single adults who have never had children

**(4)** newly married couples hoping to have children

**(5)** children who have had parents killed in a war

*Items 41 to 45* refer to the following passage.

## WHY IS THIS PRODUCTION SUCCESSFUL?

While acknowledging Amanda Wingfield's cruelty, Tennessee Williams also made it clear that this stage portrait of his mother in *The Glass Menagerie* was
(5) intended to be sympathetic. She is a woman of gentility and warmth, someone who acts out of love—or, rather, her idea of love—for her children. In Amanda's memory, she is still that Southern belle,
(10) who, one Sunday afternoon, received 17 gentlemen callers. Years later, abandoned by her husband, a telephone man who "fell in love with long distance," she sustains herself and the remnants of her fam-
(15) ily with dreams of her own romantic past and with hopes for the future of her crippled daughter, Laura....

In quest of Amanda, ...actresses can be led to overplay her bitterness and her fool-
(20) ishness. Even Amanda's "rise and shine" greeting can seem like the message of a termagent [an overbearing, nagging woman]. In her performance as Amanda in Nikos Psacharopoulos's production at
(25) the Long Wharf Theater, Joanne Woodward avoids all the pitfalls of this sizable character and creates a luminous portrait, one that captures the wistfulness as well as the desperation. It's a delicately
(30) shaded, grandly Southern characterization with humor, gaiety and, finally, a tragic dimension....

As she should, Miss Woodward represents the strong, single-parent center of
(35) this household. For all the detachment of her son Tom—dreaming away his days at the shoe factory—and for all the daughter's reverie, the three are closely allied. This feeling of a blood-tie complicity, a
(40) shared fate, is sensitively evoked in Mr. Psacharopoulos's production. Both Treat Williams and Karen Allen, as Tom and Laura, are secure within their characters.... Miss Allen regards her mother in
(45) awe—not as a tyrant but as a figure of lingering glamour, expressing a role that is far beyond her own aspiration.

... Playing Tom, [Mr. Williams] reveals a poetic self-awareness while underscoring
(50) the character with vibrancy. Through his acting we can feel the character's contrary impulses—his need for home, his craving for independence—as well as his increasing frustration. Eventually we see the self-
(55) ishness that will drive him to leave the family to follow his artistic goals, as the playwright did himself....

**41.** Which of the following best states what this review is about?

**(1)** The author is praising the performances in an autobiographical play by Tennessee Williams.

**(2)** The author is praising the writing in a novel by Tennessee Williams.

**(3)** The author is comparing Joanne Woodward's performance to Amanda Wingfield's.

**(4)** The author is condemning the quality of plays at the Long Wharf Theatre.

**(5)** The author is commenting on the family members in Tennessee Williams' autobiography.

**42.** How does Treat Williams' acting affect the audience?

   **(1)** They become frustrated.

   **(2)** They better understand Tom's character.

   **(3)** They become confused about the idea of the play.

   **(4)** They see how selfish he is on stage.

   **(5)** They are amused by his comic portrayal.

**43.** What is the author's purpose in beginning his review by discussing Tennessee Williams' intentions?

   **(1)** He wants explain why he dislikes the way Tennessee Williams writes about Southern women.

   **(2)** He wants to suggest a question that he will answer in the rest of the review.

   **(3)** He wants to support his own opinion of this performance.

   **(4)** He wants to attract the reader's attention.

   **(5)** He wants to contrast the playwright's ideas about how the play should be performed with the quality of the performance that the author himself saw.

**44.** Why does the reviewer mention that "...actresses can be led to overplay [Amanda's] bitterness and her foolishness" (lines 18-21)?

   **(1)** to comment that generally there are more bad actresses than good ones

   **(2)** to prove that the role of Amanda was poorly written

   **(3)** to emphasize the difficulty of the role

   **(4)** to acknowledge that acting is a very personal art

   **(5)** to admit his own uncertainty about the central meaning of the play

**45.** If the reviewer went to another play with the same cast, he would probably expect

   **(1)** to be bored

   **(2)** to see a light comedy

   **(3)** to see strong dramatic performances

   **(4)** to see a play about Tennessee Williams' family

   **(5)** to be annoyed by the way the actors refused to work together

Answers are on page 339.

# Practice Test

## Performance Analysis Chart

**Directions:** Circle the number of each item that you got correct on the Practice Test. Count how many items you got correct in each row; count how many items you got correct in each column. Write the amount correct per row and column as the numerator in the fraction in the appropriate "Total Correct" box. (The denominators represent the total number of items in the row or column.) Write the grand total correct over the denominator, **45**, at the lower right corner of the chart. (For example, if you got 40 items correct, write 40 so that the fraction reads 40/**45**.)

| ITEM TYPE | Nonfiction (page 14) | Fiction (page 90) | Drama (page 168) | Poetry (page 210) | Commentary (page 246) | TOTAL CORRECT |
|---|---|---|---|---|---|---|
| Literal Comprehension | 28, 30 | 2, 25, 32, 34, 35 | 6 | 20, 38 | 15, 16, 41 | /13 |
| Inferential Comprehension | 10, 11, 29 | 1, 3, 24, 26, 27, 33 | 5 | 37 | 17, 18, 42 | /14 |
| Application | 12, 13 | | 9 | 23, 40 | 19, 45 | /7 |
| Analysis | 14, 31 | 4 | 7, 8 | 21, 22, 36, 39 | 43, 44 | /11 |
| TOTAL CORRECT | /9 | /12 | /5 | /9 | /10 | /45 |

# SIMULATION

# Introduction

You've completed the material on the Interpreting Literature and the Arts Test. By this time, you're probably asking yourself, "Am I ready to take the GED test?" How well you do on the Simulated Test will help you answer this question.

The test is as close as possible to the actual Interpreting Literature and Arts Test. There are the same number and types of questions. The time limit and the mixed order of test items are the same as well. Taking the Simulated Test will give you valuable test-taking experience and help you judge just how ready you are to take the actual GED test.

## Using the Simulated Test to Your Best Advantage

Unlike the Practice Test, there is only one way you should take the Simulated Test—under the same conditions as the actual GED test.
- Set aside 65 minutes to complete the Simulated Test. Work in a quiet place without interruption.
- Do not use any outside aids such as books when you complete the test. If you have a question, speak with your instructor.
- If you are not sure of an answer, take your best guess. As with the actual GED test, you will not be penalized on the Simulated Test for guessing. This means that guessing the correct answer can improve your score, while guessing the wrong answer will not affect your score any more than leaving the answer blank.

When you take the Simulated Test, record your answers neatly on a sheet of paper or use an answer sheet provided by your instructor. If you run out of time before you complete the test, circle the last item you answered. Then continue working on the test. This way, when you score the test, you will be able to judge how much time influenced your results.

## Using the Answer Key

Refer to the Answer Key (page 345) to score your answers. Put a check mark next to each item that you answered correctly. Even if you answered the item correctly, read the explanation for each answer. This will reinforce your testing skills and help you understand the material more completely.

## How to Use Your Score

If you got 36 or more items correct, you did 80% work or better. This tells you that you are working at a level that will allow you to score well on the actual Interpreting Literature and the Arts Test. If you got a few less than 36 items correct, then you should review the material. If your score was well below the 80% mark, then you should consider spending time reviewing the lessons that contain material you missed on the test. The chart at the end of the test will help you identify the areas you should review.

# Simulated Test

**TIME:** 65 minutes

**Directions:** Choose the one best answer to each question.

<u>Items 1 to 5</u> refer to the following passage.

## HOW IS THIS ANIMAL SAVED?

I made good time to the farm and found Phin waiting with his three sons. The young men looked gloomy but Phin was still indomitable.... He even managed a little tune
(5) as we crossed to the bull pen but when he looked over the door his head sank on his chest and his hands worked deeper behind his braces.

The bull was standing as though rooted to
(10) the middle of the pen. His great rib cage rose and fell with the most labored respirations I had ever seen. His mouth gaped wide, a bubbling foam hung round his lips and his flaring nostrils; his eyes, almost starting from his head
(15) in terror, stared at the wall in front of him. This wasn't pneumonia; it was a frantic battle for breath, and it looked like a losing one ....

What in the name of God was this? Could be Anthrax ... must be ... and yet ... I looked
(20) over at the row of heads above the half door; they were waiting for me to say something and their silence accentuated the agonized groaning and panting. I looked above the heads to the square of deep blue and a tufted cloud
(25) moving across the sun. As it passed, a single dazzling ray made me close my eyes and a faint bell rang in my mind.

"Has he been out today?" I asked.

"Aye, he's been out on the grass on his teth-
(30) er all morning. It was that grand and warm."

The bell became a triumphant gong. "Get a hosepipe in here quick. You can rig it to that tap in the yard."

"A hosepipe? What the 'ell ... ?"
(35) "Yes, quick as you can—he's got sunstroke ...."

I enjoyed myself after that. I can't think of anything in my working life that has given me more pleasure than standing in that pen directing the life-saving jet and watching the bull
(40) savoring it. He liked it on his face best and as I worked my way up from the tail and along the steaming back he would turn his nose full into the water, rocking his head from side to side and blinking blissfully.
(45) Within half an hour he looked almost normal ....

Excerpt from *All Creatures Great and Small* by James Herriott. Copyright ©1972 by James Herriot. Reprinted by permission of St. Martin's Press, Inc.

1. At the beginning of the passage, how does Phin feel?

    **(1)** sure that the bull will recover on his own
    **(2)** worried by the bull's illness
    **(3)** worried about the vet's bill
    **(4)** embarrassed by his sons
    **(5)** relieved by the vet's arrival

2. What effect does the author intend by writing "Could be Anthrax ... must be ... and yet" (lines 19-20)?

    **(1)** to show how nervous the vet is
    **(2)** to suggest there is no cure for Anthrax
    **(3)** to indicate that the vet is unsure about this diagnosis
    **(4)** to emphasize how sick the bull is
    **(5)** to gain the reader's sympathy

3. Which of the following clues helps the author to make his diagnosis?

    **(1)** the color of the water in the bull's pen
    **(2)** the appearance of the sun
    **(3)** the ringing of a bell in the distance
    **(4)** the bull's difficulty in breathing
    **(5)** the foam around the bull's lips

**4.** Which of the following activities that involve children would probably give the author the kind of pleasure he describes in this passage?

**(1)** repairing a child's broken toy
**(2)** holding a newborn baby
**(3)** seeing a child's good report card
**(4)** teaching a child to ride a bicycle
**(5)** watching a baby take its first steps

**5.** Based on this passage, what can you tell about the vet's way of dealing with sick animals?

**(1)** He makes a show of his specialized training as he works.
**(2)** He tries to make friends with each animal he treats.
**(3)** He refuses to be moved by the sight of a sick animal.
**(4)** He is careful to consider causes that might not be obvious at first.
**(5)** He prefers to treat an animal without its owner watching.

Items 6 to 9 refer to the following passage.

### HOW HAS NORA BEEN WRONGED?

NORA: In all these eight years—longer than that—from the very beginning of our acquaintance, we have never exchanged a word on any serious subject.

(5) HELMER: Was it likely that I would be continually and for ever telling you about worries that you could not help me to bear?

NORA: I am not speaking about business matters. I say that we have never sat down in
(10) earnest together to try and get at the bottom of anything.

HELMER: But, dearest Nora, would it have been any good to you?

NORA: That is just it; you have never under-
(15) stood me. I have been greatly wronged, Torvald—first by papa and then by you.

HELMER: What! By us two—by us two, who have loved you better than anyone else in the world?

(20) NORA: (*shaking her head*). You have never loved me. You have only thought it pleasant to be in love with me.

HELMER: Nora, what do I hear you saying?

NORA: It is perfectly true, Torvald. When I was
(25) at home with papa, he told me his opinion about everything, and so I had the same opinions; and if I differed from him I concealed the fact, because he would not have liked it. He called me his doll-child, and he played with me
(30) just as I used to play with my dolls. And when I came to live with you—

HELMER:. What sort of an expression is that to use about our marriage?

NORA (*undisturbed*): I mean that I was simply
(35) transferred from papa's hands into yours. You arranged everything according to your own taste, and so I got the same tastes as you—or else I pretended to, I am really not quite sure which—I think sometimes the one and some-
(40) times the other. When I look back on it, it seems to me as if I had been living here like a poor woman—just from hand to mouth. I have existed merely to perform tricks for you, Torvald. But you would have it so. You and
(45) papa have committed a great sin against me. It is your fault that I have made nothing of my life.

Excerpt from *A Doll's House* by Henrik Ibsen. Copyright ©1959 by Bantam Books, Inc. Reprinted with permission of J.M. Dent , Ltd., London.

**6.** From Helmer's responses, you can conclude that he

**(1)** has always taken Nora seriously
**(2)** has been as unhappy as Nora
**(3)** is not a serious person
**(4)** agrees with Nora
**(5)** is surprised by what Nora is saying

**7.** According to Nora, how has her life with Torvald been like her life with Papa?

**(1)** Nora has lived according to the "rules" of both men.
**(2)** Both men have been unwilling to express their affection for her.
**(3)** Nora frequently has argued with both men.
**(4)** Nora has been unwilling to express her affection for either man.
**(5)** Both men have loved her very much.

8. When Nora says that Papa treated her as "his doll-child" (line 29), she means that she was expected to

   **(1)** dress nicely
   **(2)** say little
   **(3)** be idle at home
   **(4)** have no thoughts of her own
   **(5)** play like a proper little girl

9. If Nora were alive today, which of the following causes would she be most likely to support?

   **(1)** the fight against world hunger
   **(2)** planned parenthood
   **(3)** women's liberation
   **(4)** federal aid to education
   **(5)** the movement to combat terrorism

Items 10 to 13 refer to the following passage.

## HOW DOES SANFORD FIND HAPPINESS IN THE ARMY?

In the beginning, Sanford Carter was ashamed of becoming an Army cook. This was not from snobbery, at least not from snobbery of the most direct sort. During the two and a
(5) half years Carter had been in the Army he had come to hate cooks more and more. They existed for him as a symbol of all that was corrupt, overbearing, stupid, and privileged in Army life. His anger often derived from noth-
(10) ing: the set of a pair of fat lips, the casual heavy thump of the serving spoon into his plate, or the resentful conviction that the cook was not serving him enough. Since life in the Army was in most respects a marriage, this
(15) rage over apparently harmless details was not a sign of imbalance. Every soldier found some particular habit of the Army spouse impossible to support.

Yet, Sanford Carter became a cook and, to
(20) elaborate the irony, did better as a cook than he had done as anything else. In a few months he rose from a Private to a first cook with the rank of Sergeant, Technician. After the fact, it was easy to understand. He had suffered
(25) through all his Army career from an excess of eagerness. He had cared too much, he had

wanted to do well, and so he had often been tense at moments when he would better have been relaxed. He was very young, twenty-one,
(30) had lived the comparatively gentle life of a middle-class boy, and needed some success in the Army to prove to himself that he was not completely worthless....

So he took an opening in the kitchen. It
(35) promised him nothing except a day of work, and a day of leisure which would be completely at his disposal. He found that he liked it. He was given at first the job of baking the bread for the company, and every other night he
(40) worked till early in the morning, kneading and shaping his fifty-pound mix of dough. At two or three he would be done, and for his work there would be the tangible reward of fifty loaves of bread, all fresh from the oven, all clean and
(45) smelling of fertile accomplished creativity. He had the rare and therefore intensely satisfying emotion of seeing a the end of an Army chore the product of his labor.

Excerpted from "The Language of Men." by Norman Mailer. Copyright ©1959 by the author. Reprinted with permission of Scott Meredith Literary Agency, Inc..

10. Which of the following statements best describes Sanford's change of attitude in this passage?

   **(1)** Sanford, originally passive and reserved, learns to speak out for what he believes is right.
   **(2)** Sanford begins by treating all his work with lazy indifference, but he learns to be both responsible and enthusiastic.
   **(3)** Sanford at first is hostile toward the other soldiers, but eventually he comes to accept and even respect them.
   **(4)** Sanford, originally eager and hard-working, is stripped of these characteristics by the demeaning lifestyle of the Army.
   **(5)** Sanford, originally resentful and ashamed of his life in the Army, finds satisfaction in his new accomplishments.

11. Which of the following civilian jobs would

Sanford probably be most likely to enjoy?

(1) house builder
(2) accountant
(3) restaurant manager
(4) bus driver
(5) police officer

**12.** Sanford is probably the kind of man who

(1) is overcritical and judgmental
(2) lacks incentive and enthusiasm
(3) takes pleasure in small tasks done well
(4) has difficulty obeying authority
(5) is concerned only with power and self-advancement

**13.** When the author refers to "the Army spouse" (line 17), he is making a comparison to imply that most soldiers

(1) want to get out of the military
(2) enter the military without taking their commitment seriously
(3) learn to love their military careers
(4) find that military life makes many of the same demands on them as marriage does
(5) feel that life in the military is degrading

Items 14 to 18 refer to the following passage.

## WHAT MAKES *HUCKLEBERRY FINN* A MASTERPIECE?

*Huckleberry Finn* is *the* American Classic. Uneven and bitty, it is no masterpiece in the ordinary sense .... Yet it is the only novel in American literature that has the permanent,
(5) enchanting, and mysterious power of an ancient myth. The vision at its center—of the skin-and-bones son of the town drunk floating down the Mississippi on a raft in the company of a runaway slave—goes side by side with
(10) images like that of Prometheus chained to the rock; it embodies, as much by luck and magic as by conscious art, something fundamental in the experience of being human ....

When Twain set Huck and Jim adrift on the
(15) Mississippi, he placed them in a landscape of terrifying and topical complexity. For the river

in the book is nothing less than the current of life itself: it carries the raft along on an epic voyage in which idyll turns into nightmare and
(20) nightmare into idyll by turns.

For long stretches, the boy and the slave are quite alone, living by instinct, as at home in nature as a pair of raccoons; then the river spits them out abruptly into the middle of soci-
(25) ety, where they have to deal with a multitude of con men, bigots, thieves, and kindly aunts. As the current quickens under them, so Huck has to deal at firsthand with the dilemmas of America in the 19th century: the issue of slav-
(30) ery, the divide between the North and the South, the limits of individual liberty and the steady encroachment in the wilderness of "civilization" in the form of the narrow, philistine, god-fearing, law-abiding small town.
(35) No wonder that Huck gets into such a tragic muddle. The boy from Pike County is confronted by the Mississippi with questions that continue to defeat Presidents and their cabinets. Trying to work things out on his finger-ends,
(40) painfully naming his experience to himself in his own plain words, Huck fails as an ethical philosopher, but he succeeds—dazzlingly—in defining what it means, in Henry James' phrase, to share the complex fate of being an
(45) American.

Excerpted from "Why 'Huckleberry Finn' is *the* American Classic" by Jonathan Raban. Copyright ©1992 by News America Publications, Inc. Reprinted with permission from *TV Guide*® magazine.

**14.** Which of the following statements best summarizes the author's opinion of *Huckleberry Finn*?

(1) It was well written for its day, but it has little to say to contemporary Americans.
(2) It is a masterpiece chiefly because Twain vividly depicts scenes of everyday American life.
(3) It is interesting mainly because of Twain's skillful description of characters.
(4) It fails to live up to the standards of ancient mythology.
(5) It is important because it reveals basic human issues.

**15.** How does the reviewer see Huck's character?

  **(1)** Huck is an idle dreamer who will never amount to anything.

  **(2)** Huck is a simple person whose wisdom goes far beyond his formal education.

  **(3)** Huck is a tragic figure who deserves the reader's pity.

  **(4)** Huck is a fool who is constantly at the mercy of others.

  **(5)** Huck is a symbol of the childlike qualities that remain in adults.

**16.** Huck's experiences suggest that he

  **(1)** never fully resolves the problems he encounters

  **(2)** has solved the problems that governments can't figure out

  **(3)** eventually becomes a slave

  **(4)** drowns at the end of the book

  **(5)** is the opposite of what America represents

**17.** When the author refers to "civilization" invading the wilderness (lines 31-33), he is

  **(1)** emphasizing the loneliness of the individual in society

  **(2)** drawing the reader's attention to the changes that are taking place in America

  **(3)** indicating that the town surprises both Huck and Jim

  **(4)** questioning whether the town is as civilized as it seems

  **(5)** reminding the audience of the disappearing wilderness

**18.** If the character Huckleberry Finn were able to see a movie, which kind would he most likely identify with?

  **(1)** a nature film
  **(2)** a comedy about city life
  **(3)** a war movie
  **(4)** a science-fiction epic
  **(5)** a biography

Items 19 to 22 refer to the following passage.

## WHAT DOES RAINY MOUNTAIN SYMBOLIZE?

A single knoll rises out of the plain in Oklahoma, north and west of the Wichita Range. For my people, the Kiowas, it is an old landmark, and they gave it the name Rainy
(5) Mountain. The hardest weather in the world is there. Winter brings blizzards, hot tornadic winds arise in the spring, and in summer the prairie is an anvil's edge. The grass turns brittle and brown, and it cracks beneath your feet.
(10) There are green belts along the rivers and creeks, linear groves of hickory and pecan, willow and witch hazel. At a distance in July or August the steaming foliage seems almost to writhe in fire. Great green and yellow
(15) grasshoppers are everywhere in the tall grass, popping up like corn to sting the flesh, and tortoises crawl about on the red earth, going nowhere in—the plenty of time. Loneliness is an aspect of the land. All things in the plain are
(20) isolate; there is no confusion of objects in the eye, but one hill or one tree or one man. To look upon that landscape in the early morning, with the sun at your back, is to lose the sense of proportion. Your imagination comes to life,
(25) and this, you think, is where Creation was begun.

I returned to Rainy Mountain in July. My grandmother had died in the spring, and I wanted to be at her grave. She had lived to be
(30) very old and at last infirm. Her only living daughter was with her when she died, and I was told that in death her face was that of a child.

Her name was Aho, and she belonged to
(35) the last culture to evolve in North America. Her forebears came down from the high country in western Montana nearly three centuries ago. They were a mountain people, a mysterious tribe of hunters whose language has never
(40) been positively classified in any major group. In the late seventeenth century they began a long migration to the south and east. It was a journey toward the dawn, and it led to a golden age. Along the way the Kiowas were befriend-
(45) ed by the Crows, who gave them the culture and religion of the Plains. They acquired horses, and their ancient nomadic spirit was sud-

denly free of the ground. They acquired Tai-
me, the sacred Sun Dance doll, from that
(50) moment the object and symbol of their worship, and so shared in the divinity of the sun.
Not least, they acquired the sense of destiny,
therefore courage and pride. When they
entered upon the southern Plains they had
(55) been transformed. No longer were they slaves
to the simple necessity of survival; they were a
lordly and dangerous society of fighters and
thieves, hunters and priests of the sun.
According to their origin myth, they entered the
(60) world through a hollow log. From one point of
view, their migration was the fruit of an old
prophecy, for indeed they emerged from a sun-
less world.

Excerpted from *The Way to Rainy Mountain*.by N. Scott
Momaday. Copyright ©The University of New Mexico Press,
1969. Reprinted with permission.

19. Which of the following words best
describes the author's general attitudes
toward Rainy Mountain?

(1) respect
(2) frustration
(3) uncertainty
(4) dread
(5) joy

20. The author uses the expression "going
nowhere in plenty of time" (lines 17-18) to
express his

(1) belief that life is meaningless
(2) criticism of those who fail to use
opportunities
(3) concern for his own seeming hope-
lessness
(4) fear of what Rainy Mountain represents to his people
(5) feeling that time seems to stand still at
Rainy Mountain

21. Which of the following pieces of art would
be most similar in theme to the author's
description of Rainy Mountain?

(1) a pastel drawing filled with large pink
and white flowers
(2) a pencil sketch of a baseball player at
bat
(3) a watercolor of sailboats passing a
lighthouse
(4) an oil painting of an abandoned shack
under a red sky
(5) a charcoal drawing of a busy city
street

22. Based on this passage, where is Rainy
Mountain's place in the migration of the
Kiowa?

(1) at the end of the migration
(2) at the beginning of the migration
(3) in the late 17th century
(4) where the Kiowa met the Crow
(5) where Montana is now located

Items 23 to 26 refer to the following passage.

## WHAT HAS MR. COVEY TAUGHT THE AUTHOR ABOUT SLAVERY?

If at any time of my life more than another, I was made to drink the bitterest dregs of slavery, that time was during the first six months of my stay with Mr. Covey. We were worked in all
(5) weathers. It was never too hot or too cold; it could never rain, blow, hail, or snow, too hard for us to work in the field. Work, work, work, was scarcely more the order of the day than of the night. The longest days were too short for
(10) him, and the shortest nights too long for him. I was somewhat unmanageable when I first went there, but a few months of this discipline tamed me. Mr. Covey succeeded in breaking me. I was broken in body, soul, and spirit. My
(15) natural elasticity was crushed,—my intellect languished, the disposition to read departed, the cheerful spark that lingered about my eye died; the dark night of slavery closed in upon me, and behold a man transformed into a
(20) brute!

Sunday was my only leisure time. I spent this in a sort of beastlike stupor, between sleep and wake, under some large tree. At times I would rise up, a flash of energetic freedom
(25) would dart through my soul, accompanied with a faint beam of hope, that flickered for a moment, and then vanished. I sank down again, mourning over my wretched condition. I was sometimes prompted to take my life, and
(30) that of Covey, but was prevented by a combination of hope and fear. My sufferings on this plantation seem now like a dream rather than a stern reality.

Our house stood within a few rods of the
(35) Chesapeake Bay, whose broad bosom was ever white with sails from every quarter of the habitable globe. These beautiful vessels, robed in purest white, so delightful to the eye of free-men, were to me so many shrouded
(40) ghosts, to terrify and torment me with thoughts of my wretched condition. I have often, in the deep stillness of a summer's Sabbath, stood all alone upon the lofty banks of that noble bay, and traced, with saddened heart and tear-
(45) ful eye, the countless number of sails moving off to the mighty ocean. The sight of these always affected me powerfully. My thoughts would compel utterance; and there, with no audience but the Almighty, I would pour out my
(50) soul's complaint, in my rude way, with an apostrophe to the moving multitude of ships:

"You are loosed from your moorings, and are free; I am fast in my chains, and am a slave! You move merrily before the gentle gale,
(55) and I sadly before the bloody whip! You are freedom's swift-winged angels, that fly round the world; I am confined in bands of iron! O that I were free!"

Excerpted from Frederick Douglass, from *Narrative of the Life of Frederick Douglass, An American Slave*. First printed May 1845 by the Anti-Slavery Office in Boston. Reprinted with permission from *The Norton Anthology of American Literature* (New York: W.W. Norton, 1989).

23. What did the author lose during his stay with Mr. Covey?

(1) his freedom
(2) his fear of punishment
(3) his basic self-respect
(4) his ability to work
(5) his children

24. How does the use of a first-person point of view help the author to make his point?

(1) It underscores the slaveowners' strength.
(2) It helps the reader to understand the personal hardships of slavery.
(3) It allows a discussion of both sides of the question.
(4) It symbolizes the struggle of all people to be free.
(5) It enables the reader to appreciate the slave's pride in his work.

25. How does Douglass feel about the ships on Chesapeake Bay?

(1) They give him great delight.
(2) They give him a feeling of energetic freedom.
(3) They make his experiences on the plantation seem like a dream.
(4) They have no effect on him at all.
(5) They make him feel the power of his enslavement more cruelly.

**26.** If Mr. Covey were a manager in a present-day factory, and one of his employees fell ill, what would he be LEAST likely to do?

(1) make his employee stay at his station and keep working

(2) tell someone else to do both the other employee's job and his own

(3) work the employee until late in the day and then send him home

(4) tell the employee to keep his mind on his work

(5) see that the employee received immediate medical attention

Items 27 to 30 refer to the following passage.

**WHAT KIND OF PLAN
IS BEING CONSIDERED?**

AMANDA: Character's what to look for in a man.

TOM: That's what I've always said, Mother.

AMANDA: You've never said anything of the kind and I suspect you would never give it a
(5)     thought.

TOM: Don't be so suspicious of me.

AMANDA: At least I hope he's the type that's up and coming.

TOM: I think he really goes in for self-improve
(10)     ment.

AMANDA: What reason have you to think so?

TOM: He goes to night school.

AMANDA: [beaming] Splendid! What does he do, I mean study?

(15) TOM: Radio engineering and public speaking!

AMANDA: Then he has visions of being advanced in the world! Any young man who studies public speaking is aiming to have an executive job some day! And radio engi
(20)     neering? A thing for the future! Both of these facts are very illuminating. Those are the sort of things that a mother should know concerning any young man who comes to call on her daughter. Seriously or not.

(25) TOM: One little warning. He doesn't know about Laura. I didn't let on that we had dark ulteri or motives. I just said, why don't you come and have dinner with us? He said okay and that was the whole conversation.

(30) AMANDA: I bet it was! You're eloquent as an oyster. However, he'll know about Laura when he gets here. When he sees how lovely and sweet and pretty she is, he'll thank his lucky stars he was asked to dinner.

(35) TOM: Mother, you mustn't expect too much of Laura.

AMANDA: What do you mean?

TOM: Laura seems all those things to you and me because she's ours and we love her.
(40)     We don't even notice she's crippled anymore.

**27.** What are Tom and Amanda discussing?

(1) the personality of the man Tom invited to dinner

(2) the personality of Laura's fiance

(3) Tom's interest in becoming like the man who is coming to dinner

(4) Amanda's distrust of Tom's judgment

(5) helping out Tom's friend by giving him a good meal

**28.** To what does Amanda refer when she tells Tom, "You're eloquent as an oyster" (lines 30-31)?

(1) Tom's ability to speak well

(2) Tom's lack of talkativeness

(3) Tom's good taste in clothing

(4) Tom's good manners

(5) Tom's cautiousness

**29.** Amanda's willingness to predict the dinner guest's reactions and future without knowing much about him indicates that she is

(1) unusually perceptive

(2) afraid to find out the truth about him

(3) extremely imaginative

(4) very eager to match him with her daughter

(5) careless

**30.** What fact does Tom think might get in the way of their plans?

(1) The guest is too serious.
(2) Amanda is too suspicious of his motives.
(3) Laura is crippled.
(4) Amanda wants an up and coming type.
(5) Laura is too good for the young man.

Items 31 to 35 refer to the following poem.

## WHAT MAKES THIS PLACE SO IMPORTANT?

### Facing It

My black face fades,
hiding inside the black granite.
I said I wouldn't,
dammit: No tears.
(5) I'm stone. I'm flesh.
My clouded reflection eyes me
like a bird of prey, the profile of night
slanted against morning. I turn
this way—the stone lets me go.
(10) I turn that way—I'm inside
the Vietnam Veterans Memorial
again, depending on the light
to make a difference.
I go down the 58,022 names,
(15) half-expecting to find
my own in letters like smoke.
I touch the name Andrew Johnson;
I see the booby trap's white flash.
Names shimmer on a woman's blouse
(20) but when she walks away
the names stay on the wall.
Brushstrokes flash, a red bird's
wings cutting across my stare.
The sky. A plane in the sky.
(25) A white vet's image floats
closer to me, then his pale eyes
look through mine. I'm a window.
He's lost his right arm
inside the stone. In the black mirror
(30) a woman's trying to erase names:
No, she's brushing a boy's hair.

From "Facing It" from *Dien Cai Dau* by Yusef Komunyakaa.
Copyright ©1988 by Yusef Komunyakaa. Reprinted with permission of University Press.of New England..

**31.** Which of the following best describes the situation of the speaker in this poem?

(1) A dead soldier is trying to communicate with the living.
(2) A black man is watching reflections in the Vietnam Veterans Memorial wall.
(3) A man is weeping for a friend who died in Vietnam.
(4) A man is turning into part of the stone memorial.
(5) A visitor to the memorial is reliving his wartime experiences.

**32.** Which of the following is NOT reflected by the wall?

(1) the speaker's own face
(2) a woman's blouse
(3) 58,022 names
(4) a plane
(5) a bird's wings

**33.** Which of the following is probably true of the speaker in this poem?

(1) He has no emotional reaction to the Memorial.
(2) He is a Vietnam veteran.
(3) He died in Vietnam.
(4) He was an anti-war protester during the sixties.
(5) He resents the other visitors to the Memorial.

**34.** Which of the following statements best explains why the poet ends the poem with the image of the woman and boy?

(1) to make a sharp contrast to the white veteran
(2) to indicate that the simple acts of living continue even next to a reminder of tragic death
(3) to show why the woman was trying to erase names
(4) to shock the reader
(5) to make the reader realize that the woman is mourning the death of the boy's father

**35.** Which of the following words best describes the feelings of the poem's speaker?

   **(1)** anger
   **(2)** happiness
   **(3)** sadness
   **(4)** hope
   **(5)** despair

<u>Items 36 to 40</u> refer to the following passage.

### WHAT IS WRONG WITH PEARL?

I was fourteen, full of anger and cynicism. My mother, brother, and I were sitting by ourselves in an alcove, a half-hour before the service was supposed to begin. And my mother
(5) was scolding me, because I refused to go up to the casket to see my father's body.

"Samuel said good-bye. Samuel is crying," she said.

I did not want to mourn the man in the cas-
(10) ket, this sick person who had been thin and listless, who moaned and became helpless, who in the end searched constantly for my mother with fearful eyes. He was so unlike what my father had once been: charming and
(15) lively, strong, kind, always generous with his laughter, the one who knew exactly what to do when things went wrong. And in my father's eyes, I had been perfect, his "perfect Pearl," and not the irritation I always seemed to be
(20) with my mother.

My mother blew her nose. "What kind of daughter cannot cry for her own father?"

"That man in there is not my father," I said sullenly.

(30) Right then my mother jumped up and slapped my face. "That bad!" she shouted. I was shocked. It was the first time she had ever struck me.

"Ai-ya! If you can't cry, I make you cry." And
(35) she slapped me again and again. "Cry! Cry!" she wailed crazily. But I sat there still as a stone.

Finally, realizing what she had done, my mother bit the back of her hand and mumbled
(40) something in Chinese. She took my brother by the hand, and they left me.

So there I sat, angry, of course, and also victorious, although over what, I didn't know.

And perhaps because I didn't know, I found
(45) myself walking over to the casket. I was breathing hard, telling myself, I'm right, she's wrong. And I was so determined not to cry that I never considered I would feel anything whatsoever.

(50) But then I saw him, colorless and thin. And he was not resting peacefully with God. His face was stern, as if still locked in his last moment of pain.

I took so many small breaths, trying to hold
(55) back, trying not to cry, that I began to hyperventilate. I ran out of the room, out into the fresh air, gasping and gulping. I ran down Columbus, toward the bay, ignoring the tourists who stared at my angry, tear-streaked
(60) face. And in the end, I missed the funeral.

Excerpted from *The Kitchen God's Wife* by Amy Tan. Copyright ©1991 by Amy Tan. Reprinted with permission of the Putnam Publishing Group.

**36.** Who is Samuel?

   **(1)** the dead man
   **(2)** the little brother
   **(3)** the dying man
   **(4)** "perfect Pearl"
   **(5)** the narrator's father

**37.** What does the mother do to try to make her daughter cry?

   **(1)** talk about the dead man's goodness
   **(2)** leave her daughter behind
   **(3)** refuse to let her daughter stay
   **(4)** curse her daughter in Chinese
   **(5)** slap her daughter

**38.** Why does the narrator in this passage refuse to go to the casket?

   **(1)** She knows the dead man is not her father.
   **(2)** She is crying too hard to appear in public.
   **(3)** She doesn't want to say goodbye to Samuel.
   **(4)** She wants to remember her father before he became ill.
   **(5)** She wants to irritate her mother.

**39.** Why does the girl run away at the end of the passage?

   **(1)** She is overwhelmed with grief after seeing her father.

   **(2)** She wants to prove that her mother is wrong.

   **(3)** She is afraid of her father's anger.

   **(4)** She is embarrassed by her earlier behavior.

   **(5)** She wants to hide her dry eyes.

**40.** After the experience described in this passage, the narrator probably will

   **(1)** believe her father is at peace with God

   **(2)** continue to have disagreements with her mother

   **(3)** begin to hate the memory of her father

   **(4)** start to agree with her mother

   **(5)** become happier about life

<u>Items 41 to 45</u> refer to the following passage.

### WHY IS THIS BOOK SO SURPRISING?

Fairy tales and Amy Tan seem to keep close company. Two years ago Tan was just another struggling, unpublished, 37-year-old writer, making up brochures for computer companies (5) while composing stories on the side. By the end of 1989 she was the author of the most admired novel on the best-seller list, her *Joy Luck Club* having conquered critics and the public alike. A literary star had been born (10) overnight—and, in her wake, a fairy tale's difficult postscript: How could she ever live up to what felt like a once-in-a-lifetime success?

At the outset of *The Kitchen God's Wife* (Putnam; 415 pages; $22.95), one's apprehen- (15) sions begin to gather like avenging furies: the opening pages introduce us to a young Chinese-American woman, her all-American husband and her inalienably Chinese mother, living around San Francisco—precisely the (20) contemporary scene that made up the least transporting parts of *The Joy Luck Club*. For two chapters the young woman tells a pleasant but unremarkable tale of sweet-and-sour tensions, haunted by her nagging mother—and by (25) her nagging sense that her mother and she are speaking different languages. Then, on page 61, the mother takes over, and suddenly the book takes flight.

For almost all the pages that follow, the (30) yeasty old woman unpacks the rich and terrible secrets of her past, as a young girl in Shanghai growing up amid a plague of sorrows; how her own mother abandoned her and she was married off to an ogreish ne'er-do- (35) well; how they hid in a monastery famous for dragon-well tea while the Japanese invaded Manchuria; how somehow she endured the war, losing friends and children along the way; and how, in the end, indomitable as pain, she (40) escaped China and her husband just five days before the communist takeover.

Almost every page of the old wife's tale is lit up with the everyday magic of a world in which birds can sound like women crying and (45) sweaters are knit in the memory of spider webs. Yet all the storybook marvels are grounded in a survivor's vinegar wit ("In Nanking, snow is like a high-level official— doesn't come too often, doesn't stay too long"). (50) And in front of the watercolor backdrops are horrors pitiless enough to mount a powerful indictment against a world in which women were taught that love means always having to say you're sorry. In traditional China, the old (55) widow recalls, "a woman had no right to be angry."

Yet the end—and the point—of Tan's novel is forgiveness, and the way in which understanding the miseries of others makes it harder (60) to be hard on them. And as the story all but tells itself—so seamlessly it feels as if Tan's ancestors are speaking through her—it bestows on us a host of luminous surprises. The first is that the dowdy, pinchpenny old (65) woman has a past more glamorous than fairy-tale, and more sad. The second is that in the light of her trials, her curious superstitions come to seem as sound as legal evidence. The final surprise may be the best of all: Tan (70) has transcended herself again, triumphing over the ghosts, and the expectations, raised by her magnificent first book.

**41.** To what does the phrase "once-in-a-lifetime success" (line 12) refer?

(1) the best-selling first novel
(2) Amy Tan's computer brochures
(3) a fairy tale
(4) a literary critic
(5) Amy Tan's new book

**42.** Most of *The Kitchen God's Wife* is about

(1) a young Chinese-American woman
(2) life in San Francisco
(3) the mother's life in China
(4) women's rights
(5) Chinese superstitions

**43.** From the reviewer's comments, you can conclude that the first two chapters of the book are

(1) unusual and contemporary
(2) suspenseful and disturbing
(3) powerful and exciting
(4) likable and ordinary
(5) surprising and puzzling

**44.** Which of the following does the reviewer imply about the mother in this book?

(1) She wishes she had never left China.
(2) She did not learn anything from any of her troubles.
(3) She never learned how to speak English.
(4) She wants her daughter to have a better life than her own.
(5) She could not completely accept traditional Chinese values.

**45.** In what way does the reviewer use the idea of a fairy tale?

(1) as a negative criticism
(2) as a positive comparison
(3) as a suggestion that the book is for children
(4) as a warning to readers
(5) as evidence of his own reading habits

Answers are on page 345.

# SIMULATED TEST

# Performance Analysis Chart

**Directions:** Circle the number of each item that you got correct on the Simulated Test. Count how many items you got correct in each row; count how many items you got correct in each column. Write the amount correct per row and column as the numerator in the fraction in the appropriate "Total Correct" box. (The denominators represent the total number of items in the row or column.) Write the grand total correct over the denominator, **45,** at the lower right corner of the chart. (For example, if you got 40 items correct, write 40 so that the fraction reads 40/**45.**)

| ITEM TYPE | Nonfiction (page 14) | Fiction (page 90) | Drama (page 168) | Poetry (page 210) | Commentary (page 246) | TOTAL CORRECT |
|---|---|---|---|---|---|---|
| **Literal Comprehension** | 3, 25 | 10, 36, 37 | 7, 27, 30 | 31, 32 | 14, 41, 42. 43 | /14 |
| **Inferential Comprehension** | 1, 5, 22, 23 | 12, 13, 38, 39 | 6, 29 | 33 | 15, 16, 44 | /14 |
| **Application** | 4, 24, 26 | 11. 40 | 9 | | 18, 21 | /8 |
| **Analysis** | 2 | | 8, 28 | 34,35 | 17, 19, 20, 45 | /9 |
| **TOTAL CORRECT** | /10 | /9 | /8 | /5 | /13 | /45 |

# Answer Key Chapters 1-5

## Chapter 1: Nonfiction

### Lesson 1

1. **(2)** *Literal Comprehension/Nonfiction.* In lines 18-20, the author tells us that a person who is telling a humorous story tells it "gravely" and "does his best to conceal the fact that he even suspects that there is anything funny about it." In other words, he acts as if there's nothing funny. You might predict, then, that *gravely* means *acting as if there's nothing funny.* The best match for this is (2): *in a serious and solemn manner.* (1) is incorrect, then, since it is exactly opposite what you predict; telling something in a humorous manner means acting as if there *is* something funny. (3), (4), (5) are wrong because clues in the words around *gravely* point to the seriousness of the storyteller, not his speed or loudness. (Watch out for (3); it sounds like something later on in the passage "casual and indifferent." While it may be *true* that the teller of the humorous story speaks in a slow, quiet manner, it doesn't answer the question: What does **gravely** mean? Stick with clues right around the word *gravely*.)

2. **(1)** *Literal Comprehension/Nonfiction.* Notice the parallelism clues. In lines 28-29, the author states that one way of *to divert attention* is by acting "in a casual and indifferent way." Think about your own experience. When people act casually about something, they are usually not trying to call your attention to it. (2), (3), and (5) are incorrect because they have nothing to do with acting casually even though they are words used elsewhere in the passage.

3. **(5)** *Literal Comprehension/Nonfiction.* In lines 31-32, you are given a contrast clue: "the teller of a comic story does not slur the nub; he shouts it." *Slur* must mean the opposite of *shout.* Only *mumble* is the opposite of *shout.* (2) is incorrect, since it means almost the same thing as *shout.* (1), (3), and (4) don't have anything to do with shouting: *consider* and *remember* are ways of thinking, while *wisecrack* is a way of joking.

### Lesson 2

1. **(3)** *Literal Comprehension/Nonfiction.* This is a restatement of what the author tells us in line 7-9: "if dial clocks disappear, so will the meaning of those words for anyone who has never stared at anything but digitals." (1), (2), (4), and (5) are all incorrect because the statements are untrue or unsupported. (1) Reading dial clocks has nothing to do with reading digital clocks. (2) People will still be able to hover about a pole, but they will just have more difficulty describing the direction of rotation. The terms mentioned in (4) will still be useful to astronomers, since they do not refer to the motion of a dial clock. (5) The author talks about difficulty in *talking* about the motion; there is no evidence that the ability to *study* the motion will be affected by loss of the terms "clockwise" and "counterclockwise."

2. **(1)** *Literal Comprehension/Nonfiction.* This is a restatement of lines 11-13, immediately following line 11 where the author describes the loss of terms as "no minor matter." (2) and (5) are incorrect because you can tell that they are obviously untrue by using common sense and the passage; people will still be able to tell time and digital clocks will be one means of doing this. (3) is an accurate restatement of a detail from the passage, but it doesn't answer the question; it doesn't explain why losing the terms is a problem. (4) is incorrect because it merely jumbles phrases from the passages: comparing the south pole and direct motion is nonsense.

3. **(5)** *Literal Comprehension/Nonfiction.* According to the last sentence, "Astronomers speak of 'direction motion' and 'retrograde motion,' by which they mean counterclockwise and clockwise, respectively." Restated, direct motion means *counterclockwise* and retrograde motion means *clockwise.* Therefore, these terms are opposites. Choices (1), (3), and (4) are contradicted by the passage; each member of the pair means the same thing as the other. Choice (2) is incorrect because the pole of rotation, according to the paragraph, could be either clockwise (if the south pole) or counterclockwise (if the north pole).

## Lesson 3

1. **(5)** *Literal Comprehension/Nonfiction.* This idea—that the school's strength was that it allowed students to be proud of becoming Americans while being proud of their background—is what the author wants us to come away with. (5) is the only sentence general enough to include all of the details in the paragraph. (1) is a true detail, but it only tells part of the story. According to the last line, the author was allowed to feel proud to be a Mexican American, but nothing suggests that he felt more pride in his background than the other students felt about theirs. (2) and (3) contradict the main idea of the paragraph, which stresses that Lincoln High allowed students to retain their foreign backgrounds while becoming Americans. (4) is true, but it is only a detail. The stories told by Matti, Encarnacion, and the author, plus the sharing of the Chinese scroll, show that students often told stories about their native lands and that Asian and Spanish students shared experiences.

2. **(3)** *Literal Comprehension/Nonfiction.* When you locate the line describing how the teacher widened her eyes to show how interested he was, examine the clues from the two or three sentences before that. The author has been listing examples of the types of stories and objects students shared from native lands: Matti's story about the quilt, Encarnacion's skit about fishing, the author's story about the stagecoach, the Chinese scroll that someone showed. These examples have something in common: they are all stories and objects from the children's native lands. "These matters" must refer, then, to the various stories and objects. (1), (2), and (5) are close, but not quite on target. The teacher expressed to the children that she was enthusiastic about their backgrounds, about what they had to show and say. The author doesn't say how she reacted to the field trips (1) and the museum pieces (5). She encouraged the narrator to tell about his experiences in a stagecoach, not about the stagecoach in the museum at Sutter's Fort (5). Likewise, she responded to the Chinese scroll one student showed, not to all the historic paintings in Crocker Art Gallery (2).

3. **(3)** *Literal Comprehension/Nonfiction.* McNeil states his main idea in the first sentence: "The trouble with television is that it discourages concentration." (3) is the only statement that expresses this

idea. (1), (2), and (4) are wrong because they are not supported by any information in the paragraph. (5) directly contradicts what the author says in lines 2-3: "Almost anything interesting and rewarding in life requires some constructive, consistently applied effort."

## Lesson 4

1. **(2)** *Literal Comprehension/Nonfiction.* All of the main ideas of the paragraphs develop the main point stated in the last sentence of the passage: that Mrs. Flowers was "one of the few gentlewomen I have ever known, and has remained through my life a measure of what a human being can be." None of the other choices is general enough to include all the details in the passage. (1) restates the last sentence of paragraph one, which states that Mrs. Flowers gave the author "my first lifeline." (3) is not stated in the paragraph, but you might conclude it from paragraph one. However, it is not the main reason the author thinks so highly of Mrs. Flowers. (4) summarizes statements in paragraphs three and four: that Mrs. Flowers "didn't encourage familiarity," (line 16) that she never laughed although "she smiled often," (lines 18-19) and that her smiles for the author were "graceful" and "benign" (line 22). (5) is also a detail, not the main idea.

2. **(4)** *Literal Comprehension/Nonfiction.* (4) is a faulty restatement of a detail found on lines 7-8: "it seemed she had a private breeze which swirled around, cooling her." All the other choices restate details that are true. Choices (1) and (5) are reinforced in lines 17-18: "I don't think I ever saw Mrs. Flowers laugh, but she smiled often." Choice (2) comes from line 5, "Mrs. Bertha Flowers was the aristocrat of [the town of] Black Stamps." Choice (3) is stated in lines 6-7: "She had the grace of control to appear warm in the coldest weather...."

3. **(1)** *Literal Comprehension/Nonfiction.* The topic sentence appears in the first sentence of the paragraph: "Mrs. Bertha Flowers was the aristocrat of [the town of] Black Stamps." All the details of this paragraph contribute to this idea. The other choices are either supporting details or faulty restatements of details. (2) is a faulty restatement of the second sentence of the second paragraph, which says that "She had the grace of control to appear warm in the coldest weather . . ." This says nothing about her controlling people around her. (3) correctly restates part of

line 9, but it is only one detail describing Mrs. Flowers's "grace." (4) is incorrect because we are told that she dressed well—she wore "printed voile dresses and flowered hats"—but not that she was the best-dressed woman in town. Her elegance and dignity make her seem to the author "our side's answer to the richest white woman in town" (lines 11-12). This means that despite her poverty, she was equal in grace and dignity to the richest woman in town  not that she *was* the richest woman in Stamps.

## Lesson 5

1. **(1)** *Inferential Comprehension/Nonfiction.* In the second sentence, the word "indeed" signals a context clue of contrast: an infant *prodigy* must mean the opposite of a dullard. Only (1) describes someone who is the opposite of a dullard. (2), (3), and (4) are incorrect because they describe someone who *is* a dullard. (5) is incorrect because there is no evidence in the passage that crying easily had anything to do with being a prodigy.

2. **(4)** *Inferential Comprehension/Nonfiction.* There is nothing in the paragraph that directly states that Einstein took time to explore his interests. However, the paragraph does state that he taught himself calculus (math) and later studied physics (science) on his own. The question can be answered by putting the clues together and reading between the lines. It is implied—but not directly stated—that Einstein was interested in science and math, and so made time for them. (1) is incorrect because the paragraph states that Einstein went beyond his regular work at school to master physics  not that he ignored the work he was supposed to be doing. (2) is incorrect because we read that young Einstein was unable to get any academic positions. (3) is contradicted by the information about how young Einstein taught himself calculus and asked questions. Choice (5) is wrong because it makes too broad a leap from the information given. True, Einstein produced brilliant ideas while working in the patent office, but it does not follow that working at the patent office in any way sparked his ideas.

3. **(3)** *Inferential Comprehension/Nonfiction.* The second sentence of the final paragraph explains how Einstein's two theories reconciled seemingly contradictory forces. The final sentence tells us that Einstein was correct in his opinion. From this we can infer that his theories were extraordinary because they brought together what appeared to be opposing ideas, waves and particles. Only (3) states this. (1) is wrong because it is incomplete; just because the theories did not seem to fit together does not make them extraordinary. (2) is incorrect because it is also too narrow. (4) is wrong because it is illogical: just because theories are new does not make them valuable in any way. To be extraordinary, the theories must show something important. (5) is wrong because from the information in the passage we cannot infer that he made any money at all. Even if he did, that would not make the theories extraordinary.

## Lesson 6

1. **(3)** *Inferential Comprehension/Nonfiction.* By putting the author's statement that he "cannot preserve [his] health and spirits" without walking regularly with his statement that walking is the "enterprise and adventure of the day" you can infer the main idea: the author considers walking a necessary and enjoyable part of his routine. (3) is the only sentence that expresses an idea general enough to cover all the details in the passage, which explains why the author feels this way about walking. The author implies that he would not give up walking and accept a job in a shop, but this is a detail, not his main idea, eliminating choice (1). (2) is an incorrect restatement; actually, the author claims that his type of walking "has nothing in it akin to exercise"—in other words, cannot be compared with exercise. Reject (4) for the same reason; the author states that you cannot compare his type of walking with exercise taken like medicine. (5) is wrong because it is only a detail—not the main idea.

2. **(2)** *Inferential Comprehension/Nonfiction* From what the author says about how he would have "committed suicide long ago" if he had a job like some of the mechanics and shopkeepers he knows, you can infer that he could not tolerate a full-time indoor job. (1) is wrong because there is no evidence that the author works in an office even for less than four hours a day. (4) is wrong because in lines 10-15 the author implies he is "astonished" people do not "rust" in regular office jobs. (3) and (5) are illogical; the author likes walking, not "exercise." He doesn't seem to like weight-lifting—the formal sort of exercise an instructor might well lead.

3. **(1)** *Inferential Comprehension/Nonfiction.* The last sentence of the first paragraph states that "People who enjoy being outdoors in the summer need to be aware of the effects of getting too much sun." The other two paragraphs of the passage mainly concern sensible protection: the second paragraph is about the use of sunscreens, and the last paragraph is about sunbathing wisely. (1) therefore covers both main topics of the passage—knowledge and protection regarding harmful effects of the sun. (2) clearly covers only one detail of the paragraph on sunscreens; in fact, it misstates that detail because the paragraph does not say that you should use only sunscreens with high SPF. Skin cancer (3) and premature aging of the skin (4) are two harmful effects of sunbathing mentioned in the first paragraph; since neither choice discusses the knowledge and protection against the sun described in the other two paragraphs, neither can be the main idea of the passage. No statement in the passage describes a "gradual increase of ultraviolet rays" (5).

## Lesson 7

1. **(2)** *Inferential Comprehension/Nonfiction.* To answer this question, it is important not to focus too much on any one detail such as the hard weather, the brown grass, or the "great green and yellow grasshoppers… everywhere," but rather on how the author seems to *feel* about the mountain he describes. His purpose in describing this place which might be labeled by someone else as "terrible," "cluttered," "dead," and even "worthless"— is revealed in the last four lines: it is a place that makes you feel inspired. His observation that "your imagination comes to life" is the key. This contradicts the idea of a place that has no meaning or is uninspiring, so (1) and (4) are wrong. The detail about the grasshoppers everywhere might imply that animals compete for food, but this is only a detail, not the author's general attitude, so eliminate (3). Nothing about the people in surrounding areas is either stated or implied, so (5) is incorrect.

2. **(2)** *Inferential Comprehension/Nonfiction* …"hickory and pecan, willow and witchhazel" (lines 8-9) are examples of trees, so groves must be groups of trees—not meadows (1), nuts (3), streams (4) or ditches (5). The word "creeks" appears near "groves" and might mislead you into thinking that groves are streams, so look carefully at *all* of the clue words around "grove." The

word *grove* looks a lot like groove, so you might think that the answer is "a group of ditches"; make sure you read the question *carefully.* Likewise, don't make the mistake of thinking groves must be nuts just because you know about hickory and pecan nuts. The groves are *linear,* so it makes more sense to assume that they are groups of trees.

3. **(3)** *Inferential Comprehension/Nonfiction.* Details in the last six lines of the passage—the author's thoughts about the loneliness of objects and about the way Creation must have been—suggest that the author feels thoughtful when looking out upon the lonely land. Choice (1) is wrong because it is contradicted by line 15: "there is no confusion…" There is nothing to suggest that he feels lost, so eliminate (2). Nor does he seem to feel frightened (5) or hopeful (4). Rather, his tone suggests a person thinking, and his purpose seems to be to convince us how thoughtful and meditative that lonely land makes a person feel.

## Lesson 8

1. **(4)** *Inferential Comprehension/Nonfiction.* The first sentence says "American entrepreneurs are cashing in on AIDS." The second paragraph describes the need of the AIDS patients for "ready cash," which makes them easy "victims." The third paragraph's first sentence says: "the fact that the entrepreneurs are making money out of mortality is brushed aside." The rest of this paragraph describes the way each investor can "place his bet" on which AIDS patient is likely to die first. All these statements put together suggest that the author's attitude toward this business is that it "exploits people in need for the sake of profit" (4). The author obviously does not believe (5), therefore, or that the recent recession is the main cause of this type of greed (2). However, he does not suggest all American business is like this (3); his comment, "It is the American way," is a sarcastic rejection of these entrepreneurs' argument that they are doing the patients a favor while making a profit. Clearly, (1) is only a detail.

2. **(2)** *Application/Nonfiction.* From his negative comments on the insurance-buying business, we can infer that the author feels AIDS patients are being exploited mainly because "once they contract their illness, they typically lose their jobs or other sources of income" (line 10-11). Therefore, to protect them from exploita-

tion he would favor giving them financial support. Since he realizes that without other support the AIDS victims are forced to sell their life insurance policies, he cannot think no one should ever sell them at a discount (3). If he believes they are being unfairly exploited, (1) cannot be true, and the passage also makes clear that (4) is false. Ending the recession (5) would not protect dying AIDS patients because they have not lost their income because of the recession but because of their illness.

3. **(1)** *Application/Nonfiction.* The main characteristic of the businessmen who are buying up the life insurance policies of dying AIDS patients is that they present themselves as people who are "doing the victims a favor" when in reality they are interested only in taking advantage of them in order to make a profit. In this way they resemble a wolf disguised as a grandmother, who presents himself as a kindly old lady when he really wants to devour the person he pretends to want to help. Though these "entrepreneurs" are liars, the article suggests that their lies do *not* expose them to ridicule, so (2) cannot be correct. The other choices touch on parts of the entrepreneurs' behavior but are not "most similar" to it because all of them omit the characteristic of pretending to be good and helpful while really having selfish and evil motives.

## Lesson 9

1. **(2)** *Inferential Comprehension/Nonfiction.* You may want to find the answer to this question by eliminating the incorrect choices first. (1) and (3) are wrong because the owl makes noises (lines 5-6) by snapping its beak and flapping its wings and it first becomes aware that a predator is near when it "hears a noise." That it relies on hearing rather than its ability to see in the dark or its sense of smell allows us to infer that it has a good sense of hearing. If the first sentence tells us the owl "sits perched on the limb of a tree," we can infer that it can fly, so (4) cannot be true. Nothing suggests that owls are about to die out, and therefore (5) is wrong. On the other hand, you may be able to infer from the owl's whole behavior that it "is not big and strong," because none of its defenses rely on displaying itself as big or strong; on the contrary, it first tries to hide and be silent, and then makes noises so it will appear to be a more frightening animal than it really is.

2. **(2)** *Application/Nonfiction.* Like the owl, the kitten scares away a predator. None of the other behaviors accomplish the same result: the deer doesn't scare the lion, it avoids him (1); likewise, the lizard avoids the hawk (2) and the kingfisher avoids its enemies (4). The seagull attracts a mate (3).

3. **(1)** *Application/Nonfiction.* In answering this question you would put together what you already know with what you can infer from the passage. You probably already know that the phrase "being cool" is often used by teenagers and others to describe what is considered popular within a certain group at a certain time—what is "in" according to the majority opinion of the group. Therefore, someone who scored high on the teens' test for "coolness" would want to be liked by other teens (3). To think video games and cameras are "cool" and books and reading are "uncool" probably would not make these teens popular with teachers (1), but that would not be the main motive for scoring high on the test. Nothing suggests these teens mainly want to provoke negative reactions in publishers (2), win a present (4), or compete over intelligence (5).

## Lesson 10

1. **(3)** *Analysis/Nonfiction.* Suspense is tension created when a story raises questions in the reader's mind. After learning that Doug "would have but one jump" to reach the crevice or he would "go hurtling down some 600 feet onto the rocks," you wonder: Will Doug make it up to the ledge? You want to read on for the answer. Choices (1), (2), and (4), are all incorrect because they are contradicted by the passage. The narrator couldn't boost Doug because of his own unsteady balance—not because he was too far away (1). The author never describes Doug's weight (2). The author doesn't state that Doug could not land safely on the crevice (4): on the contrary, a safe landing is what he is hoping for.

2. **(3)** *Analysis/Nonfiction.* (1) is the correct answer because the dialogue gives us a glimpse into Doug's mind, which helps flesh out Doug's character and make him more real. This, in turn, makes his situation more emotional because now we can better identify with Doug and put ourselves in his place. (2) and (3) are wrong because Doug's words do *not* show that Doug is afraid and his speech *does* make

sense. (4) is inaccurate because dialogue doesn't make the favor clear; again, that can be done as well with third-person narration. Finally, (5) doesn't make sense because first-person dialogue is not the most effective way to describe a person.

3. **(5)** *Analysis/Nonfiction.* Choice (5) is the only true statement. The final statement, "I wept," gives you a sense of how upset the narrator is upon hearing Doug's brave words. A good way to answer a question about why a particular opening or ending is effective is to ask yourself: Why wouldn't the story have been as good without this? Without the last brief sentence, you wouldn't have been so struck by the complete anguish of the narrator. Many of the other sentences in the passage *do* show emotions—Doug's love, pride, courage,—so (1) is wrong. The ending makes the reader feel for the narrator—not question his bravery; so reject (2). The narrator's tears might indicate that he hasn't *shown* his emotion up to this point, but he has felt it; so (3) is wrong. Nothing supports (4); the reason for the narrator's tears is clear and his weeping raises no new questions in the reader's mind. The big question is still whether Doug will survive.

## Lesson 11

1. **(1)** *Analysis/Nonfiction.* The writer is telling about the series of events that happened before the *Titanic* sank. He has chosen to arrange his sentences in time order, and uses signal words such as *now* and *then* to show how one idea moves to the next in time. The writer simply reports what happened and who said what. He does not concern himself with blaming people (2) or analyzing the officers (3), nor does he provide his own opinions about what happened (4) or about where ships should be operated (5).

2. **(2)** *Analysis/Nonfiction.* This writer's purpose is to tell a story, not persuade his audience of a viewpoint. Like most storytellers, this writer offers readers the chance to experience another place and time—the dangerous moments aboard the *Titanic* before it sinks. (1) and (3) are incorrect because the writer deal with "usual problems" but an unusual situation, nor does he imply that we should blame anyone in particular for the accident. Although the time order used in the passage might make you consider (4), it is wrong because the author only mentions

one or two details about guiding a ship, such as reading indicators. If he wanted to have readers understand how to pilot a ship, he would have used time order to arrange several steps in the process. Choice (5) is not correct because the author presents facts about what happened on the ship—what the crew and passengers saw, heard, felt, did, said—not facts about icebergs.

3. **(5)** *Analysis/Nonfiction.* The ending makes a strong impression on us because we know something that the passenger doesn't: Despite the steward's calm words, something terrible is about to happen and many lives are about to be lost. (1) is incorrect because the ship *did* hit the iceberg: "a slight shock… shell ice… fell on the foredeck." (2) is wrong because this isn't a surprise ending. (3) is not correct because the final lines do not review what has happened. Eliminate (4) because there is no evidence that the victims know the extreme danger they're in; they merely seem puzzled.

## Lesson 12

1. **(5)** *Analysis/Nonfiction.* Throughout the piece, the author describes the results of the flood: the creek rises out of its banks, obliterates everything, and rushes by. (1) is incorrect because only one detail refers to the *cause* of the flood—lots of rain from a hurricane demoted to a tropical storm. (2) is not correct because the passage describes what happened during, not before, the flood. (3) is wrong because only two details describe neighbors' reactions: the Atkins kids come out in their rain gear and the neighbors gather. The writer describes only immediate effects, not any long-term ones, so (4) is incorrect.

2. **(3)** *Analysis/Nonfiction.* By switching to the present tense—"Everything *looks* different"—the writer takes the reader back with her as she relives the whole experience in memory. It is as if we are watching over her shoulder, and seeing the events unfold as they happen. There is no evidence that things happened any differently from the way she or others remember them. Her memory seems reliable; therefore, (1) and (5) are incorrect. There is no mention of past floods or future ones, so (2) and (4) are not correct.

3. **(2)** *Analysis/Nonfiction.* The details of the last paragraph illustrate the topic sen-

tence, "Everything looks different"—the new and different appearance of the land-scape. Though the Atkins kids and the neighbors appear, they are not described as frightened (1) or as helping each other (4).The last words of the passage, "I go out," do not suggest that the narrator is abandoning her home (5). Nowhere in the passage is the noise of the flood waters (3) mentioned. Although you might expect her to describe sounds of such a powerful movement of water, the author is concerned only to give us a visual description of the changed appearance of the land.

## Lesson 13

1. **(1)** *Nonfiction/Analysis.* The author makes several philosophical statements about the new understanding he reached: The "world was simple—stars in the darkness" (lines 11-12). "We realized... all that was real and that mattered were the same today as they had always been and would always be." His attitude as he describes the voyage is reflective as he meditates on the important truths he came to know. (2) is wrong because the author is fascinated by what he sees, not bored. For example, he calls the waves "an impressive movie," which shows that he is impressed, not disappointed. (3) is incorrect because the author does not judge what he sees; rather, he accepts it with joy, thrilling to the "alert intensity" he feels. Do not be confused by (4); the author is thoughtful, not playful. He does not "play" with his environment. Instead, he reflects on what he experiences. Finally, (5) is wrong because he is clearly awed by what he sees, not objective. He realizes some eternal truths about people and their world and is impressed by his experiences.

2. **(4)** *Analysis/Nonfiction.* "We lived, and that we felt with alert intensity." "Time and evolution ceased to exist." These are the statements of a man who felt vigorously alive. The words suggest vitality and a sense of being connected to the moment not anger, weariness, or homesickness, so (1) (2) and (3) are wrong. The author mentions feeling safe while looking at the waves from inside the raft—not while looking at the stars from the rubber boat—so (5) is not correct.

3. **(2)** *Analysis/Nonfiction.* The author's purpose is to explain how he felt and what he thought about while on his voyage. All the details in the passage—feeling the safety of a "cozy lair," seeing the world as "simple," understanding that life in the past had been "full" for people—describe the impact of the trip on the author's mind. (1) is incorrect because nothing is said about the raft's capsizing. (3) is incorrect because the author implies nothing about being afraid. (4) is incorrect because we are told only that the voyage was long, not what preparations were made. Similarly, (5) is incorrect because the details tell about the voyage itself, not what led up to it.

## Chapter 2: Fiction

## Lesson 1

1. **(5)** *Literal Comprehension/Fiction.* The main event is the disastrous dumping of snow on the fire. This is the life-threatening problem to which the main character reacts by planning another fire. The man does not actually hear himself sentenced to death, so (1) is incorrect. (2), (3), and (4) are details—not recaps of the main action. In addition, (2) and (4) neglect to tell how the problem comes about. (3) does not make clear what the problem is.

2. **(2)** *Literal Comprehension/Fiction.* Only (2) is not part of the action. There is no avalanche; the author uses the word "avalanche" to describe the snow falling from the spruce tree to convey how disastrous the loss of the fire is to the man. The snow falling from the tree "grew like an avalanche," but cannot be an actual avalanche because a relatively small amount of snow is falling a small distance from a spruce tree to a fire. (1) is part of the action according to lines 8-9: "Each time he pulled a twig he had communicated a slight agitation to the tree." (3) is true, because of lines 15-17: "... and the fire was blotted out. Where it had burned was a mantle of fresh and disordered snow." (4) is true, as is clear from lines 23-25: "... it was up to him to build the fire again, and this second time there must be no failure." The man wishes that he had listened to "the old-timer on Sulphur Creek" (line 21) and taken a trailmate along, so (5) is also part of the action.

3. **(4)** *Literal Comprehension/Fiction.* We are told at different points in the passage that the man "should have built it in the open" instead of "under the spruce tree" from which "it [snow] descended without warn-

ing upon the man and the fire." (4) puts these details together and restates them. (1) is a false statement, even though it contains some words from the passage. The falling snow—not the fire—kept him from cutting the strings. (2) is wrong because it contradicts the passage. Having the fire under the tree—not in the open—made pulling twigs easiest. The story mentions that the tree is spruce, but doesn't suggest a comparison between spruce and brush, so (3) is wrong. (5) contains accurate information, but does not explain the man's mistake.

## Lesson 2

1. **(3)** *Literal Comprehension/Fiction.* The answer comes from the phrases "spruce valley" and "now in the winter." Details that support this conclusion include the description of how Gordon has to make "snow camp" in "the deep woods near the valley's head." Don't be fooled by the word "haunted" used in line 10 to describe the woods; Gordon is in the forest, not a house, so (1) is wrong. You can eliminate (2) because the valley is "a mile from home," not two. The setting is clearly described as a "valley," so (4) cannot be correct. Gordon's shelter is "the bark-covered, half-faced lean-to he and his father had set up for the storage of trapping gear," not a small but well-equipped cabin in a valley, so (5) is incorrect as well.

2. **(2)** *Literal Comprehension/Fiction.* The first line directly states the atmosphere: "that sinister feeling in the pine shadows and a sense of something watching, waiting among the dense trees up ahead." This is echoed in the second line:"This spruce valley was a dark, forbidding place even in the summer; now in the winter silence under the blue-black trees was more than silence—it was like a spell." There are no details in the passage that are cheerful at all, so eliminate (1). Paul feels "filled with dread from the first," but he is not panic-stricken (3) or horrified (4). The calm is not peaceful; rather, it is deeply upsetting, eliminating (5), too.

3. **(5)** *Literal Comprehension/Fiction.* Gordon, the sixteen-year-old-boy, has to go "twice a week he had to make snow camp in the deep woods near the valley's head" (lines 19-20) to tend the "trapline [they had laid], just a week before his father had come down with flu-pneumonia" (lines 7-8). This had left "Gordon to cover the long line during the worst weeks of winter." There is no

mention of an animal of any kind, so eliminate (1). The "faint gray lichen" is the description of Gordon's first growth of beard, nothing that he is clearing from the forest, so (2) is wrong. We are told that his father has "come down with flu-pneumonia," but not that he is dying, eliminating (3). (4) confuses several details from the passage. Gordon feels that the forest is a "haunted place," but we are not told that it is in fact haunted. Rather than trying to "escape," he is dutifully carrying out his responsibilities.

## Lesson 3

1. **(1)** *Literal Comprehension/Fiction.* Barry "flexed his shoulders… and was surprised again by the unexpected weight of his muscles, the thickening strength of his body" (lines 6-9); he is "strongly made" (lines 13-14). Lines 16-17 ("Sometimes a devouring restlessness drove him from the house to walk long distances in the dark") show he is energetic. (3) describes the way Barry used to be (lines 9-10) and (2) better describes Jackie (see lines 20-25). Eliminate (4) because Barry is "tall, strongly made," so he cannot be "weak and powerless." The same is true of (5). Barry is "strongly made," with an "unexpected weight of (his) muscle," so he cannot be "delicate."

2. **(3)** *Literal Comprehension/Fiction.* Jackie is described (lines 20-25) as "tall and suave, his thick, pale hair sleekly tailored, his gray suit enviable." The "enviable" suit shows that he is well-dressed; the word "suave," that he is confident. Eliminate (1) since Jackie's hair is "pale," not dark, and he is "suave," not quiet. (2) is also wrong because Jackie is not clumsy. The narrator calls him "suave" and says he waves a "graceful" hand. It is Barry, not Jackie, who "walked solidly now, and often alone," eliminating (4). Finally, Jackie is described as "tall," and talks a great deal, so (5) is wrong.

3. **(3)** *Literal Comprehension/Fiction.* Barry "walked the High Street among the morning shoppers," showing that the passage is set on High Street in the morning. According to the first sentence, the "brisk April sun" has dispersed the overnight frost, so you know that the story takes place in spring. (1) and (2) are incorrect because Barry's walk and conversation with Jackie take place on High Street. Eliminate (4) because you know Barry and Jackie are standing among "the morning

shoppers," so the story must be set in the morning. Since Barry jarred his shoulder in a "tackle," he had to be playing football, not baseball. Further, Barry is "quiet," but there is no evidence in the passage that the street with its "morning shoppers" is quiet, so (5) is incorrect.

## Lesson 4

1. **(2)** *Inferential Comprehension/Fiction.* Several details clue you in to the fact that the man is trying to capture a fish. Descriptions of the fishing line, the man's thoughts, and the man's and fish's doings all serve as clues to the action. For example, "He knew that if he could not slow the fish with a steady pressure the fish could take out all the line and break it." (1) and (3) are incorrect because details about the fish's sword and "scythe blade" tail suggest that this is a swordfish, not a whale or shark. Words like "fast," "slow the fish," and "if he made his run" might seem to suggest a race. However, closer inspection of the story shows that the man is one of those "who kill" fish, not race with them. (4) is incorrect because while the man is on a "skiff," there is no suggestion that he is trying to sail it. His energies seem to be going into handling the fishing line. (5) is incorrect because it twists a detail from the story. The sword is part of the fish, not a weapon used by the man.

2. **(3)** *Inferential Comprehension/Fiction.* The "ocean bulged ahead of the boat and the fish came out" suggests that the the boat is out at sea. The fish and man both have hold of a racing line, so the man must be on the boat. (1) is incorrect because we are told that the body of water is an ocean, not a river. (2), (4) and (5) are incorrect because the man seems to be watching the fish from a moving boat, not from the shore, from a point underwater, or from a dock.

3. **(5)** *Inferential Comprehension/Fiction.* According to lines 6-7, the fish's "sword was as long as a baseball bat and tapered like a rapier." His tail is described as a "great scythe-blade." You can infer that this is a swordfish, based on these clues and any personal experience you may have had with swordfish or their pictures. Although striped bass have stripes and some sharks, whales, and dolphins have sharp tails, none of the fish mentioned in (1), (2), (3), and (4) has a sword.

## Lesson 5

1. **(5)** *Inferential Comprehension/Fiction.* The storyteller—an unnamed third-person narrator—looks in on the villagers from the outside and reports back to us on what has been seen and heard. The narrator describes the words and actions of Mr. Graves, Mrs. Summers, Mrs. Hutchinson and others without being directly involved in the story. (1), (2), and (3) are incorrect because we learn about what Mr. Graves, Mr. Summers, and Mrs. Hutchinson do from an outside observer, not from the characters themselves. These characters are quoted, not actually telling the story. If Mr. Summers were the storyteller, for instance, the passage would read, *"Tessie," I said*—NOT, as it does—*"Tessie," Mr. Summers said.* (4) is incorrect because the narrator does not take part in the story being told, and never says, "I."

2. **(1)** *Literal Comprehension/Fiction.* We know that Tess chose the marked paper from lines 12-14: "Bill Hutchinson went over to his wife and forced the slip of paper out of her hand. It had a black spot on it, the black spot Mr. Summers had made the night before …" The details in the end of the passage describe her stoning: "A stone hit her on the side of the head" (lines 32-33). (2) is incorrect because it contains a false detail: the rocks are collected for throwing, not to make a clearing in the village. (3) is wrong because it contains two details from the story but not a general summary of the action. The first half of (4) is true, but the second half is false: Mrs. Hutchinson's paper has to be forced from her hand because she does not want to display it. (5) describes two events that occurred prior to the action of the passage.

3. **(4)** *Inferential Comprehension/Fiction.* Mrs. Hutchinson does not want to be killed. Since her outcry comes when the villagers close in on her armed with stones, it is logical to assume that she is protesting against the stoning. The villagers turned on her after they saw her paper, so you can conclude that she is being stoned for having the paper with the spot. Although Steve Adams's position at the head of the crowd is mentioned right before Mrs. Hutchinson cries out a second time, nothing indicates that his position *caused* her outcry; therefore, (1) is incorrect. (2) is incorrect because it contradicts common sense. Why would someone who is a target complain that she hadn't helped collect

the ammunition? (3) describes an accurate detail, but not a reason for Mrs. Hutchinson's scream. The end result of Mr. Summers's action—the stone-throwing—is what makes her cry out. Mrs. Hutchinson became a victim instead of a stone-thrower because she chose the paper with the spot, not because she showed her paper last. Also, Mrs. Hutchinson was terrified about being stoned—surely NOT about being left out of the stone-throwing ritual. Therefore, (5) is incorrect.

## Lesson 6

1. **(2)** *Inferential Comprehension/Fiction.* Mrs. Clarke shows that she is a determined person by keeping at what she wants—food from various homes—until she gets it. Her words show her to be rather sneaky and conniving: The narrator believes that Tony is a good provider, but Mrs. Clarke complains that "Tony don't fee-ee-eee-ed me!" (1), (3), and (4) are incorrect because Mrs. Clarke begs and complains loudly—NOT the actions of a solemn, timid, or cheerful person. Mrs. Clarke seems concerned about food and sneaky about getting it, so (5) is incorrect.

2. **(1)** *Inferential Comprehension/Fiction.* You can infer Mrs. Clarke's opinion that Mr. Clarke is stingy from what the narrator tells you about her remarks as she leaves the store: "meat in hand, she departs, remarking on the meanness of some people who give a piece of salt meat only two-fingers wide"(lines 21-23). Mrs. Roberts grumbles about Mr. Clarke's stinginess—she does not praise him. Since (2), (3), and (4) describe praise, they are incorrect. Don't be fooled by (4). Hoping to get a big piece of meat, she *acts* as if he were an "angel on earth." However, we hear her express her *real* opinion of his miserliness when she leaves. Mr. Clarke is reading when Mrs. Roberts comes in, but she does not comment on that, so (5) is incorrect.

3. **(1)** *Inferential Comprehension/Fiction.* Putting together clues from near the word "keening," you can tell that the word describes Mrs. Roberts's high voice as she begs for meat. Since the "keening" annoys Mr. Clarke, it makes sense that "keening" is complaining. (2) is incorrect because Mrs. Roberts is clearly not happy. Since a groan is a *low* moan, and Mrs. Roberts has a *high* keening voice, keening cannot be groaning; so (3) is not correct. If Mrs. Roberts has a high keening voice, she is clearly not whispering; so (4) is incorrect. The word "scrape" is used by the narrator

to describe how Tony Roberts collects what he can for his wife, not to describe her voice, so (5) is incorrect.

## Lesson 7

1. **(4)** *Inferential Comprehension/Fiction.* The man's main concern is "the knowledge that each instant his feet were freezing. This thought tended to put him in a panic" (lines 6-7). On the other hand, he "felt a great surge of envy" (line 15) when he saw how the dog in the snow, with "its tail curled around warmly over its forefeet" (lines 13-14), "was warm and secure in its natural covering" (lines 16-17). Since he and the dog deal with the cold differently, (1) cannot be true. No comparison is stated or suggested between the intelligence of the man and the dog, so (2) and (3) are incorrect. From the description of the man's efforts to get warm in lines 8-11), by threshing his arms and beating his hands, first sitting and then standing, it is clear that the author does not mean for us to think that "human beings easily master natural difficulties" (5).

2. **(5)** *Inferential Comprehension/Fiction.* In lines 7-10, we are told that the gulls "stared at the men with black, beadlike eyes. At these times they were uncanny and sinister... and the men hooted angrily at them..." One gull has "black eyes... fixed upon the captain's head" and its desire to light on the captain's head is described as menacing (the oiler calls it an "ugly brute"). The last two lines of the passage sum up the impression that this gull, and the other gulls, make on the man: "somehow gruesome and ominous." All these details suggest that the men think the birds are waiting for them to die so they can feed on them and that the men may not survive. The fact that the "wrath of the sea was no more to them [the gulls] than it was to a covey of prairie chickens a thousand miles inland" does not make the men accept the gulls matter-of-factly and calmly; it is clear that they fear and hate them. Nothing supports (4) or suggests that the men see the gulls as a sign that help is coming (1) or that the sea is getting calmer (2).

3. **(2)** *Inferential Comprehension/Fiction.* References to storms ("the wrath of the sea"), to the men's anger, and to the gulls' sinister qualities all create tension in the air. The men seem disturbed, as if something bad might happen; the mood is not calm, hopeful, or joyous or happy, so (1), (3), (4) and (5) are incorrect.

Copyright ©1993 Regents/Prentice Hall, a division of Simon and Schuster, Englewood Cliffs, NJ 07632

## Lesson 8

1. **(4)** *Inferential Comprehension/Fiction.* A body is like a clock because each "loses time." Like a clock that loses more and more time until finally it stops, the body slows down until it stops at death. None of the other choices mentions the similarity between clocks and bodies—that both lose time. (1) is a detail suggested by the passage—that old people tend to rise early, in the summer and other times. However, (1) does not explain why the narrator compares bodies with clocks. (2) is incorrect because it is a detail contradicted by the passage; the old "have lost the gift of sleep" (line 2). (3) is a nonsense statement made by scrambling phrases from lines 3-5, so it is incorrect. Because (5) contradicts the idea that everyone's life ends, it is wrong.

2. **(2)** *Inferential Comprehension/Fiction.* The speaker compares death to an express train rushing toward him. Both rush onward and cause inevitable fatality. None of the other choices mentions the key reason the speaker uses the phrase—to emphasize how fast and unstoppable death is.

3. **(4)** *Inferential Comprehension/Fiction.* The theme of the passage—the lesson the lifeguard has learned—is that we all die. You can figure out this message from many details describing the lifeguard's thoughts about old people and about his own death. (1) is incorrect; while lines 1-2 state that "the old… are idle," the passage overall does not support the message that old people waste their energy. (2) is an opinion that is neither supported nor contradicted by the passage. (3) is contradicted by the passage. The speaker's description of relentless time, smiling "old ladies," and "old roosters" suggests that aging catches up with all people no matter how they feel. Most of the details suggest something about aging and death—not about swimming—so (5) is incorrect.

## Lesson 9

1. **(4)** *Application/Fiction.* Despite the noisy fighting, Julia calmly greets her husband, reminds the children to wash their hands, and lights the candles as she probably does every day at this time. Based on what we see of Julia on this one occasion, she seems to be a cool-headed woman who tries to keep her family on an even keel by ignoring conflict and sticking to civilized routine. Such a composed woman would probably try to maintain order by ignoring her children's fighting in a store and continuing her shopping routine. It is difficult to connect our mental image of calm-and-collected, proper Julia with a mother publicly yelling at or spanking her children, so reject (1) and (2). There is a partial connection between the idea that Julia calmly says hello and the idea that Julia would quietly say goodbye. However, it would be irresponsible and improper to leave children in a store, so eliminate (3). You can also build a partial bridge of ideas between your mental picture of Julia and the description of the controlled mother who takes her children home quietly. However, the Julia we know from the passage does not punish her children by denying them dinner—or any other way—even when they fight at dinnertime. You cannot logically connect that idea of Julia with the idea of a mother who would use such a punishment for fighting at another time, so reject (5).

2. **(4)** *Application/Fiction.* Based on how the children act in the passage, you can see that they are a rowdy bunch. Based on what you are told by the speaker, that rowdiness does not usually keep them from greeting their father warmly: "Nine times out of ten, Francis would be greeted with affection." (4) best describes the sort of warm and rowdy greeting you might expect from the children on another more typical night. What you know of the children transfers only partly to the other choices. While (1) describes a spirited Louisa, it does not describe an affectionate greeting. While you do see Henry kick his sister in the passage, this would not be an affectionate way to welcome his father home. Further, there is no evidence that Henry would be that disrespectful to a parent, so (2) is incorrect. (3) does describe a warm greeting, but one that you would expect from a polite older person. It does not connect with our image of Toby as a very little boy, so discard (3). (5) is not correct because it describes a repeat of the performance described in the passage—behavior which, you are told, is not usual.

3. **(1)** *Application/Fiction.* Francis happens to come home in the middle of the children's squabbling and is drawn into the clash. The bear's situation is most like the father's: in both cases, innocent bystanders get "stung" by being in the wrong place at the wrong time. Like the correct choice, (2), (3), and (4) all describe noisy rackets. Unlike the correct choice, none describes the *innocent bystander* and *unhappy uproar* that are described in the

passage. In (2) and (3) and (4), the cat food, rock star, and soldier all *cause happy uproar.* While (5) does describe uproar and distress, the prankster is the cause—not an innocent bystander.

## Lesson 10

1. **(4)** *Application/Fiction.* The details the author chooses to describe suggest that he looks on the grandmother positively. By having her ask the young man about himself, the author shows her to be interested in him and supportive of his plans. By having her reflect aloud on her grandson, the author shows her to be encouraging and caring. (1), (2), and (3) all express negative attitudes and are therefore wrong. While the author seems to respect the grandmother, it is doubtful that he shares certain of her beliefs;so (5) is incorrect. For instance, he may not share her religious beliefs or her opinion that it is "sinful" to bet. Also, he may not agree with her about the relative merits of being a doctor, dentist, foot-doctor, or undertaker.

2. **(2)** *Application/Fiction.* Several of the woman's comments reveal the woman's religious faith: "Thank the Lord for that," "That's sinful," "Keep you acquainted with the house of the Lord." It is logical to predict that the author would show her bringing up religion as a topic in a later discussion. There is no evidence that the woman is interested in politics, relationships, or crime, so (1), (3), and (5) are not logical choices. It doesn't sound as if the woman does much traveling, since she seems to spend most of her time with the "home-folks," so (4) is not a good choice.

3. **(3)** *Application/Fiction.* The author has the woman explain how she advised her grandson: "....whatever you do, like a church steeple: aim high and go straight." This suggests that the author believes that people should aim high at whatever career they choose—best expressed by (3). The woman does suggest careers that require college, but she never refers to college and seems to feel that success depends on innate ability, effort, and religious fate. Therefore, (1) is not something the author would likely endorse. None of the careers in the passage *require* going to a big city, so (2) is not valid. In the same way, none of the careers discussed involve travel, so (5) is wrong. While the woman does suggest medicine, she speaks of it as a way to do what the "Lord... see fit," not because it pays well. Therefore, (4) is incorrect.

## Lesson 11

1. **(4)** *Analysis/Fiction.* Details about the action, setting, and characters in paragraph two all suggest a tone of sympathy and hope. The man is optimistically planing to meet people he has greeted from a distance for years. He feels "tenderness" for them and for their "little house." His image of them has been "carved sharply in his heart" and their lives have been "wrought into his own." You can almost hear the optimism and tenderness in the speaker's voice as he describes the man's feelings and thoughts. While his tone is serious, nothing suggests gloom and fear, anger, or sarcasm so (2), (3), and (5) are incorrect. Nowhere does the speaker poke fun at anyone or anything, so (1) is wrong.

2. **(3)** *Analysis/Fiction.* As the action in the story proceeds, the engineer's feelings about the characters do an about-face and the tone changes sharply. After meeting the woman and seeing how old and unfriendly she really is, "his heart, which had been brave and confident... was now sick with doubt and horror." You can hear the sad, discouraged tone of voice; in fact, if you really "listen," you might imagine you hear him sigh. There is no evidence of any humor, including sarcasm, so choices (2) and (5) are incorrect. Nothing suggests a tone of distrust (1) or of anger (5).

3. **(4)** *Analysis/Fiction.* The engineer's problem is that reality does not match his imagination. The author's purpose is to describe how the engineer's feelings change from hope to despair as he confronts this problem. (1), (2) and (3) are wrong because neither the town nor the engineer's work is described, and the only 'story of travel' told concerns the engineer passing the same house on his routine train-run, which cannot be described as 'entertaining.' Since the whole point of the story is that the value the engineer has given to his past experience (his memory of the woman and her daughter waving to him from the porch) is an illusion, the author's purpose cannot be (5).

## Lesson 12

1. **(2)** *Analysis/Fiction.* By including dialect, complete with grammatical errors, the author makes you feel that "Squeaky" is talking right to you. If the same information had been put into more formal language, the writer would still have conveyed that the race is important to the narrator; so (1) is incorrect. Nothing suggests that

Copyright ©1993 Regents/Prentice Hall, a division of Simon and Schuster, Englewood Cliffs, NJ 07632

the narrator is weak (5). In fact, her statement that "I much rather just knock you down and take my chances even if I am a little girl with skinny arms and a squeaky voice" (lines 15-17) shows that she is exceptionally brave and aggressive. Her willingness to fight, as well as her running ability, shows that she is not physically weak, either. Nothing suggests that she is confused (3). (4) and (5) are too general; the language reveals something about this one girl, who happens to be athletic and may be poor.

2. **(4)** *Analysis/Fiction.* "In the first place, no one can beat me and that's all there is to it." The author's purpose throughout has been to describe Squeaky through her own eyes. The final sentence sums up Squeaky's self-impression—her supreme confidence in her ability—with ringing finality. Therefore, (5) is wrong. There is no doubt that the track meet is "tomorrow," so (1) is incorrect. Squeaky's statement couldn't be more clear and to the point, so (2) is incorrect. There is nothing new about Squeaky's idea that she will win, as she has stated the same idea in several forms throughout the piece. Therefore, (3) is incorrect.

3. **(1)** *Analysis/Fiction.* Anyone who can boldly state that "I much rather just knock you down and take my chances even if I am a little girl with skinny arms..." is confident. Her statements: "I'm the fastest thing on two feet" (lines 19-20) and "no one can beat me and that's all there is to it" (lines 37-38) show her to be boastful. Such self-descriptions certainly don't come from someone who is shy, so (3) is incorrect. Although she is direct, there is no evidence that she is disrespectful or rude, so (2) is incorrect. Similarly, she brags about her ability, but with good cause, since she is an excellent runner. Therefore, her bragging is neither snobbish nor deceitful, so (5) is incorrect.

## Lesson 13

1. **(3)** *Analysis/Fiction.* The narrator says that "whenever she smiled at—at him, at a chicken liver, at nothing—it disturbed him that her smile could have no root in mirth, or even amusement" (lines 4-6). From this you can infer that the author lists different things she smiles at in a series to emphasize that she is not amused but sad about something (3). We are told she has "a moody expression" (line 1) and "petulance" [irritation] in her voice (lines 2-3), but nothing she says or does shows her to be angry at Dexter (2) or to be thinking "he is a nobody" (4). The details she smiles at in a series do not suggest (1) or (5).

2. **(1)** *Analysis/Fiction.* Dexter calls himself "nobody" (line 28) but then admits he is rich ("I'm probably making more money than any man my age in the Northwest"... lines 30-31). The other man did the opposite—at first he gave the woman no hint he was poor, and then he told her that he was (lines 13-15). Since Dexter tells the woman the truth and the other man concealed his poverty from her, (2) states the opposite of the truth about the two men. Though the other man disappointed the woman, nothing suggests that Dexter makes her happy (3). We are not told the ages of Dexter and the other man so (4) cannot be correct. As for (5), it was the woman's interest in the other man that "wasn't strong enough to survive the shock" (line 22) of finding out he was poor; there is also no suggestion that she is rejecting, or going to reject, Dexter. In fact, since Dexter is rich, and is 'starting right' with her by being honest, she is likely *not* to reject him.

3. **(1)** *Analysis/Fiction.* Dexter at first says "I'm nobody" (line 28 ) and then admits he is very rich (lines 30-31). The last line of dialogue in the passage indicates that his motive for contradicting himself in this way is that at first he does not want to tell the truth about his wealth because he feels that it is "an obnoxious remark" to say how rich he is; on the other hand, he wants to start right by telling the woman the truth about his financial status. (5) is a detail and part of this meaning. The main reason he contradicts himself is a conflict between a desire not to boast about his wealth and a desire to be honest with the woman. If to 'start right' means to be honest, (3) cannot be true. Everything in the passage suggests that Dexter wants to get closer to the woman, not get away from her (2); contradicting himself is a part of his struggle to make a good impression on her. Nothing about Dexter's age appears in the passage and his contradiction does not concern his true or false age; so (4) is wrong.

## Lesson 14

1. **(3)** *Analysis/Fiction.* In lines 3-4 we are told Anne "felt sorry for her [Mrs. Davenport]" when she found her asleep in front of the television, and in lines 5-7, we are told that "For the first time, she saw Mrs. Davenport as old and vulnerable and unfortunate rather than aggressive and unpleasant and ill-bred." From these statements, you can infer that Anne gives Mrs. Davenport extra money in lines 7-9 because she feels guilty for not having sympathy for the older woman before—for, in fact, disliking her. Since she disliked her earlier, (1) is wrong. (4) states true details, but they do not explain why Anne gives Mrs Davenport extra money. Nothing suggests that Anne feels Mrs. Davenport has no place to sleep and needs rent money (2), or that Anne feels a guilt over her relative wealth and wants to give money to poor people in general (5).

2. **(2)** *Analysis/Fiction.* Anne's reaction to finding the cookie right where Mrs. Davenport said it was "covered with dust hair" (line 28) must be one of embarrassment that the old woman's criticism of her is correct. Anne's fury shows that she is unusually sensitive to criticism— or the comment of an "unpleasant and ill-bred" old woman would not enrage her so much. (Of course, she is also angry at overtipping Mrs. Davenport and feeling sympathy for her.) Since "the [children's] room was a mess" (lines 25-26), (1) cannot be true. Nothing suggests her anger is motivated by hostility to all older women (3), or comes from an unhappy marriage (4), or is caused by overprotectiveness toward her children (5).

3. **(4)** *Application/Fiction.* From the statement in lines 30-31 ("How had she allowed that woman in her house with her children, even for a moment?"), we can infer that Anne's main intention in going to the phone is to tell Mrs. Davenport never to come to her house again. Since so much of Anne's anger springs from the fact that Mrs. Davenport's criticism was justified, she is not likely to accuse Mr. Davenport of lying about her; we also have no reason to believe that Mrs. Davenport has accused Anne of treating her children badly. Therefore, (5) is not correct. Anne gave Mrs. Davenport the five dollars voluntarily, and she is not at all likely to call the police about so small a sum, so (3) can be rejected. (1) refers to an attitude of sympathy and guilt toward Mrs. Davenport which Anne felt in the first paragraph of the last passage; it is not the attitude she has going to the phone in the last paragraph. (2) is obviously false.

## Chapter 3: Drama

### Lesson 1

1. **(3)** *Literal Comprehension/Drama.* After Lee refers to the plates and spoons and things as "the same crap we always had around," Austin responds, "I guess they have personal value to her." That is another way of saying, "I guess I understand her feelings. She feels attached to these things." (1) is incorrect, since it is Lee's line, not Austin's. It gives Lee's ideas about his mother's feelings, not Austin's idea. None of the other choices except for (3) say anything about the mother's feelings, so (2), (4), and (5) are incorrect.

2. **(2)** *Literal Comprehension/Drama.* Lee states that he "never realized the old lady was so security-minded." He says that he "made a little tour this morning. She's got locks on everything." In other words, it is just this morning that he discovered his mother's concern with the safety of her things. Lee doesn't say anything about her buying expensive furniture or replacing the furnishings with different ones—so (1) and (4) are incorrect. The plates with Idaho stickers are part of the "same crap we always had around," so the mother's interest in Idaho would not be news to Lee; (3) is therefore incorrect. Nothing is said about anyone's caring about healthful food—just that Lee does not care to eat off plates with Idaho decals—so (5) is incorrect.

3. **(3)** *Literal Comprehension/Drama.* The words "junk" and "phony" convey dislike. You can tell that Lee is talking about his mother's antiques because no one has changed the subject since line 10, where Austin first suggested that his mother considers her antiques valuable. (1) and (2) don't give Lee's opinion about antiques, so they are incorrect. (4) is wrong because it is Austin's line and expresses understanding, not dislike. (5) is a statement about where Lee is and how he wants to feel when he eats—not about his general dislike for his mother's antiques—so it is incorrect.

### Lesson 2

1. **(2)** *Literal Comprehension/Drama.* The stage direction, indicated by italicized words and in brackets (lines 24-25), is

Copyright ©1993 Regents/Prentice Hall, a division of Simon and Schuster, Englewood Cliffs, NJ 07632

[*Tom gives a long ring.*]. (1) is incorrect. Jim states, "I think we just beat the rain." This is a line of dialogue, not a stage direction. Nowhere in the stage directions does it state who answers the door (although Laura states that she will), so (3) and (4) are incorrect. The stage directions indicate that Laura—not Amanda—turns on the phonograph. (LAURA: Oh, Oh, oh… [*She returns through the portieres, darts to the Victrola, winds it frantically and turns it on.*] Therefore, (5) is incorrect.

2. **(2)** *Literal Comprehension/Drama.* The stage directions, along with the dialogue, make it clear that Amanda's attitude is one of anger. She "*stares furiously at Laura. She points imperiously* [domineering, arrogant] *at the door*" (lines 10-11). She says "(*in a fierce whisper*): What is the matter with you, you silly thing?" (lines 13-14). Her words and gestures do not express any of the attitudes listed in the other choices.

3. **(4)** *Literal Comprehension/Drama.* in lines 1-12, Laura is shown to be paralyzed by fear, unable to go to the door and pleading with her mother to open it for her. She begs her to do so again in line 18, and in lines 20-21 cries "(*despairingly*)" that she is "sick!". Her stark terror cannot be described as excitement (1), which suggests positive emotion. None of the other choices are supported by descriptions of her behavior in the dialogue and stage directions.

## Lesson 3

1. **(3)** *Inferential Comprehension/Drama.* Mac admits that he tried to kill Sue Anne's mother, so they didn't get along very well. Mac's comment that "Courts gave her complete jurisdiction" over Sue Anne indicates that he and Sue Anne's mother were divorced. They may or may not have sung in the same band. However, the violence, anger, and drunkenness that Mac recalls show that the marriage was neither perfect nor close and loving. Therefore, (2) is incorrect. Since Sue Anne's mother threatened to have her arrested if she saw Mac, (5) is wrong. Mac's statement in lines 12-13 shows that her mother won custody long ago so (1) is incorrect. Nothing suggests the mother ever was an alcoholic, so (4) is also wrong.

2. **(2)** *Inferential Comprehension/Drama.* Sue Anne reveals that "the other night," Mama threw the whiskey in a woman's face after that woman had praised Mac's singing. From Mama's reaction you can infer that Mama is still angry with Mac. (1) is incorrect because the divorce was not recent; Mac wonders whether his daughter still recognizes him, so he hasn't seen her in a long time. (3) can be rejected because nothing is said about Mac's song-writing, just his singing. (4) is incorrect because it contains a false detail. Mac states that he tried to kill Sue Anne's mother, not the reverse. (5) is incorrect because Mac's statement, "I wrote you a few letters," does not suggest a recent event, like the whiskey-throwing "the other night.'

3. **(5)** *Literal Comprehension/Drama.* Sue Anne mentions to Mac that "Mama says you tried to kill her once," and Mac agrees, "I did." (1) and (2) may or may not be true, but neither is *stated in the passage*, so all three should be rejected. Mac admits that he drank, but does not state that his drinking was the reason Sue Anne's mother left him. Sue Anne mentions "Mama's band," but does not state that Mama is a great country-and-western singer. Sue Anne did not tell her mother she was meeting Mac, but may have told someone else; so (4) is wrong. No one states that Mac is a devoted father and his long absence contradicts that idea, so (3) is not correct.

## Lesson 4

1. **(5)** *Inferential Comprehension/Drama.* Alicia and Bill have gotten a divorce and are splitting up their furniture. It is logical to assume that the furniture is in the living room they once shared. They are remembering a French restaurant and an art gallery from their past—not visiting them now—so (1) and (4) are incorrect. They are deciding who gets what familiar, used furniture—not buying new furniture—so this is not a furniture store (2). There is no evidence that the conversation takes place is a court of law, although we can infer that the couple probably visited one in the past during their divorce, so reject (3).

2. **(3)** *Inferential Comprehension/Drama.* In lines 19-30, Alicia and Bill argue. Bill accuses Alicia of having an "acquisitive streak." Alicia starts to lose control as she says sarcastically, "In my naive way, I thought we were going to spend our lives together." These are two angry people and the mood is certainly not hopeful, happy, quiet, or peaceful. Therefore, you should reject (1), (4), and (5). Though the quarreling couple are not happy, they are not expressing sadness, but anger, so (2) is wrong.

3. **(4)** *Inferential Comprehension/Drama.* Since the couple had time to collect furniture and memories, they must have been married for quite a while. Alicia, not Bill, is the one with the "acquisitive streak," so (1) is wrong. Alicia and Bill argue freely now, and they probably argued when they were married. In any case, there is no indication that they argued "seldom" while married, so reject (2). (3) contains a false statement, since it is clear that the Alicia and Bill have gotten a divorce. There is no evidence to support the idea that another woman caused the divorce, so (5) is incorrect.

## Lesson 5

1. **(4)** *Application/Drama.* In lines 30-32, Ken says: "When I say something really awkward [disturbing] you just pretend I haven't said anything at all." Ignoring his disturbing statements is most like not listening to an unhappy child. The hospital staff has not refused him service (1), or deserted him (5); in fact, his complaint is that they continue to give him service and keep him alive when he wants to end his suffering by dying. His miserable situation is not due to a failure of his (3) or to his inability to make use of what the hospital staff gives him (2).

2. **(4)** *Application/Drama.* Mrs. Boyle tries to convince Ken not to give up. She advises him to "make the best of the situation" (line 6) and to realize that his depression is normal. She isn't the sort of person who would suggest that a friend stop trying ("throw in the towel"). (1), (2), (3) and (5) are all hopeful, optimistic sayings that Mrs. Boyle might use, so they are incorrect. (Remember: the question asks for the choice that you would *not* match with Mrs. Boyle.)

3. **(5)** *Inferential Comprehension.* Ken's answers are angry and sarcastic. For example, he contradicts Mrs. Boyle sharply, "No. 'We' don't have to do anything," and uses a curse—"You're all the bloody same." He is stirred up and pessimistic, not hopeful, philosophical, or calm. Therefore, (2), (3), and (4) should be rejected. You might think at first that (1)— resigned (obediently accepting one's fate)— is right because Ken wants treatment stopped. However, he states fiercely that he "cannot settle for" waiting until the depression lifts (line 18), so (1) is incorrect.

## Lesson 6

1. **(4)** *Analysis/Drama.* In this scene, Chris blames Keller for causing the deaths of young airmen by irresponsibly selling faulty parts. The author's message is that people have responsibility to others. All the details in the scene emphasize that theme—how important that lesson is to Mother and to Chris and how horrified they are that Keller ignored it. (1) and (3) are incorrect because they are contradicted by the passage. Throughout the scene Chris makes it clear that Keller was *wrong* to do what he felt was best for his company. The reactions of Chris and Mother show that Keller should *not* have considered his work more important than the lives of others. (2) should be discarded because there is no support for it in the passage. The author shows us Chris's anger, but does not seem to make the point that Chris's anger is useless or wrong in any way. (5) is incorrect because it is only a detail mentioned by Keller, not the overall message.

2. **(5)** *Analysis/Drama.* Chris's words ("God in heaven, what kind of man are you?"), tone ("*deadly insistence*"), and gestures ("*pursuit and escape*") all indicate lack of respect and dislike. Chris has a negative attitude toward his father, not a positive one (respect) or even a neutral one (indifference), so (1) and (3) are incorrect. Chris is shocked and probably saddened by his father's actions, as you can tell from all the disbelieving questions he asks ("Then... you did it?" "Then why'd you ship them out?" "Then why didn't you tell them?"). Nevertheless, Chris shows more contempt overall than amazement or sorrow, so (5) is a better answer than (2) or (4).

3. **(3)** *Application/Drama.* Throughout this scene, Chris has shown concern for airmen whose lives were endangered by unsafe planes. Therefore, he would probably show a similar concern for those fighting during wartime and might go into a business to help them. There is no evidence in the passage to suggest that he would take any direct role in the fighting as an enlisted person, a spy, or a pilot, so (1), (2), (4) and (5) are incorrect. Considering his concern for men in the war, Chris would not be likely to reject military service (2).

Copyright ©1993 Regents/Prentice Hall, a division of Simon and Schuster, Englewood Cliffs, NJ 07632

## Lesson 7

1. **(4)** *Analysis/Drama.* The mother's protests come while her son gently tries to convince her to face facts: her daughter has a disability. Amanda's problem is that she doesn't want to hear the truth because it hurts, so (3) is flatly wrong. (1) is incorrect because it is unsupported and goes against common sense. Why would Amanda be worried about improving Tom's vocabulary at a time like this? There is no evidence that Amanda—Tom's own mother—considers Tom an intruder, so (2) is incorrect. (5) is too general. Just because Amanda cannot tolerate hearing these things about her daughter does not make her an intolerant person, so it should be eliminated.

2. **(3)** *Analysis/Drama.* Throughout the entire scene, Tom takes pains not to come on too strongly ("Just one little warning, Mother"… "just one thing…" "she's ours and we love her"). He seems to care about both his mother and his sister and not to want to hurt either. Therefore, when he says that his sister's differences are "not quite all" in her favor and that she is "a little" peculiar, you can infer his sympathetic but realistic attitude. He is trying to be reasonable, and would not sound angry, resentful, or sarcastic, so (1), (2), and (5) are incorrect. There is no evidence of humor in his tone—joking would be out of place in this serious conversation—so (4) is incorrect.

3. **(3)** *Analysis/Drama.* Amanda seems absorbed in her children—not in herself. Apparently she has had Tom invite a friend over in the hope that he will hit it off with Laura. Her tears arise from sadness because Laura does not have the happiness she deserves. (2) and (4) are incorrect because they describe someone who acts falsely, out of self-interest. There is no evidence that she says one thing and does another (that is, is a hypocrite) or will do anything to get what she wants. She just wants Laura to be happy. Fools and crybabies cry for little or no reason, and Amanda certainly has reason to be upset, so (1) and (5) are incorrect.

## Chapter 4: Poetry

### Lesson 1

1. **(2)** *Literal Comprehension/Poetry.* The topic of the poem is the father's death. Every detail in the poem helps build the idea that the children need to go on living despite their father's death. (1) is incorrect because the speaker says nothing about everyone remembering her husband's death. (3) is incorrect because the mother says nothing about obedience in connection with the father's death. (4) is too general and is not supported by the poem. By saying that she will use her dead husband's clothes, the woman implies that they are of value to her even if they aren't worth a lot of money. (5) is incorrect because it is a general opinion about children and death that may or may not belong to the poet. In the first two lines, the mother does tell two specific children about the death of their father, but the rest of the poem is about carrying on after the death of a loved one.

2. **(3)** *Literal Comprehension/Poetry.* The speaker says: "Life must go on,/Though good men die;/Anne, eat your breakfast;/Dan, take your medicine" (lines 17-20). She tells her children that she plans to make jackets and trousers from their father's old coats and pants, not buy new clothes. Therefore, (1) is incorrect. She mentions the pennies and keys that she will take from the pants and give to Dan and Anne. However, she does not give the children presents, so (2) should be eliminated. (4) is incorrect because she talks about using the dead man's clothing, not throwing it away. The mother says nothing about parties or noisemakers. She just states that Anne shall make a "pretty noise" with the keys, so (5) is incorrect.

3. **(1)** *Literal Comprehension/Poetry.* A "lament" is an expression of grief or regret, so the title prepares the reader for a poem about someone's sorrow. There is nothing in the definition of "lament" to suggest forgetfulness, so (2) is incorrect. You can lament many things other than death such as the absence of someone you love or the foolish way you acted—so the title does not necessarily suggest a story about death. Thus (3) is not the best answer. (4) is a false statement since the poem *is* a woman's lament. The woman's sorrow is clear, especially in the last two lines when she says, "Life must go on;/I forget just why." (5) is incorrect because it is unsupported by the poem. The woman's matter-of-fact approach to her husband's death shows that she is sad but bearing up, not angry.

## Lesson 2

1. **(3)** *Inferential Comprehension/Poetry.* the first two lines of the poem show that the speaker is hesitating: first he says he is too young to love, then he says he is old enough to love. Then in lines 3-6, he tosses a penny—either flipping a coin to see if it comes up heads or tails, or throwing a coin into a "wishing well," making a wish. He imagines the well or the flipped coin "answering" him by saying "Go and lov, go and love, young man/If the lady be young and fair' (lines 5-6). Deciding whether to love by tossing a coin shows hesitation about loving—but also shows an eagerness to love. The second stanza expands on this attitude. It begins with a expression of fear and wonder about love: "Oh love is the crooked thing,/There is nobody wise enough/To find out all that is in it" (lines 9-11). But the next three lines imply that being carried away by love is desirable and wonderful as well as frightening ("For he [the lover] would be thinking of love/Till the stars had run away/ And the shadows eaten the moon"). The last two lines stress that despite his doubts and fears, the man is eager to love. The man is not confident (1), angry and proud (2), sad and disappointed (4), or carefree (5).

2. **(4)** *Inferential Comprehension/Poetry.* The last lines of the poem ("But O that I were young again/And held her in my arms!" reveal that the speaker is older than "that girl standing there" in the first line. Therefore, (2) cannot be correct . The "travelled man" (line 5) and the "politician" (line 7) are men the speaker points out as having a different point of view from his own. Their points of view agree with the quotation by Thomas Mann under the title of the poem which declares the meaning of human life is basically political. The last two lines of the poem show that the speaker does not agree with that opinion; he thinks the meaning of life is concerned with love. For this reason it is wrong to infer that the speaker is Thomas Mann (3), a politician (1), or a world traveller (5).

3. **(3)** *Inferential Comprehension/Poetry.* The poem presents a conflict of two points of view. One considers politics the most important thing in life—involving nations and "war and war's alarms" (line 10). The other point of view considers love to be the most important thing in life, which is the speaker's point of view. In the first four lines, the speaker asks how he can fix his attention on politics when he sees "that girl standing there." Notice that the speaker does not say politics is unimportant. In lines 5-9, he says that the travelled man "knows/What he talks about/ And there's a politician/That has read and thought,/And maybe what they say is true." But for him, the real meaning of life is the experience of love. Since the speaker does not condemn his feelings of love, (5) is wrong. Nothing suggests that politicians interfere with love (1), or that love's happiness makes up for politicians' broken promises (2), or that love can solve the world's political problems (4).

## Lesson 3

1. **(5)** *Inferential Comprehension/Poetry.* In lines 20-21, the speaker describes joy with words usually used to describe people: "...shy, unique,/Friendly to a few." (1), (2), (3) and (4) are incorrect because they are phrases that have nothing to do with joy in the poem. The phrase "proud and confident" (lines 13-14) refers to "man", and "shining and unsheathed,"(line 27), "diverse yet single," (line 11), and "fused and mingle" (line 10) refer to grief.

2. **(1)** *Inferential Comprehension/Poetry.* The first two stanzas (lines 1-12) convey the idea that people should share their grief. The third stanza emphasizes that idea by comparing unshared grief to an unshared "little tent:" "Let no man be so proud/And confident,/To think he is allowed" to live alone. (2) is incorrect because the poet is using figurative language to talk about isolation, not literally talking about living in tents. (3) is incorrect because "Let no man be so proud" is another way of saying, "Do *not* be so proud..." (4) is incorrect because it is contradicted by the speaker, who is telling you *not* to try to find a place for yourself. (5) is incorrect because it is not supported by the poem, which suggests that none of us really can live alone.

3. **(2)** *Inferential Comprehension/Poetry.* A crown is a symbol of honor and respect. The speaker compares the sorrow he shares with another to a crown laid on that person's head. With this comparison, the speaker implies that the sharing of sorrow, like the wearing of the crown, is honorable. (1) is incorrect because the last two lines are about shared sorrow ("My sorrow... on your head")—not self-pity. (3), (4), and (5) can quickly be eliminated because none of them mentions sorrow at all. The last line is about shared sorrow— not real crowns, royalty, or joy.

## Lesson 4

1. **(5)** *Application/Poetry.* The two lines repeated throughout the poem are "Do not go gentle into that good night" and "Rage, rage against the dying of the night." The attitude that the poet is calling for from his dying father is one of brave defiance of approaching death. Every stanza of the poem describes a type of man who fails or is defeated in life but who still declares his strength of spirit, struggling to the last. The poet therefore would not urge a dying AIDS patient to simply look forward to death as a relief (4), to sleep as an escape from pain (3), to wait for a cure (1), or just be patient with the doctors (2).

2. **(2)** *Application/Poetry.* The speaker wants his father to "rage," so he would *not* like his father to calmly give up and accept death. (1), (3), (4), and (5) are all strong, spirited refusals, so the speaker would probably not mind hearing any of them. (Note: Be careful to look for what the *speaker* would dislike, not you. *You* might not want to hear your father upset about dying or angry with you, but the speaker *does* want to hear that fighting spirit.)

3. **(3)** *Application/Poetry.* The title of the poem and the two lines repeated throughout the poem (see answer to question 1), affirm the expression of personal strength in the face of defeat and death. None of the images or statements in the poem support the other choices.

## Lesson 5

1. **(5)** *Analysis/Poetry.* All the images in lines 3-6 suggest poverty (stairs with tacks, splinters, "boards torn up/And places with no carpet on the floor—"). The single word line, "Bare," sums up the effect of these lines. (2) and (3) are therefore not true. Since it is the climax of a series of images of poverty, it does not make those images seem exaggerated (1), but makes them more convincing. Nothing in line 7 suggests the speaker's struggle is almost over (4); the images all suggest the opposite.

2. **(1)** *Analysis/Poetry.* Most of the images in the poem are of a dark stair that requires a long, hard climb to get up and which is (see answer to question 1) dirty and poor; the image of a crystal stair contrasts with this central image of a long, hard struggle. There is no mention in the poem of a reward in heaven (2) or a religious faith (4). The speaker in no way suggests that her present, past, or future are different from each other—all are the same hard

struggle; so (3), is wrong. The whole point of the poem contradicts (5); she wants her son to know he will face the same struggle.

3. **(2)** *Analysis/Poetry.* You may want to figure out the answer to the question by eliminating the choices that do not seem to characterize the speaker. Given her emphasis on life as a long, hard struggle, she does not seem optimistic (5), and given her emphasis on never giving up, she does not seem defeated (3). She is giving sympathetic and supportive advice to her son, so she is not demanding or domineering (4), and since she tries to help him face life by giving him many examples from her experience, she does not seem impatient or irritable (1).

## Lesson 6

1. **(4)** *Analysis/Poetry.* The b-sounds are used to emphasize images describing the cruelty of trapping the mother fox: "forbear the bitter blow" and "blood." The fox is described as it is trapped, not as it escapes the trap (5). Neither the pain of the mother fox giving birth or raising her cubs (3) nor the mechanism of fox traps (2) are described in the second stanza. The dangers of foxhunting (1) would concern the risks faced by men who hunt foxes with guns and packs of hunting dogs.

2. **(3)** *Analysis/Poetry.* The first line, "Speak gently, Spring, and make no sudden sound," expresses a desire for nature to be gentle with the "New-born foxes squirming on the ground" (line 3). The s-sounds go along with the literal expression of this desire for peace and quiet ("make no sudden sound") that will be protective of these helpless animals. Since the speaker is concerned for their safety, he is not mainly happy for the little foxes (1), and certainly he is not afraid of them (2). Nothing supports (4) and (5).

3. **(4)** *Analysis/Poetry.* The literal meaning of the words quoted show that the speaker sees the little foxes as weak, frightened, and helpless. The last stanza describes them as unprotected against pain, rain, and the "rampant hurricane" of the windy month of March. As he does repeatedly in the poem, the speaker asks nature to be gentle ("Step softly") with the little foxes. Though the situation makes him sad, his main feeling is pity, not depression (1). The other choices have no support.

# Chapter 5: Commentary on the Arts

## Lesson 1

1. **(2)** *Literal Comprehension/Commentary on the Arts.* The author states that "no one connected with 'The Game'... seems to have a clue about how a movie is put together." The film is "hopelessly amateurish in the writing, the direction and... the performances." Since amateurish performances are poor acting, (1) is incorrect. (3) is only half-right. The original idea was "clever," but the resulting story is "witlessly composed." It is funny at times by accident, not from cleverness. Since the author makes the point that one first-time filmmaker (former ad executive Curtis Brown) has *not* been particularly successful, (4) is not supported. The critic says nothing about David Dinkins, so (5) is incorrect.

2. **(3)** *Literal Comprehension/Commentary on the Arts.* Both sentences in the second paragraph build the author's main idea, his opinion that the movie is weak. The first sentence presents what the movie might have been but fails to be, and the second sentence tells why the movie fails. The plot is summarized in the first paragraph, so (1) is incorrect. Nowhere in the second paragraph—or anywhere in the article—does the author give specific examples of how the movie is funny, so (2) is incorrect. The author gives background on the filmmaker, but that is in the third paragraph, so (4) is incorrect. The setting, New York, is described in the first paragraph, not the second one, so (5) is incorrect.

3. **(3)** *Analysis/Commentary on the Arts.* The critic's main opinion is that the film is poorly made, and one of the details supporting this opinion is stated in lines 18-20—that the "film dawdles over unnecessary details and skimps on the important ones" so "that it brings laughs in the wrong places...." The other choices restate details which are in fact in the excerpt, but they neither support nor contradict the author's main opinion.

## Lesson 2

1. **(2)** *Inferential Comprehension/Commentary on the Arts.* The critic refers to people who "always want music to have a meaning" as "[simple]-minded souls." From this negative [comment, y]ou can infer that the author [is not, or] leaning, against those peo[ple. (1) is incorre]ct because it states the [opposite of what is] true. He is *with* those [people who believ]e that music does not always have concrete meaning; he is not biased against them. (1) and (4) are incorrect because they are too general. He describes the attitude of "one timid lady" toward music as wrong and refers to people like her as "simple-minded," but he isn't necessarily biased against all timid people or all simple-minded ones. (3) is wrong because it twists the critic's words. He points out that the "timid lady" is wrong to blame herself for being unable to "connect" *music* with *concrete meaning.* He does *not* say anything about *people* who can't connect with *music.*

2. **(3)** *Inferential Comprehension/Commentary on the Arts.* A commentary that is entirely objective would consist only of facts that can be proven. By beginning with the words "My own belief..." the critic admits that his is only one of several possible opinions. (1), (2), (4) and (5) describe objective portions of the article that the critic uses to support his opinion. (How musical commentators, musicians, and others view music is factual information that can be collected through interviews, questionnaires, and so forth. An author could write an objective commentary that simply summarizes what commentators, musicians, and others think about music.) Therefore, these four choices are incorrect because they describe the opinions of others, but do *not* reveal that the critic offers his own opinion throughout the article.

3. **(5)** *Inferential Comprehension/Commentary on the Arts.* The topic of this article is the meaning of music. Each paragraph supports the idea that *music's meaning cannot necessarily be put into words.* In the first paragraph, the critic states that there is meaning, but that you cannot "state in so many words what the meaning is." In the second paragraph, the critic explains his viewpoint with examples. He points out how wrong commentators and music lovers are to assume that music's meaning is connected with definite words and ideas. In the third paragraph, the critic summarizes and emphasizes his opinion by ending with the view of some musicians. According to the critic, musicians sometimes believe that "no appropriate word can be found" to express the meaning of any piece of music. (1), (2), (3), and (4) are all contradicted by the commentary. The critic states that *all music has certain meaning,* but that the meaning can not necessarily be summed up in words. He suggests that people like the "timid lady" who can't use words are *wrong* to worry that something is lacking in their appreciation.

## Lesson 3:

1. **(3)** *Application/Commentary on the Arts.* On one hand, the critic praises the author's "brilliant reconstruction of his experiences" during World War II. On the other hand, the critic faults the author for the way he unravels the mystery through a "series of take-it-on-faith implausible events." In other words, he likes the war story because it is realistic, but dislikes the mystery because it is hard to believe. Therefore, he would probably enjoy a TV mystery that is set during war time and believable, a show best described by (3). (1), (2), (4), and (5) are incorrect because they all describe stories that are hard to believe. The critic would probably object to the unlikely coincidences through which the woman marries her father's murderer, the poor boy grows rich, the time traveler falls in love with his great-grandmother, and the twin sisters marry twin brothers.

2. **(2)** *Application/Commentary on the Arts.* The critic praises the author for writing about something he understood well from personal experience  war: "The author... was a Royal Marine Commando officer... and his brilliant reconstruction of his experiences illuminates and authenticates the war sequences." In another situation, a class on writing, the critic would probably convey the same view: it is good to write about things that you know well. (1) is not the best choice because it does not go far enough. The critic points out that stories with an air of mystery can be weak and unintriguing if the mystery is not believable. Therefore, if he were a writing teacher, he might suggest writing *plausible* mysteries that intrigue the audience. Likewise, (3) and (4) are not the best choices because they each leave out something important. The critic would probably advise writing about war or about rich people *only if the writer really knows about war or the rich.* (5) is incorrect because it contradicts one of the ideas the critic expresses in the article. He *criticizes* the author for the way he "trips over his own feet in unraveling a complicated and mind-boggling series of... events." Therefore, the critic is not likely to advise students to make their writing complicated and mind-boggling.

3. **(3)** *Application/Commentary on the Arts.* Four-letter words are obscenities. The critic is saying that the author uses obscenities throughout the story—sometimes for no good reason. The critic is implying that the author should use better judgment in deciding when to use obscenities. You don't know the critic's views on obscenity in other books, but it is a safe bet that he would have same view against unnecessary obscene language in them. (1) and (2) are incorrect because they are statements of the author's *strengths*, while the critic's statement about obscenities is designed to reveal one of the author's *weaknesses*. (4) is incorrect because it is based on a misunderstanding of the critic's remark. The critic is objecting to excessive use of "four-letter" words because they are obscene, not because they are short or simple. (5) is incorrect because it is not supported by the critic's statement about four-letter words—or anywhere else in the article, for that matter. Nowhere does the critic suggest that readers lose sympathy for soldiers who curse—just that the cursing is not always "called for" in this novel.

## Lesson 4

1. **(2)** *Analysis/Commentary on the Arts.* The author is talking to typical movie-goers like you and me. She uses the sort of language that the average viewer can understand. You don't have to be a filmmaker or scientist to understand general descriptions like the following: "large, lavish and absolutely sincere," "lovable," "nuttiness," "lots of electronic gadgetry," "scientific gibberish," and "his technical expertise leaves much to be desired." If the author were addressing scientists or filmmakers, she would probably to give specific examples using the special language of these experts. However, she does not use such specialized language, so (1), (4), and (5) are incorrect. The author refers to the "20-year-old hit" in the first line and compares the new movie repeatedly with the old *Star Trek* show. Since the show was originally on TV before today's teenagers were born, the review is probably *not* intended primarily for people under 20. There are *some* people under 20 who watch re-runs of the *Star Trek* and can therefore understand those references to the original TV show, but (3) is not the best answer.

2. **(4)** *Analysis/Commentary on the Arts.* The author gives her opinion of the movie in the beginning. In the first paragraph, she says that: it is "large, lavish, absolutely sincere..." created by minds that must be beginning "to play strange tricks." In the next paragraph she states her main opinion, that "it isn't the rationality of the *Star Trek* series that has made it loveable. It's the nuttiness, which is in extremely good supply this time" (lines 6-7). In most of

the rest of the excerpt, the author supports her opinion with examples and explanations. She explains the film's sincerity by summarizing the save-the-whales plot. She gives example of the film's "nuttiness," with talk about Klingons one minute, talk about whales and parking spots in San Francisco the next. Then, in the final sentences, she summarizes the opinion stated at the outset: there is "levity" [comedy or humor] in this "sincere" film which keeps alive the "durable" Star Trek mystique. None of the other choices follow this structure and are therefore incorrect.

3. **(2)** *Inferential Comprehension/Commentary on the Arts.* The author states that "it isn't the rationality of the *Star Trek* series that has made it lovable. It's the nuttiness..." In other words, the *series* is enjoyable because of its craziness. She goes on to state that "nuttiness is in extremely good supply" in this movie. Putting these details together, you can infer that the author likes the movie, too, because of its craziness. The author does state that "it begins to look as if this film may remain... impenetrable" [impossible to get into or understand]. However, "lo and behold," the movie quickly becomes comprehensible and lively when its story turns to whales. Therefore, (1) is incorrect. (3) and (4) are incorrect because they are contradicted by the author. Although the characters speak "scientific gibberish" at the beginning, the author finds the movie as a whole quite meaningful ("absolutely sincere"). She does not consider the movie to be expert, since he states that the director's "technical expertise leaves much to be desired." Nowhere does she call the movie frightening , so (5) is incorrect.

# Answer Key Practice Items

1. **(4)** *Inferential Comprehension/Nonfiction* The author explains Kelly's lack of "any sense of fitness" through a series of examples. In each example, the author implies that Kelly is exhibiting abnormal behavior for a dog. For instance, Kelly chases swans instead of playing with the other dogs (lines 11-13); he refuses to swim with a dog-paddle stroke as other dogs do (lines 15-20); and he even ignores the kinds of things that most dogs like to chew on (lines 35-41). (1) is wrong because the passage does not state that Kelly is badly out of shape; on the contrary, he is capable of attempting a complicated swimming stroke. In the same way, there is no evidence in the passage that Kelly gets into fights (2); he avoids other dogs and will not nip at their heels. (3) and (4) name examples of his unfit behavior but do not summarize their general meaning.

2. **(3)** *Literal Comprehension/Nonfiction.* The author says Kelly growls at the suede brush "just to show" her. This refers back to her statement in the first sentence of the passage that she "never met a dog that didn't have it in for [her]." She is not trying to show that dogs like leather (1), or are always hungry (2), for neither of these ideas is discussed in the passage. There is no evidence that Kelly is mistreated (4) or sad (5).

3. **(2)** *Inferential Comprehension/Nonfiction.* The author clearly states that Kelly will never catch a swan (lines 13-14), so you can eliminate (3). The statement "he always sinks" (lines 19-20) implies that rescuing Kelly from the millpond is a regular event. In other words, Kelly keeps trying, with the same result every time. Apparently, he is not a dog who learns from his mistakes (2). While the author implies in lines 8-11 that Kelly does not spend much time in the company of other dogs, (1) is not related to Kelly's experiences at the millpond.

4. **(5)** *Analysis/Nonfiction.* Although Kelly's actions might be annoying or embarrassing, the author writes about them in an amusing way. You can tell from the way she makes him seem human. For example, "he has to show off," (line 17); "he simply lost his head" (line 31); and he

plans to "get even" (lines 35-37). She doesn't take her dog's unusual behavior seriously enough to be angry (1), bitter (2), or resentful (4). Instead of being sad about Kelly's inability to learn from his experiences (3), she laughs at him in a good-natured way.

5. **(1)** *Literal Comprehension/Nonfiction.* In lines 4-7, the author states that the truck is decorated with a small piece of turquoise and sage added for long trips (line 11). These additions are not a lot, but they are more than none at all (4). The truck still looks like any other truck, not a ranch (3) or a home (5). Nothing supports (2).

6. **(2)** *Inferential Comprehension/Nonfiction.* The author states that Coke High came with his name (line 21) and the Dodge came with its name (line 39-40). Eliminate (1) because Coke High is most likely a cowboy name. (3) is wrong because the author does not know if they are named after men. While Coke High is an unusual name, Dodge is not, so (4) cannot be correct. (5) is wrong because the author states in lines 28-29 that Coke High had an owner, while he is the owner of the truck.

7. **(4)** *Inferential Comprehension/Nonfiction.* Knowing how Coke High got his name would "spoil" what he calls "the spirit of his inquiry" (line 30). In other words, that would take the fun out of the mystery. Since the author has spent time thinking about the horse's name, (1) cannot be correct. (2) is wrong because the reason is not that the owners wouldn't tell him; he states that he did not ask. (3) and (5) are not supported by information in the passage.

8. **(4)** *Application/Nonfiction.* Since the author does not cover his truck with a lot of decoration, and says that he likes his truck to look like all the other trucks, you can conclude that he would leave his motorcycle the way it was (4). Because he does not care for decoration, he would not repaint it (2) or add chrome (3). Since he did not name his truck, he probably would not name his motorcycle, so (1) is wrong. Eliminate (5) because the author would be unlikely to join a motorcycle club because of his preference for privacy (lines 15-16).

9. **(2)** *Analysis/Nonfiction.* The paragraphs about Coke High and the other horses on the ranch provide an example of the author's attitude toward names. He includes the names on purpose, so (1) cannot be correct. While the author does refer to whites, this does not explain why he includes a discussion of horses while talking about his truck, so (3) is wrong. (4) is not a good choice because there is no evidence that he knows more about horses than he does about trucks. Finally, if his purpose had been to interest readers in horses, he would have eliminated nearly all the material about trucks. Therefore, eliminate (5).

10. **(3)** *Literal Comprehension/Fiction.* Gruber explains the reason for the eviction by saying, "If the tenants don't take care they have to go. You don't take care and you fight with my janitor, so you have to go" (lines 20-23). So Gruber believes that Kessler doesn't behave the way a good tenant should. Kessler states that he pays his rent (lines 11-12), so that cannot be the reason for the eviction. Therefore, (1) is wrong. The building is not being torn down, so eliminate (2). Gruber tells Kessler that the problem is "not personal" (lines-18-19), which tells you that (4) is wrong. (5) is wrong because there is no evidence of anti-semitism on Gruber's part.

11. **(1)** *Inferential Comprehension/Fiction.* By his words and actions, Gruber shows his sympathy with Kessler's situation. At first, he seems genuinely uncomfortable about discussing the eviction with Kessler (lines 1-2 and 16-18). Gruber then offers to let Kessler stay the night without fear of trouble (lines 23-24). He tries to find an alternative for Kessler and thinks of trying to place him in a public home, even though he has no legal responsibility for Kessler (lines 35-38). In short, Gruber feels that he can no longer allow the man to stay, but he does everything possible to make leaving easy for Kessler. There is no evidence for the other choices.

12. **(3)** *Inferential Comprehension/Fiction.* Ignace's nervousness in this passage is related to his report that he hasn't seen Kessler leave the apartment, nor has he seen any movement within the apartment. He is afraid to voice his fear about why there is no movement. Kessler had said that he would die before leaving the apartment (lines 27-28), which was apparently the last thing Ignace heard

him say. There is no evidence for the other choices.

13. **(5)** *Application/Fiction.* In the passage, Kessler is a tenant who is being evicted by his landlord. If Gruber were an employer, Kessler's position would be most like that of an employee who is being fired. When confronted by Gruber, Kessler responds by saying, "Are you a Hitler or a Jew?" (line 14). Kessler is saying, "How can you persecute me when we have a common background?" Only (5) reflects the idea of being sent away. Since Kessler is not a cooperative tenant, (1) and (3) cannot be correct.

14. **(1)** *Literal Comprehension/Fiction.* In lines 9-11, the author says that Hetty "did not exist" for her children because "they were all respectable people... And Hetty was not respectable." There is no mention of any inheritance (2) or of how Hetty treated her children (3). (4) and (5) are wrong because Hetty's children feel embarrassment, not blame or resentment.

15. **(2)** *Literal Comprehension/Fiction.* The phrase "dislocation from the normal" is explained by the example of Hetty's visit to the train station. This is an odd way to act (2). Her family fears that this foreshadows even more peculiar future behavior, lines 41-44. Eliminate (3) because this is Hetty's defense for her odd way of behaving. There is no support in the passage for the other choices.

16. **(5)** *Analysis/Fiction.* Among the details that indicate Hetty's strong-mindedness are her insistence on visiting the train station despite her husband's teasing (line 34) and her free response to those who ridiculed her in public (lines 50-54). Her oddness is seen in her children's fears about her behavior becoming stranger (lines 41-44); in the author's description of her state as "dislocation from the normal" (line 22); and in the author's description of her desire to visit railway stations (lines 23-34). Hetty is not confused or afraid, so eliminate (1). Fred, not Hetty, is steady and hardworking, so (2) is wrong. Although Hetty is odd, that does not mean that she is crazy (3). (4) is wrong for two reasons. First, we are told that in "her prime" she was "handsome." Second, even though her children "were fearful that her gypsy blood might show itself in worse ways than haunting stations," nothing suggests that she is a frightening person.

17. **(4)** *Application/Fiction.* The author states that Hetty's visits to the railway stations "were for her a drug, like other people's drinking or gambling" (lines 31-34). This suggests that she is addicted to these visits, as a smoker is to cigarettes. None of the other choices express this addiction, only feelings of like or dislike that may be positive or negative.

18. **(2)** *Analysis/Fiction.* Hetty's shout that she was "none the worse for that" (lines 53-54) shows her pride at having gypsy blood. Thus, (1) cannot be correct. Eliminate (3) because standing up for herself does not mean that she is crazy. Since her husband was proud of her independence (lines 38-41), he would not have been wrong about her (4). Her shout is directed at the people who criticize her, not her children, so eliminate (5).

19. **(4)** *Inferential Comprehension/Drama.* Even before Willy voices his concern in line 27, there are clues that he is losing control. He is irritated at only slight questioning (lines 8-9), for example. He repeats, "I couldn't make it" (lines 13-14). He wonders if he is having a reaction to coffee (line 19). He tells Linda that he was unable to control the car (lines 21-23). When he places the blame on himself rather than on the car (line 27), Willy admits that he has been losing his concentration. All these signs point to someone who is losing control of his life. Willy's own words show that (1) and (2) are wrong. There is no mention of a physical illness (3). Even though Linda does not understand at first, Willy keeps explaining until she does grasp the problem (lines 37-39), so (5) is wrong.

20. **(3)** *Inferential Comprehension/Drama.* In lines 4-5, Linda keeps asking Willy what has happened to bring him home. She obviously had not expected him. In response to her question on lines 15-16, Willy tells Linda that he did not get very far before he had to return home. Willy is early, not late, so eliminate (1). (2) is not correct because Linda is clearly more worried about him than about the car. There is no mention of drinking (4) or a previous argument (5).

21. **(3)** *Analysis/Drama.* Linda reacts with concern and understanding to Willy's problem. She worries that he has had an accident (line 7) and that he is ill (line 10), because he looks "terrible" (line 16). She tries to find an easy explanation for his problems (lines 24-26). Her desire to support Willy is also indicated by the stage directions: she speaks "very carefully, delicately" (line 15) and "helpfully" (line 24). She is not enthusiastic (1), foolish (2), irritable (4), or irresponsible (5).

22. **(3)** *Analysis/Drama.* The dashes break up the sentence to show that Willy is hesitating because he is confused about what is happening to him. There is no indication that he has a speech problem (1) or that he had a stroke (2). Since Linda tries to help Willy express himself, eliminate (4). There is no connection between the dashes and the Florida vacation (5).

23. **(3)** *Literal Comprehension/Drama.* Although the children first seem to be reporting that they are getting a warm welcome from the residents in the new community, their sarcasm becomes clear at the end of the passage when they talk about threats and hatred. The true intent of the "Welcoming Committee" is clear in lines 52-54 when Ruth explains that the committee is trying to buy back the family's house. Therefore, the situation is the opposite of (1). At this point the family is not making a decision about moving, as suggested in (2) and (5). They are not reacting to actual threats (4), but to the hypocritical way they are being treated.

24. **(4)** *Analysis/Drama.* The stage directions make heavy use of words that emphasize how the family teases Mama about the hypocrisy of the Welcoming Committee. These words include "teasingly" (line 7), "saucily" (line 9), "devilishly" (line 16), and "mockingly" (line 34). These words show that the children's words cannot be taken at face value. Even Mama's recognition that they are not telling the truth appears in a stage direction (line 19). Although the situation is serious (1), the stage directions suggest mockery. The directions also indicate that the family is wise to what is happening, so reject (3). There is no evidence for the other choices.

25. **(2)** *Inferential Comprehension/Drama.* Mama is expressing her feelings about the racial prejudice her family encounters. Her prayer-like exclamations show her sadness and distress. The stage directions (lines 19 and 42) show that she understands what is going on, and that has caused her to feel sad, not thankful (3). She agrees with the way her children acted, so she cannot be angry at them (5) or be setting an example (1). She cannot be praying for physical protection (4), because Beneatha reassures her that they have not been threatened physically.

26. **(3)** *Application/Drama.* Since everyone but Mama is speaking facetiously, the "welcome" from the Clybourne Park Improvement Association becomes clear: A black family is not welcome in the neighborhood. Of the choices given, only the possibility of a halfway house for recovering drug abusers would depart from the norm. That group would probably receive a similar "welcome."

27. **(3)** *Inferential Comprehension/Poetry.* Line 2 explains that the child is "A cabinet-maker's son," so (2) cannot be correct. On line 15, the cabinetmaker is identified as "Papa," which tells you that the answer is (3). The speaker's father—not the speaker—was "alone and wild," so eliminate (1). There is no mention of the speaker's son or grandfather, so (4) and (5) are wrong.

28. **(5)** *Inferential Comprehension/Poetry.* In the lines 3-6, the speaker explains that his father turned away from his own father's profession, cabinetmaking. On line 9, you find out that he turned to music. The son has followed in his father's footsteps, for he is a musician, too (lines 9, 19-20). You do not know if the son left home, so (1) cannot be correct. Eliminate (2), (3), (4) as well, for there is no evidence in the passage about these issues.

29. **(5)** *Literal Comprehension/Poetry.* The son says that he inherited his father's love of music (line 9), stories of the road (line 10), freedom to make his own decisions (line 11), and discipline (line 14). The only "gift" the speaker does not mention is (5), the love of working with wood.

30. **(5)** *Analysis/Poetry.* Just before line 23, the speaker says "My life has been a poor attempt/ To imitate the man" (lines 21-22). The phrase is not a statement of what the speaker has achieved (1) or what he expects in terms of money (4). The phrase "living legacy" suggests that he admires rather than resents his father, so eliminate (2). Even though he may not be as good as his father, there is no suggestion that he considers himself a complete failure (3).

31. **(1)** *Literal Comprehension/Poetry.* The past is full of "shame" (line 9) and "pain" (line 11), which suggests injustices. This idea is reinforced in the first two stanzas, as the speaker describes history's "bitter, twisted lies" (line 2). Eliminate (2) because it refers to the speaker ("I'm a black ocean"), not to history. The history is dramatic, filled with "terror and fear" (line 15), so (3) is wrong. The history can-

not be a source of pride (4) because it is full of "bitter, twisted lies," so eliminate (5) as well.

32. **(2)** *Literal Comprehension/Poetry.* The speaker states that she is the "dream and the hope of the slave" (line 20). She also refers to herself as being black on line 13. Thus, she represents the future of the black race, not a group of historians (1), imagination (3), or abused women (4). (5) is an image of movement, not what she actually represents.

33. **(2)** *Application/Poetry.* The main idea of the poem is that blacks are rising up and establishing themselves despite the obstacles of the past. They are overcoming prejudice, cruelty, and hatred. An appropriate title would be one that focuses positively on this idea. The dark nights are in the past (1), and the speaker appears to have no intention of giving up. (3). Although the speaker may feel that history should be rewritten (4), that is not what she is talking about. Nor is that past at all glorious (5).

34. **(3)** *Analysis/Poetry.* "Daybreak" stands for a new and better way of living. It is the opposite of the "nights of terror and fear" (line 15) which are part of "history's shame" (5). The poet uses the word as a metaphor, a comparison, not as a reference to the dawn of an actual day (1), (2) and (4).

35. **(5)** *Analysis/Poetry.* The repetition emphasizes the idea of rising or overcoming again and again. The lack of commas between the words adds to the suggestion of a continuous and building movement. Although three may be a lucky number (1), the speaker is not depending on luck to achieve her goal. That goal is practical, not religious (3). There is no support in the structure or content of the poem for (2) or (3).

36. **(3)** *Literal Comprehension/Commentary.* The reviewer states that di Suvero arranged the leasing and financing (lines 17-22). The fact that he operated the crane (1) is less important. Although he may have donated a sculpture (2), supplied the steel (4), or planned future shows (5), none of these are mentioned in the review.

37. **(5)** *Literal Comprehension/Commentary.* The reviewer follows his statement that the "park is a realization of a dream" (line 26) with an explanation. In addition to helping other sculptors, Di Suvero wanted to "create an active role for sculpture in

the community" (lines 29-30). The out-door sculpture allows the public to see art all year round (lines 7-9). Even the building of it involved young people from the community (lines 33-35). New York did not sell the land for the park, so (1) is wrong. While sculpture competitions may be held in the future (2), that was not the purpose for building the park. The only thing Socrates (a long-dead Greek philosopher) had to do with the park (3) was to inspire the creator's with his writings about truth. (4) has no support in the passage.

38. **(5)** *Inferential Comprehension/ Commentary.* The author uses the word "raw" immediately after he mentions clearing and landscaping the grounds and before his comment that "there is no sense yet of a clear guiding vision" (lines 22-23). Thus, the context of "raw" is the author's concern that something about the way the park looks suggests there is room for improvement. He develops his concern in lines 41-46. The passage offers no evidence for the other choices.

39. **(2)** *Analysis/Commentary.* The reviewer's only negative comment about the Socrates Sculpture Park is that it lacks an organization in the way it has been landscaped and how the first show is displayed (lines 41-45). What the park needs, he feels, is better planning, "the sense of a touch, clearly defined guiding vision" (lines 47-48). There is no suggestion that an outdoor park can be dangerous (1), or that the entire plan is poor (4). He is not warning that the park may decay (3), only that it needs a firm controlling vision. (4) cannot be correct because what the author appreciates the most about this park is the chance it will give people to study sculpture up close (lines 55-60).

40. **(1)** *Application/Commentary.* What the reviewer appreciates the most about the Socrates Sculpture Park is the opportunity it provides for people to study sculpture in person. It is in this sense that the park has both awakened and realized dreams. If the reviewer is attracted by the interaction between the individual and the subject matter, then it would be reasonable to assume that he would appreciate the chance for people to interact with science, as provided in a "hands-on" science museum, (1). None of the other choices allows people the chance to interact with material in the same personal way.

41. **(3)** *Inferential Comprehension/ Commentary.* The critic gives a generally favorable review of "Murder, She Wrote," noting how the show can "flirt with the fact of violence" (line 37) and that it is "played... with perhaps a hint of a wink" (lines 42-43). he also calls it "good entertainment, the electronic equivalent of a good read" (line 57). This means that the show is not great art, as suggested by (5). What is fun cannot be called dull (2) or not worth watching (4). There is no suggestion that the viewer has to concentrate to enjoy the show (1).

42. **(1)** *Literal Comprehension/Commentary.* The critic contrasts the "cerebral" style of "Murder, She Wrote" with the physical action of "screeching tires and shootouts" of the "standard police show" (lines 3-6). Therefore, "cerebral" must mean "thoughtful" because the closest opposite to "thoughtful" is (1), "physical." Since the cerebral approach to solving mysteries is thoughtful, (2) cannot be the opposite of "cerebral." (3), (4), and (5) describe Jessica Fletcher, not the style of her mystery show.

43. **(4)** *Literal Comprehension/Commentary* Miss Marple is described as "terribly proper and sedate" (lines 22-23). Jessica Fletcher, on the other hand, is "a no-nonsense, practical woman" (line 25-26). This shows that Jessica Fletcher is more down-to-earth than Miss Marple, (4). (2), (3), and (5) do not fit these descriptions. Neither detective is violent, so (1) cannot be correct.

44. **(1)** *Analysis/Commentary.* The reviewer obviously finds the episode entertaining (line 56) but uses several phrases to indicate that it was predictable. He refers to the "local rednecks" (line 44), a predictable set of characters. He also says that the "jailed suspect... was, of course, innocent" (lines 51-52). The phrase "of course" shows that the reviewer knew the outcome was predictable all along. Because of the dependable nature of the show, the reviewer would not find it original (3). While Jessica may have found the town terrifying, there is no suggestion that the viewer will be terrified by the show, so reject (2). The reviewer's account of the plot sounds believable (although slightly comical), so reject (4). It is also clear and not at all disturbing so (5) is wrong.

45. **(4)** *Application/Commentary.* The reviewer approves of "Murder, She Wrote" in clear opposition to "action" shows that rely on car chases and gunfights. Of the choices given, (4), the disaster movie comes closest to the "action" shows that the reviewer dislikes. Since the reviewer enjoys complicated mysteries, he would probably enjoy watching quiz shows (1) and current events shows (5) as well, making these poor choices. Since he clearly put a high value on entertainment, he would like the comedy special (2) and the live jazz performance (3).

# Answer Key Practice Test

1. **(4)** *Inferential Comprehension/Fiction.* The boy wants to win his mother's affection. To do so, he imitates as many of the father's habits as he can, one of which is smoking a pipe. His main reason is not to start smoking (1); the boy is only pretending to smoke. That he thinks smoking is attractive (2) is mentioned only as a comment, not as the primary reason for stealing the pipes. The boy does not destroy the pipes (3), nor does he want to appear grown up to his father (5).

2. **(2)** *Literal Comprehension/Fiction.* In lines 24-26, the boy states that he is waiting to continue a fight. He believes that when he is grown up he can break his father's hold on his mother by marrying her. That is when the real fight would begin again. He tells his mother he will marry her now; he does not wait to do this (3). The boy does not consider the possibility of his father's death (1). The other two choices are not related to the boy's decision to wait.

3. **(2)** *Inferential Comprehension/Fiction.* The boy is not indifferent toward his father, nor does she fear him, as illustrated by his proposal to his mother in his father's presence (lines 32-35). He admires his father's habit of smoking (lines 11-13) but also states that all of his father's characteristics are less attractive than his own (lines 5-6). He does not say that he hates his father; rather, his words and especially his actions indicate that he resents his father's influence over his mother, imagines that his mother resents it as well (lines 38-41), and looks for an opportunity to secure that influential place for himself.

4. **(5)** *Analysis/Fiction.* Telling the story from the child's point of view highlights for the reader the child's limited understanding. This immaturity leads to the child's naive conclusions and outbursts, which are the source of the humor. The point of view does not affect the ease of reading (1) or the descriptions (3). No lesson for parents on how to handle children (2) is evident. If the child was exceptionally intelligent, he would understand his situation better, so (4) is not a good choice.

5. **(3)** *Inferential Comprehension/Drama.* Tevye states that he has had to take his horse to get a new shoe. The stage directions show him as having just pulled his cart to the house. The combination of the two ideas allows us to infer that he has to do the work his horse would normally be doing. He is not actually a horse (1), and his attitude suggests that he would not want to be one (2). The other two choices may be true, but they do not explain what Tevye means.

6. **(5)** *Literal Comprehension/Drama.* Tevye says that he is starving (line 28) and that God made many poor people. The first line tells us that Tevye has a home so (1) is wrong.The sickness referred to in line 26 is not an illness, but is a colorful way of saying how Tevye is thinking about Golde (2). A man who talks to God must believe in Him at least a bit (4), although he doesn't believe that conditions will improve soon (3).

7. **(1)** *Analysis/Drama.* Tevye's comments are laced with humor. For example, he tells God that he has been "blessed" with having to provide for five daughters and having to live in poverty (lines 8-9). He speaks about God's mischief-making in causing Tevye's horse to lose its shoe; he explains the same situation to Golde by saying that the horse has accepted the blacksmith's invitation for Sabbath dinner (lines 18-19). He is critical about his situation in life, as well as other things, but he accepts what goes wrong instead of giving up (3). The passage does not give any evidence for (4) or (5).

8. **(2)** *Analysis/Drama.* The song is about what Tevye would do if he had a lot of money. As a result, the song does not explain how Tevye lives as a poor person (3), nor does it compare him to other poor people (5). The song does not mention Golde (1). The song clearly does not change the setting (4).

9. **(5)** *Application/Drama.* Throughout the passage, Tevye has appealed to God in a humorous manner about the difficulty of his life. It is reasonable to assume that Tevye would continue to act this way if he had a problem with Golde. None of the other choices are supported by the way Tevye acts in the passage.

10. **(3)** *Inferential Comprehension/Nonfiction.* In these lines, the father defines a fool as someone who keeps "looking for something that is never there." Then, after the shell game, the father states his fear that his son will spend all his life "lookin' for a pea that ain't there" (line 31). The father implies that his son fits the definition he himself has helped to create. Mr. Jimmy is the con man who first showed the narrator the shell game (1), and he is shown to be a sharp person. The father is not talking about an uneducated person (4), only one who acts foolishly. In the same way, he is not talking about New Yorkers (5) or himself (2).

11. **(4)** *Inferential Comprehension/Nonfiction.* It is evident throughout the passage that the father is worried about his son as shown by his references to his son as a fool for looking for something that he can never have. On lines 2-6 we learn that the father has been trying to straighten out his son for a long time, but the young man doesn't listen to his father at all. The son will be leaving the streets of New York (lines 14-16). Line 18 explains that the son has been stealing. From these clues you can infer that the son is going to be sent to a reform school to straighten him out. There is no evidence about California (1), the army (2), or becoming a magician (5). Since the boy has been stealing and not listening to his father, it is very unlikely that he would be going off to college (3).

12. **(1)** *Application/Nonfiction.* The father's demonstration of the shell game shows that he believes that people should learn to take care of themselves, to see what is really happening rather than what appears to be happening. Since he has tried—without success—to teach his son to be mature and self-reliant, he would probably believe that people should work to support themselves rather than relying on welfare. This belief contradicts (2). There is no evidence in the passage for (3), (4), or (5).

13. **(5)** *Application/Nonfiction.* The father's basic message to his son is to be realistic about his expectations (lines 52-56). He expresses his hope that his son will take the initiative and change his ways (lines 16-20). This "help yourself" attitude is expressed in (5). If the father believed that success was just a matter of luck (2), he would not be trying to straighten out his son. He clearly is not using the shell game to emphasize the skills of gamblers (1), entertain his son (3), or show that people in general are dishonest (4); rather, he wants to show his son that he must set realistic goals.

14. **(3)** *Analysis/Nonfiction.* The son's attention suddenly switched after this phrase. Before that, he had been indifferent to what his father had to say. Clearly, the father had said something that caught his son's attention, in contrast to all the father's other attempts at communication. (1) and (2) refer to how the son avoids listening to his father, the opposite of what the question asks. (4) and (5) have nothing to do with how the boy is paying attention.

15. **(2)** *Literal Comprehension/Commentary.* The author states his opinion throughout the passage. In lines 20-21, for example, he says that "The Story of English" is "public television at its best." It is "a delight to the eye and ear" (lines 24-25) and "a triumph" (line 51). (1) is wrong because it refers to his opinion about another PBS program, a literacy campaign (lines 10-12). (3) is incorrect because it is what he says in lines 24-29 the program is *not*. There is no support for (4) or (5) in the passage.

16. **(2)** *Literal Comprehension/Commentary.* The author quotes the Carnegie Commission's directive that public television should provide a "fuller awareness of the wonder and vitality of the arts" (lines 54-55). In other words, public television was meant to show people that a rich, varied world of cultural experience awaits them. The other choices are not correct because they name specific ways in which public television tries to fulfill this directive.

17. **(3)** *Inferential Comprehension/ Commentary.* Robert MacNeil finds people who create rap music on the streets of Philadelphia. He calls these musicians "ghetto Homers" (lines 46-47) because they live in the slums and create legendary songs in the style of the ancient Greek poet Homer. This has nothing to do with baseball players (1), television personalities (2), or the series' co-authors (4). There is no support in the passage for (5).

18. **(1)** *Inferential Comprehension/ Commentary.* The author explains how the series taught him the historical development of Gullah (lines 33-38). It also changed his mind about rap music (lines 47-51). Before the show, the reviewer

thought that rap was "deficient in the merits of either music or speech" (lines 49-50). The show persuaded him that his opinion was wrong (lines 50-51). This statement is the opposite of (2). Instead of influencing the reviewer against public TV (4), the series seems to have strengthened his belief in its value. There is no evidence that the show encouraged him to become an historian (5), or to pursue any other field, for that matter. Likewise, here is no evidence for (3).

19. **(2)** *Application/Commentary.* The author values "The Story of English" for the way in which it enriches the viewer's cultural life (lines 52-56). As a result, he would most likely view a program about artists to be culturally enriching. He probably would not consider sports bloopers (1), musical variety shows (3), presidential addresses (4), or comedies (5) to be "cultural" in the same sense.

20. **(1)** *Literal Comprehension/Poetry.* In line 6, the speaker states "Oh, a girl, she'd not forget him." The rest of her description suggests the opposite of choices (2) and (5); he seems to be happy and unconcerned with what may happen tomorrow; so (2) is wrong. Despite her glowing description, the speaker makes it clear that her love is less than perfect (3) through her comments in the last line of each stanza. The reference to the flag (line 5) is a comparison to the joyous waving motion, not a suggestion of patriotic feeling (4).

21. **(2)** *Analysis/Poetry.* The last line of each stanza is a comical surprise in contrast to the loving sentiment of the next to the last line. Even though there is a hint of bitterness, this contrast is not serious enough to suggest tragedy (1) or to make the reader sad (3). The contrast also indicates a problem, not true love (4). The poem as a whole seems to be a private expression of the speaker's feelings, not an appeal to her lover (5).

22. **(4)** *Analysis/Poetry.* The line is a metaphor that compares the speaker's love to the child of a fairy-tale creature, a spirit of nature. He, like the wild animals, doesn't seem bound by human rules of behavior. The line is not supposed to be taken literally as talking about his mother (1) or where he grew up (2). There is no

suggestion of his attitude about nature (3), nor is there any evidence of shyness (5).

23. **(2)** *Application/Poetry.* The subject of love is serious, but the poet's approach is humorous. The subject of raising teenage children is also serious, but its frustrations and trials can be approached in a lighthearted manner. None of the other subjects could be treated comically.

24. **(4)** *Inferential Comprehension/Fiction.* The first paragraph describes the way the woman wakens on the train. The rest of the passage reveals that her husband is cold and motionless. The idea that he has died is reinforced by the way his hand feels like a dead thing (line 36). The woman is travelling with her husband, not meeting him (1), and her husband does not waken (2). There is no hint that the woman had anything to do with the man's death (3), and the way he is described in the last two paragraphs suggests something much more serious than illness (5).

25. **(5)** *Literal Comprehension/Fiction.* The first paragraph traces the woman's feelings as she awakens. At first she is stiff (line 1), but gradually she begins to feel "more hopeful" (line 13). When she is fully awake, her natural cheerfulness asserts itself: "It was always a struggle for her not to be cheerful in the morning" (lines 13-15). There is no suggestion of exhaustion (1), fear (3), or crankiness (4). Eliminate (2) because it describes the landscape, not the woman.

26. **(5)** *Inferential Comprehension/Fiction.* The woman is worried not because she is left alone (1) but because she suspects that her husband is dead. There are clues that the husband may have been ill for some time. The woman is described as continually struggling not to look cheerful in the morning (lines 13-15), as if she has had long practice looking serious for someone. Bringing her husband an early glass of milk (lines 21-23) implies that she supervises his diet and thus worries about his health. Nothing in the passage indicates the husband's job (3) or how long the couple has been married (4). The woman seems to be cheerful, but since nothing is said of the husband's temperament, eliminate (2).

27. **(2)** *Inferential Comprehension/Fiction.* The woman's concern for her husband's glass of milk (lines 21-23) suggests that she is used to taking care of him, watching over what he eats. When she looks at her watch (1), she is simply thinking about the time of day. Likewise, drawing up the shade (3) is just to help her see better. (4) and (5) refer to normal actions in waking someone, not special care.

28. **(4)** *Literal Comprehension/Nonfiction.* There are several places in the passage where Mrs. Chapin states her opinion that people don't appreciate the beauty around them. She notes that people ignore the plan to tear down the water tower, a landmark that appeals to her because of its historical value (lines 7-9). She also points out that people don't take the time to notice everyday beauty that they could see while walking (lines 24-26). "People's eyes are closed," she complains on lines 28-29. In talking about parks and museums, she concludes, "These things are in our hands and we don't use them" (lines 35-36). The passage does not mention that Mrs. Chapin has a fear of taking walks (1); on the contrary, she enjoys her walks very much. Although (3) may be true, it is not an example of how Mrs. Chapin feels about people. The same is true of (5). The visit to the Art Institute is an example of how people don't make time for art, not an of their inability to understand art. There is no evidence for (2) in the passage.

29. **(3)** *Inferential Comprehension/Nonfiction.* Mrs. Chapin states that the water tower should be kept because it was considered beautiful in its own time (lines 7-9). She contrasts the plan to tear down the historical water tower with the pride people in other countries feel toward their historical monuments. Other countries, she implies, know how to take care of things that represent their past. Eliminate (4) because it is directly contradicted by Mrs. Chapin's comment that it is wrong to live in the past (line 6). (2) is incorrect because she does not mention selling the water tower. She never discusses the beauty of buildings in other countries, so eliminate (1). There is no support for (5) in the passage.

30. **(3)** *Literal Comprehension/Nonfiction.* Mrs. Chapin defines "provocative" in the preceding sentence: "It refreshes your mind again" (lines 39-40). While she does indicate that the Art Institute is a good place to visit (2) and that it is ignored by many Chicago residents (4), she uses "provocative" to describe the way the Art Institute "refreshes your mind" (lines 39-40). She never discusses what paintings are displayed there, so eliminate (1). The length of the visit is not important, nor is it mentioned, so eliminate (5).

31. **(5)** *Analysis/Nonfiction.* The main idea of the passage is that people should appreciate the beauty around them, both in the everyday things of the present and the reminders of the past. That Mrs. Chapin has a geranium garden reveals her love for simple, everyday beauty. None of the other choices show how Mrs. Chapin lives according to her opinions. She never states that Chicago is the best place to live (1). That she was born in Chicago (2), was widowed (3), and had seen her children marry (4) has nothing to do with the question.

32. **(4)** *Literal Comprehension/Fiction.* The plans Jeff and his wife have to end their lives is clear from several references in the passage. First, the passage opens with the couple reminding each other to be brave and not "scairt" to do what they have planned (lines 1-5). Jeff considers death a lesser evil than facing what the future probably holds (lines 30-36). Lines 38-47 list each detail in their plan, as Jeff deliberately drowns them both in their car. The end of the passage makes choices (1) and (5) unlikely. (2) is wrong because the only future they plan for is death. Jeff and his wife lose their car (3), but more importantly, they lose their lives.

33. **(1)** *Inferential Comprehension/Fiction.* As he prepares for his death, Jeff recalls pleasures of the past. He remembers having been part of a "gay young crowd" that visited the Mardi Gras celebration in New Orleans (lines 15-22). He does not consider his past wicked, for "it did not make him sad" (line 22-23), so (4) is wrong. The other choices occur late in the passage, not early. Jeff fears the future late in the passage (lines 30-35), not early, so eliminate (2). The same is true of (3); his concern for his wife's disabilities and his decision (5) occur later in the passage.

34. **(4)** *Literal Comprehension/Fiction.* Jeff's present image of himself is stated in lines 30-31. Choices (1), (2), and (3) refer to Jeff and his friends when they were young. Jeff's wife is the one who is described as now being frail and blind (5).

35. **(5)** *Literal Comprehension/Fiction.* Only after Jeff compares his past and present does he begin to feel brave. The choices that deal with his youth and his time at Greenbriar are not connected to a mention of bravery. He felt brave (line 40) just before he began to drive into the river, not after the car hit the water (4).

36. **(2)** *Analysis/Poetry.* First, the use of quotation marks is a standard way of signalling a conversation. By enclosing each stanza in quotation marks, the poet creates the impression of more than one speaker. Second, stanzas one and three contain questions that are answered in stanzas two and four, underlining the idea of a conversation. The choices in (1) and (3) do not occur in the poem. (4) is a common poetic form and in no way says anything about the number of speakers. The conversation seems to take place in the bedroom (lines 1-2), not in the garden; but more important, the place does not indicate anything about the speakers.

37. **(4)** *Inferential Comprehension/Poetry.* The speaker recalls her children walking in the garden when they were younger. This memory helps her treasure the past and their love. The speaker states that the children are dead and buried in a foreign land (lines 16, 20) so (1), (3), and (5) are wrong. The speaker is looking to her memories rather than hoping to find ghosts, so eliminate (3).

38. **(2)** *Literal Comprehension/Poetry.* The first speaker asks twice why his partner is out of bed (lines 1-2, 15-16). He thinks that the two of them should close the doors and stay in bed, so eliminate (5). This shows that he doesn't understand why his partner is walking in the garden. On line 9 he says that "The sons we know were slain" so (1) cannot be correct. He is not indifferent (3); he just doesn't understand. (4) is wrong because there is no doubts that the children are dead.

39. **(3)** *Analysis/Poetry.* The comparison suggests the wife's sadness that her children died far from home. The image of the moth suggests the fluttering soul of a creature trying to find the place it can finally rest. The light at the door represents their home. Choices (1), (2), (4) and (5) are literal statements with no support in the poem.

40. **(1)** *Application/Poetry.* Other parents who have lost children in a war would probably understand the wish that at least the spirits of the children were near. For the one speaker, the fact that the children died in a foreign land makes the deaths more difficult to live with. There was no real parting; the parents were left to "only know them dead." The groups in the other choices would probably not be as emotionally moved.

41. **(1)** *Literal Comprehension/Commentary.* (1) identifies what is being reviewed, the playwright's name, the play's background, and the performance. (2) and (5) misinterpret the point of the review and confuse the play with a novel and an autobiography. Because Woodward plays the fictional Amanda, their performances cannot be compared (3). The reviewer is praising only one play, not condemning several, so eliminate (4).

42. **(2)** *Inferential Comprehension/Commentary.* The reviewer speaks from the point of view of the audience. He sees Tom's frustration and selfishness revealed through Williams' acting. This is the opposite of (1) and (3), as Williams' performance clarifies Tom's character. The selfishness is the character's, not the actor's, so eliminate (4). The reviewer has also made it clear in lines 29-32 that this is *not* a comic performance (5).

43. **(3)** *Analysis/Commentary.* The reviewer feels that the role of Amanda should be performed "with humor, gaiety, and finally, a tragic dimension" (lines 31-32). This view is supported by Tennessee Williams' view that "this stage portrait... was intended to be sympathetic" (lines 3-5). The reviewer uses the playwright's own words to support his opinion of the performance. Since he shows how the performance fulfills the playwright's intentions, (5) is wrong. The introduction is not a negative criticism (1) or a question (2). Finally, however informative the discussion is, it is not mainly a device to grab the reader's interest (4).

44. **(3)** *Analysis/Commentary.* The lines suggest that the role of Amanda is often poorly played, but the reviewer continues by describing how well Joanne Woodward has captured the essence of the character in her performance. Perhaps the reviewer's key thought in this regard is that Woodward has avoided "all the pitfalls of this sizable character" (lines 25-27). (1) and (2) do not address the idea of acting technique. (4) and (5) are not supported in the passage.

45. **(3)** *Application/Commentary.* The way the reviewer praises the performances of this cast suggests that he would expect to find the same level of fine acting if they appeared together in another play. He would thus not be bored (1) or annoyed (5). As the three actors are primarily dramatic performers, he would not expect to see a comedy (2). Seeing the same actors would not lead him to think the play was same as *The Glass Menagerie*, so eliminate (4).

1. **(2)** *Inferential Comprehension/Nonfiction.* Although Phin tries to seem cheerful at first, his worry about the bull is shown by his actions (lines 5-8), so (1) and (5) are wrong. There is no support for Phin's concern about a bill (3) or his sons (4).

2. **(3)** *Analysis/Nonfiction.* The sentence begins with an initial diagnosis but then is interrupted by dashes and phrases that show that the vet is questioning himself. The "and yet" (line 19) indicate a change of mind. This type of self-questioning is the mark of a good vet, not a nervous one (1). There is no hint about a cure (2). The statement is about what ails the bull, not the intensity of his illness (4). The vet's questioning may appeal to the reader's curiosity, not to a sense of sympathy (5).

3. **(2)** *Literal Comprehension/Nonfiction.* Lines 23-27 make it clear that the appearance of the sun from behind a cloud starts the author thinking about sunstroke, the correct diagnosis. The deep blue color (line 24) refers to the sky, not the water, so eliminate (1). The reference to the bell means that the author had an idea, not that he is hearing a real bell (3). (4) and (5) are symptoms that could come from many causes, and so do not help the author make his diagnosis.

4. **(1)** *Application/Nonfiction.* The author says that he never had more pleasure in his work than when he watched the bull getting better. All the choices deal with some aspect of pride; only (1), however, deals with pride that comes from returning to normal something that has gone wrong.

5. **(4)** *Inferential Comprehension/Nonfiction.* The author's thought processes described in this passage illustrate his willingness to keep looking for answers, especially answers that might not be obvious at first. Since he is moved by the sight of the suffering animal, eliminate (3). He is not showing off his education, so (1) cannot be correct. (2) and (5) may be true of his methods, but they are not shown in this passage.

6. **(5)** *Inferential Comprehension/Drama.* Note that most of Helmer's responses are in the form of questions. This shows that he doesn't understand what Nora is saying to him and suggests that he is surprised by her comments. His surprise is shown in lines such as "Nora, what do I hear you saying?" (line 23). Thus, (4) cannot be correct. Her responses show that (1) is wrong as well. Helmer's astonishment at Nora's discontent shows that he was content in their marriage, so (2) is false. There is no evidence that Helmer is not serious (3).

7. **(1)** *Literal Comprehension/Drama.* In lines 24-28, Nora explains that both her father and Torvald have forced her to live by their rules. Both men have "greatly wronged" her (line 15). (2) and (4) are wrong because the matter of affection is not discussed. Torvald's astonishment shows that he is not used to hearing her speak this way. This suggests that she probably has not argued with him often, if at all, so eliminate (3). (5) is wrong because Torvald, not Nora, states that both Papa and he loved her.

8. **(4)** *Analysis/Drama.* The playwright uses the comparison between a child's toy and the woman to emphasize Nora's lack of power over her own life. Her father and husband treat her as she used to treat her dolls: as playthings incapable of original thought. There is no mention of her dressing well (1), saying little (2), or playing as a proper child (5). Likewise, she is not expected to be idle (3), just submissive.

9. **(3)** *Application/Drama.* Nora expresses the idea that women should be allowed to think, speak, and act for themselves. This belief forms the basis of women's liberation. Some or all of the other causes might appeal to Nora, but they are not discussed in the passage.

10. **(5)** *Literal Comprehension/Fiction.* Sanford originally had held a "resentful conviction" about Army cooks (line 12) and felt "ashamed" about becoming one himself (lines 1-2). By the end of the passage, however, Sanford has come to enjoy his work (line 37), and to be satisfied at seeing the "fertile accomplished creativity" of his labor (line 44). This change in his attitude is the opposite of (4). Eliminate (1)

because his attitude has not changed from passivity to assertive. There is no evidence that he is lazy (2). (3) is wrong because his anger is directed toward cooks as symbols of Army life, not toward other soldiers.

11. **(1)** *Application/Fiction.* Sanford's satisfaction comes from his ability to be creative in his work and to see the product of his labor. Being a house builder (1), might allow him some creativity and would let him see the results of his work. (2), (4), and (5), would not allow him the same kind of creative satisfaction. Although Sanford works in an Army kitchen, he probably would not enjoy managing a restaurant, for he seems to have trouble handling authority (lines 6-9), so eliminate (3) as well.

12. **(3)** *Inferential Comprehension/Fiction.* Like most soldiers, Sanford is somewhat critical of Army organization and management, (1) and (4), and thus may sometimes lack enthusiasm (2). The characteristic the author develops most fully, however, is that Sanford achieves a sense of worth by doing a job that usually goes unnoticed. (5) is wrong because Sanford's job does not involve power or self-advancement, although he does well enough to be promoted.

13. **(4)** *Inferential Comprehension/Fiction.* The author prefaces his remark by commenting that "life in the Army was in most respects a marriage" (lines 13-14). By this he means that "Every soldier found some particular habit"—that is, routine—of Army life unbearable, just as every husband has a specific complaint against his wife. None of the other choices refers to a comparison of the Army to a wife.

14. **(5)** *Literal Comprehension/Commentary.* The reviewer says that the novel reveals "something fundamental in the experience of being human" (lines 12-13). The novel deals with "the dilemmas of America and the 19th century" (lines 27-28), with "questions that continue to defeat Presidents and their cabinets" (lines 36-37). Ultimately, the novel defines "what it means… to share the complex fate of being an American" (lines 44-45). The author feels that the novel still has a lot to say to Americans, so (1) is wrong. The adventure is not one that would happen to most people, so (2) is not correct. Eliminate (3) because the reviewer is interested in the issues involved, not in Twain's development of character. The reviewer does not expect the novel to represent ancient myth (4). The comparison

to mythology refers to the novel's underlying message about basic human issues.

15. **(2)** *Inferential Comprehension/Commentary.* The reviewer describes Huck's encounters with the less appealing aspects of society in his day and then reminds the reader of Huck's lack of formal education (lines 39-41). The reviewer concludes that in dealing with these experiences, Huck "fails as an ethical philosopher" (lines 41-42) but succeeds in "defining what it means… to share the complex fate of being an American" (lines 44-45). This shows that Huck is a simple person whose wisdom goes far beyond his formal education. Huck teaches the reader what it means to be an American. Huck may be something of a dreamer (1), but he is not a failure or a fool (4), Likewise, he does not live in a fantasy world (5). There is nothing tragic about him; on the contrary, in his wisdom he is worthy of admiration, not pity (3).

16. **(1)** *Inferential Comprehension/Commentary.* The author states that Huck confronts many moral and social problems, but there is no suggestion that he solves them, so (2) is wrong. The author does not supply any information about Huck's situation at the end of the book (3 and 4). Choice (5) is wrong because the reviewer seems to see Huck as representing the ordinary American.

17. **(4)** *Analysis/Commentary.* Even as the author refers to "civilization" as symbolized by the "god-fearing, law-abiding small town" (lines 33-34) he describes it as "narrow" and "philistine". Putting quotation marks around "civilization" also implies that the author is questioning whether the town is as civilized as it seems. The author's choice of words is the key here. The contrast is based on the group, not the individual (1). It also suggests the opposite of change; it implies that progress is not happening (2). Choices (3) and (4) have no support in the passage.

18. **(1)** *Application/Commentary.* As a youngster, Huck might enjoy the fantastic elements in science-fiction movies (4), but such movies would go far beyond his experience. A comedy (2), a war movie (3), and a biography (5) would deal with aspects of society that Huck might have trouble understanding. The author explains that society is what gives Huck trouble. He also states that Huck and Jim are "as at home in nature as a pair of raccoons" (lines 22-23). Huck would probably feel some sense of familiarity with a nature film.

19. **(1)** *Analysis/Commentary.* The author describes a mountain that is important to the history of his tribe (lines 3-5) and thus is worthy of respect. Despite the harshness of the landscape, the description does not make him feel frustration (2) or uncertainty (3). The author is not afraid of Rainy Mountain (4), nor does he find it joyful (5).

20. **(5)** *Analysis/Commentary.* The expression suggests that Rainy Mountain is timeless, complete, and never-changing. It looks today as it did centuries ago when his ancestors first walked the earth. That time stands still does not suggest life is meaningless (1) or hopeless (3). The phrase describes the mood of the setting, not human actions or choices (2). The author feels comfort in the area's time-lessness, not fear (4).

21. **(4)** *Application/Commentary.* The author uses such words as "loneliness" (line 18) and "isolate" (line 20) to describe his subject. Of the choices given, only the painting described in (4) would convey the same combination of desertion and grandeur as the author's description of Rainy Mountain. All the other choices convey either vibrant life (1) or human action (2), (3), and (5).

22. **(1)** *Inferential Comprehension/Nonfiction.* Rainy Mountain was the home of the author's grandmother. She is a descendant of the Kiowa who made the long journey, not one of those who began it. This would suggest that rainy Mountain is at the end of the journey. The starting place was Montana (5). Therefore, (2) cannot be correct, and since Montana was the starting place of the migration, (5) is also wrong. If the entire migration took place in the 17th century, (3) cannot give us any answer to the question. The time of the meeting with the Crow tribe (4) took place "along the way" (line 44), before the Kiowa "entered upon the Southern Plains" (line 54)—where Rainy Mountain is located—so (4) is incorrect.

23. **(3)** *Inferential Comprehension/Nonfiction.* The author's loss of physical vitality, intellectual interest and hope add up a loss of self-respect. As a slave, the author had no freedom to lose (1). There is no support in the passage for (2), (4), or (5).

24. **(2)** *Application/Nonfiction.* The first-person narrative helps the reader share the experience of slavery and to see that slavery was more than a political philosophy, that it was a personal tragedy. Douglass expresses no pride in his work as a slave (5). The first-person point of view has nothing to do with the other choices.

25. **(5)** *Literal Comprehension/Nonfiction.* Douglass sees the ships as "so many shrouded ghosts." The ships "terrify and torment me with thoughts of my wretched condition" (lines 40-41) he writes. Since they have this powerful effect, (4) cannot be correct. The ships clearly have exactly the opposite effect of (1), great delight. Neither do the ships give him a feeling of energetic freedom (2). His experiences on the plantation, not his feelings about the ships, seem like a dream (3)—a bad dream .

26. **(5)** *Application/Nonfiction.* Mr. Covey is portrayed as a manager who does not have any sympathy for his workers. He works his slaves even in the most brutal weather and during the night (lines 4-10). (1), (2), (3), and (4) express a similar lack of concern; only (5) expresses sympathy.

27. **(1)** *Literal Comprehension/Drama.* The first half of Amanda's and Tom's conversation is about someone's character. Lines 27-29 reveal that the man they are discussing has been invited to dinner. There is no suggestion that Laura is engaged (2); in fact, the conversation suggests that Laura and the man have never met. Tom shows no interest in being like this man (3), nor do the pair seem to be doing the man a favor (5). (4) is only a passing comment in the conversation.

28. **(2)** *Analysis/Drama.* The phrase is a figurative comparison based on the idea that oysters are silent. Amanda is saying that Tom is as close-mouthed as an oyster by not telling the man much about the dinner invitation (lines 27-29). (1) is the opposite of the intent of the comparison. (3), (4), and (5) have nothing to do with speech habits.

29. **(4)** *Inferential Comprehension/Drama.* Throughout the passage, Amanda combines her eagerness to have the guest meet Laura with her insistence that he will like Laura. She does reveal some imagination (3), but it is within the context of her hopes and expectations about the dinner. Amanda is too eager to be very perceptive (1). She shows no sign of suspecting that the man might have hidden secrets (2). Amanda may be jumping to conclusions, but it is out of hope rather than carelessness (5).

30. **(3)** *Literal Comprehension/Drama.* In lines

Copyright ©1993 Regents/Prentice Hall, a division of Simon and Schuster, Englewood Cliffs, NJ 07632

35-36, Tom warns that they can't expect much of Laura and in line 40 states that Laura is crippled. Eliminate (1) and (4) because they are the guest's good points, supplied by Tom. Amanda's suspicions of Tom's motives have nothing to do with the plan for dinner, so eliminate (2). (5) is not correct because Tom shows no signs of evaluating Laura's worth.

31. **(2)** *Literal Comprehension/Poetry.* The man describes his face as black in Line 1. In line 11, the speaker states that he is at the Vietnam Veterans Memorial. Throughout the poem, he describes objects reflected by the wall's surface. The speaker is alive and thinking only to himself, so (1) cannot be true. In line 4, he makes it clear that he will not allow himself to cry (3). By saying "I'm stone" in line 5, the speaker is talking about his desire to hold back his tears, not actually becoming stone (4). Although there is a brief vision of war in line 18, it is not enough to be called reliving the experience.

32. **(3)** *Literal Comprehension/Poetry.* Of all the items and people described, only the names are actually on the wall. All the others are reflected images: the speaker's face (lines 1 and 6), a woman's blouse (line 19), a bird's wing (lines 22-23), and a plane (line 24).

33. **(2)** *Inferential Comprehension/Poetry.* The speaker's veteran status can be inferred from his "half-expecting" (line 15) to find his own name on the wall. He is not dead yet (3), but he can visualize how Andrew Johnson died. His reaction to the memorial is very emotional (1), but with no apparent resentment for other visitors (5). There is no support for choice (4).

34. **(2)** *Analysis/Poetry.* The mother's action is an ordinary part of bringing up a child, a new life. Her movement is a dramatic contrast to the reason for the wall's existence. There is no such contrast with the white veteran (1). The speaker states that he is mistaken about thinking she is trying to erase names (lines 29-31) (3). Such a simple gesture is not shocking (4) or suggestive of mourning (5).

35. **(3)** *Analysis/Poetry.* The speaker's struggle with tears, his momentary "entrapment" in the wall, and the bleakness of the images suggest sadness instead of happiness (2) or hope (4). There is no sign of a violent emotion such as (1) anger or (5) despair.

36. **(2)** *Literal Comprehension/Fiction.* On the first line, the narrator says that she, her mother, and her brother are sitting by themselves before the service is supposed to start. The mother is scolding the narrator because she will not go up to the casket to see her father's body. "Samuel said good-bye. Samuel is crying," the mother says. Since the only other person there is the little brother, he must be Samuel. There is no dying man (3), and the narrator's father has already died (5). A dead man cannot say goodbye or cry as Samuel does (1), and "perfect Pearl" is the narrator (4).

37. **(5)** *Literal Comprehension/Fiction.* The mother says that she will make the girl cry (lines 34-35) and slaps her repeatedly. Choices (1), (3) and (4) do not occur. The mother leaves the girl (2) after she realizes that things have gotten out of control.

38. **(4)** *Inferential Comprehension/Fiction.* The girl states that she does not want to mourn the man in the coffin (lines 9-10). Her following description of how she remembers her father suggests that is the way she would prefer to think of him (lines 14-17).She says she has always irritated her mother (lines 19-20) but that is not why she refuses to go up to the casket (5). Nothing supports the other choices.

39. **(1)** *Inferential Comprehension/Fiction.* The girl's physical and emotional reaction in the last paragraph is triggered by the sight of her father. At this point, she is not concerned about her mother (2) or how she appeared earlier (4). Her emotion is grief, not fear (5). Part of her running away is based on the fact that she is crying, not that she can't.

40. **(2)** *Application/Fiction.* Before this episode, the mother and daughter have not gotten along (lines 19-20). This incident has done nothing to draw them together (4). It is most likely that they will continue to disagree. The girl says her father is not "resting peacefully with God" (line 51), (1) and she has resolved nothing that will make her happier (5).

41. **(1)** *Literal Comprehension/Commentary.* Amy Tan's first novel was a major success and is the only book mentioned in this paragraph. So the phrase does not refer to the new book, mentioned in the next paragraph. (5). The other three choices don't qualify as successes.

Copyright ©1993 Regents/Prentice Hall, a division of Simon and Schuster, Englewood Cliffs, NJ 07632

42. **(3)** *Literal Comprehension/Commentary.*
The mother's story begins on page 61 of
the novel. The reviewer spends most of
his time summarizing her experiences.
Only the first two chapters are about the
younger woman (1) or San Francisco (2).
The other two choices may be mentioned
in the novel, but they are not the primary
subjects.

43. **(4)** *Literal Comprehension/Commentary.*
(4) restates the reviewer's comment that
in the first two chapters "the young
woman tells a pleasant but unremarkable
tale" (lines 21-23). Although the setting of
the first part of the book is called contemporary (lines 19-20), this "scene" is not
described as unusual but as like the
"least transporting parts"—that is, least
exciting parts—of Amy Tan's first novel.
Writing this uninteresting is not likely to
be unusual. No statements by the reviewer support the other choices.

44. **(5)** *Inferential Comprehension/*
*Commentary.* By including several details,
the reviewer suggests that the mother
had trouble with some traditional Chinese
values. In addition to saying that she left
her husband, he includes two remarks
the mother made about women's limited
rights: "a powerful indictment against a
world in which women were taught that
love means always having to say you're
sorry" where " 'a woman has no right to
be angry' "(lines 51-56). (1) and (2) are the
opposite of what is suggested about the
woman's character. Lines 66-68 indicate
that from her suffering the old woman
has gained a kind of knowledge or wisdom "as sound as legal evidence," even
though it takes the form of "curious
superstitions." The "different languages"
(line 26) spoken by mother and daughter
are not Chinese or English (3), but their
different ways of looking at life. The mother may indeed want a better life for her
daughter, but there is no mention of this
in the review (4).

45. **(2)** *Analysis/Commentary.* The references
to a fairy tale are used to describe the
miraculous, overnight success of Amy
Tan as an author (lines 1 and 10). The
fairy tale here seems to stand for magic
and dreams come true, not for anything
negative (1) or something to be avoided
(4). Since the novel is clearly for grown-up
readers, (3) cannot be correct. There is
no suggestion within the commentary
that the reviewer reads fairy tales, so (5)
is wrong.